Freud in the Pampas

Freud in the Pampas

The Emergence and Development
of a Psychoanalytic Culture in Argentina

Mariano Ben Plotkin

Stanford University Press
Stanford, California 2001

Stanford University Press
Stanford, California

© 2001 by the Board of Trustees of the
Leland Stanford Junior University

Printed in the United States of America
On acid-free, archival-quality paper

Library of Congress Cataloging-in-Publication Data

Plotkin, Mariano Ben
    Freud in the Pampas : the emergence and development of a
psychoanalytic culture in Argentina / Mariano Ben Plotkin.
        p. cm.
    Includes bibliographical references (p.) and index.
    ISBN 0-8047-4054-2 (cloth : alk. paper) —
    ISBN 0-8047-4060-7 (paper : alk. paper)
        1. Psychoanalysis—Argentina—History—20th century.
    I. Title.
    BF173.P6427   2001
    150.19′5′0982—dc21   00-040730

Typeset by TypeWorks in 10.5/13 Bembo

Original Printing 2001

Last figure below indicates year of this printing:
10   09   08   07   06   05   04   03   02   01

To the two P's of my life: Zíngara and Cachito
and to my parents

Contents

Preface

This book originated in a conversation I had with my aunt Alicia (a psychoanalyst) back in 1986, when I was a first-year graduate student at the University of California, Berkeley. During my Christmas visit to Argentina, she asked me how much it cost a graduate student to live in the United States. After a quick calculation I came up with a monthly figure. My aunt could not hide her surprise. How could anyone live on so little? I itemized my expenses: so much for food, so much for rent, so much for clothing, and so on. Finally she nodded. "Oh, now I understand—there you don't need to budget for psychoanalysis."

My aunt's remark did not surprise me. After all, I had grown up in Buenos Aires and had already been through many years of psychoanalysis. Everybody I knew in Argentina was or had been in analysis. Yet my aunt's words stuck in my mind. Only later, after a few years in the United States, where virtually no one I met had undergone psychoanalysis, I realized that my aunt's observation had a double meaning. She was telling me not only that psychoanalysis was considered a normal expense in Argentina but that "there"—that is, anywhere else—it was acceptable not to allocate money for therapy. In her view, going to the psychoanalyst was a natural thing to do in Buenos Aires, though not necessarily elsewhere.

At that time I was thinking about a dissertation topic that ended up having nothing to do with psychoanalysis. The longer I lived outside of Argentina, however, the more my aunt's statement intrigued me. By the time I finished and published my dissertation, it had become clear to me that what I and my aunt and many other Argentines had taken for granted—that lying on an analyst's couch four times a week at great financial sacrifice was one of any normal human being's activities—was in fact a problem that required explanation. Indeed, it became clear that it was an Argentine problem. More surprising was my discovery that virtually nothing had been written until then on the development of an Argentine psychoanalytic culture. It seemed that it had never occurred to Argentine historians and intellectuals that there was anything peculiar about Argentines' devotion to Freud. Only in recent years have Argentine intellectuals started to see it as a phenomenon worth investigating historically.

Whereas in other countries, particularly in the United States, enthusiasm for Freud has receded and even given way to an anti-Freudian backlash among the intelligentsia, in Argentina Freud's works are still gospel. Despite a series of economic crises that made it difficult for many people to bear the expense of orthodox psychoanalytic therapy, psychoanalysis both as a therapy and as an interpretive system is still a vital component of Argentine urban culture. Although the proliferation of short-term therapies and even some New Age practices have eroded the monopoly that psychoanalysis once enjoyed in the realm of psychotherapy, in Argentina many of those practices are deeply influenced by psychoanalysis. Freud and the cult of Sai Baba seem to be able to coexist more easily there than elsewhere. Psychoanalysts host political and cultural TV shows and are routinely interviewed by writers for popular magazines. Psychoanalytic jargon permeates Argentines' everyday speech.

Sometimes psychoanalysis shows up in unexpected places. In July 1999 I was invited by a private university in Argentina to deliver a talk on my research on the history of psychoanalysis. I arrived early, and one of the members of the audience introduced himself as an economist. Since an ongoing seminar on economics met in the room next door, I suggested that perhaps he had gotten the wrong room, that probably the meeting he wanted was the one next door. To my surprise, he said no, he was coming to my seminar because he was interested in and in fact had written on the convergence between Lacanian psychoanalysis and economic theory! As an American colleague pointed out, the development of psychoanalysis in a country where even economists think in psychoanalytic terms deserves at least one book.

Writing the history of psychoanalysis poses special challenges for the historian, for psychoanalytic institutions are very zealous in keeping their internal affairs beyond the reach of the lay public. Psychoanalytic archives are generally difficult or impossible to access.[1] A substantial portion of Freud's papers at the Library of Congress is still off limits. Moreover, analysts in general are more used to listening than to talking. I was fortunate enough to have access to limited parts of the Argentine Psychoanalytic Association's archive and almost unlimited access to the archive of the Asociación de Psicólogos de Buenos Aires (APBA). For reasons that perhaps merit a psychoanalytic study of another kind, however, memory is a problematic concept in Argentina. Archives do not receive much attention and are generally in poor condition. Like most researchers in Argentina, then, I had to rely heavily on private archives and collections.

During the years of working on this book I have collected so many debts of various kinds to so many people that any attempt to name them all is bound to lead to unfair omissions. All the same, I will try. First I want to express my gratitude to the institutions whose financial support made this book possible. The research for it was more than generously funded by a grant from the National Endowment for the Humanities (NEH) and supplemented by another grant from the Joint Committee on Latin American Studies of the Social Sciences Research Council (SSRC) and the American Council of Learned Societies, with funds provided by the NEH. I am grateful to both institutions and particularly to Daniel Jones of the NEH and to Eric Hershberg of the SSRC for the continuous help with administrative issues before, during, and after the period covered by the grants. I owe a special debt of gratitude to Colby College, and particularly to Robert Weisbrot, Jorge Olivares, and Robert MacArthur, for granting me a two-year leave of absence to devote myself to research for this project after only one year of actual teaching there. I am also grateful to Peter Berger, director of the Institute for the Study of Economic Culture at Boston University, for the ideal working conditions he created at the Institute, for his continuous support, and for the opportunity for active intellectual exchange. I also thank William Keylor, chair of the History Department at Boston University. My thanks to the Argentine Psychoanalytic Association, especially to Dr. Moisés Kijak and Dr. Carlos Mario Aslán, and to the librarian I remember only as Anita; to the Asociación de Psicólogos de Buenos Aires, especially to its president, Julio Tollo, and to the staffs of the Wellcome Institute for the History of Medicine in London, the British Psychoanalytic Society, the archives of the Rockefeller Foundation in Tarrytown, New York, the New York Psychoanalytic Institute, and the Library of Congress.

Many people helped me in various ways throughout my research. My wife, Piroska Csúri, and my son, Pascuel, played essential roles in this project, as in all other aspects of my life. I thank Hugo Vezzetti for his generosity in sharing with me sources and material from his own research and for his suggestions and advice (though I did not always take it). Many thanks to Germán García, director of the Centro Descartes of Buenos Aires, for his help. Drs. Juan Carlos Stagnaro and Emiliano Galende gave me free access to what is left of the archive of the Federación Argentina de Psiquiatras, and Dr. Martha Rosenberg allowed me to use material from her personal archive. Eva Giberti also shared with me her recollections and her archive. Horacio Tarcus gave me unrestricted access to his impressive collection of Argentine cultural and political periodicals. He also gave me permission to photocopy his father's letter to Freud and the latter's response. Washington Luis Pereyra gave me permission to use his collection of periodicals. Jorge Balán gave me encouragement and advice at the beginning of my research. Dr. Emilio Rodrigué shared his recollections with me in what he calls a "cybernetic" dialogue via the Internet.

While I was writing this book I was invited to present some preliminary results of my research in various places, including the seminar on intellectual history led by Oscar Terán at the University of Buenos Aires; the history workshop of the David Rockefeller Center for Latin American Studies, headed by John Coatsworth; the history workshop of the Center for Latin American Studies of Princeton University, chaired by Jeremy Adelman; the Argentine Psychoanalytic Association, the Latin American Centre of St. Antony College at Oxford University, the Universidad Torcuato Di Tella in Buenos Aires, the History Department of the Consejo Superior de Inves-tigaciones Científicas in Madrid, the Museu Nacional of the Federal University of Rio de Janeiro, and the Fundación Descartes / Antena Tucumán in San Miguel de Tucumán, Argentina. My appreciation to all those institutions and to the participants in those seminars.

I am deeply grateful to those analysts and intellectuals who spent time with me, sharing their memories and interpretations in sometimes long interviews. They are all named in the bibliography.

Many people read parts of the manuscript and suggested changes and improvements; I thank them all. Tulio Halperin read and commented on an early version of the entire manuscript. He has been and is a permanent source of inspiration. Jeremy Adelman and Ariel de la Fuente also read and commented on the whole thing and offered useful suggestions. Thomas Glick expressed his confidence in the project from its early stages. His comments on early drafts of some chapters were very enlightening. Lila Caimari, Jorge Cañizares, Ricardo González, Joel Horowitz, Jorge Myers, Federico Neiburg, and Kristin Ruggiero made important suggestions on how to give coherence to what was a shapeless mass of information. My friends Samuel Amaral, María Fernanda Arias, Anahí Ballent, Victoria Cerrudo, Raúl García Heras, Claudia Gilman, Pablo Kreimer, Adrian Lerner, Telma Liberman, Jorge Myers, Federico Neiburg, Raanan and Mónica Rein, Norma Santo-andré, and Hugo Vezzetti all helped me more than they probably imagine. Three assistants helped me efficiently in the collection of information both in Argentina and in the United States: María Isabel Fontao in Buenos Aires, Felipe Santos at Harvard University, and Gerardo Pérez at Colby College. My thanks to them.

I thank very specially Muriel Bell, my editor at Stanford University Press, for the confidence she had in the project when it was still only a project, and for her constant support and encouragement; and thanks to Barbara Salazar, the copyeditor.

Finally, I am deeply grateful to my parents for their encouragement in this and in other projects and, of course, to my Aunt Alicia for her inspiring remark back in 1986.

Parts of Chapter 1 have appeared in two articles: "Freud, Politics, and the Porteños: The Reception of Psychoanalysis in Buenos Aires, 1910–1943," *Hispanic American Historical Review* 77, no. 1 (1997): 45–74; and "Tell Me Your Dreams: Psychoanalysis and Popular Culture in Buenos Aires, 1930–1950," *The Americas* 55, no. 4 (1999): 601–29.

M. B. P.

Freud in the Pampas

Introduction

One of the things that foreign visitors to any major city in Argentina find most surprising is the enormous presence of psychoanalysis in the urban culture. With four analytic societies affiliated with the International Psycho-analytic Association (IPA) and twenty-nine IPA-affiliated analysts per mil-lion inhabitants, Argentina today has one of the highest incidences of Freudian analysts in the world. Argentina also vies with France for first place in the number of Lacanian analysts—those who follow the doctrines of Jacques Lacan.[1] Moreover, in 1995 almost two of every 400 *porteños,* as the citizens of Buenos Aires are called, were psychologists, and if they were practicing, they were probably using some kind of psychoanalytically in-spired therapy. From politicians to bank clerks, from soap opera stars to cab drivers, and even a few generals—everybody seems to use psychoanalytic language to express the concerns of everyday life. As an American colleague pointed out, anyone who questions the existence of the unconscious or of the Oedipus complex at a social gathering in any large Argentine city is made to feel as if he or she were denying the virginity of Mary before a synod of Catholic bishops. For broad sectors of Argentine society, psycho-analysis has become an interpretive system—a map, in the words of the Brazilian Sérvulo Figueira—used to understand various aspects of reality.[2] Psychoanalysis is also a permanent presence in the Argentine media. Several major newspapers feature widely read weekly sections on psychoanalysis, and psychoanalysts regularly host TV shows. Although, as one might expect, psychoanalysis has spread more broadly through the middle class, it has pen-etrated all sectors of society.

The Argentine psychoanalytic movement has had a deep impact on the rest of Latin America and on Spain. Most members of the first generation of IPA-affiliated Brazilian psychoanalysts were trained in Argentina. The Uru-guayan Psychoanalytic Association is an offshoot of the Argentine Psychoanalytic Association (APA), and the Mexican association was originally placed under APA supervision. The first Lacanian associations in Spain were founded by Argentine exiles in the 1970s. The impact of Argentine psychoanalysts has been so great that the "Argentine psychoanalyst" has become a social stereotype in Madrid and Barcelona.[3]

In spite of the relative weight of Argentine psychoanalysis in the international psychoanalytic movement and of its centrality in Argentine culture, researchers working on the evolution of the international psychoanalytic movement have largely neglected the study of the development of Argentine psychoanalysis.[4] Until recently Argentines themselves did not think the diffusion of psychoanalysis in their own country was worth studying.[5] This lack of curiosity suggests that psychoanalysis has become so deeply rooted in the culture of the country that for a long time it was simply a given, part of an Argentine's "world taken for granted."

Aside from the general emphasis on Europe and North America in the historiography on psychoanalysis, the neglect of Argentina's psychoanalytic movement may be related to the fact that, unlike their American and French colleagues, Argentine analysts have not produced a distinctively national psychoanalytic school. The reception of psychoanalysis in Argentina—a country that, as the literary critic Adolfo Prieto has suggested, formed its national identity through the view of the "other"—was mostly derivative. Until the late 1960s Argentine psychoanalysis was very much under the influence of the theories of the London-based analyst Melanie Klein and the British school. For years the APA took pride in its ultra-orthodox Kleinism. Since the late 1960s, although Klein continued to be influential among affiliates of the IPA, Lacan has gained a wide following. Therefore, Argentine psychoanalysts have gone from (British) Kleinianism to (French) Lacanianism.

The derivative nature of Argentine psychoanalysis does not imply that psychoanalytic theory has been accepted blindly or uncritically. No body of ideas is ever absorbed passively. As we shall see, there were creative deviations, elaborations, and selective appropriations of foreign theories in the process of reception and diffusion of psychoanalysis in Argentina. Moreover, Argentine psychoanalysts made some truly important innovative theoretical contributions.[6] As members of the analytic community have recognized many times, however, the Argentine psychoanalytic movement has not evolved into a distinctive Argentine school.

The reasons for this failure to create an identifiable Argentine school of psychoanalytic thought are complex, and at this point I can only speculate.

Argentina, a country of immigrants, has a long tradition of admiring all things European. France and England have been sources of inspiration for the Argentine intellectual elite since the nineteenth century. Moreover, unlike France and the United States, at the time psychoanalysis started to be discussed, Argentina did not have strong and autonomous psychiatric and psychological traditions that could shape the reception of psychoanalysis. Furthermore, psychoanalysis was not seen as something exotic or foreign that needed to be adapted for Argentine consumption. In France the psychoanalysis promoted by Lacan has been interpreted as a truly French (meaning not Jewish and not German) version of psychoanalysis, a French "return" (as he and his followers have claimed) to Freud. Most members of the first generation of prominent U.S. psychoanalysts were European exiles who had already established outstanding careers in Europe and now had to work their way through a different and already consolidated cultural fabric. European psychoanalysts, like other foreign intellectuals, found in the United States a society receptive to their theories and ideas, but they also found themselves forced to adapt their thought to deeply rooted values of their new home—to "Americanize" them—if they were to gain acceptance. In some respects, their intellectual production was deeply influenced by the new environment in which they had to live.[7]

The APA, by contrast, founded in 1942, was constructed as a microcosm of Argentine society, composed of large numbers of European immigrants and their first-generation Argentine children. The six founding members were a Spanish émigré with family roots in Argentina, an assimilated Austrian Jewish émigré, an Argentine-born child of Jewish immigrants, an Argentine-born descendant of Italians, a Swiss-born psychiatrist who grew up in the interior of Argentina, and a Catholic member of the landed local oligarchy. Even before the APA was formed, psychoanalysis had arrived in Argentina through French, Italian, and Spanish sources. It could be said that psychoanalysis, in typically Argentine fashion, was imported to Argentina from France, Italy, and later England (countries for which the Argentine middle and upper classes have traditionally felt deep admiration) by Spaniards. Unlike the United States, Argentina did not receive a wave of eminent European analysts during World War II, so there was little to "Argentinize." There were some European émigrés in the early Argentine psychoanalytic community, but most of them completed or even started their psychoanalytic training in Argentina. The Argentine psychoanalytic community was therefore largely self-reproducing and mostly locally generated. Furthermore, by the time the APA was founded, psychoanalysis already occupied a prominent space in Argentine culture; psychoanalysis was already in demand.

The failure to create a native school may help to explain psychoanalysis' lasting popularity: as a prominent analyst has suggested, by following the changing international theoretical currents, Argentine practitioners enabled psychoanalysis to adapt to an ever-changing and highly unstable political context, and thus to be always relevant.[8] A more structured national school could have collided with the changing reality.

Whatever the reasons Argentine analysts did not produce an original school of psychoanalytic thought, the Argentine case is worth studying. Psychoanalysis is much more than a psychological theory; it constitutes, in W. H. Auden's words, "a whole climate of opinion." As John Forrester points out, the presence of psychoanalysis in the West is "so constant and pervasive that escaping its influence is out of the question." In spite of the current wave of anti-Freudian sentiment in the United States and elsewhere, going back to pre-Freudian beliefs is as likely as "going back to pre-Copernican beliefs."[9] The study of how this system of thought made its way into different cultures is essential if we are to understand why and how it became so influential.

Here I must define my terms. Throughout this book the term "psycho-analysis" refers not (or not only) to a particular psychological theory or therapeutic technique but to those discourses and practices that find legitimacy in their Freudian inspiration, thus generating what could be called a psy universe—whether the notions of Freudianism conveyed by those discourses and practices are accurate or not. As we shall see, psychoanalysis was read in many ways for different purposes by a variety of social groups, each of which tried to use it to satisfy its own needs. Psychoanalysis thus spilled into fields far removed from the therapeutic realm. In some countries, Argentina among them, psychoanalysis has become a central element of culture, one could say a belief system. A history of psychoanalysis, then, cannot be limited to its theorization or its institutions. This book is an attempt to explore the diffusion of psychoanalysis in a specific society as a general cultural phenomenon and to analyze the conditions for its dissemination.

The history of psychoanalysis as a cultural phenomenon is a result of the combination of its reception and diffusion in different cultures and societies. It has been understood differently in early Soviet Russia, in Japan, in the United States, in France, and in Argentina, and all those patterns of reception and diffusion are constitutive elements of its history. The history of ideas is also the history of their implantation, appropriation, and elaboration by different cultures. An exploration of the way psychoanalysis was disseminated in a particular society and culture tells us something important about both psychoanalysis and that culture. As a body of knowledge, psychoanalysis has influenced and changed the cultures in which it was introduced. And like all scientific theories or bodies of knowledge, it has suffered transformation and adaptation in the process. Moreover, the ways in which ideas adapt to the complex social and political fabric of the society where they are implanted is, as Nancy Stepan points out, a subject of interest in its own right.[10] Despite the claims of some of its practitioners, there is no "real psychoanalysis" that can serve as a yardstick against which all others must be compared.

How do we explain the diffusion of psychoanalysis in a given culture? Sociological studies generally agree that Western culture's receptivity to psychoanalysis originated in the anxieties provoked by rapid modernization, secularization, disruption of traditional forms of social interaction, and the emergence of a new concept of subjectivity. Psychoanalysis, according to this perspective, fills the gap created by the split between public and private identities that occurred with such changes as industrialization and the loss of traditional community feeling. Psychoanalysis provides security in rapidly changing societies undergoing a crisis in "civilized morality," when traditional ways of interpreting collective experience seem inadequate.[11]

Psychoanalysis has also been seen as a secular substitute for religion. According to Clifford Geertz, religions are essentially ordering systems that are concerned not with how to avoid suffering but how to endure it, turning it into something bearable, understandable, and expressible. What religious systems offer is a framework of *intelligibility* for sufferance.[12]

From its beginnings, psychoanalysis was meant to provide "sufferableness" rather than relief. Freud himself pointed out that the goal of psychoanalysis was to turn neurotic misery into ordinary unhappiness through a deeper understanding of the unconscious. Like religious faith, psychoanalysis can also provide interpretive tools for understanding and giving order to the elements of an otherwise chaotic reality. The framework of intelligibility that psychoanalysis provides can be applied to diverse situations. Thus psychoanalysis, as Sherry Turkle points out, is an "appropriable theory": it generates concepts and ideas that are easily manipulable, or, as she puts it, "objects to think with." Dreams and slips of the tongue provide interpretive tools that can be applied to a large variety of human behaviors.[13]

General sociological explanations, however, explain only part of the story. The factors delineated above could constitute the necessary factors that facilitate and explain the emergence of a psychoanalytic culture, but they are far from sufficient. Otherwise, how could we explain the fact that the massive diffusion of psychoanalysis took place since the 1930s in the United States, only in the late 1960s in France, and since the late 1950s in Argentina? And nothing of the same proportions happened in England, where some of the most innovative psychoanalytic theoretical developments originated and where Freud himself spent his last days. Psychoanalysis was widely popular in the early days of the Soviet Union but was later suppressed for political and ideological reasons. It would be difficult to argue, however, that Soviet society was in any way more "modern" in the early 1920s than the British or French society in the 1950s. Moreover, the purely sociological approach cannot explain why psychoanalysis was from the beginning medicalized and absorbed by the psychiatric establishment in the United States but developed a much more philosophical and linguistic orientation in France.[14]

Only a historical approach can yield an answer to such questions. By "historical approach" I mean something that is quite obvious but that has sometimes been overlooked. First, the diffusion of psychoanalysis develops over time—it is a process, not a direct consequence of the establishment of a psychoanalytic institution or of an orthodoxy that fights and overcomes society's "resistance," as some histories produced within the psychoanalytic community have argued.[15] Second, the diffusion of psychoanalysis in each society is the result of a unique combination of social, cultural, economic, intellectual, and political factors; it responds to the logic of each setting and satisfies its particular social needs.[16]

There is always a temptation to look for the single or at least the principal factor that can explain the diffusion of psychoanalysis in a given society. Why was psychoanalysis so widely disseminated in Argentina and not, say, in Paraguay or Mexico? Argentines have always prided themselves on being different from other Latin Americans. Members of the elite and of the middle class have seen themselves as Europeans in exile. European, particularly French and English, culture has had deep influence on Argentina's intellectuals and on the country's large middle class. At least during the first part of the century, this self-perception had some grounding in reality.

Like the United States, Argentina is a country of immigrants. In fact, Argentina received more immigrants (mostly from Southern Europe but from Central Europe as well) in proportion to native-born population than the United States. By 1914 over a third of Argentina's population was foreign-born. In Buenos Aires, which accounted for roughly a third of the country's population, the proportion was even higher. There, at the beginning of the century, over 60 percent of the working-class male population had been born in foreign countries. Large proportions of present-day Argentines are children or grandchildren of European immigrants. Argentina also housed (and still does) the second largest Jewish community in the hemisphere, after the United States.

Few would dispute that until the 1920s Argentina's history had been a success story and that the Argentine horizon was bright. Since the 1860s the country had enjoyed a relatively stable political system and impressive rates of economic growth based on the export of agrarian products to Europe— so overwhelmingly to England that economically Argentina was almost an informal British colony. Moreover, a modern and efficient education system had reduced illiteracy to a level comparable to those of European countries. By the end of the nineteenth century Argentina was essentially an urban country. The census of 1895 showed that over 50 percent of Argentines lived in urban concentrations.

By the 1930s, as a result of drastic changes in the international and domestic environments, the long period of prosperity and stability came to an abrupt end. Argentina, which started as a promising project and fulfilled that promise, suddenly became a problem. Argentines found to their surprise that they had absolutely no control over the forces that had made them prosperous. In the following decades Argentines, who were accustomed to believe that their country was a European enclave and therefore was immune to the problems that affected the rest of Latin America, suffered dictatorship, exclusion, violence, war, and poverty. In the 1970s Argentina was ruled by one of the most murderous military regimes on the continent. A feeling of crisis and disappointment became widespread among intellectuals. In the 1930s a new narrative genre emerged, consisting of essays that tried to explain what went wrong in Argentina and when it happened. Given this history, a variety of factors have been conjured up as *the* factors that explain the development of a psychoanalytic culture in Argentina. Among those alleged "causes" we find the European background of most of the population and the crisis of identity provoked by its foreign roots; the presence of a large Jewish community; a permanent feeling of disappointment originating in unrealistic expectations; and even the national tradition of the tango and the guitar-strumming gaucho.[17]

Hugo Vezzetti warns us against writing the history of the diffusion of psychoanalysis in Argentina from the end backward. If Argentina (particularly Buenos Aires) is recognized today as a world capital of psychoanalysis, it is tempting to look to history for the reasons, as if the status that psychoanalysis has in Argentine cultural life today had been there in embryo from the beginning. The burgeoning of psychoanalysis in Argentina began in the late 1950s. Until then, psychoanalysis had occupied an important but not central place in the cultural life of the country, and there was nothing that could have led anyone to predict what came later. Although there is evidence of a demand for psychoanalysis when the APA was founded, that demand was far from massive. Brazil and Peru had been more receptive to psychoanalysis in the 1910s and 1920s than Argentina was. So I think Vezzetti is right in pointing to the danger of a teleological approach to the problem, but I do not necessarily agree with his remedy. Vezzetti emphasizes the almost random character of the Argentine reception of psychoanalysis. According to him, such reception occurred in different cultural areas and did not respond to a system: as he examined the reception of psychoanalysis he found "neither a system nor a 'field' nor a grid, and as research progressed it became clear that an interpretive grid that emphasized some 'structural' dimension of that horizon of discourses would leave aside a fundamental aspect of those histories."[18]

Vezzetti's stress on the compartmentalized character of the reception of psychoanalysis is, as he points out, a methodological choice that he made in order to avoid the teleological trap. Although the reception and early dissemination of psychoanalysis was not a "structured" process, it seems to me that focusing on different areas of reception as compartmentalized spaces impoverishes the analysis. Society's assimilation of a new system of thought can only be understood in its deep cultural dimension only if we see it as a complex phenomenon that occurs at different times and at various depths at different levels. A history that acknowledges the existence of different levels of reception and acceptance and that deals with the "diversity of problems and the heterogeneity of sources," however, does not necessarily have to limit itself to independent case studies. *Only a multidimensional approach that integrates into the narrative the complex of conditions that facilitated the phenomenon can explain why and how a psychoanalytic culture emerged.* A study that recognizes the problems caused by the complexity of the phenomenon being investigated, but that at the same time explores the interconnections of the different areas of diffusion of psychoanalysis—as all levels of culture are intertwined—does not necessarily become "history told from the end," as Vezzetti fears. If I am unable to convey those interrelations properly, it is only because of the limitations of my narrative ability and because, as Jorge Luis Borges has suggested, one is always forced to use successive images to convey phenomena that in reality evolve simultaneously.[19]

This book explores the reception and diffusion of psychoanalysis in Argentina, analyzing the multiple dimensions of the phenomenon. It follows the development and diffusion of a complex and heterogeneous doctrine with scientific claims, the creation and broadening of a professional field, and the evolution of the cultural, political, and social environment that has facilitated its dissemination. Because all these developments were part of the same complex political, cultural, and social process, the reader will find some unavoidable overlapping and repetition throughout the chapters. Chapter 1 discusses the reception of psychoanalysis by medical and intellectual circles early in the twentieth century. It also analyzes the ideological uses that intellectual groups made of psychoanalysis. I argue that the fact that intellectuals at opposite ends of the ideological spectrum could appropriate psychoanalysis for their own purposes and at the same time could belong to the same scientific institutions and publish in the same journals suggests the existence of a relatively autonomous scientific sphere. The scientific value and possible uses of psychoanalysis were discussed within the realm of science. Chapter 1 also focuses on the early diffusion of psychoanalysis among an expanded public, and follows its path through widely read newspapers and popular publications. It shows that by 1942, when the Argentine Psychoanalytic Association was created, psychoanalysis was already in demand.

Chapter 2 focuses on the creation of the Argentine Psychoanalytic Association in 1942 and on the origins and expansion of psychoanalysis as a professional field. It also analyzes the political and ideological conditions under which the young psychoanalytic association developed. By the late 1930s and early 1940s Argentine society was deeply polarized. Political and ideological differences were invading most areas of public discourse and practice, including science. By then the peaceful coexistence of people loyal to opposing ideologies was no longer possible. This polarization had an impact on the early development of the Argentine psychoanalytic movement. Chapters 1 and 2, then, analyze the impact of political and ideological developments on the psychoanalytic field.

Chapter 3 takes a different tack. It analyzes the psychoanalytic boom of the 1960s and the emergence of a psy culture. It traces its origins to the convergence of social, economic, political, and cultural factors. It explores the multiple meanings of psychoanalytic discourse. The chapter also discusses the consolidation of the APA and the expansion of the supply of psychoanalytically inspired therapeutic techniques, such as group therapy and psychodrama. The introduction of these techniques made psychoanalytic discourse and ideas available to a larger portion of the population. Moreover, group therapy promoted a dialogue between psychoanalysis and the social sciences.

Chapter 4 looks at the psychoanalysis boom from a different point of view. It analyzes the role of "diffusers"—people who played an active part in disseminating the Freudian system through various media. Some were part of the psychoanalytic establishment and some were not. Among the former were prominent analysts whose works reached a broad public. Among the latter were writers on child rearing and contributors to popular magazines and other publications. I argue in this chapter that the attraction that psychoanalysis exercised in Argentine society may be partially explained by the fact that the theories of the most visible representatives of the analytic community constituted a modern channel to validate deeply rooted social values. This was particularly important in a society that was pulled between a longing for modernity and the persistence of conservative social mores.

Chapters 5, 6, and 7 discuss specific areas of reception and diffusion of psychoanalytic thought. Those areas opened confluent lines of dissemination and facilitated the increasing social legitimacy of the discipline. Chapter 5 focuses on the acceptance of psychoanalysis by progressive sectors of the psychiatric establishment. It explores the evolution of psychiatry in Argentina, its constitution as an autonomous medical specialty in the 1950s, and its politicization in the late 1960s and early 1970s. The chapter also explores the convergence of psychoanalysis and psychiatry, and the emergence of conditions for the introduction of psychoanalysis into public general hospitals in the 1960s. This development was particularly important because it dramatically increased the availability of analytic therapy for broad sectors of the population.

Chapter 6 examines the impact that the creation and massive expansion of the psychoanalytically oriented program of psychology at the University of Buenos Aires and elsewhere had on the diffusion of psychoanalysis. It also analyzes the complex process of the professionalization of psychology. In particular the chapter explores the complicated relations between psychologists, psychiatrists, and psychoanalysts and the role that gender played in those relations. The fact that psychologists were overwhelmingly women and most psychiatrists and psychoanalysts were men fostered the subordinated position that psychologists occupied within the psy professions.

Chapter 7 deals with the gradual infiltration of psychoanalysis into the mental artillery of the influential intellectual left that emerged in the 1960s. Although traditionally the left had rejected psychoanalysis, the emergence of a new critical left in the 1960s opened an important space for the diffusion of psychoanalytic thought. The new left was receptive to the social sciences in general and to psychoanalysis in particular. The chapter also discusses the works of three influential leftist intellectuals and the way each of them appropriated selected aspects of psychoanalytic theory.

Chapter 8 explores the politicization and radicalization of society and culture in the late 1960s and early 1970s, when the intellectual sphere of activity became cannibalized by politics. The chapter analyzes the changing place of psychoanalysis in the leftist culture of those years. In particular, it explores the politicization of psychoanalysis itself, the emergence and spread of Lacanian psychoanalysis, and the place of psychoanalysis in the discourse of oppression and liberation that was then in fashion. Finally, Chapter 9 discusses the aftermath of the process explored in Chapter 8, focusing on the consequences for the psy universe of the military dictatorship established in 1976. It ends with some reflections on the practice of psychoanalysis in a highly authoritarian political context.

Although I am supposedly dealing with psychoanalysis in Argentina, a large part of the discussion concentrates on the city of Buenos Aires. This is not an arbitrary choice. Argentina is a macrocephalic country. Buenos Aires holds almost a third of Argentina's population and by far the largest number of psychoanalysts and psychologists in the country. The psychoanalytic movement started simultaneously in Buenos Aires, Córdoba, Rosario, and Mendoza, but developed mainly in the capital city. Analysts from Buenos Aires traveled to the interior periodically to train analysts in the provinces. It was mostly from Buenos Aires (and to some extent from Córdoba) that psychoanalysis spread throughout the country.

ONE   The Beginnings of Psychoanalysis
       in Argentina

Psychoanalysis took root and spread in Argentina on multiple levels simultaneously. By the late 1920s local psychiatrists were discussing Freud's theory
and methods (generally with more enthusiasm for the methods than for the
theory), and popular magazines and other publications were disseminating
popularized versions of psychoanalysis. At the same time psychoanalysis occupied an expanding place in the teaching of psychology at the University
of Buenos Aires and of psychiatry at the University of Córdoba. Psychoanalysis thus entered into public discourse through many paths. It was discussed as a psychiatric technique and as an object of cultural consumption,
subject to many readings. For many years, however, it was perceived more as
something to talk about—either for or against—than as an integrated body
of knowledge.

   Although it is tempting to distinguish a medical reception of psychoanalysis from its cultural and psychological receptions, it would be misleading to do so. Until the late 1940s psychiatry (and certainly not psychoanalysis) was not really defined in Argentina as an autonomous and legitimate
medical specialty. Although some respected psychiatrists were highly visible in society and politics, psychiatry was considered a minor subspecialty of
medicine. A chair of psychiatry had been established at the School of Medicine in the late nineteenth century, but a graduate program in the field was
not offered until the 1940s. Despite their efforts to be recognized as full-
fledged members of the scientific community, psychiatrists were seen not as
specialists but as curious conglomerations of hospital administrators, dilettantes, scientists, and philanthropists. The most prestigious practitioners,
moreover, cultivated the image of savant by stepping into such other fields as
literature, the arts, and philosophy. Fernando Gorriti, for instance, a well-re-
garded psychiatrist, not only attempted to analyze literary works from the
psychiatric (and later psychoanalytic) point of view but, more interesting,

discovered new mental pathologies in characters in works of fiction.[1] Furthermore, because the care of psychiatric patients had social and political repercussions and was closely linked to another emerging field, criminology, it attracted the attention of nonspecialists. The roster of the Liga de Higiene Mental, founded in 1929, and that of the Asociación de Biotipología, Eugenesia y Medicina Social, founded in 1932, reveal a large number of lay members. Psychiatrists who taught psychology and wrote fiction coexisted with writers and politicians interested in problems related to mental illness.

The reception of psychoanalysis went through three distinct periods after its introduction in Argentina. From the late 1910s through the early 1920s psychoanalysis was known and discussed primarily in medical circles, and as a foreign doctrine. Knowledge of it came principally from French sources. In general, psychoanalysis was conceived as a medical theory. From the mid-1920s until the late 1930s, psychiatrists gradually incorporated it in their therapeutic arsenal (or argued against what already had secured its inclusion among the available therapies). At the same time, popularized versions began to circulate among the general public. Psychoanalysis came to be recognized as an important current of thought even by those who opposed it. It was impossible to ignore Freud and his theories. By the late 1920s psychoanalysis was not only a medical technique but also an object of cultural consumption. Finally, from the 1930s into the 1940s, psychoanalysis and psychiatry became established as autonomous specialties in a highly polarized society. By 1942, when a group of doctors founded the Argentine Psychoanalytic Association, psychoanalysis already occupied an important place in the country's urban culture.

Psychoanalysis as a Foreign Idea

Argentina was not so receptive to psychoanalysis during the first decades of the twentieth century as France or even Brazil. Although many Argentine doctors considered psychoanalysis more appropriate for artists than for scientists,[2] the first group that started a serious discussion of Freud's ideas was the psychiatric community. The first mention of psychoanalysis in a scientific forum in Argentina probably came in 1910 when Germán Greve, a Chilean physician, read his paper "Sobre psicología y psicoterapia de ciertos estados angustiosos" at the Congreso Internacional Americano de Medicina e Higiene in Buenos Aires. Greve and his paper acquired historical status when Freud mentioned them in *On the History of the Psychoanalytic Movement*. Greve praised Freud's theory of the sexual etiology of neuroses and recommended an unorthodox version of the psychoanalytic method. Conscious that he was breaking a paradigm by introducing a new and controversial psychological theory, Greve tried to fit his approach into an established tradition: the French school, which was extremely influential in the development of Argentine psychiatry. "Let us compare Freud's opinion about the primary etiology of neuroses and the one [Pierre] Janet has expressed on the same question, because we need to note the agreements between the two in order to reconcile [Freud's theory] with such a distinguished opinion [as Janet's]."[3]

Thus Greve started a tradition that would shape the early reception of psychoanalysis in Argentina. Freud would be read in French, by both sympathizers and detractors, and mostly at second hand, through commentators. This continued to be the case even after Antonio López Ballesteros's translation of Freud's *Obras completas* became available in the 1920s.[4] We do not know how his colleagues reacted to Greve's paper, but we do know that by the late 1910s psychoanalysis was being discussed among psychiatrists and some intellectuals.

During the first decades of the twentieth century Argentine psychiatry was not very hospitable to the new discipline. Unlike their Brazilian colleagues, who appropriated psychoanalysis in the hope of applying it to their concerns about subduing the exotic and "savage" components of their culture, Argentine psychiatrists were reluctant to accept the Freudian system.[5] Modern psychiatry emerged in Argentina in the last decades of the nineteenth century under the influence of positivism, which since the 1880s had been the received wisdom of intellectuals in Argentina, as elsewhere in Latin America. In 1886 a chair of mental diseases was established at the School of Medicine at the University of Buenos Aires. The first holder, Lucio Meléndez, had been the director of the Hospicio de las Mercedes, the local madhouse, since 1876. He is considered the first Argentine alienist, the person who introduced the ideas of Philippe Pinel and Jean-Etienne-Dominique Esquirol in Argentina. A chair of psychiatry was established in Córdoba in 1888. Domingo Cabred, appointed to succeed Lucio Meléndez in Buenos Aires in 1893, set out to modernize psychiatry in Argentina. He transformed the Hospicio into a research institution, hiring qualified staff in Argentina and Europe. Moreover, it was at his initiative that the open-door system was established.[6] Despite these efforts, however, conditions in mental hospitals still left much to be desired.

Argentine psychiatry developed under the influence of the French and Italian schools. The Argentine elite looked to Europe, particularly to France, as a beacon of civilization, and only those professionals who could show some degree of success in Europe received recognition in the Argentine medical establishment. "From the intellectual point of view, we are French," declared Horacio Piñero, a psychiatrist who held the chair of psychology at the University of Buenos Aires, in 1903.[7] French and, to a lesser extent, Italian were considered mandatory languages for Argentine physicians, and Argentine journals routinely published articles in those languages.[8] For different reasons the Italian and French psychiatric traditions were not particularly receptive to psychoanalysis during the early years of the century. In France the deeply rooted neurological tradition, the influence of such psychologists as Pierre Janet, and anti-German (and anti-Semitic) nationalist feelings conspired against acceptance of psychoanalysis in psychiatric circles. In Italy the main factors that impeded the acceptance of psychoanalysis were the prestige of Cesare Lombroso's criminal anthropology on the one hand and the vast influence of the Catholic Church on the other. Later the emergence of fascism only made the diffusion of Freudian ideas more difficult.[9]

The theory of degeneracy, introduced by the French physician Benedict-August Morel in the nineteenth century and later modified by Valentin Magnan, remained a major current of thought in Argentine psychiatry until as late as the 1940s. This theory was based on the idea that mental and physical diseases were inherited from generation to generation, each time in a heavier and more destructive dose.[10] These ideas were combined with Lombroso's theory that criminals and madmen were atavistic remnants of previous stages of human development.[11] Until well into the 1940s the typical psychiatric examination (particularly forensic) included a search for physical stigmata of degeneration, such as flat feet, a particular shape of the ears or of the palate, and crooked teeth.

In Argentina, degeneracy theory became associated with immigration. During the last decades of the nineteenth century and the first decade of the twentieth, Argentina received large waves of immigrants, mostly from southern Europe. The demographic boom created by massive immigration was accompanied by social problems that posed new challenges to the social elite, who had originally sought European immigrants in an effort to improve the national stock. Once welcomed as a coveted seed for the country's civilization, by the 1910s immigrants were seen as instigators of class and social conflict. At the beginning of the century, citing "scientific" evidence,

nationalists argued that uncontrolled immigration would degrade the national race by incorporating large numbers of degenerates into society.[12]
The fact was that for a variety of reasons, immigrants constituted a large
proportion of patients in mental hospitals. The image of the "crazy immigrant" became an important element in the Argentine popular imagination
during the first decades of the century. According to the psychiatrist Gonzalo Bosch, a founding member of the Liga Argentina de Higiene Mental
and its long-term director, "[Juan Bautista] Alberdi would say: 'To govern is
to populate,' a concept typical of his era; today we would say: To govern is to
select."[13] Psychiatry became part of a larger medical apparatus set up by the
state to control the new urban masses and at the same time to improve their
lives. The late nineteenth and early twentieth centuries saw the apogee of
hygienism and the other interventionist conceptions in social medicine that
later combined with the widespread eugenics notions embraced by left- and
right-wingers alike.[14]

Until the 1930s and even later, psychiatry in Argentina was articulated
around what Nathan Hale calls the "somatic style." It was generally believed
that the origins of all mental illness could be discovered in the morphology
of the brain or of the nervous system, and that disorders had to be treated
accordingly.[15] Very influential in promoting this notion of psychiatry was
Christofredo Jakob, a German neurologist and fanatic somatist, hired by the
Argentine government in 1899 as head of the laboratory of clinical psychiatry and neurology of the Hospicio de las Mercedes. In 1913 he also became
director of the laboratory of the Hospital Nacional de Alienadas, the mental
asylum for women, and was appointed to teaching positions in Buenos Aires
and La Plata.

Another figure of paramount importance in Argentine psychiatry—and
in criminology, a science that developed concurrently—was José Ingenieros,
a positivist physician with broad interests in sociology, psychology, and
philosophy. He was appointed director of the Institute of Criminology in
1907.[16] Ingenieros is a typical case of a physician who moved freely among
disciplines that did not yet have clear boundaries. In 1902 he became the
editor of *Archivos de Criminología, Medicina Legal y Psiquiatría,* the influential
journal founded by his teacher Francisco de Veyga. Under a succession of
names and directors it was one of the longest-lived medical journals in Argentina. In 1915 Ingenieros founded the *Revista de Filosofía,* a very prestigious forum for the dissemination of scientific and philosophical ideas.
Although a declared somatist—for him psychology was a branch of biol-

ogy—Ingenieros introduced and promoted hypnosis and psychotherapy as early as the turn of the twentieth century.

In this context, psychoanalysis had not yet found a place for itself in the therapeutic arsenal of Argentine psychiatrists in the first decades of the century. Certainly it was known and discussed, but it was still a foreign theory that did not fit into the psychiatric tradition of the country. This is the environment in which Greve spoke in 1910, and the one that shaped the early reception of Freud in Argentina.

Most early mentions of Freud by Argentine psychiatrists were negative and based on what French psychiatrists had said about the so-called school of Vienna. A case in point was Dr. Alejandro Raitzin, a respected forensic psychiatrist who had collaborated with Cabred in the creation of the open-door psychiatric colony and who later developed an interest in psychoanalysis. In 1919 Raitzin published an article on madness and dreams in which he offered an extensive critique of Freud's theories. At the end of the article, however, Raitzin recognized that his knowledge of psychoanalysis was limited to what he had read in Emmanuel Régis and Angelo Hesnard's *Psychanalyse des névroses et des psychoses,* a book highly critical of Freud that had been published in France in 1914.[17] Similarly, in the 1919 edition of his influential *Histeria y sugestión,* José Ingenieros criticized Freud's theories using the arguments presented by the French psychologist Pierre Janet in a polemic text of 1913.[18] The version of psychoanalysis available to Argentine physicians during the first decade of the century was thus deeply influenced by its French reading: Freud's was considered a pansexualist theory that slipped into the nonscientific realm of things too practical and too mundane. For most Argentine doctors the only acceptable parts of Freud's theories were those that were compatible with the French psychiatric tradition, which in any case was credited with discovering them first. Although parts of Freud's method gradually came to be accepted, he was still criticized for his "dogmatism"—that is, for his emphasis on the preeminence of sexuality in the etiology of neuroses. And for Freud, sexuality (and Argentine doctors found this hard to swallow) developed independently of physiology.[19] While Brazilian psychiatrists were adopting and adapting psychoanalysis' emphasis on sexuality as a method for its control, Argentine doctors were less receptive to Freud's ideas.[20]

Still, psychoanalysis was something that Argentine doctors, even those most attached to a purely biological conception of mental illness, felt they had to reckon with. In 1917 Christofredo Jackob, writing in a prestigious

Argentine medical journal, devoted four full pages to psychoanalysis before dismissing it as unscientific.[21] Jackob represented the mainstream medicine of his time. By the 1920s, however, his positivist vision of the world was showing signs of a crisis.

Since the late 1910s, European idealist philosophy had been displacing positivism in Latin America, partly in reaction against what was perceived as a threat—both cultural and political—posed by the "materialist empire of the North." From the "Ateneo de la Juventud" in Mexico to the impact of such works as José Enrique Rodó's *Ariel,* published in 1900, an antipositivist / antimaterialist wave extended throughout Latin America. The decline of positivism coincided with the emergence of an increasingly although never totally independent field of cultural production linked to the professionalization of such intellectual areas as philosophy and literature.[22]

Prominent visitors also played important roles in the spread of alternative philosophical currents of thought. In 1907 a second course in psychology was introduced at the School of Philosophy and Literature of the University of Buenos Aires (the first chair had been established in 1896). The first holder of the second chair was a German psychologist, Felix Kruger, a former student and later successor of Wilhelm Wundt in Leipzig. Kruger, who stayed in Argentina only two years, emphasized the nonexperimental aspects of Wundt's work and introduced the works of such nonpositivist writers as Wilhelm Dilthey, who were little known in Argentina. Kruger's teaching was influential in triggering the antipositivist reaction of the following decade.[23] Another visitor who contributed to the decline of positivism was the Spanish philosopher José Ortega y Gasset, who visited Argentina for the first time in 1916 and introduced German philosophical views. Ortega's devastating critique of positivism found receptive ears among the younger generation of Argentine philosophers.[24] Incidentally, Ortega was to write a foreword to the first Spanish translation of Freud's *Obras completas* in 1922. Moreover, Ortega's *Revista de Occidente,* widely read by Argentine intellectuals, published several articles on psychoanalysis between 1923 and 1925, including reviews of Freud's new and recently translated works.[25]

The general crisis of long-held beliefs brought about by World War I had a great impact in Latin America, enriching (and at the same time further confusing) the ideological environment. Another factor related to the downfall of positivism was the decline of authoritarian political and academic practices that had espoused particular versions of it to legitimize themselves. In 1916 Hipólito Yrigoyen, a Krausist,[26] became Argentina's first popularly elected president. In 1918 a student movement that secured access to higher education for the middle class got under way at the University of Córdoba. The cultural impact of immigration also contributed to the collapse of positivism. Confronted with waves of newcomers who introduced new social problems, members of the Argentine elite started looking for the "real" roots of Argentine nationality, roots that some found in the Spanish Catholic heritage.[27]

The crisis of positivism was felt in the medical profession as well, and it opened the door to alternative therapeutic theories. Throughout the 1920s the hereditary degeneracy paradigm began to lose its hegemony. Psychiatrists gradually turned from a purely somatic approach to mental illness to a more global vision of mental patients, a vision that encompassed the psychic dimension, the mind as well as the brain. Psychiatrists did not abandon previous notions, however, but combined degeneracy theory with Ernst Kretschmer's constitutional psychiatry, Nicola Pende's biotypology, Adolf Meyer's psychobiology, and other theories. The decline of positivism and the incorporation of alternative therapies facilitated the acceptance of psychoanalysis within the psychiatric community and in broader intellectual circles, where Freud's ideas were generally associated with those of the French philosopher Henri Bergson.[28]

In 1929 a group of psychiatrists founded the Liga Argentina de Higiene Mental, influenced by the mental hygiene movement that had emerged in the United States and elsewhere. Mental hygienists promoted the ideas that mental illness could be prevented and cured and that psychotherapy was an effective technique. The idea of mental disorders as curable promoted an interest in exploring new forms of treatment. Moreover, the possibility of preventing mental illness was dependent on early detection and treatment. Mild neuroses were therefore a focus of the Liga's attention; thus its emphasis on outpatient treatment and on psychotherapy, among other new therapeutic techniques. Moreover, if mild neuroses were worth treating, then the boundary between alienation and "normality" became blurred. "The alienated [person] is not an 'alien' [*ajeno*]," claimed Bosch in 1941 during the inauguration of a show of artistic works done by patients of the Liga's mental institutions. "No one is absolutely sane."[29] Although Bosch did not practice psychoanalysis, he showed some interest in it and supported those who, like Enrique Pichon Rivière and E. Eduardo Krapf (both members of the Liga), introduced it in the Hospicio.

As a progressive organization promoting the renovation of psychiatry, the Liga naturally attracted young psychiatrists with an interest in new ways of approaching mental disorders. In 1940 Enrique Pichon Rivière and his wife,

Arminda Aberastury, worked in the outpatient service established by the Liga in the Hospicio together with Arnaldo Rascovsky. Later other future members of the Argentine Psychoanalytic Association who came to psychoanalysis through psychiatry, such as David Liberman and Diego García Reinoso, also worked in the Liga's outpatient services. Another member of the Liga was Mauricio Goldenberg, a young psychiatrist who did much to promote psychoanalysis in the 1950s and 1960s as director of psychiatric services at the Gregorio Aráoz Alfaro Hospital in the porteño industrial suburb of Lanús. Those who were already interested in psychoanalysis (Pichon Rivière, García Reinoso) could profit from the presence in the Liga (and in the Hospicio) of E. Eduardo Krapf, a German psychiatrist interested in Freud, who would later undergo his official analytic training at the APA. Krapf was one of the first psychiatrists to introduce serious analytic techniques at the Hospicio.

The first persons to discuss psychoanalysis (or some version of it) in a positive light, however, were foreign doctors. In 1918 Antonio Austregesilo, a distinguished Brazilian psychiatrist and an unorthodox practitioner of psychoanalysis, visited Buenos Aires to lecture on psychoanalysis at the National Academy of Medicine. Some of his lectures and articles were published in *La Semana Médica,* the most prestigious medical journal in Argentina and probably in Latin America. Austregesilo combined Freud's ideas on infantile sexuality—which he viewed as something to be educated and directed—with classic notions of degeneracy.[30]

The Peruvian Honorio Delgado was another foreigner who published articles in defense of psychoanalysis in Argentine journals. He considered himself a "heterodox psychoanalyst." Delgado had developed a personal relationship with Freud and introduced psychoanalytic thought in Peru. He published extensively on the topic until the late 1920s, when he began to become disenchanted with psychoanalysis; he finally rejected it in toto. In the 1930s he became sympathetic to fascism, and from then until the end of his life he was a fervent opponent of psychoanalysis.[31] Delgado's version of psychoanalysis was very eclectic. He never accepted the theory of libido and in fact was more Adlerian than Freudian.[32] In 1918 the *Revista de Criminología* (the successor to Ingenieros's *Archivos*) published two articles by Delgado on psychoanalysis in the same issue.[33] Delgado's books on psychoanalysis, including a biography of Freud, received admiring reviews in Argentine journals. At one point, Alejandro Raitzin proposed that he be invited to Argentina to lecture on the subject; the invitation never materialized.

Another important foreign introducer of psychoanalysis in Argentina was a well-known Spanish psychiatrist and neurologist, Gonzalo Rodríguez Lafora. In 1923 Rodríguez Lafora, a disciple of the Nobel laureate Santiago Ramón y Cajal, visited Argentina and lectured at the School of Medicine of the University of Buenos Aires on a variety of topics ranging from physiology to psychoanalysis. His lectures attracted a large audience of students, faculty, lawyers, and criminologists, some of whom became interested in applying psychoanalysis to criminology.[34] Some of his lectures were published in various journals and newspapers.[35] Lafora was by no means an orthodox psychoanalyst. He started one of his lectures by claiming that he was a psychoanalyst but not a Freudian. He was critical of what he called Freud's excesses and dogmatism. Many people in his audiences became interested in psychoanalysis, and at least one of them, Dr. Juan Ramón Beltrán, became an enthusiastic if eclectic practitioner.[36]

In the meantime, psychoanalysis began to be discussed in nonmedical circles. The *Revista de Filosofía,* under the direction of José Ingenieros and later of his disciple Aníbal Ponce, also published Delgado and other writers favorable to psychoanalysis, though both Ingenieros and Ponce rejected psychoanalysis in the name of positivism and biological monism. Ponce referred to psychoanalysis as "the monstrous clinical apparatus of Vienna," but he had no problem with publishing the views of psychoanalysis' supporters in his journal.[37]

Ingenieros's role in opening new areas for the reception of psychoanalysis has been thoroughly studied by Hugo Vezzetti. Although Ingenieros opposed psychoanalysis in principle, his interest in hypnosis and psychotherapy and his writings on sexual pathology and hysteria, which reached a public beyond the limited circle of specialists, generated and at the same time responded to an interest in topics that were close to psychoanalysis. His discussions of psychotherapy promoted the idea that the mental patient had to be heard. In other words, the patient's discourse had a meaning; it should not be dismissed as delirium.[38] Moreover, his *Tratado del amor* constituted a modern discourse on love in which the erotic dimension of sexuality was endowed with its own value. In this new discourse Ingenieros not only broke with traditional Catholic notions of family and love but also abandoned his allegiance to positivism.[39] For Ingenieros, love should be detached from domesticity. Although he never cited Freud on the subject, Ingenieros was also interested in the interpretation of dreams. He died prematurely in 1925 without really founding a school of psychiatric thought; but it was through

their readings of Ingenieros's works that at least two important practitioners of psychoanalysis, Jorge Thénon and Celes Cárcamo (the latter a future
founding member of the APA), became interested in psychoanalysis.[40]

Between 1904 and 1919 Ingenieros taught psychology at the School of
Philosophy and Literature of the University of Buenos Aires. From the beginning the psychology courses had a clinical and psychopathological bias
that would continue throughout the decades. Although he did not explicitly discuss psychoanalysis, Ingenieros did cover subjects that were related to
some aspects of psychoanalytic theory. Among the subjects listed in his 1909
syllabus, for example, were "suggestion and psychotherapy" and "dreams:
mythic and psychological interpretations." Since I could not find the reading list for this syllabus, I do not know what works he assigned. He may well
have used writings by the Italian psychiatrist Santo de Sanctis, whom he admired, and whose theories partially coincided with Freud's in many respects.

Until the mid-1920s, then, psychoanalysis was known and discussed but
was not part of the normal mental equipment of Argentine psychiatrists,
who were still very much under the influence of the French school. Psychoanalysis, moreover, did not yet arouse much interest in artistic or literary
circles. The boundaries of psychiatry were still vague, since the specialty was
not yet thoroughly professionalized.

The Spread and Internalization of Psychoanalysis

As positivism lost its hold over the elite and the idea that degeneracy was
hereditary gradually lost favor among psychiatrists, psychoanalysis made
some headway in medical circles. In the 1930s new psychiatric therapies became available all over the world, including electroshock and chemical therapies. For the first time psychiatry had something better to offer than classi-
fications of mental diseases. Therapies became more effective, though they
were not always firmly anchored in theory. Although the practice of psychiatry was still centered in the Hospicio, some Argentine hospitals began to
offer outpatient services, often at the urging of the Liga Argentina de
Higiene Mental. Moreover, some progressive-minded doctors started questioning the very foundations of psychiatric (and by extension medical) practice. They had a broader conception of medicine, in which the psychological dimension of disease and medical treatment could not be ignored. From
doctors who recommended a more human approach to patients ("little psychotherapy") to those who promoted specific psychotherapeutic techniques
("major psychotherapy"), there was a trend toward accepting alternative

uses of psychotherapy and a recognition that patients should be listened to. Many therapists saw psychoanalysis as one of the alternative therapies available, the one with the strongest theoretical foundation.[41] Psychoanalysis could even offer a theoretical foundation for some somatic therapies. In the late 1930s, while psychiatrists in Argentina and elsewhere admitted they did not know why shock therapies worked, Enrique Pichon Rivière, a pioneer in the use of electroconvulsive therapy in Argentina and later a founding member of the APA, came up with a psychoanalytic explanation. Shock therapy worked in cases of "melancholy" (which Pichon would later consider the origin of all mental illness) because it fulfilled the patient's wish for punishment, thereby reducing his or her psychological tensions and anxieties.[42]

Perhaps more important, other spaces opened for psychoanalysis. Aside from its status as a psychiatric technique, psychoanalysis started to be considered one of the most important spiritual currents of the day (for better or for worse).[43] As we have seen, some intellectuals were comparing Freud with Bergson (though Freud always denied any connection). By the 1930s psychoanalysis was being discussed in new contexts. The popular magazine *El Hogar,* for instance, published several articles on the subject as early as the 1920s, and Freud was often mentioned as one of the important thinkers of the day.[44] Freud's ideas were becoming well known to the general public. The references to psychoanalysis in *El Hogar* appeared in discussions of such popular subjects as hypnosis and current literature. Basic psychoanalytic terms were introduced without explanation; it was assumed that the reading public had some familiarity with Freud.[45]

Acknowledgment of psychoanalysis as an important intellectual current did not always imply a positive evaluation of it. In the 1920s and 1930s Aníbal Ponce, then a professor of psychology at the Instituto Nacional del Profesorado before he was dismissed for allegiance to Marxism in 1935, wrote articles—some of them published in *El Hogar*—denigrating psychoanalysis as a frivolous fad in vogue in the Parisian salons but lacking any scientific foundation.[46] In one way or another, psychoanalysis was associated with modernity.

By the late 1920s some Argentine psychiatrists started to internalize psychoanalysis and incorporate it in their theoretical artillery, not as an exclusive method but as a tool that could be added to and sometimes combined with more traditional techniques and theories. Traditional psychoanalytic historiography produced by the psychoanalytic community dismisses this eclectic use of psychoanalysis as evidence of the resistance that Freudian theories encountered in the medical profession.[47] This kind of partial acceptance, however, should be seen as a natural development for any new discipline that challenges the accepted canon. If anything, the combining of psychoanalysis with already accepted theories shows a great deal of flexibility on the part of psychiatrists and contributed to its legitimization. As Richard Whitley points out, the process of popularization of a scientific discipline implies a redescription and change in the body of knowledge.[48]

Throughout the 1920s and 1930s a few prominent psychiatrists felt attracted by the Freudian doctrine. Even those who took a generally dim view of psychoanalysis recognized that at least some of Freud's ideas were worth taking seriously. Nerio Rojas, who had characterized psychoanalysis as a "doctrine between scientific and pornographic," admitted the usefulness of Freud's dynamic conception of the unconscious, along with some aspects of his dream theory.[49] In 1930 he even visited Freud in Vienna and published his respectful though critical impressions in *La Nación,* one of Argentina's most prestigious newspapers at the time.

One eminent psychiatrist who started using psychoanalysis was the Paraguayan-born Fernando Gorriti, who served as deputy director of the open-door colony in Luján, in Buenos Aires province, and was a founding member of the Liga Argentina de Higiene Mental and of the Sociedad Argentina de Medicina Social. In 1926 Gorriti delivered a paper before the Sociedad de Neurología y Psiquiatría titled "Reparos al complejo de Edipo" (Objections to the Oedipus complex), in which he denied the existence of infantile sexuality but nonetheless recognized the value of the psychoanalytic method. A few years later, Gorriti started using psychoanalytically oriented methods himself. In 1930 he published a book on his experience of analyzing a patient's dreams.[50] He sent a copy to Freud, who was very pleased to see that knowledge of psychoanalysis had made its way to such an exotic land.

Gorriti's book on dream analysis exemplifies a conservative interpretation of psychoanalysis. Gorriti claims that although psychoanalysis deals with the worst aspects of sexuality, it is not immoral because it provides the elements for its better control and reeducation. Following the Argentine tradition, Gorriti felt compelled to legitimize his sympathy for Freudianism by pointing out that French doctors also used psychoanalytical methods successfully. His many references to Ernest Jones, however, suggest that perhaps it was through a reading of the English psychoanalyst that Gorriti became acquainted with the discipline. Meanwhile, study groups were established to explore psychoanalysis in Córdoba, Rosario, and elsewhere in the country.

Moreover, although psychoanalysis was not included in the formal curricula of the medical schools (except in Córdoba, where Gregorio Bermann had been teaching classes on various aspects of psychoanalytic theory since the 1920s), it was known among curious students, at least one of whom corresponded with Freud.[51]

Ideological Appropriations of Psychoanalysis

Now that psychoanalysis was becoming integrated into Argentine culture, it became subject to ideological appropriation. Although the liberal consensus that had constituted a unifying myth for the Argentine (and Latin American) elite through the second half of the nineteenth century suffered a crisis in the 1920s from which it never completely recovered, peaceful coexistence was still possible for people at opposite ends of the ideological spectrum.[52] Whereas in Republican Spain, for instance, psychoanalysis was appropriated by leftists as a tool for sexual and political liberation and was rejected by conservatives as immoral, in Argentina it was embraced by both progressives and conservatives. At that time Argentina was much less ideologically polarized than Spain, and there was still room for civil discourse in science. This civil discourse, which Thomas Glick defines as "the possibility of open discussion of scientific concepts without requiring that they fit into a preexisting ideological struggle," permitted ideological appropriations of science but would subject them to the rules of scientific discourse and practice.[53] People made partial and ideological readings of psychoanalysis (as they could do of anything else), but the validity of the body of thought was in general not linked to its compatibility with a certain ideology, except for the radicals of right and left. This situation was to change in the late 1930s, particularly after the beginning of the Spanish Civil War and later of World War II, events that deepened an already existing polarization of Argentine society. The political polarization of the country was to become unbridgeable after the emergence of the Peronist movement in 1945 and would affect all areas of public discourse.[54]

In the 1930s a few leftist doctors saw psychoanalysis as compatible with their ideology. It is not possible, however, to identify a consistent leftist reading of Freud in those early years. Some intellectuals on the left, such as Aníbal Ponce and the writer Elías Castelnuovo, opposed psychoanalysis, the latter on the grounds that it was an idealistic doctrine that substituted sex for hunger as the motive force of human behavior.[55] Many socialists had a rigid discourse on sexuality that emphasized sexual abstinence and were not receptive to Freud's ideas.[56] Others, however, such as the poet Raúl González Tuñón, a fellow traveler of the Communist Party, accepted psychoanalysis as a liberating doctrine that could be combined with socialism.[57] Still, there is no evidence of a structured Freudian-Marxist movement in Argentina such as emerged in France and Germany. Leftist doctors who approached psychoanalysis in the 1930s did so with the idea of using it as the foundation for a restructured psychiatry, as well as a method of social criticism.

One such doctor was Gregorio Bermann, a long-time fellow traveler of the Argentine Communist Party who taught forensic medicine and toxicology at the University of Córdoba. Bermann had developed an interest in psychoanalysis in the 1920s, and had published on the subject.[58] Holder of degrees in medicine and in philosophy, he had been a disciple of José Ingenieros and had taken an active part in the reform movement at the University of Córdoba in 1918. He had lectured on psychoanalysis in Córdoba since 1922. Bermann was interested in applying psychoanalysis to criminology, and he thought it should play a large role in the long-overdue modernization of psychiatric methods in Argentina.

In 1936 Bermann founded a journal, *Psicoterapia: Revista de Psicoterapia, Psicología Médica, Psicopatología, Psiquiatría, Caracterología, Higiene Mental*. He published only four issues before he left for Spain to fight for the Republic, but those issues revealed a high degree of theoretical eclecticism: in the first issue, published in January 1936, the editors proclaimed their admiration not only for Freud, "whose name cannot be remembered here without admiration and gratitude," but also for Carl Gustav Jung, Alfred Adler, Wilhelm Stekel, Ernst Kretschmer, Karl Jaspers, Pierre Janet, Ivan Pavlov, and "hundreds of others." The third issue was devoted to Freud, as a tribute to him on his eightieth birthday; the fourth and last, published in May 1937, was a tribute to the Spanish Republic. Eminent psychiatrists, including Gonzalo Bosch, published notes on the creator of psychoanalysis in *Psicoterapia*. The journal's editorial board represented a wide rage of ideas: among its members were the French psychoanalysts René Allendy and Rudolph Loewenstein (who was Jacques Lacan's analyst for a time), the American psychoanalyst A. A. Brill, Honorio Delgado (who by that time had become an opponent of psychoanalysis), Paulina H. de Rabinovich (who tried to combine psychoanalysis with Pavlov's reflexology), Emilio Pizarro Crespo, and Aníbal Ponce.[59] By the second issue Juan Ramón Beltrán (a right-winger close to antidemocratic military groups, who, as we will see, also played an important role in the diffusion of psychoanalysis) had also become a member of the board. Although the ideological bias of the journal was clear from the start, the involvement of open right-wingers shows that there was still room for civil discourse. As we shall see, right-wing journals were similarly open to people with other views. Journals and institutions could openly declare their political preferences, but the value of scientific theories was argued within the framework of scientific discourse.

For *Psicoterapia,* psychotherapy was a modern response to modern problems originating in the critical conditions of the time. Psychotherapy was going to play an expanded role in the construction of a new society, a role far beyond the mere cure of neuroses: "At this crucial moment in world history, there is an increase in man's incertitude and instability as well as in his anguish and vacillation, and in his desire for clarification of the processes that impel [his behavior]."[60] Psychotherapy would facilitate this clarification.

The journal was proposing a break with traditional psychiatry. The scientific and modern psychotherapy it promoted was "as far from the one usually taught [in the university] as the localization of faculties proposed by Gall [can be] from the knowledge of the cortical functions elaborated by von Monakov and Pavlov, by Vogt and Brodtman."[61] It was the first journal in Argentina to publish works by Freud and Jung in translation.[62] Incidentally, it was in *Psicoterapia* that the Spanish psychoanalyst Angel Garma, later the founding father of orthodox Argentine psychoanalysis but at that time still in Europe, published his first articles in Argentina.[63]

Psicoterapia's program was much more ambitious than the promotion of psychotherapy as a technique. It included a progressive political agenda. Psychiatry had to be totally renovated. Psychotherapy was a crucial component of this renovation and also part of a political program, since it was a tool for the better understanding of the crucial historical and social conditions the world was living through.

Bermann, in part influenced by the French Marxist psychologist Georges Politzer, who had been interested in psychoanalysis for a time but then publicly rejected it, finally found psychoanalysis incompatible with his political convictions, as other leftist thinkers had done.[64] In the late 1940s Bermann finally denounced psychoanalysis as bourgeois-idealist science, although in 1940 he participated in the preliminary meetings that led to the founding of the Argentine Psychoanalytic Association in 1942.[65] In the 1950s and 1960s Bermann continued to promote nonpsychoanalytic forms of psychotherapy and the modernization of the psychiatric establishment.

Emilio Pizarro Crespo's position in the medical establishment was more marginal than Bermann's, although he published extensively in prestigious journals. As his friend and associate Lelio Zeno remembered, Pizarro Crespo was better known in artistic and bohemian circles than in the medical community; yet he was one of the first Argentine doctors to work and write on psychosomatic medicine.[66] He had graduated from the University of Córdoba and later moved to Rosario, where he practiced psychotherapy. Like Bermann, with whom he collaborated on *Psicoterapia,* Pizarro Crespo was active in politics. He sympathized with communism and visited the Soviet Union in 1935. Also like Bermann, Pizarro Crespo left for Spain in 1937, but he soon became disenchanted with the Republicans and with leftist politics in general. He died in 1944, after making a 180-degree turn in his political thinking. His last work, *Afirmación gaucha,* was a right-wing nationalist pamphlet.

Like many other doctors of his time, Pizarro Crespo admired France. There he had an opportunity to deliver a paper on psychosomatic medicine at the Société Psychanalytique de Paris, to which he was elected an associate member.[67] Lacanian analysts credit him with being the first to introduce Lacan's name in Argentina. In an article published in *Psicoterapia* on the uses of psychotherapy in France, Pizarro Crespo praised Lacan's 1932 doctoral thesis on paranoia.[68] In 1934 an associate of Pizarro Crespo's wrote to Freud to inform him that a group of doctors interested in psychoanalysis were seeking affiliation with the International Psychoanalytic Association (IPA). Freud's response was cold: until they abandoned Stekel's theories, they would not be welcome in the IPA. He advised them to seek a duly trained (European) teacher. Pizarro Crespo wrote later to Ernest Jones that they had "cleared up certain defects in the active technique—similar to Stekel's."[69] In the late 1930s he published articles in such popular magazines as *El Hogar* on family issues that were not directly related to psychoanalysis but that he approached from a psychoanalytic viewpoint.[70]

Before his conversion to right-wing nationalism, Pizarro Crespo tried, like other leftist doctors acquainted with psychoanalysis, to use psychoanalysis as a tool for the modernization of psychiatry and as a methodology for social criticism: "It is to the psychoanalytic school—particularly to the work of its founder and master, Sigmund Freud—that we owe the incalculable boon of having removed . . . the obsessive neurotic, hysteric, and phobic disorders from the shadowy realm of genetic destiny . . . to which the current medical doctrines of heredity and degeneration condemned them."[71]

Of the doctors who attempted to combine Freud and Marx, Pizarro Crespo was the most persistent. In 1934 he explained narcissism as a bourgeois disease that could be overcome only by the establishment of a socialist society.[72] His theoretical eclecticism was not uncommon among his col-

leagues. In his later articles Pizarro Crespo defended a "materialist and dialectical monism," although he also recognized the primacy of the unconscious.[73] Before turning to the right, he tried to make Freudian psychoanalysis compatible with Pavlov's theory of conditioned reflexes, the official
psychiatric theory in the USSR.

Jorge Thénon was younger than both Bermann and Pizarro Crespo. His
interest in psychoanalysis came as a result of his experiments with hypnosis
after he had read Ingenieros's works. Like other progressive psychiatrists,
Thénon promoted a psychiatry that was, as a colleague and fellow member
of the Communist Party expressed it, at the opposite pole from the "official
psychiatry" practiced at the Hospicio.[74] For Thénon, as for Pizarro Crespo
and Bermann, the psychic and even spiritual dimensions of disorders had to
be integrated into medical practice.

In 1930 Thénon published his psychoanalytically informed doctoral dissertation, *Psicoterapia comparada y psicogénesis,* which was awarded a prestigious
prize upon its publication—an indication of some degree of acceptance of
psychoanalysis within the medical profession. Thénon sent a copy of the
book to Freud, who, more concerned about promoting psychoanalysis in
faraway places than in protecting orthodoxy, suggested that he summarize it
for publication in the *International Journal of Psycho-Analysis.*[75] Although the
book is subtitled *Contribución al estudio psicoanalítico del sueño en las neurosis*
(Contribution to the psychoanalytic study of dreams in the neuroses), dreams
are treated in only one chapter. In fact, almost half of the book is devoted to
hypnosis and suggestion as therapeutic techniques.[76] *Psicoterapia comparada*
cannot be considered a psychoanalytic book in the orthodox sense. Freud is
cited alongside Jung, Adler, and Stekel, his theory as one among others.
Thénon's knowledge of Freud seems to be limited to the early works, particularly *Studies in Hysteria, The Interpretation of Dreams,* and *Three Essays on
the Theory of Sexuality,* which he cites in a French translation.

Like Ingenieros before him, Thénon emphasized the importance of psychotherapy as a general therapeutic technique. He saw psychoanalysis as requiring a higher level of specialization than other techniques, but he thought
general clinicians ought to know its basic principles because it would give
them a better understanding of hysteria and other conditions that could be
psychic in origin. *Psicoterapia comparada* thus constitutes a break with the
hereditary degeneracy paradigm.

In 1935, the year he won a fellowship for study in France, Thénon published another important book, *La neurosis obsesiva,* which Gregorio Bermann gave a good review in *Psicoterapia* in May 1937; he praised Thénon's

efforts to become a psychoanalyst: "The effort he [Thénon] has successfully completed was doubtless great, especially when we realize how hard the road is for any of us who wants to become a psychoanalyst, not only for lack of a favorable environment but principally for want of teachers, and thus the impossibility of [undergoing] a training analysis."

La neurosis obsesiva clearly reveals that Thénon's knowledge of psychoanalysis had improved greatly over the past five years.[77] Now more committed to Marxism—at some point he joined the Communist Party—Thénon made explicit his disagreement with the "metaphysical aspects" of Freud's theory. Although Thénon accepted Freud's method, he dismissed his theory as metaphysical speculation. The materialism in which Thénon's psychiatric ideas were rooted convinced him that an organic factor lay behind every form of disease. However, he also recognized the importance of research on the psychic dimension.

Like Pizarro Crespo, Thénon offered a sociological reading of some aspects of psychoanalytic theory: "The psyche expresses the subject's social way of being. This fundamental principle must be the leading line of research in the process of psychological integration."[78] Whereas for Pizarro Crespo, for instance, narcissism was a disease associated with a specific stage of social development (bourgeois capitalism), for Thénon the Oedipus complex was associated with the patriarchal family:

> The [Oedipus] legend symbolizes the appropriation of the government (Oedipus incarnates power) and of the product of labor through elimination of the rival during the hegemony of the patriarchal regime. The myth is reproduced in dreams because the circumstances that led to the creation of the popular legend are still related to the maintenance of inequality of power that justifies revenge . . . and crime.[79]

Thénon's political activities cost him his job at the Hospicio de las Mercedes. He remained interested in psychoanalysis and continued to write about it until the early 1940s. Banned from the university as well, he lectured on psychoanalysis at the Colegio Libre de Estudios Superiores, a kind of parallel university founded by his friend Aníbal Ponce, among others. In the tense and rigid ideological environment of the Cold War, however, his political sympathies eventually proved to be incompatible with psychoanalysis. In the late 1940s he turned from psychoanalysis to Pavlovian psychiatry. In a lecture at the Colegio in 1952 he denounced psychoanalysis as an unscientific bourgeois method: "In the abstraction 'private property' that they [psychoanalysts] associate with the oral and anal libido . . . lurks the process that runs from Fabrizio's hut to the Rockefeller Trust, that dramatic process which begins with the primitive community . . . and continues with feudalism and the bourgeoisie."[80]

Thénon, Bermann, Pizarro Crespo, and some others gave psychoanalysis a leftist reading in the 1930s. Although they rejected some of its theory, psychoanalysis was for them one of the methods available (perhaps the most important one) for a general and overdue modernization of psychiatry at a time when the classic hereditary paradigm was in crisis. Moreover, it could provide some tools for social criticism. It was put to very different uses by some doctors on the right of the political spectrum, most notably Juan Ramón Beltrán.

Beltrán taught at several institutions, among them the Military Academy, the Colegio Nacional, and the schools of medicine and philosophy of the University of Buenos Aires. He wrote extensively on psychoanalysis and was very influential in its diffusion in Argentina. Ideologically, he was close to right-wing Catholic and military groups, yet he collaborated with leftist psychiatrists in many organizations related to mental health and even served on *Psicoterapia*'s editorial board.[81] Beltrán characterized himself as a psychoanalyst. In 1939 he founded and became the first president of the Sociedad de Psicología Médica y Psicoanálisis, a branch of the Argentine Medical Association. Beltrán published profusely on psychoanalysis, mostly on its uses in criminology. His point of view, however, was highly eclectic. A convinced Lombrosian, he combined psychoanalysis with criminal anthropology and degeneracy theory.[82] In an article published in 1927, for instance, after citing such authors as Freud, Janet, Morel, and Charcot and listing the physical characteristics of a particular criminal he was analyzing, Beltrán concluded that the man was a classic example of a degenerate, with an abundance of physical stigmas. However, "What makes this observation all the more interesting," he went on, "is the patient's sexual history. . . . This constitutes a serious argument in favor of the much-attacked Freudian thesis, which in this case we accept completely."[83] Beltrán's biological reading of psychoanalysis was paradoxically close to that of some leftists. According to Beltrán, Freud's theory of libido confirmed the "biological thesis of the foundations of our personality."[84] Like many others, Beltrán did not jettison his earlier ideas but, in the French tradition, added psychoanalysis to them.[85] He gave an idiosyncratic reading to Freud's ideas. In 1936 he claimed that one of the most important findings of psychoanalytic theory was that "the child, far from being something chaste, pure, morally spotless, is immoral, impure. Education, society, custom, the family, and so on will purify the child, will give it, with time, the necessary morality, will elevate its temperament and its natural tendencies."[86] The agents of social control, far from engendering pathology, had for Beltrán a "purifying" effect. Beltrán viewed psychoanalysis as a tool for social order, with an educative purpose. Despite his eclecticism and his sometimes perfunctory knowledge of basic psychoanalytic concepts, Beltrán had credibility as a psychoanalyst because of his election to associate membership in the Société Psychanalytique de Paris.[87] He was instrumental in putting psychoanalysis into discourse in Argentina.

Pizarro Crespo, Bermann, Thénon, and Beltrán were only four of the people who read psychoanalysis in ways congenial to their ideologies. All of them combined Freudian theory with other psychiatric theories. The goal of the leftists was a general renovation of psychiatric practice. They also suggested that psychoanalysis could be used as a tool for social criticism. Beltrán and other rightists combined psychoanalysis with hardly compatible theories in an effort to use it as an instrument of social control. Rightists and leftists, however, did not debate; they coexisted. Beltrán and Bermann did not see eye to eye on either politics or theory, yet they agreed on the need for a more comprehensive medicine that would incorporate the psychological dimension. The lack of an official psychoanalytic association and the ideological fluidity of the 1920s and early 1930s made peaceful coexistence possible. None of the psychiatrists interested in psychoanalysis could claim to represent "true" psychoanalysis, because orthodoxy was not yet defined in Argentina. They were approaching an open field that had room for all perspectives.

Another case in point is the Asociación de Biotipología, Eugenesia y Medicina Social and its *Anales,* founded in 1931.[88] The association was inspired by the ideas of Nicola Pende, an Italian doctor and supporter of Mussolini. Pende claimed that the human population could be divided into types, each with its own characteristic illnesses and psychological profile.[89] Biotypology became very influential and the association was a highly respected institution. It had its own hospital and training institute, which was formally dedicated in 1933 with Argentine President Agustín Justo and the archbishop of Buenos Aires in attendance.

The connections between Pende (who visited Buenos Aires in the early 1930s) and fascism should not mislead us. The association's board of directors was a curious mixture of such notable psychiatrists as Gonzalo Bosch, Osvaldo Loudet, and Juan Obarrio; progressive educators such as Víctor Mercante, Ernesto Nelson, and Rosario Vera Peñaloza; conservatives such as F. Julio Picarel, who promoted "nationalist education" in the primary schools;

and anti-Semites such as the writer Gustavo Martínez Zuviría. The association's first president was the highly respected Dr. Mariano Castex. The organization's sympathy with Nazi Germany and especially with Fascist Italy was clear from the start,[90] yet many of the writers who contributed articles to the journal (including the socialist politician Alfredo Palacios) and even a few members of the board of directors could hardly be considered philofascists.[91] To make things even more confusing, the association established not only a Latin Culture section unofficially sponsored by profascist groups but a Spanish section whose honorary president in 1935 was the ambassador of the Spanish Republic.[92]

For Pende mental diseases were determined by biotype, but many contributors to *Anales* thought otherwise. In an article published in the first issue, for instance, Federico Aberastury acknowledged that some mental diseases had no somatic cause, and he referred to Freud as the "genius of the century."[93] In a series of articles published in the same journal between 1934 and 1936, however, Arturo Rossi, director of the Institute of Biotypology, approached the issue from a radically different perspective. Whereas Aberastury saw Freud's chief merit as his return of sexuality to the realm of science, for Rossi the merit of psychoanalysis (not of Freud, whom he dismissed) lay in its provision of an alternative to materialist psychiatry, which, according to Rossi, denied the existence of God. Whereas Rossi found Freud unacceptable because of his "pan-sexualism," Adler's individual psychology represented a more palatable version of "psychoanalysis."[94] When Freud died in 1939, however, *Anales* published an obituary, lamenting the loss of the great scientist.[95] The next chapter will show how this coexistence became impossible in the polarized environment of the late 1930s and 1940s.[96]

Psychoanalysis for the Expanded Public

PSYCHOANALYSIS AND OTHER DISCIPLINES

In the meantime, psychoanalysis received broad acceptance in other areas. Although the University of Buenos Aires did not establish a psychology program until the late 1950s, it had had a psychology chair since the 1890s. The first time psychoanalysis was mentioned in a syllabus had been in 1914, when Horacio Piñero, a psychiatrist (until the 1940s most professors of psychology were psychiatrists), introduced a discussion of Freud and Josef Breuer's theory of hysteria in comparison with Janet's work on the topic. The clinical-psychopathological orientation of the first course (a second course offered since 1907 was more philosophical in orientation) and the decline of positivism among Argentine intellectuals made room for Freud in the psychology curriculum. Credit for a broader discussion of psychoanalysis in the psychology course, however, should be given to Enrique Mouchet, a psychiatrist who was a prominent socialist. Mouchet occupied the chair in psychology first as an adjunct professor, then after 1919 as full professor.

In 1924 Mouchet devoted his entire course to a discussion of psychoanalysis. Mouchet saw psychoanalysis as one of the modern methods of psychological research, and he discussed it in conjunction with other methods of experimental psychology. For Mouchet, then, psychoanalysis was less a clinical technique than a research method. Psychoanalytic thought indirectly informed his own attempt to systematize a new "vital psychology," which he defined as "biological introspection." For Mouchet instinct and intelligence could not be separated, so he appreciated psychoanalysis' emphasis on instinct. At the same time, he criticized Freud's "one-sidedness and exaggeration" in ignoring the physiological, anatomic, and histological aspects of mental illness. Mouchet also welcomed psychoanalysis as an innovation in the field of psychology and as a bridge between psychology and psychiatry. Mouchet's course on psychoanalysis appears to have been very popular.[97] In 1930 he reopened the Sociedad de Psicología de Buenos Aires, which had been founded by Ingenieros, Piñero, and others in 1910 and closed in 1914. Freud was among the foreign corresponding members of the reconstituted society.

While Mouchet was introducing psychoanalysis to his psychology students, Víctor Mercante was pondering its uses in pedagogy. Mercante was a positivist who held several official posts, including the deanship of the school of pedagogic sciences at the University of La Plata. Although psychoanalysis seems to have made no impact on actual pedagogical practices in Argentina until the 1960s,[98] Mercante's approach to psychoanalysis is worth noting because it represents yet another way of reading Freud. Mercante was a reformer in education, educated at the positivist Escuela Normal de Paraná. He interpreted Freud as a biologist.

Three chapters of Mercante's 1927 book *Paidología* discuss psychoanalysis. Chapter 3 associates Freud's theory of instinct with the tradition of what Mercante calls "genetic psychology," among whose practitioners he mentions Lombroso, Antonio Marro, Georges Sorel, and Lascassagne. The juxtaposition of Freud and Lombroso delineates a path of entry for Freud's ideas that is particularly evident in the works of Juan Ramón Beltrán. The other two chapters in which Mercante discusses psychoanalysis relate conversations he claims he had in Europe with Santo de Sanctis on dreams and with Freud himself on psychoanalysis.[99] Mercante claims he became acquainted with Freud's work in 1911 through translations that appeared in Theodule Ribot's *Revue Philosophique*. At first Mercante questioned Freud's emphasis on sex, he says, but he came to recognize the value of psychoanalysis for education. He also recognized the existence of sexuality in young children and the importance of not repressing it. Here Mercante diverged from most rightist readers of Freud, who emphasized the usefulness of psychoanalysis as a means to control "dirty" sexual activity.

Meanwhile, some criminologists were also taking notice of psychoanalysis. Beltrán, as we have seen, was the most visible of them but not the only one. In 1935 two members of the Patronato de Recluídas y Liberadas, an institution that promoted the welfare of imprisoned and recently released women, traveled to Brazil and there met Dr. J. P. Porto Carrero, one of the early champions of psychoanalysis in Brazil. They invited him to lecture in Buenos Aires, and he gave a talk at the law school of the University of Buenos Aires later that year.[100] Throughout the 1930s many articles on the application of psychoanalysis to criminology were published in Buenos Aires,[101] and forensic psychiatrists increasingly cited Freud and took care to listen to inmates with potential mental disorders.

PSYCHOANALYSIS AND THE AVANT-GARDE

Mercante's interest in psychoanalysis stemmed from his personal and professional curiosity, but also from a growing perception of it as not only an innovation in psychology and psychiatry but an essential component of modernity in general. Psychoanalysis was becoming less a psychiatric theory than an object of cultural consumption. In the 1920s critics claimed that the "literary nature" of psychoanalysis was evidence that it lacked a scientific foundation; in the 1930s, the same "literary nature" was seen as cause for positive evaluation. It was not through avant-garde literature, however, that psychoanalysis would reach an expanded audience, at least not until much later.

In Argentina psychoanalysis had no noticeable influence on the artistic avant-garde during the 1920s and 1930s. Elsewhere—in France, for instance— the Surrealists made explicit the close relationship between their artistic conceptions and psychoanalytic theory; some Surrealist artists even sought personal contact with Freud.[102] French artists and writers welcomed psychoanalysis before the medical community was ready to accept it. In Brazil the Modernistas, who were influenced by Dadaism and Surrealism and were eager to emphasize the "exotic elements" of their native culture in order to nationalize it and shake up the bourgeois aesthetic, sang the praises of psychoanalysis and its creator. Brazilian avant-garde circles welcomed psychoanalysis not only as a controversial doctrine appropriate to *épater les bourgeois* but also as the body of ideas that dealt with the wild and savage tendencies in human nature. With this view psychiatrists interested in psychoanalysis agreed, though what they sought in psychoanalysis was an instrument for domesticating those tendencies, whereas the Modernistas wanted to use it to exalt them. Freudian theory provided the Modernistas not only with a new vocabulary but also with inspiration for their aesthetic ideas.[103] Similarly, in Peru, José Carlos Mariátegui wrote favorably on the connection between psychoanalysis and literature.

The Argentine avant-garde, however, would have none of it. Neither Surrealism nor psychoanalysis was particularly influential in literature (or in painting) until later. References to psychoanalysis could be found in literary works, but literature did not serve as a channel through which psychoanalytic discourse infiltrated Argentine culture. Even decades later, when writers began to deal with psychoanalysis more openly, they did so in response to the public's acceptance of it. Argentine avant-garde writers, even those most eager to shake up the establishment, such as the group associated with the magazine *Martín Fierro* in the 1920s, were much more moderate in their goals than their counterparts elsewhere.[104] One has only to compare the magazine's manifesto with any of the contemporaneous Brazilian Modernista manifestos. While *Martín Fierro* claimed that it represented a break with "traditional" literature—not only that of the decadents but the modernism represented by Rubén Darío[105]—it recognized that this attitude was not incompatible with having—"as in the best families"—an album of family pictures to laugh about but also to revere. Even if parts of the magazine's manifesto seem to have been inspired by F. T. Marinetti's "Futurist Manifesto," *Martín Fierro*'s tone was certainly more tame.[106] Similarly, the homage *Martín Fierro* paid to the founding father of Futurism during his visit to Argentina in 1926 described Marinetti as a man who "is approaching fifty years of age, has a bald head, and is now married"—no longer the iconoclast poet of the previous decade.[107]

As Beatriz Sarlo points out, the people who participated in the *Martín Fierro* project and its successors wanted to free literature from its social and ideological foundation, and in that sense they were at the opposite extreme from such movements as Surrealism, Futurism, and even Brazilian Modernism. The break that *Martín Fierro* claimed to represent was defined in purely aesthetic terms.[108] This project, with its strong antipsychological component, could make no use of psychoanalysis, though its value as "a new system of psycho-therapy" was recognized.[109]

Unlike *Martín Fierro, Nosotros,* the most important mainstream literary journal of the 1920s and early 1930s, did discuss Freud and psychoanalysis on several occasions. The tone of those references, however, suggests two things: first, that psychoanalysis was considered more as a curiosity, a new system of thought that was fashionable in Europe, than as an analytic or literary tool;[110] second, that it could not be ignored by anyone with intellectual pretensions. Other literary journals also published articles on the connections between psychoanalysis and literature, but very few attempts were made to incorporate psychoanalysis into actual literary practice.[111]

Later in the 1930s, *Sur,* the prominent literary journal published by Victoria Ocampo, also published some articles on psychoanalysis, and in June 1936 a tribute to Freud on his eightieth birthday praised the literary aspects of his doctrine.[112] This article, by the Spanish critic Guillermo de Torre, was published in response to a request that *Sur* join in an international tribute to Freud on his birthday signed by Thomas Mann, Romain Rolland, Jules Romains, H. G. Wells, Virginia Woolf, and Stefan Zweig. These names suggest not only the international following that Freud had acquired but the cultural areas in which his work was most influential.

Ocampo herself was interested in psychoanalysis (at least in the Jungian version) and became acquainted with Jung. She visited him in 1934 and invited him to lecture in Buenos Aires, but he declined almost disdainfully.[113] During the 1930s she was also introduced to Jacques Lacan, and they corresponded through the 1960s. *Sur's* publication of notes on psychoanalysis was consistent with its project of disseminating European currents of thought in Latin America.

Despite some attempts to read psychoanalysis as literature, psychoanalytic concepts made a very superficial impact on literary criticism during those decades.[114] Only a few novelists, most notably Roberto Arlt, used some psychoanalytic concepts. Arlt, however, wove popular versions of psychoanalysis into his novels in the same way he incorporated popular technical knowledge—as a manifestation of his fascination with the modern rather than as a literary or analytical tool.[115] In some areas of porteño culture, however, psychoanalysis had some influence relatively early. In the early 1930s, some writers published widely read essays on what they perceived as an Argentine cultural and moral crisis, and some of them used psychoanalytic concepts as interpretive instruments. One example is Ezequiel Martínez Estrada's

Radiografía de la Pampa (1933), in which he sought to explain the traumas that led to the Argentine crisis. Martínez Estrada himself recognized the central influence of Freud on that book.[116] More interesting is the reception of psychoanalysis in those areas that are usually thought of as "popular culture."[117]

PSYCHOANALYSIS IN POPULAR CULTURE

Publications directed to the general public proliferated in the 1910s and 1920s, products of a dramatic increase in literacy. Hugo Vezzetti has analyzed some of the channels through which Freudian concepts made their way into Argentine popular culture: a growing interest in sexology, Stefan Zweig's widely read biography of Freud, and inexpensive editions of Freud's works.[118] Dream interpretation was another. The spread of psychoanalytic discourse was made possible by the social and cultural changes that Buenos Aires was undergoing.

The influx of European immigrants (the city's population doubled in less than twenty-five years), rapid economic modernization, and an impressive expansion of the educational system had important effects in the city's cultural fabric.[119] Lower rates of illiteracy (comparable to those of Western European countries) greatly expanded the group of potential consumers for popular literature, and the popular publishing market enjoyed an unparalleled expansion during the interwar years. New publishing houses issued inexpensive editions of works ranging from the classics to more or less scientific works on sexology to popular versions of psychoanalysis.[120] Some of those publishers also published popular literary magazines that enjoyed a wide readership. These publications were at the same time building a reading public and responding to its demand. Some of the new publishing houses, most notably Claridad, owned by the Spanish socialist Antonio Zamora, were conceived as part of a larger project of mass education and were very active in the diffusion of major currents of thought.

These demographic and cultural changes were turning Buenos Aires into a modern city. Customs and mores that had once been rejected became acceptable. Relations between the sexes and sexuality in general could now be discussed openly. The erotic dimension of love was now discussed apart from its role in reproduction, thus materializing a discursive space that José Ingenieros had done much to open.[121] This was evident not only in the wave of popular works on sexology published in cheap editions put out by publishers such as Claridad and *Tor* during the 1920s and 1930s, but also in discussion of eroticism in general stimulated by popular weekly novels and even in some works of avant-garde literature. Sex education for children also became a topic discussed in general-interest magazines.[122]

Another effect of the social and cultural changes was the emergence of what Beatriz Sarlo calls "the knowledge of the poor," which she defines as "the unpolished mixture of discourses on chemistry and engineering, metallurgy and electricity, exotic visions and visions that announce a future metropolis."[123] This knowledge, transmitted through newspapers and popular magazines, and other nonacademic channels, was the basis for a "technical imagination" that was sometimes closer to fiction than to reality. The popular technical imagination often revamped such old obsessions as faith healing, telepathy, and communication with the dead into a new language. All these well-worn themes could now be expressed and legitimized through the discourse of science.[124] This technical and semiscientific knowledge provided an opportunity to reorganize the social hierarchy of knowledge: "Literary culture," Sarlo writes, "which did not include technical knowledge as a central value, could now be seen from without and confronted with the discourses learned in popularized books or in magazines and newspapers. Technical knowledge compensated for the absence of knowledge and of know-how in different dimensions."[125] In a constantly changing world, this "technical knowledge" could be valuable to people who were excluded from the high culture of literature.

Portions of this technical knowledge converged with nontraditional medicine. Although Ingenieros had promoted a "scientific" use of hypnosis, for example, the technique was not universally recognized as a valid medical technique. The fact that it was generally associated with entertainment conspired against its acceptance in academic medical circles. A large part of the public was interested in hypnotic phenomena, however, and in some cases this general interest overlapped with scientific medicine in a kind of gray area. Consider the case of James Mapelli, an Italian hypnotist who arrived in Argentina in the 1920s with an established reputation as an illusionist. He started demonstrating hypnosis and thought transference in theaters in 1925. Soon he gained access to medical circles, and was so well received that some doctors started referring patients to him. Mapelli even published articles in such prestigious professional journals as *El Día Médico*.[126] He was also a member of the editorial board of Bermann's *Psicoterapia*. Mapelli opened a private office and started seeing patients. He invented a therapeutic technique that he called *psicoinervación,* which consisted of inducing several emotional shocks in a patient through suggestion until the symptom disappeared. At some

point he was offered a consulting room in a public hospital, but medical authorities eventually closed it.[127] Similarly, when Jorge Thénon started his research on hypnosis in the late 1920s, a friend well connected with the media
offered him broad coverage and the possibility of instant fame. Thénon, as a
serious scientist, declined.[128] The large number of articles published on hypnosis in mass-circulation magazines such as *El Hogar* makes clear the public's
interest in the topic.

To some extent, pschoanalysis too belonged to that medical gray area.
Federico Aberastury, brother-in-law of the psychoanalyst Enrique Pichon
Rivière, did not have a medical degree, yet he was widely accepted in medical circles, published in professional journals, and presented papers at conferences. Arminda Aberastury, Federico's sister and Pichon's wife, also had an
interesting relationship with the medical world, although she had no medical degree, either. As we shall see in Chapter 2, in the 1940s she became one
of the first to psychoanalyze children. Before that, however, she was publishing reviews of books on psychiatry in *Index de Neurología y Psiquiatría,* a highly
respected psychiatric journal (her husband was on its editorial board).[129]

Thus psychoanalysis found a place in the popular imagination at the
convergence of a more open discourse on sexuality with new "scientific"
forms of knowledge. Psychoanalysis could be introduced as one of the new
technologies available for the modernization of social mores, a modern version of hypnotism, a new cutting-edge psychological theory, and at the same
time a new instrument to deal with traditional but highly popular themes,
such as the interpretation of the mysteries of dreams.[130]

In 1931 the newspaper *Jornada* introduced a column on psychoanalysis.
Jornada was the new name of *Crítica,* the most modern and popular newspaper in Buenos Aires, closed by the military government that took power
in September 1939. In July 1930 *Crítica*'s circulation was estimated to be
274,676 copies a day.[131] Since the early 1920s it had shown a growing interest in scientific and technical subjects. In 1925, when Albert Einstein visited
Argentina, the paper published nine articles on him plus an exclusive interview. It also had regular sections on auto racing, radio, and inventions. Its
coverage of technical and scientific matters (including the possibility of in-
terplanetary travel) was matched by its interest in topics that had fascinated
the public since the nineteenth century: Siamese twins, monsters, experiences with animals, and so on.[132] At the crossroad where cutting-edge technology met old-style curiosities, new areas of interest emerged—alternative
medicine, graphology, biological experimentation, medical miracles.[133] *Jornada* established a clear though somewhat arbitrary distinction between what

it considered real science and fraud. Together with fierce campaigns against "false seers" and healers, we find articles discussing "scientific spiritism" and parapsychology.[134]

This was the context in which *Jornada* introduced a column on psychoanalysis and dream interpretation under the by-line of "Freudiano." While the new column provided a more or less accurate idea of what psychoanalysis was about, its core consisted of the dreams that readers were invited to submit for analysis by Freudiano. Readers were also advised to submit personal information—age, sex, civil status—and their free associations with their dreams. What is interesting about this column is the way it presented psychoanalysis and the kind of discussions it invited. As *Jornada* presented it, psychoanalysis was situated precisely at the confluence of the modern and the archaic. It was "a modern science of interpretation of the phenomena of the soul." Though the phenomena of the soul hardly constituted a new area of interest, their study was legitimized in *Jornada* by the characterization of psychoanalysis as a "modern science." "What does this science, which is followed passionately in Europe and North America but among us is still confined to the scientist's study, consist of?" asked Freudiano rhetorically. Freud was presented as a child of the machine era, just like Henry Ford.[135]

Psychoanalysis was thus attractive because it was modern. Its claim to status as a science was in part legitimized by its close ties to medicine.[136] Slips, repeated jokes, and weird dreams had to be closely monitored because they could be symptoms of a "lesion in the subconscious." Readers were advised to consult a specialist if they suspected the existence of such a lesion, and were discouraged from trying to cure themselves. Freudiano's analysis of dreams was described as an "autopsy of the soul." Freudiano also took pains to differentiate psychoanalysis from quackery. When readers asked about the possibility of premonitory dreams, Freudiano reminded them that "psychoanalysis is a real and profound science, and its true nature cannot be confounded with absurd prophesies."[137]

According to Freudiano, psychoanalysis would also play a role in the modernization of archaic social mores. Parents were urged to send letters discussing their children's character so Freudiano could recommend ways to improve their education. He almost always emphasized the importance of early sex education. In Freudiano's view, it was necessary for society (following psychoanalytic teaching) to rid itself of religious preconceptions in the name of science.[138]

Although *Jornada* thus associated psychoanalysis with modern science and technology, many of the readers who consulted Freudiano were young women who were having problems with their boyfriends or husbands. They probably saw Freudiano as a substitute for the traditional sentimental consultant of women's magazines. At the same time, the "scientific character" of the column, which permitted a more or less open discussion of sexual topics, also attracted young men who wanted to discuss their sexual problems. In this sense, Freudiano's column has to be seen in the context of the growing interest in sexology that porteño society was experiencing.

I could not determine Freudiano's identity. He was certainly acquainted with some well-known progressive psychologists. Once he advised schoolteachers to expand their knowledge of child psychology by attending the lectures of Aníbal Ponce, who, as we know, made no secret of his opposition to psychoanalysis. Freudiano also mentioned Jorge Thénon in friendly terms, this time in order to distinguish true scientific psychoanalysis from quackery.[139] It seems clear that Freudiano had some knowledge of current psychological theories and psychoanalysis, though sometimes he substituted Janet's or Adler's ideas and terminology for Freud's. His responses to readers' questions were a mixture of common-sense advice and elemental psychological theory. The "therapies" he recommended ranged from camphor bromide and cold showers to a more active sex life.[140]

Jornada thus introduced psychoanalysis as a modern response to modern problems, since, according to Freudiano, modern society repressed sexuality.[141] Psychoanalysis was also introduced as an instrument for the overdue modernization of traditional psychiatry at a time when some progressive psychiatrists were trying to use it for just that purpose. According to Freudiano, whereas old psychiatry was interested only in symptoms, psychoanalysis was interested in the whys of mental diseases.[142] In *Jornada*, however, psychoanalysis had a double character. While Freudiano took pains to emphasize its modern and scientific character—after all, it was its modernity that legitimized its discussion in *Jornada*—the interpretation of dreams, an ancient theme of interest, placed it close to the archaic. This ambiguity helps to explain the diversity of Freudiano's readers. Interest in dream interpretation grew through the 1940s and 1950s, and other popular publications introduced columns that dealt with it.[143]

The late 1920s and early 1930s were a period of relatively broad diffusion of psychoanalysis in Argentine culture. The crisis of positivism and more specifically of the hereditary degeneracy paradigm in psychiatry facilitated its acceptance in medical and intellectual circles. Social and cultural changes made people in other sectors receptive to it. A change in mores, a revival of interest in sexology, and the spread of knowledge in the population at large generated interest in a popularized version of Freud's theories, as witness Freudiano's column and the catalogs of general-interest publishers. In 1935 one of those publishers, Tor, put out a series called *Freud al alcance de todos* (roughly, "Freud for everyone") that was reissued many times until 1946. The author, "Dr. J. Gómez Nerea," was actually the Peruvian avant-garde poet Alberto Hidalgo, who, pushed by economic needs, accepted the commission.[144] Needless to say, all the cases were invented. Freud had become so popular that almost anything purporting to explain his theories would sell.

The Founding of the APA
and the Development of the
Argentine Psychoanalytic Movement

In 1942 a new era opened for the diffusion of psychoanalysis in Argentina.
In that year a group of doctors led by the Spanish émigré Angel Garma
founded the Argentine Psychoanalytic Association (APA).[1] The new association received recognition from Ernest Jones, president of the International
Psychoanalytic Association (IPA). The recognition was only provisional, however, since acceptance had to be submitted to a vote at the next IPA congress, and with war raging in Europe, no one could say when that would be.
Only in 1949, when the first postwar congress met in Zurich, did the APA
become a full-fledged member. In 1943 the APA launched the first psychoanalytic journal in the Spanish language, *Revista de Psicoanálisis;* it has continued without interruption since then. The APA was founded by fairly
young progressive doctors who were only marginally connected to the psychiatric establishment; they constituted a particular professional group,
distinctive from those psychiatrists who had shown an interest in psychoanalysis in the previous decades.

Since the late 1930s Arnaldo Rascovsky, a young pediatrician with an interest in psychosomatic medicine and endocrinology, had been meeting in
his office on Sunday afternoons with a group of people, not all of them
physicians, to discuss psychoanalysis and read Freud's works. The meetings
were informal, and members of Rascovsky's and his wife's families took
part. At some point Rascovsky was introduced to Pichon Rivière; the two
mingled with the same avant-garde artistic groups, which by then had become interested in psychoanalysis as a cultural artifact.[2] Pichon Rivière and
his wife, Arminda Aberastury, soon joined Rascovsky's group, and gradually
the group expanded. Rascovsky's wife, Matilde Wenceblatt, and the other
women, none of whom had university degrees and whose role at first was
limited to serving tea, soon became interested in the men's discussions and

joined the study group. Later they were admitted to the APA and in time became training analysts.[3]

Psychoanalysis was a passion for these people, and it became a mandatory topic of conversation at Rascovsky family gatherings. "After lunch, Arnaldo and some of Matilde's brothers stayed, and then—they were all in-laws and very family-oriented [*familieros*]—they started telling each other their dreams and analyzing them," remembers Carlos Mario Aslán, a nephew of Rascovsky's and himself a senior analyst member of the APA. Psychoanalysis even permeated conversations with the children of the family. "On Saturdays Arnaldo took a nap after he finished work, and at five he'd take Raquelita [his daughter] and me and some other kids to the movies. After the film we went to eat pizza . . . and he interpreted the film. I felt embarrassed by the things he said. . . . I wasn't even in my teens then."[4]

At that early stage psychoanalysis was not considered a profession, and Pichon Rivière was the only member of the group who had any connection to the psychiatric establishment. It was an intellectual passion shared by people of different professional and personal backgrounds. Rascovsky used psychoanalytically oriented therapies in his work with overweight children. For Simón Wenceblatt, Arnaldo's brother-in-law and a lawyer, psychoanalysis had no immediate professional application beyond its possible links to criminology.

Other than psychoanalysis, these people seem to have had little in common. Rascovsky was a Jewish doctor from a liberal family of immigrants. He grew up in a highly educated environment and graduated in medicine very young. By the 1930s he was a respected pediatrician with a large clientele, particularly in Buenos Aires' large middle-class Jewish community. He also worked at the prestigious Children's Hospital, where he had to contend with growing anti-Semitism. Pichon Rivière, born in Switzerland, had been brought to Argentina as a young child. His family settled in the province of Corrientes. As a young man he moved to Buenos Aires, where he joined bohemian and avant-garde artistic circles. He was interested in Surrealism and particularly in the works of the nineteenth-century French-Uruguayan poet Isidore Ducasse, known as the Count of Lautréamont. By the time he joined the psychoanalytic study group, Pichon Rivière was a well-established psychiatrist under the mentorship of Dr. Gonzalo Bosch, director of the Hospicio de las Mercedes. His wife's family were wealthy intellectuals of Basque origin. One of Arminda's brothers, Federico Aberastury, studied medicine, developed an interest in psychoanalysis, and published on the subject in medical journals and popular publications, though apparently he never finished his medical studies.[5] In Federico's case we see an example of the gray area that psychotherapy occupied at the fringes of the medical profession. He was not a doctor but was widely accepted in medical circles. Arminda's other brother, Pedro, a lawyer, also became interested in psychoanalysis. He joined the Rascovsky group and later became the APA's legal counselor. In 1957 he was appointed Argentina's undersecretary of education. Other members of the group, such as Luisa Alvarez de Toledo and Alberto Tallaferro, were students or recent graduates of the local medical school. Later Konstantin Gavrilov, a Russian émigré who had studied conditioned reflexes with Pavlov and wrote a book on the relationship between psychoanalysis and conditioned reflexes,[6] also joined the heterogeneous group, although he never joined the APA.

In 1938 Dr. Angel Garma emigrated to Buenos Aires. Garma was a Spanish psychiatrist who had undergone formal psychoanalytic training in Berlin under Theodor Reik. In Spain he had been a student of the Nobel Prize–winner Santiago Ramón y Cajal and of the physiologist Gregorio Marañón, who was himself interested in psychoanalysis. Originally Garma had gone to Germany to specialize in psychiatry, but after a fellow student in Berlin introduced him to psychoanalysis, he abandoned psychiatry and entered into contact with Max Eitingon, then president of the Berlin Psychoanalytic Association. Eitingon referred him to Reik for his training analysis. Almost sixty years later, Garma described his encounter with psychoanalysis as "a marvelous thing. I had the feeling that it was what I had been searching for all my life, without knowing it."[7] In Germany Garma had an opportunity to supervise cases with some of the biggest names in the international psychoanalytic movement, among them Karen Horney and Otto Fenichel. Back in Spain he joined the juvenile court as a forensic expert. When the Civil War began, he sympathized with the Republic but was not ready to fight for it; he fled to France and became acquainted with members of the psychoanalytic community in Paris, among them Dr. Celes Cárcamo, an Argentine doctor who was doing his analytic training there.[8] Garma had close relatives in Buenos Aires,[9] and since the situation in Spain was deteriorating rapidly, he finally joined them there, with the encouragement of Cárcamo, who was planning his own return.

When Garma arrived in Argentina, his reputation had preceded him. He had published articles in such journals as *Psicoterapia*. Moreover, he was the only person in Argentina who had undergone complete formal psychoanalytic training. Garma was also a member of the International Psychoanalytic

Association.[10] He had psychoanalytic credentials that nobody in Buenos Aires could challenge or match. In order to legalize his situation, he revalidated his medical degree as soon as he arrived in Argentina. In 1939 Cárcamo arrived with similar credentials.

The arrival of Garma and Cárcamo energized the diffusion of psychoanalysis in medical circles. The official myth promoted by the APA and by Garma himself was that psychoanalysis confronted harsh resistance in Argentine psychiatric circles. Moreover, in 1979 Garma said that in light of his experience in Spain, he avoided any involvement with the Argentine psychiatric establishment.[11] This, however, does not seem to have been the case.

From the moment he arrived in Buenos Aires, Garma received a warm welcome from members of the psychiatric establishment. His books, including his seminal work *Psicoanálisis de los sueños,* received excellent reviews in the most prestigious medical journals, including the *Revista de la Asociación Médica Argentina.* Garma and Cárcamo soon were publishing articles on psychoanalysis in the most prominent journals in Buenos Aires, including the *Revista de Psiquiatría y Criminología,* the successor to Ingenieros's *Archivos,* and *Index.* They also participated in conferences and delivered papers before various medical and criminological societies.[12] Garma in particular was very active within the psychiatric community. In 1941 the *Revista de Psiquiatría y Criminología* introduced the category of psychoanalysis in its book review section, and Garma became virtually the only reviewer of books on psychoanalysis. In the next couple of years the category grew to become the largest in the journal. The same thing happened in *Index,* a prestigious bibliographic journal and the official organ of the Hospicio de las Mercedes, one of whose editors was Pichon Rivière. Garma had appeared in the list of contributors since 1939 and started contributing reviews of books on psychoanalysis in 1941. *Index* also published his monograph *Psicoanálisis: Presente y perspectiva.*

Rascovsky and Pichon Rivière immediately approached Garma and Cárcamo. The interest in the relationship thus established was mutual. Rascovsky and particularly Pichon Rivière could facilitate their access to medical and psychiatric circles. Since Garma and Cárcamo were the only two analysts who could boast internationally recognized credentials, they were the only ones authorized to carry out training analysis. Thus the members of the Rascovsky group started their therapeutic or training analysis with one of the two. This gave rise to confusing situations. The extended Rascovsky family, for instance, started their analysis with Garma. As one member of the family describes the situation, "They all started [analysis] and

Garma, I believe ill-advisedly, took them all. He analyzed the whole family, the seven siblings and almost all the spouses, and the children too. That was a real mess."[13]

In Buenos Aires Garma met the woman who was to be his second wife, Elizabeth (Betty) Goode. Goode's family was British, and although she had been born in Argentina, she had grown up in England. By her own account Goode was very popular in the Argentine British community as a singer and dancer. She also gave private English lessons and thus became acquainted with the Rascovsky-Wenceblatt family. Since the 1930s English had been replacing German as the official language of the psychoanalytic movement. The members of the proto-psychoanalytic group persuaded her to enter into analysis with Marie Langer, a young Austrian doctor who had had some analytic training in Austria before serving as a physician in the Spanish Republican Army during the Spanish Civil War: "All those psychoanalysts caught me: How come I wasn't in analysis? And they put me in analysis," remembers Goode. One day she was told that "the master" needed her services for some translations, and that was how she met Garma. Soon she started helping Arminda Aberastury, Pichon Rivière's wife, with her translation of Melanie Klein's works. Aberastury persuaded her to become an analyst: "'Why are you teaching English when you could be analyzing children?' And so I started analyzing children. . . ."[14] The wives of three of the founding members, Matilde Wenceblatt, Arminda Aberastury, and Elizabeth Goode, would join the APA as candidates as soon as the association was established. Later they would climb the analytic ladder to reach the rank of training analysts. Goode and Aberastury became the first to practice child psychoanalysis in Argentina.

In 1940 the informal group now gathering around Garma and Cárcamo began to consider starting a formal psychoanalytic association affiliated with the IPA. The presence in the country of two trained analysts who were members of the IPA gave credibility to the project. The preliminary meeting, in a fashionable coffee shop in Buenos Aires, was attended not only by some members of the informal group, the most senior ones, but also by some of the doctors who had been writing on and practicing psychoanalysis informally for years, such as Gregorio Bermann and Jorge Thénon. All were men and all but one were doctors.[15] The group's main idea was to give legitimacy to psychoanalysis by turning it into a medical specialty. The project fell through, however. Doctors who had been practicing for many years refused to submit to one of the IPA's requirements in the postwar era: an expensive and time-consuming training analysis. Of course the only analysts qualified to conduct such an analysis were Cárcamo or Garma, whom they considered their professional juniors.[16] As we shall see, there were also other considerations that prevented Bermann and Thénon from joining the association. In any case, according to Rascovsky, at that time there were too few people in Buenos Aires who had completed a therapeutic analysis and undergone at least three years of training analysis.[17] At last in 1942 the association was launched. Although all the founding members were medical doctors, it accepted lay members (even people without a university degree), such as the wives of the founding members.

Although some prominent Argentine analysts were immigrants, psychoanalysis developed more as a native discipline there than it did elsewhere. The founding members of the APA constituted a microcosm of porteño middle-class society. Only two of them were foreigners: Garma and Marie Langer (Pichon Rivière had lived in the country since infancy), and Garma could hardly be considered a total foreigner. He was a Spaniard, as a large proportion of the population of Buenos Aires had been during the first decades of the century, and he had family in Argentina. Celes Cárcamo was a member of the local Catholic aristocracy. Moreover, of the original members only two (Rascovsky and Langer) were Jewish. Furthermore, Argentina, unlike Brazil and the United States, received hardly any European psychoanalysts who had established careers elsewhere. In the United States popular entertainers put on a German accent to tell jokes about psychoanalysts; nothing of the sort could happen in Argentina, where most members of the analytic community (exceptions notwithstanding) were perfectly fluent in Spanish.[18] Most foreign analysts in Argentina started their analytic training in the country and so were not perceived as foreigners trying to impose their ideas on the local society. Since the early analysts were local products, their discipline was not seen as "exotic or Jewish," as it was in other countries.[19] Whereas in other countries the foreign analytic pioneers needed to adapt their thought to local values in order to attract local followers, in Argentina the pioneers were themselves locals.

None of the psychiatrists who had been interested in psychoanalysis during the previous decades joined the new association. Not even the members of the Sociedad Argentina de Psicología Médica y Psicoanálisis, a branch of the Argentine Medical Association, became members of the APA. Their absence was a unique feature of the development of Argentine psychoanalysis. Elsewhere, early informal practitioners of psychoanalysis usually joined the official association when it was founded. A typical case is that of Durval Marcondes, pioneer of psychoanalysis in Brazil. After practicing psycho-

analysis without formal sanction for decades (he had even founded the first
and short-lived Brazilian Psychoanalytic Association in 1927), Marcondes
brought the eminent German psychoanalyst Adelaide Koch to Brazil as the
nation's first training analyst. Koch analyzed Marcondes (in his own office),
and Marcondes became a leader of Brazilian "official" psychoanalysis. A
similar pattern can be perceived in the early development of American and
French psychoanalysis.[20]

Professionalization in a Polarized Society

Since the 1920s the IPA had been imposing strict standards for analytic
training, and its standards became more rigid after the war. Training in an
IPA-affiliated psychoanalytic association is expensive, time-consuming, and
rigorous. With some minor variations from country to country, the IPA required around 300 hours of training analysis, attendance at seminars for
three or four years, usually two or three cases completed under the supervision of a training analyst, and presentation of a substantial paper. After all
that, the candidate becomes an associate member, with the hope that after
years of practice and more papers, he or she may eventually be elected a full
member. The pinnacle of the psychoanalytic hierarchy is reached when one
is elected a training analyst (*miembro didacta* in the Argentine association),
who can train other analysts and does not need to be in analysis him- or
herself. Although there are variations in the internal structure and hierarchy
of each association, more or less all of them have followed this model since
World War II, at least in theory. The psychoanalytic associations also have
training institutes where the seminars are taught. Although the institutes are
component parts of the association, they sometimes have some degree of
autonomy. Thus the psychoanalytic associations become not only professional organizations but also the holders of a monopoly on the training of
future analysts and the gatekeepers of the profession.

Within each association training members have enormous power. They
not only administer the required training analysis but also are the teachers
and evaluators of candidates. In a small association, this can give rise to all
kinds of confusing situations. A training analyst who knows a candidate's
most intimate secrets is also going to evaluate the candidate's performance.[21]
Moreover, when the association has few training analysts, they have an additional source of power provided by the market: scarcity. In 1961 only 17
training analysts were available to serve 166 APA members plus the even

larger community of prospective candidates. People interested in psychoanalytic training had to wait years before one of the training analysts had an hour available. Since a certain number of hours of training analysis were required *before* one entered the institute as a candidate, the aspirant, probably already a physician with a specialization in psychiatry, had to wait perhaps four or five years just to try for acceptance as a candidate. Scarcity raised prices. Training analysts' fees were very high, and since candidates are usually not allowed to practice psychoanalysis independently during their training, the financial sacrifice is extreme. To make conditions less onerous and to attract more potential candidates, Garma decreed that candidates could see private patients at unregulated fees during their training. Still, the limited number of patients a candidate could see would hardly pay for the training.

Unlike other so-called liberal professions, the practice of psychoanalysis is in general not regulated. The titles issued by psychoanalytic associations have no legal standing. Some countries have limited the practice of psychotherapy to professionals holding degrees in medicine or in some cases in psychology or social work, but psychoanalysis is rarely legally recognized as an autonomous profession. During the APA's first years the practice of psychotherapy was not legally regulated in Argentina; thus the emergence of the gray area we have noted. In 1954 the minister of public health issued a regulation limiting the practice of any kind of psychotherapy to medical doctors. This regulation would have important consequences for the evolution of the APA. Theoretically, far from granting a legal monopoly to the members of the APA, this regulation allowed any graduate of a medical school to style him- or herself a psychoanalyst (whether or not the physician had ever seen an analyst's couch) and open a private practice. A few physicians did so, but the APA was able to impose its own hegemony over legitimate analytic training, and nobody would really challenge it until the 1970s.

It is not difficult to understand the popularity of analytic training among young psychiatrists in the United States. As a survey carried out in the late 1950s concluded:

> The analytically trained psychiatrist is the one who is sought by many
> university teaching centers, community mental health agencies, and the
> sophisticated public. This the psychiatric resident knows. There is a degree
> of factual basis in these realities since psychoanalytic theory is concerned
> with the *how* of mental functioning, which provides the springboard for
> psychotherapy—the psychiatrist's major claim as a specialist.[22]

In Argentina, however, the relationship between medicine (particularly psychiatry) and psychoanalysis was much more complicated, particularly in the early years of the association.

Psychoanalysis as a Liberal Profession

Argentina's official system of psychiatric services was based on the model of the asylum. Any attempt to go beyond that model had to incorporate psychotherapy. Among the psychotherapeutic methods available, psychoanalysis had the strongest theoretical foundation. Although the introduction of new somatic therapies, particularly the shock therapies and chemotherapy, had changed the image of psychiatry (now it could offer some hope of cure), no one was sure why they worked—sometimes. This problem was widely recognized by Argentine doctors.[23] Psychoanalysis could provide a theoretical anchorage—right or wrong—for some somatic therapies. Moreover, a growing interest in psychosomatic medicine, particularly after the beginning of World War II, when U.S. influence began to displace that of France in the Argentine medical profession, provided additional legitimacy to psychoanalysis.[24]

At the beginning the APA tried to create links with the medical community. In 1945, at a conference held by the Sociedad de Neurología y Psiquiatría de Buenos Aires, the society's president, Dr. Roque Orlando, warmly welcomed APA representatives. Pichon Rivière, as one of those representatives, reaffirmed the psychoanalytic community's commitment to keeping its ties with the psychiatric community. At the same time, he pointed out the analysts' distinctive identity: "Our group makes up the Argentine Psychoanalytic Association, a branch of the International Psychoanalytic Association."[25]

However, it was not within the institutions or structure of the medical profession that psychoanalysis would flourish. After the founding of the APA, psychoanalysts in general withdrew from the medical establishment. Until late in the 1950s they very seldom participated in nonpsychoanalytic conferences, and after the launching of the *Revista de Psicoanálisis* in 1943, they rarely published in other medical journals.[26] By 1944 the section on psychoanalysis in the *Revista de Psiquiatría y Criminología* had started to shrink, and soon it disappeared. Similarly, in 1943 *Index* removed Garma's name from its list of contributors. Both journals disappeared soon after the rise of Juan Perón.[27]

It is clear that the conditions of training and professional organization contributed to the relative isolation of Argentine psychoanalysts during the

APA's early years. Psychoanalysts derived their professional status from their membership not in a prestigious medical institution but in a private organization that had no links to the traditional medical structure but was a branch of an international organization, part of a tight international network. The analyst worked entirely within an analytic institution that defined a true subculture. Psychoanalysts spoke their own jargon and behaved in much the same way. Their friends were other psychoanalysts; they took vacations together and spent weekends together. They usually sought sex and marriage partners among themselves. Most of their talk was about the profession, even during their leisure time, and they saw the world through the psychoanalytic lens. Conflicts were explained away in terms of the neuroses of the opponents. One analyst compared the APA to a secret society.[28] They also broke some rules of medical etiquette. Unlike other doctors, psychoanalysts charged visits by colleagues at their regular rates. This practice certainly generated tensions, but that was only part of the story. To understand the APA and its complex relationship with the medical community during its first two decades, we have to turn our attention to broader developments in Argentine society and culture since the mid-1930s.

The End of Peaceful Coexistence

The malleability of psychoanalysis permitted ideologues of right and left to make what they would of it. Sherry Turkle points out that psychoanalytic concepts are "almost tangible." Dreams, slips, jokes, and so forth function as "things or objects we can play with." Because psychoanalytic ideas can be manipulated like objects, they are highly appropriable and are able to generate a culture.[29] It was social and political conditions, however, that facilitated not only these multiple interpretations but their peaceful coexistence. Until the founding of the APA in 1942, there was no psychoanalytic institutional orthodoxy in place, so nobody could claim to have the true interpretation of Freudian thought. Psychoanalysis was an open field. Moreover, the political environment of Argentina through the mid-1930s had generated conditions for the coexistence of different, even incompatible political interpretations of psychoanalysis. Thus, as we have seen, Pizarro Crespo published in Bermann's journal, on whose board of editors sat Beltrán. Psychoanalysis was appropriated by leftist and rightist doctors and intellectuals, but its validity as a scientific discipline was not automatically linked to a certain ideological position, as it would be in Republican Spain.

The cases of *Psicoterapia* and the Asociación de Biotipología, Eugenesia y

Medicina Social were paradigmatic but hardly unique. The *Archivos Argentinos de Psicología Normal y Patológica,* which published the article in which Pizarro Crespo attempted to combine Marxism and psychoanalysis, also published an editorial praising Nazi Germany's new eugenics law.[30] Two years later the journal published an article by Dr. Carlos Jesinghaus, official representative of the School of Philosophy and Literature of the University of Buenos Aires at a psychology conference in Germany, openly approving Nazism.[31] Later that year, however, the journal published in French a salute to Freud, Addler [*sic*], and Dubois, soliciting articles from "the three masters," and soon after it also published a highly positive note on Bermann's journal, *Psicoterapia.* Even *La Semana Médica,* which included many liberals on its board of directors, published an article by Héctor Stocker detailing the benefits of the German law mandating the sterilization of people the regime considered unfit to reproduce. Among the sources he cited was *Mein Kampf.*[32]

In the 1930s and early 1940s Argentine society suffered a political transformation that would have important consequences for intellectuals. A coup led by the philofascist general José Uriburu, who in 1930 overthrew President Hipólito Yrigoyen, thus ended a fifty-year period of institutional stability.[33] The Spanish Civil War, the emergence of Nazism, the radicalization of Mussolini's fascism, World War II, and particularly the military coup d'état of 1943 and the emergence of Perón contributed to the ideological and political radicalization.[34] The polarization of Argentine society also permeated the scientific realm. As Telma Reca, a renowned child psychiatrist, wrote to an officer of the Rockefeller Foundation in 1944, "the present [political] situation . . . exerts its influence upon all our activities."[35]

The radicalization of international politics forced Argentine intellectuals to take sides. Ideological differences became irreconcilable. The nationalist historian Julio Irazusta, referring to the regular gatherings of intellectuals at Victoria Ocampo's home, wrote in his memoirs: "Eduardo Mallea, Pedro Henríquez Ureña, María de Maetzu, Cármen Gándara . . . and innumerable others who do not come to mind associated with us in an environment of civilized conviviality. . . . If this experiment ceased, it was partly due to the European War, which confounded their spirits and divided them into international factions."[36]

Two clear political and cultural sides thus became defined in the Argentine cultural fabric: one liberal-progressive, the other nationalist-Catholic. Gradually the gulf between them became unbridgeable. Each side marked out its own space for expression and debate. Liberals and nationalists clustered in institutions and publications that openly expressed their ideological allegiance, and had little space for representatives of the other side.

The newly polarized ideological environment also had an impact in some areas of the scientific community.[37] In the particular case of psychoanalysis it provoked new alignments. Jorge Thénon and Gregorio Bermann, who had been able to reconcile their leftist sympathies with a particular interpretation of Freudian thought, found themselves forced to take sides. Both opted for their political loyalties and rejected psychoanalysis, which the traditional left now viewed as a bourgeois-idealist doctrine with no scientific foundation.[38] At the other end of the ideological spectrum, the Asociación de Biotipología grew increasingly homogeneous. All the progressive authors who had once contributed to *Anales* now disappeared from its pages. The journal's favorable references to psychoanalysis (now considered a Jewish science) also disappeared, with the exception of Freud's obituary in 1939.

After the emergence of Peronism in 1945, the political polarization of society increased. The government of Juan Perón (1945–55) had traumatic effects on Argentine society. The importance of the Peronist experience in redefining not only political but social identities cannot be overemphasized. Peronism made it possible for the working class to become a crucial force in Argentine politics. Perón gave them a new identity as a class and as a political entity.[39] The factions that opposed him, from socialists and communists (the latter briefly approached Perón in the early 1950s) to liberals and some conservatives, formed a heterogeneous coalition defined solely by its opposition to Perón. From its beginnings Peronism was characterized by its opponents as a political aberration, as the essential "other," and as a pathology in Argentine history. In the Perón decade politics became charged with a strong affective component on both sides, Peronist and anti-Peronist, in a way that was unheard of since the times of Juan Manuel de Rosas in the nineteenth century. One was for Perón or one was against him; there was no middle ground.[40]

This is the context in which psychoanalysis was institutionalized in Argentina. While the crisis of positivist and somatic psychiatry of the 1920s had opened a space for psychoanalysis in all of its various readings, the ideological and political crisis of the 1930s and 1940s limited those spaces. The existence of a psychoanalytic orthodoxy after 1942 restricted the areas of discussion even more.

Another consequence of the highly charged political environment of the 1930s was the loss of legitimacy and prestige of traditional academic institutions, particularly the universities. The democratic reform movement that started in Córdoba in 1918 generated a strong sense of identity in Argentine universities. Since 1918, public universities had obtained autonomy. Universities could choose their own authorities through the so-called *sistema tripartito,* which gave graduates, students, and faculty equal representation in the governance of their institutions. Although the universities became highly politicized, they did not become identified with any particular party, although in general they became hostile to the government of Yrigoyen during its last years.

The universities could not remain a protected democratic space for long, however. Throughout the twentieth century they were extremely vulnerable to political turmoil in the state. One of the first measures taken by the right-wing military government that took power in 1930 was to impose regulations on the universities, thus erasing by decree the autonomous status obtained by the Reform Movement. In an address to the nation one year after the coup, General José Uriburu spelled out his program for the universities:

> The universities cease to be institutions dedicated exclusively to the cultivation of scientific disciplines when they make room for philosophical doctrines, whether historical materialism, Rousseauan romanticism, or Russian communism, that separate them from the calm and ordered examination of the life phenomena that constitute science and turn them into focal points of proselitizing for special interests and violent passions.[41]

As the sociologist Silvia Sigal points out, however, it was the coup of 1943 that showed just how vulnerable the universities were, and how that vulnerability could turn them into major political actors. The philofascist military authorities who took power in 1943 not only appointed well-known nationalist Catholics, some of them openly fascist, to rule the universities but dismissed a large number of professors for political reasons. The government's intervention into the universities went deeper during the Perón regime and eventually became a tradition in Argentina. Between resignations and dismissals, the University of Buenos Aires lost 1,250 professors by 1946.[42] After 1943 and throughout the Perón era, the University of Buenos Aires became a focus of resistance against the regime, while the government made strenuous efforts to use the universities to promote its own cultural, political, and ideological agenda.[43]

The politicization generated by the emergence of Peronism in 1945 accelerated a process that had started in the 1930s: the burgeoning of intellectual life outside the universities. In 1930 a group of intellectuals launched the Colegio Libre de Estudios Superiores (CLES), a kind of parallel private unofficial university (there were no private universities in Argentina until the early 1960s). The creation and early history of CLES constitutes clear evidence of the beginnings of the polarization process. Five of the founders sympathized with socialism to one degree or another;[44] the sixth was a right-wing nationalist intellectual, Carlos Ibarguren. Right after the coup of September 1930 Ibarguren was appointed delegate of the revolutionary government in the province of Córdoba and became active in nationalist groups. In 1931 he resigned from the board of directors of CLES, claiming the institution had became a nest of communist sympathizers.

Throughout the 1930s and 1940s CLES constituted a privileged space for high-quality academic discussion and research in various fields; it was also a space for cultural resistance against the advances of Catholic nationalism in the public system of higher education.[45] The traditional institutions of cultural production linked to the state, particularly the university, had lost some of their prestige and, more important, their undisputed legitimacy. Liberal intellectual groups created a parallel network of cultural institutions, which they did not always succeed in protecting against the intrusion of the state.[46] The APA, like CLES, was part of that network.

Although Perón did not openly persecute cultural opponents, the regime's propaganda apparatus characterized avant-garde art, existentialism, and other "modern" intellectual currents as nonnational and nonpopular, and therefore non-Peronist. In this context, psychoanalysis, too, was perceived as part of the system of "cultural resistance." Although psychoanalysts were not openly persecuted, uniformed police were always present at APA meetings, and some psychoanalysts felt so threatened that they considered emigration. Dr. Ramón Carrillo, a neurosurgeon who served as minister of public health, missed no opportunity to denigrate psychoanalysis.[47] Under Perón, psychoanalysts were barred from the public system of psychiatric services.

In this tense cultural environment the success and growth of an institution such as the APA becomes easier to understand. The early members of the APA were identified with the liberal tradition now under assault. Garma and others had given talks and taken an active part in the Centro Republicano Español. They lectured regularly at CLES. In 1939–40 CLES organized a year-long series of courses on psychoanalysis. The following year, Garma, Rascovsky, and Cárcamo offered a course on the theory and practice of psychoanalysis there.

As standard bearers of a new and controversial discipline, psychoanalysts were not welcome in the public institutions and hospitals. The APA could be seen as part of the parallel network of educational and cultural institutions created in those years, institutions that derived their legitimacy in part from their lack of association with public institutions. Moreover, the APA, as a purely scientific and professional institution that did not have and did not need connections to the state, became perceived as a place where the cultural and scientific spheres could preserve some autonomy.

Consolidation and Evolution of the APA's Self-Image

The APA was not created in a vacuum. By the 1940s psychoanalysis occupied such a prominent place in Argentine society that in his novel *Adán Buenosayres* (1947) Leopoldo Marechal placed psychoanalysts together with theosophists, agnostics, and materialist (soulless) doctors in the eighth and deepest level of hell (reserved for souls guilty of the sin of pride) in his Dantesque Cacodelphia. In 1946 the popular writer Arturo Capdevila wrote a play titled *La consumación de Sigmund Freud,* whose plot consisted of Freud's journey through the soul and the realm of dreams and the unconscious. The play was reviewed in medical and professional journals, including the APA's *Revista de Psicoanálisis.*

The potential market for psychoanalytic therapy, however, was the cultural and economic elite. Psychoanalyst members of the APA were very active in those early years in building their own clienteles. Enrique Pichon Rivière spread the word in psychiatric circles and in the artistic community. Rascovsky's situation among progressive pediatricians had a multiplier effect: pediatricians interested in a psychoanalytic approach would in turn educate mothers and refer children to the psychoanalyst's office, thus contributing to the generation of a psychoanalytic culture among the progressive middle class.[48] Mothers recommended psychoanalysts to each other, while progressive private schools incorporated pedagogic techniques derived from psychoanalysis in order to satisfy a growing demand. The Rascovsky-Wenceblatt family reached out to the middle-class Jewish community and Celes Cárcamo attracted Catholic patients. As Rascovsky remembers, there was a true division of labor in the diffusion of psychoanalysis: "We divided the task. Pichon, who was a member of the Society of Psychiatry, worked in the psychiatric environments, while I, as a full member of the Society of Pediatricians, had influence among pediatricians."[49]

The APA immediately inaugurated a policy of inclusion / exclusion that proved to be very successful. Its inner circle of full and associate members, with the candidates on the fringes, was highly selective and became even more so over time as additional requirements were introduced for the acceptance of candidates. Its structure was extremely hierarchical. Only a full member had a vote in the governance of the institution. Training analysts gathered enormous power in the association. At the same time, the APA made an effort to expand its outer circle. In 1943, one year after its founding, the APA launched the *Revista de Psicoanálisis,* the first journal devoted exclusively to psychoanalysis in the Spanish language, and distributed it free among doctors, lawyers, and other professionals. The first issue claimed that it already had 185 subscribers, most of whom, needless to say, were not members of the APA.[50] By the time the second issue was on the streets, the *Revista* had 211 subscribers, and the number would increase dramatically in the following years. The APA also organized public conferences and a circle of "friends of the APA," for whom the institution organized special programs. During its first decade the APA secured financial support from the Fundación Francisco Muñoz, which financed not only the *Revista de Psicoanálisis* but also a program of fellowships for Latin American candidates. Francisco Muñoz was a Spanish immigrant who owned a department store. His manager suffered from agoraphobia and was treated and cured by Pichon Rivière. The foundation was his way of expressing his appreciation.[51] Thanks to the foundation, Argentina became the major center of psychoanalytic training in Latin America.[52]

Although some among the first generation of APA members did not hold medical degrees, requirements for admission soon became an issue. This was a critical item on the psychoanalysts' agenda for professionalization. As long as psychoanalysts were gathering in an informal group, the goal had been to attract as many people as possible. Once the association was founded, the priority was to give legitimacy to the new profession. As physicians, the APA's early leaders would have been happy to let psychoanalysis grow within the medical community. That it did not was more the result of the political and cultural environment than of any resistance from the medical community.[53]

The image of professional psychoanalysis that the APA founders promoted was strictly medical and closely linked to psychosomatic medicine. This orientation is reflected in the early issues of the *Revista.* Thus we read in its first issue: "Psychoanalysis was born as a therapy necessary to interpret and relieve the suffering of a certain sector of patients. Its later evolution led it to expand the scope of its medical activities and of its subject matter, at first confined to the psychoneurotic, in order to provide a deeper interpretation of the mental mechanisms of psychiatry." Moreover, its regulations required candidates to attend Pichon Rivière's lectures on psychosis at the Hospicio.[54]

Requirement of a medical degree was proposed as early as 1942, with the provision that nonmedical candidates might still be admitted in exceptional circumstances, if their candidacy were approved by two-thirds of the full members. The proposal was not adopted because the original statutes were still under consideration by the state, and the APA's leaders preferred not to introduce changes until the association's status was legally cleared.[55] In 1948 the requirement of a university degree was finally adopted: a medical degree for those who wanted to practice psychoanalysis and any other degree for those who wanted to apply psychoanalysis to other professions. Candidates must undergo a training analysis of no fewer than 300 sessions and could not be admitted as candidates until they had completed at least 250 hours.[56] Requirements became even more restrictive later, but loopholes were left for those members (mostly but not exclusively women) who had reached high rungs of the psychoanalytic hierarchy without a medical degree.

In 1954 the Ministry of Public Health issued a regulation limiting the practice of psychotherapy to holders of medical degrees. This regulation had paradoxical consequences for the APA. On the one hand, it placed psychoanalysis among the medical specialties, giving it additional legitimacy as a profession. On the other hand, it granted the right to any graduate of a medical school to call him- or herself an analyst and accept patients. In the long run, the regulation had positive consequences for the APA. When the University of Buenos Aires introduced a very popular psychoanalytically oriented program in psychology in the late 1950s, the APA psychoanalysts, who constituted a substantial proportion of the faculty, used the 1954 regulation (reaffirmed by a military government in 1967) to exclude graduates in psychology from training at the APA. As we shall see, the exclusion split the psy profession into two camps.

From the beginning the APA gave a clinical orientation to psychoanalysis. World War II marked a transition from the predominantly humanist psychoanalysis of Europe to the predominantly clinical orientation of the U.S. model. German was giving way to English as the language of psychoanalysis. In a letter to the APA acknowledging its founding, Ernest Jones noted that "knowledge of German, still desirable, was once an essential tool for the purposes of international links related to our work, but today it is yielding its place to English."[57] In 1949, 450 of the 800 IPA members were American and 122 were British; whereas German had been the mother tongue of 90 percent of IPA members in 1929, English was the primary language of 70 percent in 1949.[58] Garma, who had had his analytic training in Germany, acknowledged that he preferred to work with James Strachey's *Standard Edition* of Freud's works rather than with the original German editions. During its early years the APA was very much in tune with developments in Britain and the United States, and this tendency was reinforced by the rapid headway made by psychosomatic medicine.[59] Later the U.S. professional model coexisted with firm allegiance to the British theoretical school.

In part as a result of their inability to secure positions in the public mental health system but also as a way of constructing their own professional identity, psychoanalysts gradually defined themselves in opposition to traditional psychiatrists. When some analysts gained access to positions in mental health services after the fall of Perón, they set about to pull psychiatry out of the archaic and sclerotic structures in which it had been operating. According to Angel Garma, one of the most important consequences of the development of psychoanalysis was "the beautiful renaissance of psychiatry," which psychoanalysis turned into a "fundamental medical discipline, as opposed to what classic psychiatry was."[60] At that time the APA was divided between those who thought psychoanalytic therapy had to be limited to the analyst's couch and those who, like Pichon Rivière, wanted to see it incorporated by the psychiatric institutions. In any case, the APA discouraged its members from taking any professional responsibility outside its jurisdiction. It even formulated a pathology for those who did so: activity by APA members in institutions other than the APA was characterized as the satisfaction of masochistic tendencies.[61]

In Argentina as elsewhere in the world, psychoanalysts were extremely confident about the therapeutic possibilities of their discipline, and those possibilities were not limited to the treatment of mental illness. Psychosomatic medicine offered an almost limitless field of medical applications. As we read in the first issue of the *Revista*, "Unsuspected aspects of internal medicine became fertile ground for [psychoanalytic] research. Thus the emergence of psychosomatic medicine, today in rapid development, whose future prospects can be foreseen."

Stories of almost miraculous cures effected by purely psychoanalytic methods when traditional medicine had failed reaffirmed psychoanalysis' self-identity. One interesting case is that of Emilio Rodrigué, who in the early 1940s was a mediocre medical student with a serious thyroid disorder. After one year of psychoanalytic therapy with Arnaldo Rascovsky, who later published the case in *Revista de Psicoanálisis,* Rodrigué's medical tests showed no trace of the disorder. He went on to become a top student and later a prominent psychoanalyst himself, president of the APA, vice president of the IPA, and a leading figure in Plataforma, one of the groups that split from the APA for political reasons in 1971.[62]

As psychoanalysis became more popular, the image of psychoanalysts as pioneers struggling in a resistant world gave way to a more accurate self-image. By the mid-1960s, at least, analysts were seen (and saw themselves) as successful liberal professionals who played a central role in Argentine middle-class culture. As Madeleine Baranger, a French-born prominent non-medical member of the APA, put it in 1970, "In the days of the pioneers, becoming an analyst was an adventure. . . . That has changed, psychoanalysis has conquered the establishment. Psychoanalysis can reasonably be seen as a career in which it is possible to reach a position of prestige and relative economic comfort quickly."[63]

Gradually the APA started to promote the spread of psychoanalysis more actively, particularly during Pichon Rivière's term as president in the early 1950s. In his annual report of 1951, Pichon pointed out that one of his administration's goals for that year had been to establish contacts "with groups and medical societies in order to disseminate psychoanalysis among them."[64] Although he emphasized medical circles, his objectives were in fact more ambitious. Psychoanalysts gave informative talks in such places as art galleries and schools. In 1954, members of the National Association of Kindergarten Teachers organized a course on psychoanalysis taught by APA members. Pichon Rivière became a crucial link between psychoanalysis and the society at large. A few analysts became real diffusers of psychoanalysis. In 1959 the Revista de Psicoanálisis launched a section headed "Anchorena 1357" (the APA's street address) for the purpose of "attracting sympathizers to our home." The APA that had once perceived itself as an exclusive institution founded to educate a new elite of psychoanalysts had turned itself into a meeting place for "all people of the city of Buenos Aires interested in psychoanalysis; it is also the point of departure from which radiate a series of activities that show the penetration of psychoanalytic thought in all orders of life."[65] Garma wrote in 1959 that it was important to disseminate psychoanalytic knowledge among families and the professions.

In the more open cultural environment that emerged after the fall of Perón, analysts became public figures. The medical school officially celebrated Freud's centenary in 1956. The student union invited prominent analysts to lecture and teach courses. The psychoanalytic courses were a huge success, and many students went into analysis after attending them. In 1958 the Center for the Promotion of Psychological Education, sponsored by the student union at the medical school, launched a psychoanalytic journal called *Psique en la Universidad,* with established and future analysts on its editorial board.[66] The reason for the journal, its editors wrote in the first issue, was "the growing interest shown by students in all schools [of the university] who attended the Introduction to Deep Psychology courses taught by Drs. Angel Garma and Arnaldo Rascovsky." The articles they published show an intent to emphasize the links between psychoanalysis and other disciplines. Meanwhile, psychosomatic medicine became a focus of interest for progressive medical students. In 1958 a recently graduated M.D. who later became a well-known psychoanalyst complained about the lack of psychological training in medical school. "It is well known that in any specialty, 50 percent of the patients who visit us have 'psychic disorders' that are at the root of their organic diseases."[67] Analysts taught in the new psychology program, lectured at such places as the Ministry of the Army, and became highly visible in the media.

The general rhetoric of "opening the APA to society" was matched by the association's policies. In 1961 it opened the Racker Clinic, named for Heinrich Racker, a recently deceased APA member who was credited with developing a theory of countertransference. The clinic was run by candidates, who received no salary but were given one year of free supervision by training analysts as compensation. The original purpose of the clinic was "to make psychoanalytic treatment available to people of limited economic resources but who, because of the nature of their work, have a great impact on broader sectors of the population, such as teachers and nurses." The clinic achieved official recognition the following year.[68]

Despite the attempts to open the APA to the community, it continued to be a closed society, torn by internal tensions. The tensions derived from the almost incestuous relationships within the APA and from the lack of alternative national institutions that could have served as safety valves, as they did in Europe and the United States. In the *Revista de Psicoanálisis* in 1959 the analyst Leonardo Wender lamented the difficulties analysts experienced in interacting with nonanalytic circles. He urged his colleagues to assume responsibility for the problem and not to attribute it to other people's neuroses, as they usually did. Part of the problem, he wrote, was analysts' lack of experience in dealing with the external world. Most analysts had no institutional experience in hospitals.[69]

During the 1950s competing factions emerged among training analysts. These divisions trickled down to the candidates, who were forced to show blind allegiance to their superiors on the analytic ladder. As the APA became increasingly sectarian, analysts began to think about psychoanalysis as an ideology that defined their lifestyles. In a symposium with the suggestive title "Relations Among Analysts" in 1959, one candidate discussed how candidates reproduced the conflicts of their trainers:

> It's difficult for me to accept the teaching of those who don't share the idea that having religious beliefs, no matter what they are, is evidence of a more serious neurosis than an analyst can tolerate, that to circumcise or baptize a child is to enter into a kind of submission that we fight against in our patients. It's difficult for me to agree to use so-called toxic therapeutic techniques by administering drugs or electric shocks.[70]

It is not difficult to guess to which group the speaker belonged. Angel Garma expressed almost identical sentiments:

> Tolerance for such ideologies [as those taught by organized religions] within a psychoanalytic association implies at least some acceptance of ideas that fight against psychoanalysis. Of necessity, that has to lower the psychoanalytic level, generating internal tensions and intensifying sadomasochistic behavior among colleagues.

Marie Langer compared the APA to the Communist Party. It achieved a high level of cohesion when it was forced to fight against a hostile environment, but when it gained power, internal conflicts became evident. Like the Communist Party, the APA had an ideology.[71] The ideology Langer was referring to was the APA's allegiance to Melanie Klein's theories and techniques, as other participants in the symposium openly acknowledged.

Later, in the convulsive political and social climate of the later 1960s, some psychoanalysts became more concerned with the social role of psychoanalysts. The APA started to have a more active presence in the outside world. In 1969 and 1970 the APA issued press releases expressing solidarity with victims of police repression and support for strikes called by unions of health-care workers. In this changing atmosphere the identity of the psychoanalyst also changed. Some psychoanalysts started to see themselves more as progressive intellectuals than as professionals, while others openly questioned the social role of psychoanalysis. In 1968, when Garma was still insisting on the clinical aspects of psychoanalysis, Hernán Kesselman, a young leftist psychoanalyst, declared that psychoanalysis was not and should not be a mere therapeutic technique; it was a research technique. For him the obsession with cure was an obstacle to research.[72] By the end of the 1960s psychoanalysts were expected not only to be successful professionals, possessors of semimagical knowledge, as Mauricio Abadi had said a decade earlier, but also to have political interests, revolutionary sensibility, and a proclivity for working to change the social and economic structure.[73] Most APA analysts, however, remained attached to a purely medical-clinical conception of psychoanalysis and did not become involved in political debates of any kind.

An interesting insight on how psychoanalysts saw themselves by the mid-1960s is provided by a survey conducted at the Second Pan-American Congress of Psychoanalysis in 1967. It seems that the analysts who actively engaged in the diffusion of psychoanalysis were a (highly visible) minority. Among the three groups of analysts considered in the survey (Argentines, other Latin Americans, and North Americans), the Argentines were the least interested in contributing to nonpsychoanalytic publications. Those in the lower ranks of the profession were more interested in doing so than those in the upper. Lower-rank analysts tended to define themselves as "professionals," whereas those in the higher ranks (full and training analysts) saw themselves as "scientists."[74]

Kleinianism and Child Analysis

As I have suggested, child psychoanalysis was an important channel for the diffusion of psychoanalysis in the middle class. It was an area almost monopolized by women, without medical degrees in the beginning. This changed when more female doctors joined the APA in the 1950s and 1960s. Furthermore, child analysis paved the way for the reception of the theories and doctrines of Melanie Klein, which were to have so much influence in the APA until the 1970s.

At the time the APA was founded, child psychiatry and psychology were at the margins of the psychiatric establishment. Although the University of Rosario claims that the first chair of child psychiatry in the world was established there, in 1921, thus antedating the one in France by four years, the specialization was not much developed. Most of the emphasis on retarded children or on children with educational problems was part of the broader concern with mental hygiene that emerged in the 1930s. One of the exceptions to this pattern was Dr. Telma Reca's Centro de Psicología y Psiquiatría Infantil. Telma Reca had graduated from medical school in the early 1930s and was awarded a fellowship to study child psychology and juvenile delinquency at Vassar College, in Poughkeepsie, New York. Upon her return to Buenos Aires she was appointed head of the mental hygiene service of the medical school's department of pediatrics. Reca still maintained a good working relationship with the Rockefeller Foundation, which funded some of her projects. She established a center for research and assistance of troubled children, which offered outpatient services.

From the beginning Reca tried to modernize child psychiatry by using the dynamic methods she had learned in the United States. Moreover, she had a broad and interdisciplinary conception of how to treat children. By 1943, the center's staff consisted of three physicians, a social worker, and a speech therapist. In 1947 the center examined 250 new patients and administered 1,612 psychotherapeutic treatments, despite the Perón regime's withdrawal of state funding.[75] Reca's approach was flexible. Although she was not particularly sympathetic to what she considered the rigidity of psychoanalysis (after the APA was founded she became very critical of the new psychoanalytic establishment), her methods and theories were based largely on psychoanalytic findings.[76]

Nonetheless, the introducers of orthodox psychoanalysis for children in Argentina would be not physicians but the wives of the APA's founders. The lay leadership of child analysis was not a phenomenon unique to Argentina. Neither Anna Freud nor Melanie Klein, the leaders of the two competing schools of child analysis in the IPA, had a medical degree. In general, child psychoanalysis was perceived as a subspecialty best suited to women. The first person to practice it in Argentina was Arminda Aberastury.

According to her own account, Aberastury became interested in child therapy when she started seeing a young girl with learning problems. The girl's mother was in therapy with Pichon Rivière in the outpatient service at the Hospicio de las Mercedes. The girl caught Aberastury's eye as she waited for her mother in the waiting room, and Aburastury engaged in "long interviews" with her. At that point Aberastury was about to enroll in the pedagogy program at the University of Buenos Aires. After some time she concluded that the child could not learn because she did not want to know about her mother's psychosis and wanted to repress the memory of the painful episodes she had witnessed. As Aberastury continued to work informally with the girl, the learning problems gradually disappeared. Encouraged by her success, Aberastury wanted to study how to treat children. After reading a text by Anna Freud, she started treating other children. Taking advantage of the gray area occupied by psychotherapy in the medical profession, Aberastury (still without a degree) started seeing children at the Hospicio de las Mercedes.

After a while Aberastury started her training analysis with Garma and later discovered Melanie Klein's theories and her technique of analyzing children's play. In time she not only translated Klein's works into Spanish (with Betty Goode's help) but became a kind of informal ambassador for Klein in Latin America and corresponded with her. It was in part as a result of this early relationship that Kleinianism became the APA's (and by extension Latin America's) hegemonic psychoanalytic ideology.[77] Goode, too, started analyzing young children, some of them the children of other analysts. Later both organized therapeutic groups of mothers, pediatricians, and pediatric dentists that became very popular in the 1960s. For years to come the APA was an orthodox Kleinian institution, and although Klein herself never visited Argentina, many of her disciples and collaborators did, and many Argentine analysts went to London for training and supervision.[78]

The Kleinian choice, however, was the result more of random episodes and basic technical options than of a deliberate decision. At first APA members were also interested in the work of Anna Freud; those writings disappeared from the APA canon in the following decade. According to Elizabeth Goode de Garma, when she and Aberastury, untrained as they were, started doing child analysis (Goode analyzed Aberastury's children while Aberastury was in analysis with Garma), the two texts available to them were Anna Freud's and Klein's. They found Anna Freud's theory of defenses "very useful. In terms of technique, however, of what to do with a child who came with a conflict, with a problem, Klein gave us more instruments."[79] Klein provided a ready-made set of guidelines that could be easily followed.

Another reason for the Kleinian option was more personal. Garma had known Paula Heimann, one of Klein's closest collaborators, since his training in Germany. When he and his wife went to Zurich for the Psychoanalytic Congress of 1949, it was easy for him to put her in contact with Klein, who, interested as she was in expanding her circle of followers abroad, received them very cordially.[80]

Additional factors contributed to the APA's adoption of orthodox Kleinianism. Unlike alternative theories, Klein's puts special emphasis on technique, creating a rigid but workable analytic setting. Most of the correspondence between Klein and Aberastury turned on basic technical issues—how and how much to charge per session, whether the child's mother should be allowed to be present, what kind of toys the analyst should offer to young patients and how they should be arranged. Klein offered a set of rigid rules for both child and adult analysis. She emphasized the importance of the analyst's neutrality and detachment and of the analytic setting in general. As Jorge Balán suggests, in a small and young association such as the APA, in which the relationships between members and the internal hierarchies were difficult to define with precision, Kleinianism helped to establish clear rules. Periodic visits by Kleinian analysts from London helped to put things in order in the APA and gave Argentine analysts a feeling of being identified with a strict orthodoxy. After a visit by Hanna Segal in the 1950s, for instance, it was established that candidates in training could no longer attend their training analysts' seminars and study groups.[81]

Allegiance to Kleinianism provided an additional source of professional identity and legitimacy for Argentine analysts. Anna Freud doubted that it was possible to carry out a real analysis with a young child, because the parents were still such a very real presence in the child's life that a transference relationship could not be properly established. For that reason she considered it indispensable to link the analysis of young children to previous pedagogic work. Klein, however, claimed that transference could be established very early in a child's life, and young children were as analyzable as adults. According to Klein, libidinal trends interacted with Oedipal tendencies very early in life. She emphasized the existence of aggressive unconscious tendencies in infants and believed the superego was formed earlier than Anna Freud did. Children too young to express themselves verbally could express their unconscious fantasies through their play and drawings, so a young patient's play substituted for free association. Since in Klein's version there was no essential difference between a child's and an adult's analysis (any difference lay merely in the technique), Kleinian analysts sometimes offer brutal interpretations to very young patients. This is how Goode interpreted her twenty-one-month-old patient's play: "You're afraid your father is angry at you because you wanted to bite him in order to take away his penis so you can have it and use it with me."[82] A professional consequence could be established from this distinction. Educators could conceivably carry out Anna Freud's version of child analysis, but Klein's version required specific knowledge that only analytic training could provide. Klein's version, then, reinforced the APA's monopoly on child psychoanalysis.[83]

Allegiance to Kleinianism had another consequence: it gradually placed Argentine psychoanalysis on the opposite side of the theoretical fence from U.S. psychoanalysis, which in the 1950s and 1960s was very much under the influence of Anna Freud's ego psychology and of the native culturalist school. The APA's early interest in staying in touch with developments in U.S. psychoanalysis soon ended, except in respect to psychosomatic medicine and institutional models. Only 28 percent of the Argentines surveyed at the Second Pan-American Congress in 1967 claimed to be very up to date on developments in psychoanalysis elsewhere (versus 40 percent of the other Latin Americans and 34 percent of respondents from the United States). U.S. psychoanalysis in particular held very little interest for the Argentines: only 18 percent claimed to be very up to date on those developments (compared to 58 percent who said they were very up to date on developments in England). In fact, respondents from all countries had the general impression that there was a deep theoretical divide between U.S. and Argentine psychoanalysts.

The early history of the APA and the emergence of psychoanalysis as a liberal profession were deeply influenced by the political and cultural turmoil that the country had been living through since the mid-1930s. The society was polarized ideologically and politically. The politicization of the Perón era had important consequences for the new profession. The sharp separation of psychoanalysts from the medical community is more fruitfully seen as a result of this general environment than as a consequence of psychiatrists' resistance to Freud's doctrine.

THREE Social Change and the Expansion
of the Psychoanalytic World

The diffusion of psychoanalysis took place very rapidly. By the late 1960s popular magazines, TV shows, theater, fiction, and essays were loaded with psychoanalytic jargon and concepts. Throughout the decade psychoanalysis overflowed its original field of application and became a "nucleus of signification," a belief system that provided explanations for various aspects of social and political reality.[1] Even sectors of the Catholic Church, which had never had much positive to say about psychoanalysis, used its terminology. In 1962 the archbishop of Buenos Aires issued a pastoral letter condemning pornography not only because it was sinful but also because it could traumatize children; it could leave deep "psychical wounds" in their tender minds.[2] Catholic schools advertised "psychological bureaus" among the services they offered. Demand for psychoanalytically oriented therapies expanded dramatically.

Just a few years earlier the picture had been altogether different. A 1959 poll revealed that the majority of urban Argentines considered neuroses to be moral deficiencies instead of forms of mental illness. Only 8 percent of respondents cited psychotherapy and psychoanalysis as possible cures for mental disorders, while 32 percent cited electroconvulsive shock.[3] How and why did psychoanalysis achieve such widespread diffusion in such a short time?

The 1960s was a decade of dramatic social and cultural changes in Argentina, as it was elsewhere. What was unique to Argentina was the particular combination and timing of those changes. First, the social sector that comprised the natural potential clientele for psychoanalysis—a relatively affluent and highly educated middle class with new expectations and new patterns of consumption—expanded very quickly. Second, changes in the traditional concept of the family and of women's role in the home and in society opened another area for the reception of psychoanalysis. Third, the rapid social and cultural changes after the fall of Perón provided conditions for a general questioning of traditional customs and mores. Psychoanalysis provided an appropriate language for this questioning and for channeling the anxieties thus generated. Fourth, the fall of Perón was followed by political conflict that exploded in unprecedented violence toward the end of the 1960s. Between 1955 and 1970 the Argentine government was headed by four generals, two "democratically elected" civilian presidents, and one civilian president who took over after a military coup overthrew one of the constitutional presidents. Moreover, the political system established after the fall of Perón excluded broad sectors of the population, since the large Peronist party, which commanded a large constituency, was not allowed to participate in elections until 1972. The political system lost legitimacy and vast sectors of the population were forced to redefine their political (and more generally their public) identities. As politics was not seen as an arena in which social conflict could be regulated and channeled, some people preferred to turn inward to seek explanations that traditional concepts did not provide.

The rapid changes of the 1960s aroused a general feeling of anxiety and uncertainty.[4] "Are all of us neurotics?" the magazine *Primera Plana* asked rhetorically in 1963. *Nuestros Hijos,* a popular magazine devoted to child-rearing issues, declared in May 1961, "The ground is shaking under our feet." Catholic groups, both progressives and conservatives, debated the role the church should play in a time of such uncertainty.[5] People demanded explanations for what they were experiencing and an alternative framework for understanding it. For many people, psychoanalytic discourse provided a belief system that could bring order out of chaos.

In the 1960s psychoanalysis was simultaneously used as a therapeutic method, a means to channel and legitimize social anxieties, and an item of consumption that provided status to a sector of the population obsessed with "modernity"; later it was a tool for social revolution. Above all, it was an interpretive system.[6] Thus psychoanalysis became a kind of common denominator among different sectors of Argentine society. As *Gente,* a popular magazine, claimed in the early 1970s, psychoanalysis had became a common language that crossed class barriers.[7]

Social Change and the Expanding Market for Psychoanalysis

THE TRANSFORMATION OF THE MIDDLE CLASS

The middle class expanded significantly in the 1960s.[8] More interesting than its expansion (the middle class had grown even more quickly earlier in the century) were the changes in its composition. As a consequence of economic changes introduced by post-Perón governments, a new middle-class composed mainly of technicians and managers expanded at the expense of the more traditional and autonomous sectors. The Perón regime had emphasized the development of light industry oriented toward the domestic urban market. Light industry had accounted for the largest growth in employment during that period (after construction). After Perón was gone, through new "developmentalist" policies the government invited foreign investment and promoted the emergence of a more concentrated industrial sector oriented toward import substitution of intermediate and durable goods. The new industries targeted the upscale market. The reformulation of the economic model led to higher productivity among the industrial labor force, particularly in the most dynamic sectors. The industrial sector's ability to generate employment slowed down dramatically. Between 1960 and 1970 the service sector became the fastest-growing employer after construction. In 1947 the service sector employed 45 percent of the economically active population; by 1970 the percentage had risen to 51.7.[9] Moreover, the parts of the service sector that experienced the fastest growth after the fall of Perón were the most "modern" ones: those linked to new industries and financial institutions. Between 1947 and 1960 "services linked to industries" had grown 10.7 percent; between 1960 and 1970, its growth was 37 percent. Although in absolute terms this sector employed only 2.8 percent of the labor force in 1970, its dramatic growth shows the dynamism of a sector composed mostly of middle-class, highly educated professionals and technicians. Thus the number of independent small manufacturers and merchants, who had proliferated in the earlier decades, declined sharply in the 1960s to make way for a new salaried middle class dependent on the new modern industries. A similar development can be seen in the industrial sector itself. From 1947 to 1960 its expansion was associated with significant growth of the wage-earning working class; from 1960 to 1970, the fastest growing sector was the wage-earning middle class: technicians and professionals.[10] This was the case particularly in Greater Buenos Aires.

Thus the 1960s witnessed the rapid expansion of a highly educated and affluent middle class composed of executives and technicians linked to modern industries. This class developed specific patterns of consumption of both material and cultural goods. It is not by chance that in that decade a large number of publications emerged with the sole purpose of satisfying and at the same time orienting the tastes of that class.[11] The 1960s saw the proliferation of "experts"—sociologists, psychologists, economists, and the rest—at the service of the new model of economic development, which had American-style efficiency as one of its most cherished values.

Hand in hand with modern economic activities came the modern diseases, real or imagined. Stress, alienation, and neurosis became the new key words. In the modern world, homemakers were as vulnerable as executives to that modern disease par excellence, chronic fatigue.[12] "Neurosis is the disease of our times," declared *Primera Plana,* an outspoken promoter of cultural modernization. If neurosis was *the* modern disease, then psychoanalysis was *the* modern therapy to deal with it, and it was touted as such by numerous magazines and other publications. For some sectors, psychoanalysis became an object of consumption and, in the words of a leading analyst, even an investment. According to Angel Garma, analysands were happy to invest large amounts of money in therapy because they knew that by improving their whole personality, psychoanalysis would make them more productive and therefore would increase their future incomes.[13]

THE CHANGING PLACE OF WOMEN

Women, too, changed their patterns of participation in the labor force during the period. In 1947 women accounted for only 21.7 percent of the total working population—the smallest proportion in modern Argentine history. That figure rose modestly until 1960, then increased more rapidly between 1960 and 1970. In 1947 there were four times more men than women in the economically active population; in 1970 there were less than three times more men than women. This is an indication that throughout the years from 1947 to 1970 women were entering the labor force at a faster rate than men.[14]

The most important change, however, occurred within the female workforce. Between 1960 and 1970 the number and proportion of married and separated women entering the labor market increased significantly. Married women constituted the fastest growing group within the female labor force between 1950 and 1970.[15] Moreover, the median age of working women increased throughout the period, from 28.8 years in 1947 to 30.5 in 1970. These changes suggest that a growing number of mothers were participating in the labor force, and therefore introducing changes in the traditional family model. Psychoanalytic discourse provided a way to discuss such changes and the anxieties they generated.

Women not only were going out to work in unprecedented numbers, they were also better educated. During the Perón regime the education system had expanded dramatically. From 1945 to 1955 elementary education had reached its saturation point.[16] The number of students enrolled in secondary schools and universities also grew substantially. In 1942, 17,742 students were enrolled in the University of Buenos Aires; ten years later, that number was 41,325. By 1950 Argentina ranked third in the world in the number of university students per 100,000 inhabitants, after the United States and the Philippines.[17] The total number of students enrolled in public universities rose from 137,673 in 1958 to 207,437 in 1965.[18] Since 1950, the growth rate of enrollments has been higher in institutions of higher learning than in primary and secondary schools, much higher than the growth rate of the population. The number of women attending secondary schools and institutions of higher education also increased. By 1960 there were more female than male high school students in Greater Buenos Aires. The percentage of women enrolled at the University of Buenos Aires (by far the largest in the country) rose from 14.51 percent in 1941 to 18.03 percent in 1951.[19] In the decades after the fall of Perón the university population continued to grow, and so did the proportion of women in it. In 1950 Argentina ranked ninth in Latin America in the proportion of women enrolled in institutions of higher education. By 1970 it tied for first with Costa Rica and Panama.[20] By the early 1980s, 43 percent of the students attending Argentine public universities were women.[21] The founding of new universities, both public and private, in the 1960s also contributed to the increase in female enrollments.

Furthermore, Peronism had introduced important changes in the condition of women. In 1947 the government granted women the vote. Perón's discourse on women, however, was ambiguous. While he emphasized the importance of their newly granted political rights, women's participation in the public sphere was presented as an extension of their "natural" activities in the private realm. By joining the women's branch of the Peronist party, according to Peronist propaganda, women engaged not in political activity but in "social work."[22] Still, the enfranchisement of women and their increasing participation in the public life of the country (whatever the name Perón wanted to give it) did contribute to a dramatic change in women's social role. By the 1960s, women were much more integrated into public life than they had ever been before.

In the early 1970s a small but more radical feminist movement emerged among middle- and working-class women, who started translating works of feminist thinkers in Europe and the United States.[23] Moreover, since the late 1960s the emergence of powerful armed leftist groups that included women in their ranks and even in their leadership gave yet another twist to women's role in public life. Women who "fell in combat" while participating in guerrilla activities joined the pantheon of martyrs for the revolutionary left. The participation of women in the armed struggle also changed the state's perception of them. Until the emergence of the urban guerrilla movement, the women's prisons were administered by nuns of the Order of the Good Shepherd. The state did not consider women dangerous enough to warrant the kind of resources it invested in the men's correctional system. Since the early 1970s, when a large number of female inmates were political prisoners, the state took over the women's prisons. Female prisoners now received the same treatment as their male counterparts.[24]

The perception of the changing role of women, however, was ambiguous even among those leftist groups that accepted them as full-fledged combatants.[25] Argentines' perception of gender relations changed more slowly than the actual place of women in society. The revolutionary left demanded gender equality yet did not perceive women as equals. *Descamisado,* the journal of leftist revolutionary Peronism, claimed, "Here there are neither men nor women: there are the exploiters and the exploited," while taking it for granted that women are less politically educated than men because they "have to fulfill [their] obligations as wives and mothers, working at home and educating children."[26] Those "special tasks" assigned to women were never seriously questioned by most sectors of the revolutionary left.[27]

If radically progressive sectors were not altogether comfortable with gender equality, the more conservative sectors of the middle class were much less so. Most of the women polled by *Primera Plana* said that male infidelity was more acceptable than female infidelity, and that men needed more sexual contact than women. A similar poll taken among men showed identical attitudes.[28] These polls, although of limited statistical value, suggest the attachment of the middle class (even its most "modern" sector) to traditional values. Those values were reinforced by authoritarian legislation passed by the military regime throughout the 1960s.[29] Nonetheless, women in general were slowly breaking loose from traditional roles and social perceptions. As women became more independent, topics that had belonged to the realm of morality or medicine, such as female sexuality, acquired new meaning and were discussed in women's and popular publications.

Here psychoanalysis served two purposes. First, it provided a discourse outside of religion, morality, and the traditional language of eugenics to channel the new anxieties in a nonthreatening way. The discourse on gender employed by mainstream psychoanalysts such as Marie Langer and Arnaldo Rascovsky was less than radical. Second, psychoanalysis legitimized the discussion of certain topics in the name of science. When psychoanalysis was recognized as the science that studied sexuality, discussion of sexuality in psychoanalytic terms became more easily accepted.

Political Change

The Perón decade had had important psychological consequences, particularly for the middle class.[30] The social and economic changes brought about by the Perón government subverted traditional social hierarchies and customs. Peronist policies made the working class a crucial player in the political arena.[31] After the fall of Perón it was clear that many of those changes were going to be permanent. The Peronist experience was from its beginning a puzzle for the middle class, a puzzle that required an explanation and forced society in general to question Argentine social and political reality. The radically anti-Peronist middle class and particularly the intelligentsia perceived the Perón regime as a pathology in the historical development of the country. The fact that after the fall of Perón the working class continued to be loyal to him against all predictions added an important dimension to the problem.[32] It has been argued that the development of sociology in Argentina was closely related to the need to provide a "scientific explanation" for Peronism.[33] This need for an explanation generated more critical ways of contemplating social reality. Many things that had been taken for granted were now questioned.

The fall of Perón provoked a general feeling of confusion, particularly among young people. Peronism had redefined Argentines' political and social identities. During the Perón regime, those identities had hinged on the Perón / anti-Perón dichotomy. His fall forced Argentines to revise those identities, thus giving rise to a general feeling of uncertainty. The liberal anti-Perón consensus that had emerged during the Perón regime disintegrated when the man himself was gone, since Perón was the only element that had kept it together. This situation created a need for new interpretive tools. For some sectors of the critical left that emerged after the fall of Perón, psychoanalysis provided a theoretical tool for understanding social and political developments. This will be discussed in depth in Chapters 7 and 8. For other sectors of the middle class, psychoanalysis provided a means to explain politics in subjective terms—in other words, to psychologize politics. Psychoanalysts appeared on TV and in the print media, explaining current political events in terms of neurosis, the Oedipus complex, and the like. This is the way an expert consulted by *Primera Plana* summarized the recent Argentine past:

> Since 1930 we have suffered a series of repressive regimes, and the only sector that had twelve years in a row to "train" themselves in free expression was the Peronist one. Theirs was a paternal system, the "great nurturing mother" that gave them power, protection, security, and money. When the system fell, they felt deeply frustrated, resentful, aggressive, paranoid. . . . What is happening with them is what in individual neuroses is called "contamination." The repressive mechanisms and the repressed contents end up tainting each other and achieve a compromise.[34]

The language of psychoanalysis thus allowed the "expert" to fulfill an obsession of the anti-Perón middle class: to pathologize Peronism and at the same time to render it intelligible.[35]

The military coup that deposed President Arturo Illía in 1966 had particularly upsetting consequences for Argentine political culture. Although the coup initially had the approval of broad sectors of society, including important sectors of the left, the repressive policies of the government of the so-called Revolución Argentina had long-lasting traumatic effects.[36] The military government eliminated political debate and dissolved the public sphere. It abolished political parties and established a highly centralized and authoritarian regime.

The university was badly affected by the policies of the government established in 1966. Earlier it had become very politicized when the student movement recovered its voice after the decade of Peronist repression. In the eyes of the military, indoctrinated in the so-called national security doctrine, and their conservative allies, the university had become fertile ground for communist subversion. Soon after taking power in 1966, General Juan Carlos Onganía took over the university by police force in an episode remembered—perhaps with some exaggeration, considering future events—as "the Night of the Long Sticks." This episode ended the ten-year golden age of post-Perón Argentine universities. The University of Buenos Aires lost its autonomy once again. Professors and students were victims of police repression and some of them were badly beaten up. The result of this incident, which forced the resignation of almost a fifth of the faculty, was catastrophic.

Many of those who resigned were eminent professors who devoted their full time to research.[37] Within the first three months after the government takeover, 108 faculty members went into exile, some of them never to return.

Far from defusing the situation, military repression exacerbated it. Although this was not the first time the government had attacked the university, a variety of factors made the situation in 1966 particularly volatile. First, the politicization of the university was matched by that of the larger society. Second, the tumultuous "spirit of the sixties" had permeated the Argentine student corps. Third, the post-Perón university was perceived and cherished as an important agent of cultural and scientific modernization. Finally, by 1966 there was an important group of professional academics who devoted their lives exclusively to teaching and research and so had everything to lose by the collapse of the university. As tensions accumulated, Argentine society became radicalized after 1966. Between the late 1960s and the early 1970s, violence became an increasingly expected part of Argentina's political culture.

The university was not the only victim of the cultural policies of the Argentine Revolution. Any evidence of a countercultural movement also fell victim to police repression, carried out in the name of public morality, sometimes with public support. As long as the moralizing wrath of the police was directed against relatively marginal sectors, it was tolerable and even supported by the bourgeoisie. The real problem started when the police, not satisfied with forcibly cutting the hair of local hippies, arrested prominent artists, suppressed avant-garde art exhibits, and closed down typically bourgeois gathering places. *Gente,* a popular magazine that had never been known for a critical attitude toward military governments and had expressed benevolent amusement when the police had targeted the local hippies, became much more critical when the repression was extended to other sectors.[38] After 1966 public arenas of political and social debate were eliminated. In a highly politicized society, that move would have explosive consequences.

The interaction of political, social, and economic variables, then, generated an overall impression of endless crisis and insecurity. Although instability was a global phenomenon in the 1960s, in Argentina it had important peculiarities. The Peronist experience was deeply traumatic for Argentine society; it called for explanation and, more important, for a personalized and internalized vision of politics. Moreover, the authoritarian regimes eliminated politics as a channel for the expression of social demands and restricted the public sphere. When vast social sectors were deprived of political representation, the political system lost legitimacy. As Tulio Halperín points out, the political system, far from being a channel for the peaceful resolution of social conflicts, became their "sound box," amplifying them.[39] The political and social polarization of Argentine society was best captured in a comic strip drawn by Quino, one of the most perceptive of Argentine cartoonists. One strip shows a policeman chasing after a worker who is trying to catch a bourgeois who is running after a terrorist who is trying to throw a bomb at a priest who is about to smash a crucifix on the head of a freethinker who is pounding the back of a military officer with his book, and so on and so on.[40]

Cultural Changes

The end of Perón's repressive cultural policies in 1955 triggered the beginning of dramatic cultural modernization that was in part linked to the social changes we have seen. A vigorous intellectual and cultural movement that had been buried under Peronist anti-intellectualism emerged quickly after 1955. The university, badly damaged during the Perón decade, recovered its prestige and once again became an engine of cultural and scientific modernization.[41] New programs were introduced, including one in sociology and a psychoanalytically oriented program in psychology. The whole structure of the university was overhauled. For the first time the University of Buenos Aires (and others as well) started hiring large numbers of full-time faculty members devoted to research. The traditionally active student movement, silenced during the *peronato,* recovered its visibility as the university recovered its autonomy.

During the ten years of Perón's rule, such intellectual trends as French existentialism and avant-garde art had been, if not openly repressed, at least officially discouraged and identified with the opposition.[42] After the fall of Perón, Jean-Paul Sartre's existentialism, Igmar Bergman's films, Italian Neo-Realism, and the French Nouvelle Vague became very popular among Argentine intellectuals.[43] It was through Sartre, as we will see in Chapter 7, that many intellectuals developed a theoretical interest in psychoanalysis; and it was in search of deeper existential self-knowledge that many of them ended on the analyst's couch. Since the late 1950s, moreover, acceptance of U.S. popular culture and patterns of consumption had grown at a time when psychoanalysis was popular among an influential group of Americans.

A repressed thirst for novelty during the Perón era gave rise to the cultural explosion of the late 1950s and 1960s, when new sources of funding became available for support of cultural enterprises. The Argentine state, which historically had shown little enthusiasm for financing cultural and scientific development, began to play a much more active role,[44] and additional funding became available from foreign (mostly U.S.) foundations under the umbrella of the Alliance for Progress.

In the wake of these cultural developments, the prestige of traditional cultural institutions declined rapidly. The journal *Sur,* which had been the most respected literary forum since it was launched in the early 1930s, was now harshly criticized for its political closed-mindedness and its attachment to traditional "non-committed" literature. The same happened with the literary supplement of the newspaper *La Nación,* which had defined good taste in literature for decades. Cultural prestige shifted to new institutions such as the Instituto Torcuato Di Tella, founded in the early 1960s. The Instituto became a central reference for Argentine (and Latin American) avant-garde and pop art throughout the decade. It supported experimental arts through a system of prizes and exhibits. Dismissed by the traditional left as a snobbish promoter of frivolities and by the right as subversive, the Di Tella generated its own public among the expanding middle class.[45] In 1967, its best year, exhibits at the institute's Center for Visual Arts attracted almost 400,000 visitors.[46]

The Di Tella was one of the bridges between psychoanalysis and cultural modernization. They shared the same public, the expanded middle class with its fascination with modernity. Most people who went to the Di Tella's exhibits were readers of *Primera Plana,* a magazine that played an important role in diffusing psychoanalysis and promoting modern culture in general. Well-known psychoanalysts attended the Di Tella's exhibits and some of them bought artworks they saw there.[47] Moreover, analysts as highly visible as Enrique Pichon Rivière participated in some of the Institute's most controversial functions. Pichon was featured in the media providing psychoanalytic interpretations of "happenings" and other artistic experiences.[48] People who developed a theoretical interest in psychoanalysis, such as Oscar Masotta (more on him in Chapter 7), also developed close links to the Institute. For the intellectually progressive middle class, the Instituto Di Tella and psychoanalysis were part of the same complex enterprise of cultural modernization. The kind of art patronized by the Di Tella, art that privileged perception and feelings over thought, also contributed to a general environment favorable to the diffusion of psychoanalysis. The Di Tella other out-of-the-mainstream theaters were able to experiment with the theater of the absurd, some of it loaded with psychoanalytic overtones. The early plays of Eduardo

"Tato" Pavlovsky, a psychoanalyst who gained worldwide recognition as a playwright and actor, were influenced by psychodrama.[49]

EXPANSION IN THE CONSUMPTION OF CULTURAL GOODS

With the expansion of the middle class, consumption of everything increased in the 1960s. Modern methods of advertising were introduced, and the mass media expanded much faster in Argentina than in the rest of Latin America.[50] New periodicals (we will discuss some of them in Chapter 4) sprang up and television sets proliferated. Within two years of its introduction in 1951, there were 5,000 sets in the country. That figure rose to 800,000 in 1960 and to 3.7 million ten years later.[51] Television spawned new patterns of marketing; new material and cultural products, including psychoanalysis, were sold through this medium. New media, reaching a more educated public, became vehicles for new kinds of discussions. By the early 1960s in Buenos Aires alone there were three TV shows in prime time featuring psychoanalysts who discussed everything from child rearing to politics from a psychoanalytic point of view.[52]

Expanded consumption and new marketing techniques explain the literary boom of the 1960s, promoted by best-seller lists and modern publicity.[53] After a slump that had started in the early 1950s, the Argentine publishing industry expanded dramatically. New publishing houses sprang up, including a university press, EUDEBA, which put out large numbers of copies—some of them "cheaper than a pack of cigarettes"—of works on topics ranging from the classics to the new social sciences. In its heyday, EUDEBA published almost a book a day.[54]

Reading habits also changed. Back in the 1930s, according to a study carried out by Gino Germani, the middle class claimed to read serious literature, but only around 1 percent actually read intellectual magazines.[55] In the 1960s the picture changed. Julio Cortázar's *Rayuela,* a book not particularly easy to read, sold 25,000 copies a year from its publicaton in 1963 to the end of the decade.[56] Certain books, like certain patterns of consumption, became signs of social status.[57] The growth of the market for books in the 1920s and 1930s had been fed by the expansion of the elementary school system; in the 1960s, the market consisted of people who had access to secondary and higher education. Books and the arts in general became consumable commodities marketed through new channels and new techniques.[58]

Argentines not only read more books; they were reading books on topics that had been taboo only a few years earlier. Literature changed after the fall of Perón. Under the influence of French existentialism, the "generation of 1955" eschewed the stylistic niceties of traditional belles lettres. The writers who came of age after the fall of Perón addressed areas of human interaction that had been marginal in traditional literature. More or less open discussions of sexuality became conspicuous in novels by such popular writers as David Viñas and Beatriz Guido. It was in those years that Roberto Arlt, who had been a precursor of the new discourse on sexuality back in the 1930s, was welcomed into a newly defined literary canon. The French influence and the more open discussion of sexual behavior and mores opened a space for psychoanalysis in literature. In the 1960s a certain psychoanalytic way of thinking permeated contemporary Argentine literature, particularly the works of authors of the new generation, such as Manuel Puig. His semi-autobiographcal *Traición de Rita Hayworth,* for instance, is obviously informed by psychoanalysis, although the word never appears. The novel turns on the protagonist's discovery of his homosexuality.[59] When Pedro Orgambide edited a collection of short stories under the title *Crónicas del psicoanálisis* in 1966, even the Catholic magazine *Criterio* praised it highly.

It was not only fiction that was pervaded by psychoanalysis. Semisociological commentary, a genre with a long tradition in Argentina, proliferated again during the 1960s in response to the interest in new interpretations of the national reality. The central themes were not necessarily new, but the way they were approached certainly was. Again, sexuality occupied a central place in such works as Juan José Sebreli's best-selling *Buenos Aires: Vida cotidiana y alienación* and, more explicitly, Julio Mafud's *Revolución sexual en la Argentina,* both loaded with references to psychoanalysis.

While some sectors of society participated actively in the process of cultural modernization in an almost compulsive search for the new, vast numbers of people clung to traditional values. Ultraconservatives, nationalists, and Catholic traditionalists compensated for their numerical weakness by their influence in high places. Censorship was pervasive throughout the 1960s, even during the rule of "democratically elected" governments. After the military coup of 1966, cultural repression became more violent and open. But it was not only the most reactionary sectors of society that clung to conservative values. Several opinion polls provide evidence that Argentine society was much more bound by traditional mores than expected.[60] Modernizing and traditionalist tendencies coexisted uneasily in the Argentina of the 1960s, provoking conflicts and misunderstandings and a general feeling of unease.

★   ★   ★

The changing social, cultural, and political context of the 1960s facilitated receptivity to a system of thought that could provide the basis for a new subjectivity and answer the questions it aroused. None of these factors alone is enough to explain the emergence of a psychoanalytic culture. It is rather in the particular manner in which all the ingredients were combined that one should look for an explanation. Moreover, psychoanalysis could equip a broad range of social sectors with easily usable analytic tools to bring order out of chaos. Furthermore, psychoanalysis provided a scientific and progressive discourse that went against the grain of traditional psychiatry without threatening traditional values. It is significant that among the quasi-religious practices that proliferated during the 1960s, one of the most popular was astrology, which also claims to offer a "scientific" way to explain what seems unexplainable.[61]

In an environment in which the public sphere was very restricted, psychoanalysis provided some people with an inward-looking way to analyze the contentious reality. This phenomenon was already perceived at the time. According to the leftist psychiatrist Sylvia Bermann, psychoanalysis was a poor substitute for politics. Argentines were putting too much "anguish and creative energy" into efforts to understand themselves, she argued, when they should be using those energies to work to transform the country and overcome the current crisis.[62]

Some writers hypothesized that the birth of psychoanalysis itself was linked to the highly charged but restrictive political environment of fin-de-siècle Vienna. According to this line of thought, Freud, who was actively interested in politics, substituted a theory of inward subversion for the possibility, closed to him as a liberal Jew, of having an actual impact on political life.[63] The open political content of some of Freud's own dreams that he analyzed in *The Interpretation of Dreams* has also been noted, as well as his use of political metaphors (repression, censorship) to explain the work of the unconscious.[64]

An argument that is similar but reaches opposite conclusions has been put forward to explain the psychoanalysis boom in Brazil. According to Luciano Martins, the spread of psychoanalysis in Brazil since the late 1960s resulted from the alienation of the generation that came of age under the authoritarian military regime established in 1964.[65] In Brazil, according to Martins, psychoanalysis was also a substitute for politics, but there it testified to the alienation of the population. In Martins's view, psychoanalysis, drugs, and certain New Age practices were all parts of a cultural system that eliminated politics as a form of social expression. Brazilian analysts were not using psychoanalysis as an instrument for reflection, like those in Argentina, but rather were responding to a demand for escapism.

If Martins is correct, many factors could be invoked to explain the difference between psychoanalysis' connections with politics in Brazil and in Argentina. The Brazilian political system was much more stable than the Argentine. The generalized crisis of consensus and polarization that Argentine society suffered was not felt in Brazil with the same level of intensity.[66] Moreover, Brazil's populist experience under Getulio Vargas in the 1940s and 1950s did not pose the same kind of interpretive problems that Perón did for the Argentine intelligentsia. The appropriation of psychoanalysis as an interpretive instrument by the intellectual left was an important means of its dissemination and legitimation in Argentina. The Argentine critical left, far from being depoliticized by psychoanalysis, seized it as a tool for a better understanding of political reality.

The rapid changes that took place in Argentina after the fall of Perón defined the conditions for a broadening demand for psychoanalysis. The rapid increase in demand was matched by expansion of the supply of psychoanalysis and of psychoanalytically oriented therapies, in which the APA had a significant role to play.

The Expansion of the Psychoanalytic Realm

The diffusion of psychoanalysis affected analysts' self-image and presented some problems. The APA alone could not satisfy the rapidly growing demand for psychoanalytic training. Since the late 1950s a proliferation of unofficial study groups and "postgraduate schools" offered some kind of psychoanalytic training. Although they received no recognition by the psychoanalytic establishment, they did help to relieve the bottleneck. Some of these schools were run by junior members of the APA. As long as they were not teaching psychoanalytic techniques, their activities provoked no objection from the APA. The young junior members who started the Escuela de Psicoterapia para Graduados in 1965, however, had them worried. Although they called it a school of "psychotherapy" rather than "psychoanalysis," their idea was to offer psychoanalytic education to people who for one reason or another could not gain admittance to the APA. The APA leaders saw the school as a threat to their monopoly on psychoanalytic training, particularly because its faculty could claim the legitimacy provided by their membership in the official institution. The APA warned them to limit the scope of their teaching in order "to avoid any situation of ambiguity or incompatibility."[67]

The APA's desires notwithstanding, the school was successful, particularly among psychologists, who called it "Apita"—little APA.[68] One year later the APA convoked an extraordinary assembly to discuss "forms and possibilities of the diffusion and teaching of psychoanalysis." One of the hot topics was precisely the work of analysts in private schools, which by then had grown completely beyond the APA's ability to control.

The analysts' increasing visibility and the growing popularity of psychoanalysis after the fall of Perón combined to increase the supply of psychoanalysis both as a therapy and as a cultural artifact and at the same time responded to a preexisting demand, in a kind of self-feeding, spiral-like process. The APA's structure and internal dynamic limited its ability to satisfy the demand. Its membership, although expanding, remained small. Some prominent members, however, had been looking for alternative channels for disseminating the discipline, both as a practice and as a social theory, outside or at least at the fringes of the APA since the late 1950s.

GROUP PSYCHOTHERAPY: PSYCHOANALYSIS AS A SOCIAL SCIENCE

The introduction of group therapy in the late 1950s was a crucial contribution to the diffusion of psychoanalytic discourse and practice. Enrique Pichon Rivière had been conducting group therapy at the Hospicio de las Mercedes since the late 1940s, but these experiments ended with his ouster by the Peronist authorities. He continued to promote group therapy, and elaborated his own theories. Around 1950 another APA member, E. Eduardo Krapf, resumed group sessions at the Hospicio, with the assistance of some of his students. In the early 1950s another group of APA analysts joined the people working at the Hospicio in order to develop more orthodox group therapy techniques. One of them was Emilio Rodrigué, who had received his analytic training in England. There he had been able to study Wilfred Bion's theories of group analysis at the Tavistock Clinic. In 1954 he became one of the founders of the Asociación Argentina de Psicología y Psicoterapia de Grupo, which organized courses and successfully promoted psychoanalytically oriented group therapy.[69] In 1957 the association organized the First Latin American Conference on Group Therapy in Buenos Aires, which was a great success, and in 1962 it launched the *Revista de Psicología y Psicoterapia de Grupo*. Members of the association lectured regularly at the medical school, at the request of the student union. Various forms of group therapy were offered by the psychiatric services of public hospitals and that of the Children's Hospital, where the head of pediatrics, Florencio

Escardó, was assisted by Diego García Reinoso, a member of the APA. There psychologists worked with physicians and psychiatrists in "therapeutic teams." The forms of psychoanalysis they practiced were unorthodox, but they served the needs of a public pediatric hospital. In 1968 alone the therapeutic teams assisted over 10,000 children.[70]

The introduction of group therapy had various important consequences. First, it dramatically expanded the potential clientele for psychoanalytically oriented therapies. Group psychotherapy is much cheaper than regular analytic therapy, and public hospitals became receptive to it after the fall of Perón. Second, the definition of group psychology was expanded to permit the use of therapeutic groups not only for treatment of mental illness but also to deal with work-related and other problems. Since the late 1950s, analytically oriented groups proliferated among teachers, co-workers, and musicians who hoped to improve the dynamic of their working relationships. Third, group therapy permitted psychologists to work together with M.D.'s. The Asociación Argentina de Psicología y Psicoterapia de Grupo admitted graduates in psychology as full members. Fourth, this expanded use of psychoanalytic concepts and techniques redefined the scope and professional status of psychoanalysis. For the promoters of group therapy, psychoanalysis was not (or at least not only) a medical specialty; they placed it among the social sciences, together with anthropology, psychology, and sociology.

Since the 1950s some social scientists had attempted to incorporate psychoanalysis into their vast realm. The Italian-born sociologist Gino Germani, the founding father of modern Argentine sociology, discussed the place of psychoanalysis among the social sciences and the benefits that psychoanalytic concepts might bring to social scientists. As a young man in Italy, Germani had been interested in psychoanalysis, having read Freud as a teenager. In Argentina, beginning in the late 1940s, he organized the publication of books on sociology, social psychology, and related disciplines, many of which he translated himself. Among them were works by Erich Fromm, George Herbert Mead, and Bronislaw Malinowski.[71] In the early 1940s Germani had taught seminars on Marx and Freud. He recognized the important contribution that psychoanalytic theory, particularly in its American culturalist version, could make to the social sciences. He made it clear, however, that when he discussed psychoanalysis, he was not referring to institutional psychoanalysis as it was practiced and theorized by the APA. "The psychoanalytic contributions to the human sciences cannot be restricted to any particular current, including those that claim for themselves a certain purity and orthodoxy that exclude other currents."[72] According to Germani, the most relevant school of psychoanalysis was the American neo-psychoanalysis represented by Erich Fromm, Karen Horney, and Harry Stack Sullivan, none of whom were in the APA's official pantheon. For Germani, psychoanalysis would add the subjective dimension to social analysis. The psychoanalysis that Germani wanted the social sciences to welcome, then, was a kind the psychoanalytic establishment did not recognize. This approach had little practical consequences in Germani's later work, but it allowed for the introduction of psychoanalysis in the broader discussion of the social sciences at the university, where Germani occupied a prominent place.

With the emergence of group therapy, an attempt to place psychoanalysis among the social sciences came from within the psychoanalytic community for the first time. In 1957 three prominent analysts—León Grinberg, Marie Langer, and Emilio Rodrigué—published a textbook on group psychotherapy. Freud's revolution, they wrote, could be understood only in the context of the social sciences, although they conceded that psychoanalysis had made very few valuable sociological generalizations. Freud's social analysis was a part of his theoretical structure that had aged prematurely.[73] Thus they were recognizing that psychoanalysis, although a full member of the social sciences, did not substitute for them. Psychoanalysis nonetheless made important contributions to sociology, such as the theory of the superego and the application of the historical method to sociology's here-and-now approach to relate long-ago traumas to current problems.

The placement of psychoanalysis among the social sciences took away from psychoanalysis the mysterious and almost metaphysical edge cultivated by some conservative and powerful members of the APA. If psychoanalysis was a social science, then psychoanalysts could and should discuss their concerns as equals with sociologists, anthropologists, and the rest. Moreover, the opening of psychoanalysis to the social sciences from within the psychoanalytic establishment paved the way for its use as a tool for social analysis and for a later political reading of the discipline.[74] Rodrigué emphasized the convergence of psychoanalysis and the social sciences even more clearly in his *Biografía de una comunidad terapéutica,* in which he discussed his experiences at the Austen Riggs Center in Stockbridge, Massachusetts, in the late 1950s. He addressed the book to persons "interested in the social sciences . . . particularly those who are interested in politics as a science." For Rodrigué, then, a therapeutic community was a place where psychoanalysis, psychiatry, and politics converged. By the late 1950s, psychoanalysis was expanding beyond the purely medical and therapeutic realms.

Another important consequence of group psychotherapy was the expansion of the clientele for psychoanalytically oriented therapies, and therefore the creation of alternative channels for the diffusion of psychoanalytic concepts and ideas. Progressive clinicians in public hospitals referred patients to groups where they could receive therapy at no charge,[75] thus extending psychotherapy to working-class men and women.

This expansion of the clientele for psychoanalysis raised some interesting concerns among practitioners. First was the setting. While traditional psychoanalysts could ignore political and social conditions, or in the best of cases could view them through the psychoanalytic lens, in a hospital those conditions made themselves felt in a sometimes brutal way. One of Marie Langer's groups faced serious problems that compromised its very existence—"change of observers, difficulties in the service of nurses, two revolutions, etc." There was nothing to do but hold on until things changed.[76]

Second, the kind of relationship (including the countertransference) that therapists could establish with working-class patients, whose interests and knowledge base were obviously quite different from their own, was not the kind of analyst-patient relationship that could be established with middle- and upper-class patients in the consulting room. During the APA's first decade, many patients were in fact social acquaintances of the analyst. Some were referred by the analyst's friends. Langer, for instance, either had friends in common with many of her patients or was acquainted with some member of a patient's family. Their common social background permitted a transference relationship to develop quite easily, unhindered by cultural or social issues. As Langer points out, normally there was a deep understanding between analyst and patient. From this understanding emerged a gestalt. In this world, external factors had no impact in therapy. Analyst and patient even shared political views (both were usually strongly against Perón), which therefore could be interpreted psychoanalytically.[77]

This was definitely not the case with patients at public hospitals. Langer characterizes the patients in one such group as "of low intellectual and social level." The female patients in another group were "women of poor intellectual and physical condition." One group included a former prostitute with an acute skin disease and a schoolteacher who supplemented her income by working mornings in a mental hospital. Moreover, many patients were not just neurotic but "borderline," close to psychosis. In group therapy, according to Langer, the gestalt emerged within the group itself; patients viewed the therapist as a kind of foreign agent. Langer characterized her role as that of the group's "intellectual leader."[78] The introduction of group analysis redefined the social identity of the discipline at the same time that it dramatically expanded its market. Group therapy attracted a vast number of doctors and psychologists, as the success of a conference on group analysis in Buenos Aires in 1957 testified.

Another technique that became popular was psychodrama, introduced by two junior members of the APA: Eduardo Pavlovsky and the Colombian Jaime Rojas Bermúdez. They founded an Association of Psychodrama and Group Psychotherapy in the early 1960s. Although they followed the technique originated by the Romanian-born psychologist Jacob Moreno (they actually visited him in the United States), they gave it a psychoanalytic twist that Moreno's original technique lacked.[79] By that time Pavlovsky was also becoming famous as an actor and playwright. Although he always claimed that his careers in psychoanalysis and theater were not connected, his high visibility in the theater certainly affected his professional career, and sometimes it was difficult to distinguish his theater work from his work as a psychodramatist.[80] Psychodrama took psychotherapy outside the consulting room and turned it into a spectacle for a public that seized every opportunity for a modern expressive experience. Some psychodrama sessions were held in rented halls and attracted over three hundred participants and spectators.[81]

Other unorthodox techniques inspired by psychoanalysis proliferated as well. One that was rather successful among some politically progressive sectors was the use of psychedelic drugs, in particular LSD-25 and mescaline. Again Pichon Rivière anticipated a trend when he experimented with the use of drugs to facilitate analysis in the 1940s. A decade later, Alberto Tallaferro and José Bleger, the latter one of Pichon's closest disciples, wrote extensively on the topic. But it was Luisa Alvarez de Toledo, then president of the APA, who in 1956 organized a group to experiment with LSD. Other participants in the experience were Alberto Fontana, an associate member of the APA, and Francisco Pérez Morales, a candidate.[82] Fontana had established a clinic with Pichon, Bleger, and others, where he offered treatment with LSD. LSD was to facilitate psychoanalysis, not to substitute for it. In fact, the theoretical basis for the interpretation was still Kleinian. Usually the drug was administered in "prolonged sessions" that lasted for hours, sometimes a whole day; food and music were also introduced for therapeutic purposes. Most conservative members of the APA rejected the therapeutic use of drugs; they could accept deep theoretical deviations more easily than technical innovations.[83] Alvarez de Toledo was ostracized and held no other important posts in the APA after the end of her term as president. Pérez Morales was forced to resign when the paper he presented for promotion to associate member was rejected. Fontana resigned in protest.[84]

Fontana's clinic, where LSD was combined with psychodrama and group psychoanalysis, attracted an important group of politically committed intellectuals. For orthodox analysts, the LSD issue was serious, because it compromised the professional identity of the APA and of psychoanalysis. The media were linking psychoanalysis with drug use. In 1961 the *Revista de Psicoanálisis* published a full-page announcement that "deviations linked to the use of drugs (LSD, mescaline, Benzedrine, tranquilizers, cortisone, etc.), or to other techniques that change the way the patient's mind works . . . should not be considered psychoanalytic treatment regardless of who carries out such treatments."[85]

By 1968 such a variety of therapies were being offered that *Primera Plana* published a long article clarifying the differences between them.[86] Most therapies, even those that did not originate in psychoanalysis, became psychoanalytically oriented in Argentina. One Gestalt therapist dismissed American Gestalt clinicians because they "are not psychoanalysts. They don't interpret." Similarly, a Pavlovian reflexologist acknowledged in the early 1970s that there was no point in denying the existence of the unconscious; what reflexology offered was a new methodology for approaching it.[87]

Group therapy, psychodrama, and other psychoanalytically oriented alternative techniques expanded the psychoanalytic universe in theory and in practice. At the same time, some analysts were seeking a theoretical approach to areas other than the strictly clinical. Psychoanalysis' plasticity enabled it to be turned into different things to appeal to different audiences. The diffusion of psychoanalysis in Argentina in the 1960s was the result of a complex variety of social, cultural, and political developments that generated demand for an interpretive belief system. Because of its nature, its availability, its malleability, and its adaptability, psychoanalysis was able to fulfill the expectations and satisfy the demands of social groups beyond its "natural" constituency, the affluent middle class, and so became a common denominator for various groups in Argentine society.

FOUR

The Diffusers' Role
in the Expansion of the
Psychoanalytic Realm

If the social, political, and cultural contexts provided the necessary conditions for the diffusion of psychoanalysis, those conditions are still not sufficient to explain the phenomenon. By the 1950s psychoanalysis was already available in the Argentine market of ideas and was promoted by an active group of diffusers. By "diffusers" I mean people, institutions, and publications that enjoyed a wide audience, whose discourse had some degree of social legitimacy, and who actively spread the message of psychoanalysis: highly visible psychoanalysts, "modern" psychoanalytically oriented pediatricians regularly featured in the media, popular magazines that disseminated psychoanalytic ideas in one way or another, newspaper columnists, and so on. They tailored their versions of psychoanalysis to the expectations of their public.

Marie Langer and Arnaldo Rascovsky wrote on issues related to family life. Langer in particular claimed to be, and was perceived as, the only representative of a female version of psychoanalysis, in contrast to Freud's phallocratic ideas about women. Her writings, however, showed the scope and the limits of a woman's approach to psychoanalysis in Argentina. Although Langer pioneered work on female sexuality and motherhood, her conclusions about gender roles were not very different from those of male analysts. Rascovsky, for his part, wrote on parent-child relationships. For him the "natural" place for women was at home, taking care of their children. Both Langer's and Rascovsky's success in disseminating psychoanalysis was related to the fact that they did not challenge traditional values in such matters as gender roles and the patriarchal family. They used modern terminology and ideas to legitimize the traditional models of family and womanhood, models that were compatible with widely accepted middle-class values. Enrique Pichon Rivière contributed the most to the expansion of the psy realm and to the popularization of a psy culture. Paradoxically, he did so by moving beyond the fringes of psychoanalysis proper and the institution he helped to create.

Diffusers outside of the APA establishment addressed different publics. Since the late 1950s, the psychologist Eva Giberti had appeared regularly in the Argentine media, where she discussed issues related to child rearing and gender. Giberti's books and articles addressed essentially the lower middle class. Her best-selling *Escuela para padres* (School for parents) sold hundreds of thousands of copies. Giberti's role in Argentina can be compared with that of Benjamin Spock in the United States, although, as we shall see, her idea of a child-centered world differed from Dr. Spock's.

A group of widely read women's and popular magazines that disseminated psychoanalytic discourse and helped to shape the public image of psychoanalysis and psychoanalysts targeted members of the middle class who had hopes of social advancement, who looked up to the upper social strata and sought to emulate them. One magazine, *Primera Plana,* merits close examination because in many ways it was unique. Modeled on *Newsweek* but adapted to Argentine needs, it targeted a more affluent and educated audience.

Diffusers from the APA

Psychoanalysis broke with the traditional image promoted by classical psychiatry, which saw the family as the locus of degeneration. Psychoanalysts saw families as dynamic units defined by interpersonal links and roles. If the family was an agent of pathology, it was because of problems with assumed roles and the ways members related to one another, not because it was in the family that the process of hereditary degeneracy unfolded. Yet Argentine psychoanalysts did not challenge traditional images of the role of women in family and society. Small wonder that Rascovsky's and Langer's ideas became very popular among middle-class parents. In the early 1970s Langer would make a drastic ideological turn to the left and embrace feminism and Marxism. She also led one of the radical groups that split from the APA in 1971, as we shall see. What concerns us here is her role as a disseminator of psychoanalysis in the 1950s and 1960s.

MARIE LANGER: FAMILY AND FEMININITY

After her political radicalization in the early 1970s, Marie Langer reconstructed her past. In her writings of those years, and particularly in her autobiography, Langer claimed that feminism and Marxism had always been at the center of her thought. Moreover, she claimed that she had always been sympathetic to Perón, and that during his first regime she had almost joined the women's branch of the Peronist Party. She professed great admiration for Evita Perón. Her Peronist sympathies, she claimed, had isolated her from other members of the largely anti-Peronist APA.[1] After her split from the APA in 1971, Marie Langer was seen as the representative of a supposedly feminist and leftist reading of psychoanalytic theory in Argentina, opposed to the APA's male-centered right-wing approach. As a radical analyst she gained visibility in Latin America and in the United States.[2] In the widely read works on psychoanalysis she wrote in the 1950s and 1960s, however, neither Marxism nor feminism, much less Peronism, occupied the central place she later claimed. Although Marie Langer often expressed her Marxist sympathies in the 1950s and 1960s, she did not use Marxism as an analytic tool; and she openly rejected feminism and Peronism.[3]

Marie Langer was born in Vienna in 1910 to an assimilated bourgeois Jewish family. As a young medical student she joined the Austrian Communist Party and started her psychoanalytic training. Her early interest in psychoanalysis was more the result of external factors than of a clear vocation. At that time few Jews obtained appointments as residents in Austrian public hospitals, so it was difficult for most of them to complete their medical training. Psychoanalysis offered an alternative career. Langer was interviewed at the Vienna Psychoanalytic Institute by Anna Freud, started her training analysis with Richard Sterba, and supervised a few cases with Jeanne Lampl de Groot—all three at the top of the Viennese psychoanalytic establishment. In 1934 Freud forbade analysts to be members or even to analyze members of any illegal organization, and most political parties were illegal in Austria at that time; the Communist Party certainly was. Forced to choose—she was even threatened with public exposure, which would have placed her in real danger—Langer chose the Party. In 1936 she went to Spain with her husband to serve as a doctor in the Republican Army. Back in Vienna before the Spanish Civil War ended, Langer left Austria just before the Nazis took over and landed in Uruguay as a political exile. There she worked as a cook and took other jobs until her husband was offered work in a textile factory in Buenos Aires. In Argentina, Langer made contact with the emerging psychoanalytic community. As she pointed out in her memoirs, her psychoanalytic credentials were higher than those of almost everybody else in Argentina at the time. Years later, as we have seen, Langer became the only female founding member of the APA.

Once committed to psychoanalysis, Langer abandoned politics. As she put it, she substituted analytic militancy for political militancy. Langer became the informal leader of a group of technical purists in the psychoanalytic association. By the mid-1960s, however, she started to participate in political events again. Her militancy increased toward the end of the decade, and in 1971 she led the Plataforma group that split from the APA and played a very active role in the highly politicized Federación Argentina de Psiquiatras. Langer's political activities forced her into exile again. In 1974 she left Argentina for Mexico, where she stayed until she discovered she had cancer. She returned to Argentina to die in 1987. While in Mexico, she was an active supporter of the Nicaraguan Sandinista government, to which she offered her services in organizing a system of psychiatric therapeutic assistance and training.

Despite her reputation as a purist as far as psychoanalytic technique was concerned (she was called the "Virgin Mary" in the APA for her vocal opposition to the use of drugs in conjunction with analysis and other innovations), Marie Langer played an important role in enlarging the psychoanalytic field by promoting the combination of psychoanalytic theory with other disciplines. Her book *Maternidad y sexo* (Motherhood and sex), originally published in 1951, revised in 1964 and 1972, and reprinted several times, not only is the first analysis of female sexuality from a psychoanalytic perspective carried out in Argentina, but also goes beyond canonical psychoanalysis. Langer combines Kleinian psychoanalysis with other disciplines and intellectual traditions, such as cultural anthropology, thus encouraging the integration of psychoanalysis with the social sciences. Let us remember that she also co-authored a book on group psychotherapy. Moreover, Langer was the first analyst in Argentina to put women at the center of psychoanalytic discourse.

Hugo Vezzetti has analyzed the theoretical sources, sometimes of dubious compatibility, of Langer's work.[4] Here it is enough to say that Langer supports her arguments by a variety of theoretical approaches that qualify each other. To qualify Melanie Klein's emphasis on unconscious fantasies, for instance, Langer points to the importance of actual episodes in early childhood in the development of neuroses. She qualifies Margaret Mead's culturalist approach by a biological conception of sex differences based on Freud. According to Langer, while culture plays an important role in determining differences in gender roles, gender differences are still rooted in biological differences. Similarly, Langer uses Melanie Klein's theory to refute Freud's notion of penis envy as a primary element in the development of female sexuality.

Psychoanalysis legitimized the public discussion of subjects that had been taboo or the province of traditional medicine or of the confessional. Langer emphasized the difference between her approach to sexuality and that of such popular works of the 1930s as Theodoor H. van de Velde's *Ideal Marriage*.[5] Furthermore, Langer explicitly criticizes Freudian phallocratic notions. Following Melanie Klein and the early Karen Horney, she rejects the Freudian characterization of women as castrated males. This redefinition of the status of women in psychoanalytic theory, however, had serious limitations. Although Langer's concerns were far from those of Catholic or eugenic discourse, the kind of practical consequences that could flow from her work were disturbingly similar. According to Langer, women could find total fulfillment only in motherhood. Female sexuality could be realized only in reproduction. Langer combines the modern approaches of psychosomatic medicine and cultural anthropology with a traditional view of women and the family. This message had a strong appeal to a society that longed for modernity while it clung to conservative values. It is interesting to note that Langer, apparently sensitive to the public response to her work, deleted all mention of Marxism from later editions, along with any suggestion that women could find satisfaction in life without motherhood.

Maternidad y sexo's main thesis is that while traditional society restricted women's sexual expression, it did favor their reproductive functions. Traditional society bred hysteria, but reproductive disorders were much less common in times past than they are today. In modern society, women have achieved sexual freedom but are restricted in their maternal role. This new situation has generated psychosomatic diseases of the reproductive system. "At the sight of a mouse," she wrote, "our grandmothers climbed on a chair and raised their skirts, crying for help, but in general they had no problems with breast-feeding their children. Nowadays young women know how to drive cars, ambulances, and even airplanes, but frequently either they do not know how to feed a baby or they give up this task."[6]

Langer uses examples from Margaret Mead's work in Samoa to illustrate what is intrinsically female and what is culturally determined. She tries to show that different social attitudes toward women generate different neuroses, but she qualifies Mead's most provocative ideas by emphasizing that gender distinctions are based on anatomical differences and therefore are not culturally determined. "If we consider the human being as a psychosomatic unity, we cannot suppose that the anatomical and functional differences between men and women do not involve a deep psychological differentiation." And since for Langer, femaleness was centered on procreation, rejection of motherhood was equivalent to rejection of womanhood. Even work, according to Langer, has a totally different meaning for women than for men. While men sublimate only their sexual instinct in work, women also sublimate their maternal instinct. In Langer's view, employment for women was acceptable as long as it complemented motherhood. "A woman who gives up motherhood will not generally be happy or able to achieve full sexual enjoyment."[7]

According to Langer, mothers should breast-feed their children as long as possible and devote their energies primarily to their children. Only in the context of a healthy family can girls develop a healthy sexuality. What is a healthy family for Marie Langer? One in which harmony is based on well-defined gender roles:

> Both parents have to give [the girl] enough love so that she accepts their
> sexual relations without so much envy. A strong father [who is] full of
> tenderness toward his little daughter will help her to abandon her mother as
> a love object and to lean femininely toward him. A mother who is happy
> with her husband will not fall into the temptation of putting all her unsatis-
> fied love in her daughter, overstimulating her, nor will she reject or feel
> contempt for the daughter because she is not a boy. This is because the
> mother will be happy with her femininity. She will allow her daughter to
> identify with a mother who is tender with her children and loving with her
> husband.[8]

Despite Langer's efforts to reconstruct her past from the vantage point of her later radicalism, her ideas were more conservative and long-standing than she was willing to admit.[9] The 1972 edition of *Maternidad y sexo* includes an additional chapter dated 1969, in which Langer suggests that a rebellious counterculture emerged in the Anglo-Saxon countries because it was precisely there that mothers substituted the bottle for the breast. Regarding contraceptives (a subject that was not even discussed in earlier editions of the book), Langer (like other female psychoanalysts),[10] opposed the use of the pill. Her reason was that the pill induces hormonal changes that have psychological consequences. She also opposed the IUD, because it forced women to delegate their fertility to a gynecologist. She favored the diaphragm, because it was medically innocuous. However, although she does not say so, there seems to be more to it than that. A diaphragm forces a woman to make an explicit choice against motherhood every time she wants or expects to have sexual intercourse. Motherhood was still at the center of womanhood in 1969. The 1972 edition of *Maternidad y sexo* ends with an anecdote about a former patient of Langer's who called to ask for an appointment because she felt depressed. In the course of the session it became clear that there was no objective cause for the depression. Toward the end of the session the patient mentioned that she thought it would be a good idea to stop using the contraceptive pill that she had been taking for seven years. When Langer later met the patient again at a social gathering, she looked radiant. She had even managed to persuade her husband to buy her her dream house in the suburbs. The secret? She had stopped taking the pill. . . .

The real change in Langer's ideas came later. By 1973, according to her, the experience of Cuba had proved that women's domesticity was a social construction and not a fatal necessity. Now Langer questioned the need for breast-feeding and the importance of developing a physical bond between mother and infant. "Is it really wrong that in socialist countries many children are cared for by an institution from the second week of life? I think it is right."[11] If in *Maternidad y sexo* Langer had claimed that modernity and the abandonment of the ideal of motherhood were crucial neurogenic factors for women, in 1973, after reading the works of R. D. Laing and David Cooper, it was no longer clear to her that the family was such a healthy institution. Perhaps, Langer speculated, when women became creative in "visible" work, they would need less bonding with their children.

If Langer reformulated her ideas on feminism and women's sexuality as a result of her later radicalization, the same and more can be said for her political ideas.[12] To support her claim that her works of the 1950s had been unimpeachably leftist, she noted that *Maternidad y sexo* had received a positive review by the leftist psychiatrist Sylvia Bermann in the *Revista Latinoamericana de Psiquiatría*. In fact, Bermann's review had not been all that positive; Bermann had criticized Langer's lack of attention to class differences in discussing her cases and she dismissed psychoanalysis as a limited school of thought that lacked scientific foundation.[13]

The fact is that Marx (although mentioned) was not relevant to Langer's works of the 1950s and early 1960s. The place of Perón was more complicated. In a paper titled "El mito del niño asado," published in the *Revista de Psicoanálisis* in 1950 and included with few changes in *Maternidad y sexo,* Langer analyzed a story that circulated in Buenos Aires in the late 1940s. It seems that a young couple went out one evening, leaving their young child with a baby-sitter they had recently hired. On their return they found the baby-sitter dressed in the señora's wedding dress. She told the couple that she had prepared a surprise for them. To their horror, they found that the surprise consisted of their child served roasted at a well-set table. In the original version, Langer analyzed the myth from a purely psychoanalytic point of view. The baby-sitter was a degraded version of the Kleinian "bad mother."

In 1957, two years after the fall of Perón, Langer included the article in a book of essays titled *Fantasías eternas a la luz del psicoanálisis* (Eternal fantasies in the light of psychoanalysis). The second version, now titled "El niño asado y otros mitos sobre Eva Perón" (The roasted child and other myths about Eva Perón), was told from a new perspective: the political. The political dimension is important for two reasons. First, the APA proclaimed its political neutrality at that time (though the anti-Peronism of its members was well known), and Langer was its first prominent member to publish a piece that applied psychoanalysis to a political situation. Second, the paper shows how far Langer's later political radicalization led her in her project of reinventing her political past.

From the beginning of *Fantasías eternas* Langer claims that the scope of psychoanalysis goes far beyond the clinical realm: "[The] psychoanalytic field covers the medical, the psychological, the anthropological, and many other fields." Now she analyzes the roasted-child story in the light of Argentina's political environment at the time the story was being told. When she wrote the first version, Langer says, "I avoided analyzing the extent to which . . . the myth originated in the current political situation. I avoided it for obvious reasons, since such an analysis would have made its publication impossible at that time. Now that the political situation in Argentina has changed, I return to the issue to complete it."[14]

A few lines below Langer characterizes the Perón government as a "dictatorship," and compares Perón with Hitler and Mussolini. Pages later, however, she says she originally had doubts about the political interpretation of the myth. Her doubts provoked a "heated discussion" at the APA, in which Arnaldo Rascovsky took the lead. Her colleagues told her that "the distressing situation that intervened in the creation of the myth was obvious. It was the political situation . . . it was Eva Perón's dictatorship, the almighty mother who dominated everyone."[15] According to that interpretation, Eva Perón presented herself as her master's servant, a woman of humble origins who was doing her best to improve the lives of the poor, when in fact she was perverse, dangerous, and feared. The child was Argentina, and the myth emerged because open criticism of Evita was too dangerous.

Marie Langer's analysis of the myth introduced to psychoanalytic writing a sociohistorical dimension that was absent from most of her colleagues' writings. This dimension became more prominent in the 1960s. In a new epilogue added to the second edition of *Fantasías eternas,* Langer clearly stated her interest in linking psychoanalysis with the "external world." She expressed doubt about the validity of the word "eternal" in the title to characterize the fantasies she described, and she claimed it was high time to be finished with determinism and to start integrating psychoanalytic concepts into the social sciences. "I do not think we can afford to ignore the external world, its influence over us and ours over it. Someone said that we are in this world to change it. If this is so, we must know this world and ourselves very well."[16]

In the 1950s and 1960s Langer played an important role in the diffusion of psychoanalysis. She introduced a woman's approach to the discipline and she pioneered the application of psychoanalytic theory to the analysis of political developments. Despite her later claims, however, she was as far from tackling Peronism as she was from championing feminism. Her views were welcomed by the middle class in search of new analytic tools to render Peronism intelligible. Yet Langer also confirmed that Peronism could be understood as a pathology.

RASCOVSKY AND THE UBIQUITY OF FILICIDE

Arnaldo Rascovsky was routinely featured on TV and radio and in popular magazines, discussing the two topics that had become his obsessions: the psychic life of the fetus, a theory he had developed since the late 1950s, and filicide, the symbolic murder of a child by a parent. As we have seen, Rascovsky arrived at psychoanalysis through his work as a pediatrician and became one of the most active promoters of psychosomatic medicine. What distinguished his career from those of other APA members was his public visibility and the international reputation he attained in the early 1970s with the founding of FILIUM, an international organization devoted to research and education on child abuse and its prevention. In 1974 FILIUM was placed under the auspices of UNESCO.

According to his own account, Rascovsky's ideas on filicide originated when as a pediatrician he observed that parents usually insisted on painful or maiming medical procedures for their children even when equally effective but nontraumatic procedures were available and offered. This observation led him to do additional research and to conclude that there is a philogenetic tendency in parents to destroy their children.[17] This tendency is evident, according to Rascovsky, not only in the large number of parents who actually kill their children but also in more everyday behavior—corporal punishment, denigration, insults, abandonment, and so on.

Despite the seeming radicalness of Rascovsky's ideas, they are open to a conservative reading, and the family organization he advocated was compatible with traditional gender roles. Moreover, the theoretical twist he gave to Freud's ideas helped to soften their most controversial aspects. The murderous Freudian child who wanted to get rid of his father in order to have sexual access to his mother became in Rascovsky's version a weak victim of his parents' homicidal desire.

According to Rascovsky, filicidal tendencies are as old as civilization and are at the very root of the incest taboo. The killing of children appears in various myths and stories dating from "the origins of culture," including, of course, the Oedipus story. After all, the Oedipus tragedy originated in Laius's attempt to have his son mutilated and killed to prevent the fulfillment of the oracle's prophesy that the boy would grow up to kill his father and marry his mother. In early times, filicide was a way of imposing the parents' authority and at the same time the origin of the superego. While children were young, Rascovsky claimed, the prohibition of incest could be enforced because the parents could overpower them. The situation became more complicated as children grew up and became stronger than their aging parents: "Later, the primitive organization understood that the parents had to establish their supremacy while they still could; that is, during infancy, when children's weakness made it possible. Primitive society therefore created a technique still in use today, although hidden: the killing of some children . . . and the mutilation and cowing of the remaining children."[18]

The other purpose of filicide, broadly defined as abuse in general, is, in Rascovsky's view, pedagogical. It is socially used as a tool for the imposition of knowledge. According to Rascovsky, Freud's version of the original parricide in *Totem and Taboo* required an investigation of its antecedents. Parricidal tendencies, Rascovsky argues, are the result of filicidal tendencies, which are much more deeply rooted in the collective unconscious. For Rascovsky, filicidal tendencies explain most of human behavior, including what he viewed as mass filicide—war.[19]

Rascovsky's laudatory struggle against child abuse took form in 1971 with the founding of FILIUM and the establishment of branches in many countries of Europe and the Americas. In Argentina, FILIUM became very popular among progressive middle-class parents, and Rascovsky became a regular presence in the Argentine media.[20] His ideas were less enthusiastically received in international psychoanalytic circles, but they had much to do with the public's acceptance of psychoanalysis.

In Rascovsky's view, filicide can be seen in disguised form in almost every way adults interact with children. Sending newborn babies to nurseries, not breast-feeding them, even sending older children to kindergarten amounted for him to "micro-abandonment."[21] In the end Rascovsky proposed a conservative model of the family, centered on the mother. In this model, women, once again, should stay home and take care of their children. "The increasing participation of women in multiple industrial, professional, artistic, and scientific activities . . . has been carried out at the expense of the maternal function. The maternal function implies constant presence and emotional support during the early development of the child, not disrupted by other activities."[22]

Elsewhere Rascovsky blames feminism for the proliferation of mental diseases. Feminism took women away from their primordial role as mothers.[23] This abandonment of family duties has important social consequences because children subjected to even mild forms of filicide may develop antisocial attitudes. Why the entire burden of parenthood is on mothers and not on fathers is something that Rascovsky never discusses. In 1980 Rascovsky spelled out even more clearly his ideas about the family and about the therapist's role: "A psychologist must lead the subject to adapt to the environment in which he lives. In that sense the defense of the family is a central element. The family is the basis of social organization, and a good therapist must lead [the patient] to mental health, meaning to a good integration with the mother and father."[24]

In combination with his other pet theory, fetal psychodynamics, the filicide theory had deterministic consequences, since the parent's filicidal attitude even before the child was born would determine its later behavior.[25]

Marie Langer and Arnaldo Rascovsky, in their own ways and following their own theoretical interests, generalized psychoanalytic thought to social analysis. Both were heard beyond the closed circle of analysts and therefore played important roles in the diffusion of psychoanalysis. Psychoanalysis provided a language in which to discuss and explain both women's sexual problems and the parent-child relationship. And by using a scientific language and a modern theoretical framework, psychoanalysts appropriated those issues from their traditional authorities—the sexologist, the priest, or even the physician.

Yet as far as a woman's family role was concerned, the practical conclusions reached by the two psychoanalysts did not diverge much from those promoted by the old discourses. For both the family centered on the mother. The consequences of environmental factors overshadowed heredity, yet women could fulfill their mission in life only through motherhood. These versions of psychoanalysis certainly did not challenge traditional values. They did, however, provide a new system for understanding them and a new language to express them in. This combination of modernity and tradition goes far toward explaining the success of psychoanalysis in Argentina.

Enrique Pichon Rivière: Psychoanalysis and Bohemia

Pichon Rivière came to psychoanalysis with a solid psychiatric foundation. By the time he joined the original psychoanalytic group, he enjoyed a relatively secure position in the psychiatric establishment. Pichon was an innovator in psychiatry, always seeking new therapeutic methods and theoretical approaches. He introduced electroconvulsive shock therapy in Argentina and was the first to formulate a psychoanalytic theory (or any theory, for that matter) to explain its effectiveness. For Pichon Freudian theory ought to be the central point of departure for a modernized psychiatry.[26] Yet he was always open to creative ways of combining different theories. Gradually, after serving as its president, Pichon Rivière withdrew from the APA, establishing new institutions devoted to his main interest, social psychology. Although during the decade and a half of his active participation in the APA he formally ascribed to the institution's official ideology of Kleinianism and psychosomatic medicine, his teaching went beyond it to broader theoretical concerns.[27]

Throughout his life Pichon Rivière maintained a bohemian lifestyle and an affinity for the political left (never clearly articulated). His interest in avant-garde art and his public visibility helped to attract important sectors of Argentine intellectuals to psychoanalysis. In the 1940s his lectures at the Hospicio offered an alternative to traditional psychiatric practice, with its rigidity and its anachronistic allegiance to old paradigms.[28] Pichon Rivière was seen as someone "with *calle*," streetwise, who could see, interpret, and understand the world using psychoanalytic tools beyond the analyst's couch.

Although Pichon had been a founding member of the APA, he was perceived as an outsider: "After knowing old Pichon," remembers Isidoro Vegh, later a prominent Lacanian analyst, "how could you be an APA blockhead?"[29] The title of a collection of his writings published in 1970, *Del psi-*

coanálisis a la psicología social (From psychanalysis to social psychology), is a clear statement of his distance from the APA's orthodox psychoanalysis.[30] Analysts who, like Ignacio Maldonado, were receiving formal training at the APA but found the environment there stifling, simultaneously took part in informal study groups led by Pichon Rivière, alongside students who had no medical degrees.[31] For young progressive doctors, Pichon was the link between the legitimacy provided by the APA and the promise held out by new approaches to psychoanalysis.

Two generations of analysts and psychiatrists have claimed Pichon as their master. As one of his close disciples points out, however, Pichon Rivière's role as a teacher was paradoxically a destructuring one. "By his words and manner he made his listeners doubt their values, without preaching any good news. . . . More than being a foreigner, Pichon Rivière promoted foreignness."[32] The relationship his students established with Pichon usually went beyond training, either formal or informal. This is how Vegh remembers his interaction with Pichon Rivière in the early 1960s, when he was a young student:

> We went, let's say, to have a bite at Pippo [a cheap eatery in Buenos Aires], and the old man got the idea that one had to write . . . , and so we wrote nonsense, we were all drunk, but we had the illusion that we were doing something [important]. Afterward we went to La Paz [a typical bohemian café] until two or three in the morning, and after that we went to his office. He gave us pornographic magazines and told us to "get busy." . . . He did that so we'd stay awake, and then he started reading [Norbert] Wiener, who wasn't even known here, it was 1962 or 1963. He read Wiener, cybernetics, until seven in the morning. We started falling asleep like flies; some fell asleep at four A.M. and he went on reading. At seven A.M. he said: "OK, get out of here. I have a patient." He had a glass of whiskey, kicked us out, and got to work.

Pichon Rivière's life has become so entwined with myth that it is very difficult to separate fact from fiction. His son Marcelo has said, "My father, like Borges, sometimes preferred a good story to the bare facts. It was one of his forms of seduction. . . . He himself forgot the line between myth and reality."[33]

Pichon Rivière's interest in psychoanalysis sprang from three sources. One was his early interest in Alfred Adler's pedagogical and social ideas.[34] The second was the early interest in Surrealism he acquired during his bohemian youth as a medical student. One of his obsessions was the work and life of the Count of Lautréamont, an icon of the Surrealist movement, on whom he wrote several articles.[35] Pichon's third path to psychoanalysis was his experience as a psychiatrist in the treatment of psychotics. Freud arrived at psychoanalysis through his treatment of neurotics (hysterical women in particular); Pichon instead arrived at psychoanalysis through his dealings with psychotics, epileptics (whom he thought to be psychotic) in particular. Pichon never abandoned psychiatry. However, if psychoanalysis could provide the theoretical anchor for the new psychiatry he advocated, Pichon was rather open-minded on matters of technique, unlike other members of the APA.

Gradually Pichon developed his theory of a "single disorder" that was at the root of all other mental disorders. For him the "single disorder" was melancholy, the subjection of a masochistic ego to a punitive superego. All other pathological structures were nothing but "failed and inadequate attempts at cure."[36] The therapist's job, therefore, was to smooth the relations between ego and superego. By temporarily satisfying both the sadistic superego and the masochistic ego, epileptic attacks worked as a safety valve for some psychotics. Shock therapies were used to create this "safety valve" artificially in psychotics to whom real epileptic attacks were not "available." Thus shock therapy did not cure psychotics but temporarily turned them into neurotics, who could then be treated with psychoanalytically based therapy (which did cure). Pichon thus promoted an encounter between psychoanalysis and psychiatry as no one in Argentina had done before.

At the same time, Pichon was also interested in psychosomatic medicine and in the therapeutic and pedagogical use of functioning groups. The psychotherapeutic aspect would prepare the ground for the learning of topics that aroused resistance, as psychoanalysis did.[37] Pichon's approach combined different schools of thought and areas of interest in a creative way. By the 1950s he became more involved with the theories of Melanie Klein, which he combined (not particularly successfully) with his interest in Surrealism in his effort to analyze Lautréamont's poems.

Pichon Rivière's writings were prolific until the 1950s. After that he concentrated on lecturing and wrote very little. Admirers compared him (with some exaggeration) with Jacques Lacan. Both had a strong psychiatric background and arrived at psychoanalysis through work with psychotics (paranoids, in Lacan's case). Both relied on the spoken word in their teaching. Pichon Rivière claimed to be a personal friend of Lacan. At least according to the official myth, it was Pichon who introduced Lacan's works to Oscar Masotta, who then introduced them in Argentina.[38] It is a fact that Pichon cited Lacan's work on paranoia repeatedly in the late 1930s, but no trace of him is found in his later work.

Pichon became very popular in the 1960s in part as a result of his work with groups and in social psychology. From psychoanalysis and psychiatry his interest shifted to his *teoría del vínculo,* or link theory, and to functioning groups. Pichon defined *vínculo* as a "complex structure that includes subject and object, their interaction, moments of communicating and of learning, in a complex dialectical spiral; a process that begins only when internal images and external reality come together."[39] Pichon developed the theory that the mental patient was the designated crazy one in his or her group—that is, the family. To be effective, then, therapy has to operate on the whole group— on the role each member plays and on their relationships. Throughout the decade, the successive institutions he founded—the Instituto Argentino de Estudios Sociales (IAES), the School of Social Psychiatry, and later the School of Social Psychology—provided alternative forums for young doctors and psychologists who found the APA uncongenial. In general, the people who were close to Pichon preferred to work in an institutional setting rather than in a private consulting room. Many leftist doctors who refused to join the APA for ideological reasons became interested in psychoanalysis through Pichon Rivière's teaching. After his death in 1977, his School of Social Psychology, under the direction of his second wife, Ana Quiroga, established an open-admissions policy and it became a popular place where anyone—not only students but homemakers, soccer players, and boxers—could learn some psychoanalytically informed psychology.[40]

Among the roots of Pichon's work were some vague ideas borrowed from Marxism, particularly his concept of therapy as a dialectical process—a dialectical spiral, as he said: "The essential goal of psychotherapy is the transformation of a static situation into a dialectical situation that assumes the form of a regular spiral as it works through a determined task."[41] He also borrowed from Marxism the concept of praxis, and of course he emphasized the social aspects of psychology. The framework in which these ideas emerged was not always consistent.[42] In 1966 Pichon Rivière claimed that the task of modern psychiatry was to search for "methods or strategies to change the social and economic structure from which the mental patient emerges. . . . The mental patient expresses the anxiety and conflicts of his immediate group; that is, the family. And these anxieties and conflicts that are assumed by the sick person are economic." Yet elsewhere, in a twist that placed him close to the American culturalist school, he claimed that the goal of therapy was not to change the social and economic structure but to adapt patients to the neurogenic conditions of modern society.[43]

What did more to put Pichon Rivière in the public eye than his theories was his visibility in the media and thus in the street. In some people's view, he cast old verities in psychoanalytic language.[44] In the 1960s Pichon was the standard-bearer of a whole cultural system centered on the idea of "modernity." He joined the most frivolous aspects of psychoanalysis with politically committed psychiatry. He was perceived as, and claimed to be, a left-leaning progressive and at the same time theorized on the application of psychology to business administration.[45] He was frequently seen at the Instituto Di Tella, providing psychoanalytic interpretations of "happenings" and other events of the art world. He was also regularly seen at Mau-Mau, a fashionable boîte, until the small hours. Moreover, although he cultivated the image of the eternal outsider, Pichon was very well integrated into the progressive sectors of the psychiatric establishment.[46]

Pichon Rivière organized other visible and controversial experiences related to psychoanalysis. In 1958 he attempted to turn the whole city of Rosario into a "functioning group" so that he could perform a trickle-down psychoanalysis. He carried out the experiment with the aid of young physicians and students at the IAES in Buenos Aires and had the support of a variety of public institutions, including the School of Economics, the Institute of Statistics, the School of Philosophy, and the medical school's psychology department.[47] For an entire weekend about a thousand people took part in the experiment, coordinated by twenty analysts. One of them, then a young APA candidate, remembers that on the train to Rosario, some of the young participants asked Pichon for some technical and theoretical explanations about what they were about to experience. Pichon's reply was typical of his style: "If they throw shit at us when we get on the train back to Buenos Aires, then it means that when a group like this does what we're about to do in Rosario, they're pelted with shit when they leave."[48]

Another of Pichon's experiments was a dance to which he invited people active in the arts, politics, or society. Men and women were matched by computer according to background, social role, and physical characteristics. None of the married couples at the event were matched by the machine. Pichon concluded that the results "reinforce the idea that marriage is now in crisis" and that "the criteria for joining together and compatibility must be modified."[49]

In 1966 and 1967 Pichon Rivière wrote a regular column in *Primera Plana,* in which he analyzed various aspects of everyday life, from soccer championships to vacations, from the point of view of social psychology. The ideas he expressed on gender roles, family structure, and even relationships between social classes are quite conservative. One must adjust to the social environment. "When the impulses of a psychic structure are directed to socially approved goals, they support and reinforce the individual in his functions, because there is an adjustment between the given and the assumed roles. When those roles are incompatible, there is conflict and neurosis."[50] The task of the social psychologist, according to Pichon, is to reinforce the patient's sense of security amid the generally insecure environment generated by the modern social organization. Elsewhere he pointed to the importance of certain mechanisms of social control that provide security.[51] Pichon Rivière never questioned traditional gender roles, and he emphasized the importance of choosing a marriage partner of one's own background and social class.[52]

Pichon Rivière's death in 1977 was preceded by a long physical decline brought on by his abuse of alcohol and drugs. By then he had been stripped of his status as a training analyst by the institution he had helped to found. He had played a crucial role in expanding the psy realm. He was a bridge builder. In the APA's early years, he helped to establish connections between psychoanalysis and psychiatry. Later he became a symbol of cultural modernity and political progressiveness within the psy community. He went on forging links between psychoanalysis and progressive psychiatrists and psychologists who otherwise would have felt alienated from the discipline. He was also instrumental in turning psychoanalysis into a cultural artifact. His interest in modern art made him a habitué of cultural events and a highly visible personality. His experiments in taking psychoanalysis to the streets, widely covered by the media, did much to popularize psychoanalysis—and Pichon Rivière.

Langer, Rascovsky, Pichon Rivière, and others played important roles in the diffusion of psychoanalysis through their active presence in the media. Their broader theoretical concerns also helped to open doors for psychoanalysis outside of the therapeutic realm. Their public, however, was confined largely to the intellectual middle class. Another group of diffusers, not linked to the analytic establishment, was instrumental in disseminating psychoanalytic discourse to a wider audience.

Diffusers Outside the Psychoanalytic Establishment

EVA GIBERTI AND THE 'ESCUELA PARA PADRES'

Psychoanalytic ideas were readily accepted among people concerned with the raising of children in the 1960s. Although pedagogues and reformers had been advocating freer, nonrepressive education since the 1920s, child-rearing practices were traditionally considered a matter for the family to decide. "The relaxation of the relationship between parents and children is a factor that conspires against the institution of the family, threatened by modern influences," claimed *Para Tí,* a widely read women's magazine, in June 1950. A traditional family firmly rooted in traditional morality was a haven, whereas the intrusion of "modernity" was a danger that planted the seeds of future problems, even criminality. Children were "malleable wax," who absorbed what they learned at home.[53]

In this area things changed rapidly in the early 1960s. The modern world came to be seen not as a danger that could and should be shut out but as a factor that had to be dealt with. In 1960 *Para Tí* recommended a middle-of-the-road approach to child rearing, somewhere between modernity and tradition. After 1960 a new terminology was introduced; terms such as "trauma" and "Oedipus complex" made their appearance, although they still required explanation. Mothers were now urged to send their children to kindergarten, not only because it was important for children to learn how to socialize but also because they themselves could benefit from some free time. In this respect, popular magazines were more progressive than some analysts, such as Rascovsky, who opposed any recourse to child-care institutions.

If the times were changing, someone had to come to the aid of families struggling to cope with those changes. Thus the emergence of the expert. Regular columns on health-related issues (usually written by physicians) had been traditional features of popular magazines since the 1920s; when psychologists or psychoanalysts became the experts of choice in the 1960s, the nature of the advice the columns offered changed. Two of those experts were the pediatrician Florencio Escardó and his wife, the psychologist Eva Giberti. They played crucial roles in popularizing psychoanalytic discourse. Escardó was a well-known pediatrician, chief of his service at the Children's Hospital in Buenos Aires and a popular professor at the university. Throughout the 1960s he published articles in popular magazines and appeared regularly on TV and radio. He introduced a conception of psychoanalytically informed pediatrics that had an enormous impact on a new generation of pediatricians. Parents were urged to "understand" their children's diseases, and to avoid overmedication. Escardó discussed psychosomatic medicine and advocated such new pediatric techniques as psychological preparation of children who had to undergo surgical procedures. In general, he advocated more relaxed parenting, free of preconceptions. However, it was his wife, Eva Giberti, through her *Escuela para padres* (School for Parents), who was instrumental in diffusing psychoanalytically informed child-rearing techniques among broad sectors of society.

Eva Giberti graduated as a social worker before the university introduced a psychology program. After some years of study in Europe on a fellowship from the World Health Organization, Giberti returned to Argentina and worked for the Ministry of Social Action. In Europe, Giberti had become acquainted with the School for Parents movement. She became a widely known figure through appearances in the media. Between 1957 and the late 1960s, her column on child rearing appeared three times a week in the widely read newspaper *La Razón*. In the late 1960s she launched a TV program called *Escuela para padres,* in which actual cases were dramatized by actors.[54] Giberti also organized and ran a School for Parents at the Children's Hospital, as well as private groups.[55] A collection of her articles, originally published in a variety of popular newspapers and magazines, appeared in a three-volume book titled *Escuela para padres,* which went through many editions and sold over 150,000 copies (in Argentina a book that sells 10,000 copies is considered a blockbuster).[56] Later Giberti wrote books on sex education, divorce, and other issues, which were also reissued several times.

Escuela para padres was first published in 1961, with a foreword by Escardó in which he pointed out the importance of the publication of *Escuela* at a time when "the collective consciousness" was undergoing "mutation." The book itself is an interesting artifact. Its first edition was meant to be displayed as much as to be read. It was bound in red padded leather with gilded letters on the spine. The luxurious binding, however, hid a cheaply edited volume printed on thick paper and adorned with rough illustrations. The book was designed for people who would take pride in displaying it on their bookshelves or on a table.

The tone of the book and the examples it presents give us a hint of its intended audience. The language suggests that it was intended for readers who, although receptive to Giberti's message, were not educated in child psychology. The family of Giberti's examples is the typical (even stereotypical) lower-middle-class family. The father works but money is tight. If the mother works, it is only to make ends meet, not for her personal or professional development. She usually works in a factory or in an office as a secretary. Giberti's typical family lives in a small apartment, either with or close to their siblings, uncles, aunts, and grandparents. When Giberti discusses the behavior of parents who forbid their children to socialize with children of a lower social class, it is obvious that the intended readers are the parents of the children who are to be shunned.[57]

The book is written in colloquial language, free of jargon and technical terms. The situations and problems are the sort that parents could easily identify with. Each chapter starts with a dialogue between family members or women in everyday situations, which Giberti supposedly overheard. A typical opening sentence: "Waiting in line at the grocery store, I heard the following dialogue." The dialogues present the problem and the protagonists' confusion and mistaken interpretation. After the problem becomes clear (a misbehaving child, a child who refuses to eat, etc.), Giberti steps in with the correct explanation. As the introduction to a series of her articles published in *Para Tí* magazine in 1967 said: "Eva Giberti will communicate with you at a fundamentally human level. You will identify with her, with her vision of modern woman that looks at the world through your own eyes, with her plain language, which is backed by years of experience and study."[58]

Escuela para padres starts by problematizing parenthood. According to Giberti, psychology (meaning psychoanalysis) shows that the events of a child's first five years determine its future life. "A great percentage of criminals have grown up deprived of maternal care." Therefore, parents have the moral and social obligation to learn how to be parents. Experience is not enough; parents cannot afford to learn parenthood by doing. Certain precise knowledge is necessary, and that knowledge can be acquired only through years of study or through the shortcuts Giberti offers. *Escuela para padres* makes that knowledge available "without entering into psychological deep waters, although backed by psychological knowledge."[59]

The general tone of the book is prescriptive. There is a knowledge that can be made available only through the mediation of a specialist—Giberti—who knows how to do things and why. Unlike Spock, who was advising mothers to "trust themselves," Giberti points out that "the majority of parents don't know how to educate a child. They feel the right way, but they don't know."[60] She can share this knowledge with parents, but she alone is the ultimate repository of such knowledge. Therefore, Giberti spoke from a clear position of authority. Throughout the text Giberti uses a particular strategy. While she repeatedly points out that her cases are taken "from the street" and therefore they are not "clinical cases," sprinkled throughout the text are casual references to her professional practice and her consulting room. She is "one of us," an ordinary woman who overhears talk while she waits in line at the grocery store, and at the same time she reminds the reader that she is invested with the authority endowed by her professional activity and knowledge.

From the beginning of the book Giberti goes out of her way to emphasize the need for adequate technical knowledge to educate parents. Commenting on a recommendation made at a psychiatric conference in 1959 that parents should form cooperatives to organize courses on parenthood, Giberti advises that such courses should be left to professionals. "Blessed be all the associations and cooperatives that are building social pillars of coexistence and understanding with children! But may the gods protect us from improvised courses without adequate technical and professional supervision."[61] Giberti is clearly affirming the specialist's monopoly on a certain symbolic capital.

The purpose of the *Escuela de padres* is to "understand" things that have previously been seen as unproblematic. The first chapter concludes with a short list of things that parents could learn: that many children's illnesses stem from psychological problems, and that children's behavior has a meaning that is not necessarily evident. *Escuela para padres,* therefore, offers an organizing framework and an interpretive tool for understanding everyday problems.

Giberti's message was easily acceptable to broad sectors because it was presented as progressive and scientific but at the same time as not subversive or threatening; it was essentially uncontroversial. Giberti advocated greater liberty for children but she encouraged the setting of some strict limits. Although she opposed corporal punishment, Giberti acknowledged that sometimes punishment was necessary. Giberti explicitly warned parents against the laissez-faire attitude advocated by some "modern" psychological theories.[62]

Moreover, Giberti never crosses the threshold of traditional morality. Her discussions of sex education, for instance, are loaded with general common-sense advice (it is better to tell the truth, because otherwise other people may give the child misinformation, etc.) but contain very few concrete examples of how to deal with the subject. She provides a model discussion with children about where babies come from, for instance, but has little to say about how babies get into their mothers' wombs in the first place. The idea of children's sexuality is vaguely suggested but never explicitly discussed.

Her version of psychoanalysis dilutes the role of sexuality, particularly children's sexuality, the aspect of Freudian thought that met the most resistance. If young children touch each other and carry their "mom and dad" game beyond acceptable limits, parents should not repress them, Giberti tells us. In the best of cases, these games are a normal consequence of maturation, and in the worst, a copy of what children may have seen in their parents' bedroom. If the latter is the case, the guilt is the parents' for sharing their bedroom with their children.[63] In neither case (save in exceptional circumstances) are those games considered the result of an early sexual instinct.

Giberti uses the same cautious approach when she discusses other typically psychoanalytic issues, such as the Oedipus complex. It is interesting to compare Giberti's approach to the topic with Benjamin Spock's. Spock's discussion of the Oedipus complex and the possible consequences for the child of seeing his or her parents naked, for instance, refers to sexuality in an openly Freudian framework: "A boy loves his mother more than he loves any little girl. He feels much more rivalrous with his father and more in awe of him than he feels towards any boy. So the sight of his mother [nude] may be a little too stimulating and the chance to compare himself unfavorably with his father every day may make him feel like doing something violent to his old man."[64] Giberti declines to talk about the Oedipus complex at all, although she recognizes its importance: "The psychoanalytic school has warned us about the sexual links that invariably exist in all children. Thus appeared the famous Oedipus complex, whose handling and understanding are so delicate and to be approached with such respect that we will not attempt even a brief discussion here." In the child's view, "parents do not have visible and tangible sex like other mortals." The danger of parents' exposing themselves naked to their children has nothing to do with the possible sexual stimulation that such behavior may trigger. The danger is that the parents' nudity "is a means of imposing a sexuality that the child has not yet acquired"; it creates "unnecessary and artificial problems."[65] Giberti acquainted a wide audience with a psychoanalytically informed framework for dealing with their children. Her audience was essentially conservative, however, so she trimmed psychoanalysis to suit them: she took the sex out of it.

Giberti kept her treatment of women and motherhood within acceptable limits, too. She found work for women outside the home acceptable only as long as it did not take attention away from the children.[66] According to Giberti, a mother who works all day in a factory is still expected to keep her good humor and have enough energy to perform her duties as a mother and housewife; the possibility that men might share domestic tasks is only vaguely suggested. In Giberti's child-centered world, women do not work for their own personal satisfaction; they work only because they have to contribute to the household's support. Women's duties at home deserve respect, she wrote. Intelligence is not necessarily synonymous with intellectual work; it operates also at the level of perception and fantasy. Thus redefined, intelligence can also be applied to domestic duties. She encouraged women to educate themselves, provided they did not ignore their duties.[67]

Despite the limitations of her discourse, or perhaps because of them, Giberti played a crucial role in introducing psychoanalytically oriented discourse to a large number of Argentine homes. She adapted a psychoanalytically informed discourse to the needs of an expanded public that was becoming increasingly receptive to it.[68] Giberti's position on the fringes of the psychoanalytic establishment contributed to her popularity. As a non-medical psychologist she could not belong to the APA, and she says the psychoanalytic community largely ignored her.[69] Although Giberti held teaching positions at the University of Buenos Aires, she earned her degree relatively late, and was also considered an outsider by the community of psychologists. They considered her simplification and theoretical eclecticism a threat to their professional status.[70] This marginality gave her a measure of independence from institutional rigidities. Her message was mild enough to be well received in unions, in private and public schools, and even in a school run by cloistered nuns where she lectured on Erik Erikson's theories.[71] Her work in the Children's Hospital attracted large number of parents who knew her from TV and could not afford traditional psychotherapy. Giberti still makes regular appearances in the media. During the military dictatorship her son was imprisoned and she was banned from the media, but today she is again actively disseminating psychoanalytic discourse.

Giberti was instrumental in introducing psychoanalysis in the media. Through the 1960s, women's and child-rearing publications were loaded with psychoanalytic concepts. If children had difficulty at school, for instance, the explanation was not laziness but some psychological problem that a psychopedagogue (another new specialist) explained thus in *Para Ti*: "The girl, who felt that she was being displaced from her mother's affection, who felt that her younger brother was a powerful rival, took revenge on her mother, harming her in a way she knew would be painful."[72] Gradually topics that had been taboo a few years earlier—infant sexuality, masturbation—were discussed and legitimized by the new scientific discourse provided by psychoanalysis. A reader seeking advice from *Nuestros Hijos* was told to find a good psychoanalyst and warned away from psychiatrists, who did not practice that technique.[73] At the same time, new emphasis was put on sex education for children.

Psychoanalysis also permeated some areas of educational discourse in general. For broad sectors of the expanding middle class the psychoanalyst occupied a central place in the process of child rearing. Going to the psychoanalyst's office four times a week was considered a normal activity for middle-class children of primary school age. Several of the new private schools and kindergartens that mushroomed throughout the 1960s to satisfy the demand of the professional middle class for "modern" education incorporated psychoanalytic ideas (and psychoanalysts) in their pedagogic techniques.[74]

Magazines and Other Popular Publications

The surge in psychoanalytic discourse in the media came between the last years of the 1950s and the first years of the 1960s. The family began to be perceived as an agency for individual self-fulfillment rather than as a cell for the reproduction of the species. Similarly, sex was separated from its purely reproductive function and gained a legitimate place in the realm of pleasure. Specialists in the new disciplines such as psychology, sociology, and psychopedagogy started to be consulted as experts for advice on issues that appeared to have become increasingly complex. With the new emphasis on the individual came new technologies for self-understanding.

In this context psychoanalysis (generally in a vulgarized version) played a prescriptive and interpretive role. The 1960s were the years of "psychotests" published in women's and popular magazines to help readers "discover" hidden aspects of their personality. In 1963 *Para Tí* published three regular columns: a horoscope (also very popular), a graphology column, and a third on psychotests. The three techniques—each at its own level—seem to address an existing demand for interpretive and predictive tools. Columns on vocational orientation also appeared. "You think you know yourself very well," *Claudia,* another women's magazine, warned its readers in March 1961, "but we tell you that this is not the case." Psychologists and psychoanalysts were consulted as authorities.[75] The role of the psychologist is particularly important. Since the university introduced the psychology program in the late 1950s, psychology had become a "women's profession." Thus for the first time there was a new breed of women specialists who, unlike priests and doctors, could talk to women about women's issues in a woman's voice yet with a discourse that was legitimized by science.

Gradually the female psychoanalyst replaced the priest in most women's publications, while psychoanalytic concepts replaced the habitual religious-moral discourse. This evolution is clear even in such magazines as *Nuestros Hijos,* a publication devoted to child rearing that was originally linked to Catholic circles. When both a priest and a psychoanalyst were consulted in the 1960s, it was the priest who had to adjust his discourse to the new times. *Para Tí,* for instance, published a regular column titled "Secretos de Confesión," in which a priest responded to readers. Although in general his advice stayed within the bounds of Catholic doctrine, we can see a gradually developing tendency toward an understanding that went beyond religious issues. Father Agustín, for instance, advised a woman whose marriage could not be consummated to consult a good neuropsychiatrist. He urged another woman to overcome the psychic trauma that prevented her from marrying. Yet Father Agustín was aware that in a sense psychoanalysis was competing for the souls of his readers, and he reacted this way: "Marketed as a resource of choice, [psychoanalysis is] a pharisaical brainwashing technique and a corrupt fragment of sacramental confession. . . . Modern youth's false ideas have to be set right. . . . The most complete solution, my rebellious girls, is in the confessional of a church."[76] Yet this denunciation of psychoanalysis did not prevent him from using such terms as "projection" and "trauma." As reality and the perception of it became difficult to understand and express within traditional frameworks, psychoanalytic discourse provided new tools to do so.

THE ROLE OF WOMEN IN THE FAMILY AND SOCIETY

Generally speaking, until the mid- to late 1950s the dominant image of women presented by the typical women's magazine, school textbook, and other widely read publications was influenced by the Catholic tradition.[77] Publications talked to women through the voices of men (usually priests or doctors). The natural place for women was at home. "If she is not to neglect her obligations beyond forgetting, a woman who has a child must take care of him, devoting all her time and attention to him," claimed *Para Tí* in 1950. Motherhood was a "sacred duty" and the only source of personal fulfillment for women. A husband was the only link between the home and the external world. The role of the wife was reduced to "containing" him: "If wives were more understanding, they would not feel so hurt every time 'he' comes home worried, yells at the children, and answers in sharp monosyllables. . . . They should hurry dinner and leave him alone until, rested, well fed, and relaxed, he becomes less tense."[78] This "containment" also applied to sexual relations: "Every woman should remember that even when she is tired or consumed by worry, she should never say no to her husband," lectured *Nuestros Hijos* in July 1960. In general, modern life was seen as incompatible with women's duties at home.

Around 1960, as a result of the social changes we have seen, this traditional image started to change rapidly. What had been taken for granted with respect to acceptable roles for women became problematized and required explanation. In *Para Tí* we read:

> When we meet unfocused friends who never finish college, who learn languages without ever knowing them, who never find a job that comes up to their unjustified expectations, we feel like apprentice psychoanalysts. . . . In view of the propensity for "female narcissism" . . . the first thing a woman has to think about is the prospect of marriage. . . . A woman who does not live with the dream of marriage becomes someone who "does not know what to do."[79]

The problem was not so much that women engaged in activities outside their homes at the expense of their natural duties but that the lack of an anchor in the home "decentered" them, so that they failed in their other activities. Marriage was presented as a source of personal satisfaction beyond its reproductive function. Women's happiness at home was not only not incompatible with their success elsewhere but rather its precondition. For most magazines of the early 1960s, the ideal woman was a middle-of-the-road person, between those "defenders of existentialism, always in the hands of a psychoanalyst," and those too traditional, tied to the rigidities of the past. Gradually women's role at home was also redefined. In the new version, a woman was not expected just to please her husband but to share in his interests, problems, and activities. Her husband, for his part, should respect his wife because otherwise she would suffer a "maid complex."[80]

As the 1960s advanced, working mothers, far from being morally reprehensible women who did not take proper care of their families, became a social reality that had to be addressed and supported, if the magazines wanted to keep their readers. In 1960 *Nuestros Hijos* devoted its October issue to the problems of working mothers. Of the "specialists" consulted by the magazine, only a priest insisted that women's only natural place was at home. Eight months later the magazine urged an end to discrimination against single mothers. *Para Tí,* having insisted in the 1950s that women should stay home and take care of their children and husbands, in 1964 launched a series of psychotests purporting to indicate the kind of job a woman was best suited for, thus acknowledging that women were indeed looking for activities outside the home. One "specialist" on the staff of *Para Ti* advised a reader to study history, in view of her "cyclothymic temperament"; he explained to another troubled reader that her test indicated that her difficulty making decisions had an "unconscious etiology," and advised her to see a psychologist.[81]

Popular magazines also started publishing articles on female sexuality and contraception, most of them written by female psychologists or psychoanalysts. In 1960 *Nuestros Hijos* published a series of articles on "frigidity," suggesting that it could be cured by psychotherapy. Sexual harmony was now explicitly considered a precondition for happiness in marriage. Once sexual intercourse became accepted as a means of pleasure and not only of reproduction, contraceptive techniques were widely discussed. Until the mid-1960s, however, the question was not how to use them but to what extent their use was legitimate at all.

In 1966 the essayist Julio Mafud published a widely read book, *La revolución sexual en la Argentina,* which leaped to *Gente's* best-seller list, along with Florencio Escardó's *Sexología de las familias* and a collection called *Crónicas del sexo. La revolución sexual* claimed to explore the consequences of the sexual revolution that was supposedly taking place in Argentina. It was a rather incoherent impressionistic essay on the changes in Argentine sexual mores, supposedly based on interviews. Its scientific or even informative value was dubious at best. Yet its plain and sometimes explicit language and its vindication of women's right to sexual freedom reflected a change in the perception of women's role and helped to make female sexuality a topic for general discussion. The fact that for Mafud this sexual freedom was to be exercised only within the bonds of wedlock reveals the persistence of traditional elements in a discourse that claims to be "modern." That was precisely what made his discussion easy to accept.

Sexuality was certainly not a new topic. Books on various aspects of sexuality had been widely read in Buenos Aires since the 1920s. Most of them, however, viewed sexuality through the lens of physiology; in the 1960s it became a social problem to be analyzed by "sociologists" like Mafud in the language of psychoanalysis. "Since the influence of Freud and modern psychology in matters of sex is assumed," Mafud explained, "I will not dwell on it."[82] Psychoanalysts became representatives of "scientific" discourse in issues involving sexuality.[83]

IMAGES OF PSYCHOANALYSIS

Although psychoanalytic language permeated the media, until the mid-1960s the figure of the psychoanalyst was still surrounded by mystery. In 1966 *Gente* reported on the Pan-American Psychoanalytic Conference that was taking place in Buenos Aires. The reporter emphasized the atmosphere of silence and mystery surrounding the meeting (the press was not admitted). "*Gente* penetrates the inner sanctum and reveals unexpected details. What was said? Conclusions arrived at by the very exclusive disciples of Freud." The conference "looked like a meeting of magicians or of writers of children's stories. Their only talk was of fantasies, dreams, symbols . . . and other forces that have determined, from Freud to this day, that we are not as normal as we think we are."[84]

This way of characterizing psychoanalysts shows an interesting pattern in the diffusion of psychoanalysis. First, the fact that *Gente,* which generally showed more interest in movie stars than in scientific conferences, devoted three prominent pages to the meeting indicates that it assumed its middle-class readers had an interest in psychoanalysis and some knowledge about it. Perhaps more interesting is the article's tone, the comparison of a scientific meeting with a gathering of magicians and spinners of fairy tales. Yet the writer not only did not question the validity of psychoanalysis, he took it for granted. If the mysterious participants in the conference talked of fantasies and dreams, it was because fantasies and dreams are the "forces that have determined, from Freud to this day, that we are not as normal as we think we are." The writer distinguished between the discipline (unquestionable) and its practitioners (mysterious and exotic). Studies have shown that this was precisely the image of psychoanalysts in the popular imagination at the time psychoanalysis was gaining public acceptance.[85]

Gradually but quickly, psychoanalysts became less exotic. By 1968 they not only were routinely consulted on a variety of topics but were among the "famous" interviewed by *Gente* in Punta del Este, an exclusive beach resort in Uruguay.[86] Analysts were presented as members of a new intellectual and economic elite. Psychoanalysis, on the other hand, was characterized as an object of conspicuous consumption. *Atlántida,* another publication put out by *Gente*'s publisher and aimed at the same middle-class audience, included a humorous supplement with its issue of May 1968 titled "Agenda of an Important Man," purporting to be the appointment book of an executive. The entry of February 15 read: "Make appointment, Bleger, Pichon

Rivière, Pérez Morales: ask significance of swordfish." Apparently the publishers were unaware that Argentine psychoanalysts were traditionally unavailable in February, when they ritually took off for vacations,[87] but no matter; they took it for granted that an executive would be seeing an analyst, so one was not enough: they gave their "important man" three. They also took it for granted that their readers would recognize the names as those of the prominent and *expensive* psychoanalysts they were.

Such magazines as *Gente* and *Atlántida* presented psychoanalysis as an object of consumption by the rich and famous. In 1966 *Gente* asked a group of famous people a series of eight questions, the second of which was whether they needed psychoanalysis. Hugo Guerrero Martineitz, a popular Peruvian talk show host, was asked if he believed in God and if he believed in psychoanalysis (in that order). Needless to say, Guerrero was quick to reply that he believed in both. Psychoanalytic language became a social code. Interviews with film stars included discussions of their neuroses and the need for therapy. If a star did not use the terminology of psychoanalysis, the interviewer translated what the star had said into psychoanalytic jargon. When one young actress talked about her religious beliefs, the interviewer concluded that "all neurosis is a conflict between the conscious and the unconscious." When the actress referred to her nervousness, the interviewer was ready with an explanation: what she called "nerves" was in fact her neurosis.[88]

Throughout the decade psychoanalysis became a central component of popular culture. Two films by Héctor Olivera and Fernando Ayala, *Sexoanálisis* and *Los sexoanalizados,* made fun of the obsession with psychoanalyzing sex. By the early 1970s the main question was "Why do so many people go to the analyst?"[89] Psychoanalytic experience of one sort or another was available not only to the rich but also to the children of blue-collar families.

Psychoanalysis for Executives: Primera Plana

Primera Plana, a magazine that had enormous influence on Argentine journalism, played an important role in the diffusion of psychoanalysis. It was launched in 1962 to support the "blue" faction of the military (supposedly liberal and loyal to the government) in an internal conflict with broad political repercussions. From the beginning the magazine, under the direction of the influential journalist Jacobo Timmerman, promoted cultural modernization while endorsing an authoritarian political project that came to fruition in the coup of 1966.[90] This apparent contradiction between cultural modernization and political authoritarianism mirrored deeper tensions in Argentine society, and ended with a backlash against the magazine. In 1969 it was banned by the military regime it had helped to enthrone.

Primera Plana was patterned on U.S. and European magazines that covered political and cultural affairs.[91] Its staff of highly capable journalists wrote on national and international events and trends. For some influential sectors *Primera Plana* became not only an essential source of information but also a necessary reference for literary, artistic, and more generally cultural affairs. It was the first magazine in Argentina to introduce a best-seller list. It promoted the Latin American and particularly the Argentine literary boom of the 1960s and was one of the few places (if not the only one) in which avant-garde art was seriously discussed and appreciated.

Unlike *Gente* and *Para Tí, Primera Plana* targeted readers who were limited in numbers but economically, culturally, and politically influential. An advertisement it published in 1966 explicitly stated, "There are media whose aim is to reach a selected nucleus of readers, and therefore are interested not in showing how much they sell but rather to whom they sell."[92] Its price was 60 to 80 percent higher than *Gente*'s. The reader *Primera Plana* wanted to reach was the educated new "executive," a member of the managerial class that emerged and developed as a consequence of the industrial modernization of the late 1950s and early 1960s, culturally but not necessarily politically progressive. The magazine also targeted the intellectualized middle class, which shared with the managerial group an interest in the cultural developments flowing from Europe and the United States. The introduction of psychoanalysis in *Primera Plana* was part of a conscious program to promote cultural modernization.

Primera Plana made generous use of terminology and concepts borrowed from psychoanalysis and sociology. A review of the film *The Manchurian Candidate,* for instance, was headed "Consequences of the Oedipus Complex." Such terms as "Oedipus complex" and "transference" were introduced without explanation, with the assumption that readers understood their meaning. "Analytic technique, as is well known, generates in the patient a *transference* with the analyst, and as a consequence, there is a *countertransference* in the analyst."[93] The editors assumed also that prominent analysts were known by their readers. Enrique Pichon Rivière, who in 1966 and 1967 wrote a regular column, was introduced as someone "whose career as an analyst and researcher is so well known that he needs no introduction."

Primera Plana's first issue included an article titled "Somos todos neuróticos?" ("Are we all neurotics?"), putting forth the opinions of a variety of experts.[94] The article is paradigmatic of the general tone of the magazine. Psychoanalysis is presented as a fashion, but also as a need. The fact that psychoanalysis was fashionable and even glamorous is suggested by an accompanying photograph of Arnaldo Rascovsky and his attractive wife. They are pictured at a party, he looking well pleased with himself at this black-tie affair, she resplendent in sparkling jewelry, with a glass of champagne in her hand. They are not posing; the camera appears to have caught them by chance at this social event. Fancy parties seem to be the natural milieu of famous psychoanalysts. The photograph is more typical of a movie star or an executive than of a scientist. The caption reads: "Arnaldo Rascovsky sees Argentina sunk in a deep depression."

According to the article, neurosis was "the disease of the moment," the price to be paid for the modernization the magazine promoted. "The clear success of publications on [psychoanalysis] and the healthy financial situation of psychoanalysts (they charge between 400 and 2,000 pesos an hour and work a minimum of 66 hours a week)" indicated just how widespread neurosis was; yet Argentines did not see it as a mental disease. Acknowledging neurosis and seeking the aid of a psychoanalyst, then, far from being evidence of a mental problem, could in fact be interpreted as evidence of health. Psychoanalysis was also a cultural staple. Many people, according to *Primera Plana,* started analysis with the encouragement of family members or friends who were already in analysis and with whom they could now share a language.

Primera Plana was essentially a political magazine and a good example of the psychologization of politics, particularly of that bête noir of Argentine politics, Peronism. One of the factors that contributed to the neurosis epidemic, according to the magazine, was the current political situation, which, paradoxically, was interpreted as a result of the neurosis it was supposed to explain. This kind of dialectical relationship between politics and the need for psychoanalytic therapy was an idea shared by most experts consulted by *Primera Plana.* A physician urged his female patient to consult a psychoanalyst because "everybody lives in anxiety" as a result of the endless political conflicts.

Arnaldo Rascovsky offered the following interpretation of the situation: A wave of depression washed over Argentines as political conflicts went on and on. Governments represent parents. Societies, like individuals, have an id, a superego, and an ego. Peronism operated as a social superego, and when Perón was overthrown, nothing took its place, so the social structure fell into anarchy. The evidence of this anarchical situation was, according to Rascovsky, the proliferation of bounced checks, bills unpaid, and a general shift of values. Years later, Enrique Pichon Rivière also established a connection between neurosis and politics. During a flood in the province of Entre Ríos, the neurotic symptoms developed by some of the victims could be read politically. One of the victims, for instance, assumed the role of leader by organizing relief efforts. According to Pichon Rivière, this particular form of neurosis had political connotations because there were rumors of a coup, and the self-appointed organizer assumed unconsciously the role of its leader.[95]

Psychoanalysis (or some version of it) was an adequate instrument to explain almost all aspects of social life, as Pichon Rivière showed in his weekly column. He discussed such disparate topics as fashion, soccer, vacations, and censorship, interpreting them all in the framework of psychoanalysis. The sociologist José Miguens, too, conjured up psychoanalytic concepts to explain why the "blue" sector of the Army (the sector he advised), unlike the "reds," used the truth as a psychological weapon. Florencio Escardó, who wrote a regular column in the magazine's early years, discussed psychosomatic medicine and pointed out the importance of psychotherapy. More important, he argued that at least some sort of psychoanalytically based therapy should be made more widely available to low-income hospital patients.[96]

Primera Plana educated the public on the differences among psychoanalytic schools and on the details of the psychoanalytic career. It made clear whether the expert consulted was a psychologist, a psychiatrist who practiced psychoanalysis, or a "real" psychoanalyst who belonged to the APA. Most of the APA members consulted were training analysts. Eva Giberti, who was regularly consulted by the more popular magazines, was conspicuously absent from the pages of *Primera Plana*.

The cover of *Primera Plana*'s special issue of August 20, 1968, featured a caricature of Freud with the caption: "Psychoanalysis does not exist." The cover story discussed the nature of psychoanalysis, the criticism it received from epistemologists, and a classification of therapeutic schools, from orthodox psychoanalysis to Pavlovian reflexology. The article also included the responses of fifteen therapists of various orientations (all of them psychoanalytically educated) to a set of prepared questions, ranging from the appropriate response to a patient who wanted to have sex with the analyst to the appropriate fee to charge. The technical language used shows again that the magazine presumed a high level of psychoanalytic knowledge in its readers.

Primera Plana took for granted a public with modern attitudes toward such topics as sexuality, the family, and mental health. To its staff's amazement, however, although their readers were receptive to the message of modernity, they seemed to cling to traditional values. The results of opinion polls were surprisingly consistent. Polls showed not only that people felt more comfortable with a "strong government" under a charismatic leader but also that their attitudes toward sexuality and gender roles were far from modern.

The boom in psychoanalysis was a consequence of a variety of factors. On the demand side, it was a response to the rapid social, cultural, and political changes discussed in Chapter 3. Broad sectors of Argentine society felt that the crisis they were living through required new analytic and interpretive tools. But why was psychoanalysis the instrument of choice? By the late 1950s it was available in the Argentine market of ideas. An active and increasingly visible psychoanalytic association and other mental health institutions influenced by psychoanalysis brought it increasingly before the public eye. Like any other system of ideas, psychoanalysis requires active disseminators in order to reach broad sectors of society. As we have seen, it had many of them. They promoted a novel way of thinking about new problems in terms that did not collide with the cultural values Argentines took for granted. The diffusers' accomplishment, therefore, can be explained by their successful combination of the traditional and the modern in a society that was (and still is) lingering between these two cultures.

FIVE

The Encounter Between
Psychoanalysis and Psychiatry

Argentine psychoanalysis developed its professional identity in opposition to
classical somatic psychiatry, yet one important means of its diffusion was the
gradual convergence of psychoanalysts who developed an interest in social
issues and psychiatrists who questioned traditional psychiatry centered on
the mental asylum.[1] As they drew closer together, each discipline had to redefine its domain, its goals, and its practices.

As in the case of group psychotherapy, the introduction of psychoanalysis
in the psychiatric services of public hospitals suddenly made it available to
many people who otherwise would have had no access to it. It also encouraged a certain psychoanalytic way of thinking among doctors and the general public. Progressive psychiatrists who wanted to modernize the system
of psychiatric assistance absorbed psychoanalysis because it already enjoyed
broad social acceptance and was considered a modern, nonrepressive technique with a solid scientific foundation.

Some psychiatrists had been interested in psychoanalysis since the 1920s.
Although most of them were prominent members of their profession, they
were unable to secure a place for psychoanalysis in mainstream psychiatry;
since they lacked the training and did not belong to any official analytic institution, they were not perceived as true representatives of Freudianism
within the psychiatric community. In this anomalous situation, most of these
psychiatrists eventually abandoned Freudianism, either for ideological reasons or simply because it was incompatible with their professional work in
the asylum system. Whereas U.S. psychiatrists gradually absorbed psychoanalysis after the early founding of the first psychoanalytic association in
1911, in Argentina the two fields developed as separate disciplines, aimed at
different publics and relatively independent of each other, despite the efforts
of some APA members to secure a place for psychoanalysis in the medical
and psychiatric establishments.

After the late 1950s, however, the two domains began to come together as Argentine health services modernized and the political and cultural environment became more fluid after the fall of Perón. When at last general hospitals started to offer psychoanalytically oriented psychiatric services, they helped to change the way people thought about mental disorders and to boost psychoanalysis' scientific legitimacy in the eyes of the public.

Throughout the 1950s new theoretical approaches emerged within psychiatry. The "new psychiatry" began to question the traditional asylum model of psychiatric care and promoted a broader concept of the discipline. Now psychoanalysis began to be seen as a valid psychiatric technique. Changes were taking place in the psychoanalytic community, too. A progressive and more socially conscious group emerged at the fringes of the APA, gathered around Enrique Pichon Rivière. José Bleger, Fernando Ulloa, David Liberman, and Pichon's other disciples believed that the practice of psychoanalysis should not be confined to the analyst's private office; they wanted to move it into places where it would reach more people. Pichon Rivière's and other analysts' work with psychotic patients also cleared the way for a rapprochement between psychoanalysis and psychiatry.

The Consolidation of Psychiatry as an Autonomous Field and Its Politicization

Psychiatry went through important changes in the 1940s and 1950s. As a medical specialty it achieved increasing independence from other medical fields (particularly from neurology) and a clearer scientific status. Until the 1940s psychiatry had been perceived as the stepchild of medicine. It was an essentially empirical discipline with a limited therapeutic and theoretical arsenal.[2] In a system based on the asylum, psychiatrists were seen more as administrators and dilettantes than as real scientists. In the 1940s the introduction of new somatic techniques—particularly convulsive, surgical, and drug therapies—offered patients more than hope for the first time since Julius Wagner-Jauregg discovered the way to a cure for general paresis in 1917. Although no one could say why insulin shock and electroconvulsive therapy were often effective, the fact is that with them psychiatry finally had some methods that seemed to work for at least some kinds of pathologies.[3] The new therapies were discussed and applied surprisingly quickly in Argentina. With the new methods, psychiatry could at last claim scientific status. These changes accelerated the decline of the degeneration paradigm, with its emphasis on heredity.[4] In the postwar era, the development of psychotropic drugs and the growing acceptance of psychoanalysis and other psychotherapeutic methods, particularly in the United States, revamped the field completely.[5]

The diffusion of new therapeutic techniques sparked theoretical debates that for the first time went beyond the discussion of criteria for the classification of mental disorders. And when the first graduate program in psychiatry was introduced at the medical school of the University of Buenos Aires in 1942, psychiatrists for the first time received specific training in the discipline.

During the 1950s, psychoanalysis gradually entered into the psychiatric universe, even in journals dedicated to areas that seem remote from it. Some of the most prestigious psychiatrists, many of them members of the Liga de Higiene Mental, contributed to the Ministry of Public Health's journal *Neuropsiquiatría,* published between 1949 and 1953. Unlike other publications of the Perón regime, *Neuropsiquiatría* was a serious scientific journal, with no open political agenda. Although its general approach was defined by its title, the presence of E. Eduardo Krapf among its contributors opened the door for psychoanalytic concepts in book reviews and articles.[6]

Despite its increasing autonomy, psychiatry felt the impact of the volatile political and cultural environment of the 1950s and 1960s. Some of the new approaches were linked to political ideologies. Communist psychiatrists, for example, promoted Pavlov's reflexology. Reflexology was to have some importance as an institutionally and socially oriented alternative to psychoanalysis until the early 1960s, when progressive psychoanalysts started appropriating some of the reflexologists' social banners. Prestigious reflexologists such as Jorge Thénon, Julio Luis Peluffo, Antonio Caparrós, and Jorge Itzigsohn taught in the psychology program at the university or lectured occasionally at the medical school. Since the late 1950s they made common cause with the leftists of the psychoanalytic community, as we shall see.[7]

The Emergence of the Idea of Mental Health

The full acceptance of psychotherapeutic techniques among Argentine progressive psychiatrists was the result of a variety of factors. Probably of greatest importance was the growing influence of American and British psychiatry among Argentine professionals after World War II. Another factor was the development of psychotropic drugs.[8] According to the psychiatrist Guillermo Vidal, the acceptance of psychoanalysis in psychiatry was closely linked to the diffusion of those drugs, since both addressed the same phenomenon from different angles. While psychoanalysis contributed the idea that mental patients should be heard, psychotropic medication generated the conditions under which patients *could* be heard, because they tranquilized without hindering mental functioning. Both techniques contributed to the "personalization" of the mental patient.[9] The acceptance of psychotherapy was related also to the renewed emphasis on prevention and therefore on the treatment of neurosis. Psychotherapy was seen as the most appropriate method to deal with neurotic outpatients.

The introduction of psychoanalysis in the progressive areas of the public psychiatric system, however, was in part also the result of reforms introduced by the state in the post-Perón era. Despite the good intentions of such institutions as the Liga Argentina de Higiene Mental, conditions in public mental hospitals did not improve significantly, although the number of psychiatrists continued to grow. By 1970 Argentina had by far the largest number of psychiatrists in Latin America, followed at a distance by Brazil and Mexico.[10] Public mental hospitals, however, continued to be overcrowded. The National Neuropsychiatric Hospital for Women (later the Hospital Braulio Moyano) had 223 patients per 100 beds in 1955 and 187 in 1956. Only in 1957 did that number fall to 87. The National Neuropsychiatric Hospital for Men (the old Hospicio de las Mercedes, later the Hospital Nacional José T. Borda) had 173 patients per 100 beds in 1957. Mortality rates in mental hospitals were extremely high; of the patients removed from the rolls of the Colonia Cerdá for retarded children in 1957, 58.6 percent had died.[11] In general conditions were deplorable; mental hospitals were perceived more as warehouses than as therapeutic institutions.[12]

In the years after the fall of Perón, prominent psychiatrists published numerous articles complaining about the condition of psychiatric services and proposing improvements. Everyone agreed that the situation had to change, and there was also a relatively high degree of consensus regarding which concrete changes had to be made. The reforms proposed included improvements in training and in compensation for nurses and support staff; establishment of outpatient services in general hospitals; the use of new therapeutic techniques (the techniques proposed varied with the theoretical orientation of the doctor); and an increase in the national budget for public mental health services.[13]

More receptive to such suggestions than the Perón regime, the government that came after him founded the Instituto Nacional de Salud Mental (INSM) in 1957. The INSM was an independent government agency that centralized public psychiatric and preventive services. Its establishment has to be seen in the context of the developmental policies of the governments that succeeded Perón.[14] The goals of the INSM—whose name spoke of *salud mental* (mental health) rather than *higiene mental*—were: (a) to prevent neuropsychiatric disorders; (b) to promote scientific research; (c) to provide broad-based assistance to neuropsychiatric patients; (d) to contribute to the social rehabilitation of mental patients; (e) to provide technical advice; and (f) to coordinate the activities of national, provincial, and municipal organizations and provide technical and financial support. Psychoanalysis played a central role in the renovation of psychiatry because it was perceived as an essential component of modernity and because it was sending down such deep roots in Argentine culture. Pichon Rivière was only one of many psychoanalysts who were appointed to the INSM.

The INSM was a response to a new conception of mental health. Mental health was promoted by the World Health Organization and drew its inspiration from new ideas on psychiatric care developed in Europe (particularly in Great Britain) and in the United States after World War II. Whereas the goals of mental hygiene had been to improve treatment conditions for mental patients and to prevent mental disorders, mental health focused on improving conditions for the general population, with emphasis on health as a positive value. The idea was to work not only with people who were already afflicted by mental disorders but also (and fundamentally) with the healthy population. "Health is not only the absence of sickness, but a state of physical equilibrium and of mental and social welfare."[15] This definition of mental health brought about a whole redefinition of the psychiatric field. Mental health was no longer the province of psychiatry; psychiatry was only one of the tools available to achieve it. Mental health was one facet of the general welfare and therefore had to be approached from different perspectives and with the insights provided by different disciplines. Whereas the mental hygiene movement focused on the traditional psychiatric institutions with the aim of improving them, mental health could be meaningful only outside the asylum. Mental health was a positive condition that resulted from a variety of social, economic, and environmental factors, as the law that established the INSM in 1957 explicitly acknowledged.[16]

The emphasis on mental health was reflected in the composition of the INSM's board of directors: four psychiatrists (two specializing in child psychiatry), two neurologists, one educator, one sociologist, one lawyer, and one economist. The establishment of the INSM was a breakthrough in the public system of psychiatric care. Unfortunately, the impulse was short-lived, in part because of a perennial lack of funds and also because of the political instability that the country suffered throughout the 1960s. The INSM quickly lost relevance. Paradoxically, it was revived by the repressive military government that took power in 1966 as part of another authoritarian attempt to modernize the country. Nonetheless, the mental health movement had some important long-term consequences. It generated the conditions for a broad introduction of psychoanalytic approaches. The task was made easy by a very active group of analysts who were ready to question orthodox practice centered on the analyst's couch.

New Forums for Debate: Revista Latinoamericana de Psiquiatría *and* Acta Neuropsiquiátrica Argentina

The decline of the degeneracy paradigm and the increasing autonomy of psychiatry as a medical field gave rise to new forums for discussion and debate. In 1951 Gregorio Bermann, having promoted psychoanalysis for twenty years only to abandon it for Marx, founded a new journal: the *Revista Latinoamericana de Psiquiatría.* The year before, the *Revista de Psiquiatría y Criminología,* the heir to José Ingenieros's *Archivos* and the most prestigious psychiatric journal in Argentina, had ceased publication under pressure from the Perón government. The *Revista Latinoamericana* stepped into the space left empty by the *Revista de Psiquiatría.* Its original editorial board was a heterogeneous group, including among others the Brazilian Antonio Austregesilo, José Bleger (who was not yet a psychoanalyst), the Peruvian Honorio Delgado (who would soon quit for political reasons), the Spanish psychiatrist Emilio Mira y López, Nerio Rojas, and Jorge Thénon. The program of the new journal revealed a totally new conception of psychiatry and mental disorders. For the editors of the *Revista,* mental disorders were "a medical problem, but in no lesser degree a social and political problem."[17] Psychiatry was therefore a full-fledged member of the human sciences. Neither psychoanalysis nor purely somatic psychiatry could alone respond to the complex problem of mental disorders. The journal promoted a psychiatry that would be at the same time humanistic and social, and that in its quest for a proper understanding of mental processes would seek the aid of psychology, cultural anthropology, sociology, and even the arts. The focus was placed on what Bermann called "sociopsychiatry."[18]

Although the journal's board of editors included psychiatrists of a variety of political backgrounds, from the beginning the chief influence was clearly wielded by a group of Communist doctors (Thénon, Bleger, Peluffo) or sympathizers (Bermann himself). The third issue of the journal included Honorio Delgado's letter of resignation. The journal was too leftist for him.

It is true that after the first couple of issues the journal closely followed the Communist Party line: overwhelmingly Pavlovian and antipsychoanalytic. It is probable that the Communist doctors were taking advantage of the short honeymoon between the Party and the Perón regime. All the same, the *Revista* became an important forum outside of the psychiatric establishment centered on the Hospicio for the discussion of new psychiatric theories.

The *Revista* promoted something that had been missing from psychiatric journals: debate among representatives of different theoretical leanings.[19] When psychiatric journals had published articles on different approaches to psychotherapy in the 1920s and 1930s, the various sides had not been moved to challenge one another, but now the field had come alive, and Bermann seized the opportunity to encourage debate. Although he had turned against psychoanalysis since the 1940s, he still promoted the wide use of psychotherapy in combination with the various shock and drug treatments for cases that did not respond to any one treatment alone. More on this below.[20]

Despite its initial strength, the *Revista Latinoamericana* was short-lived; it disappeared in 1954. The reasons are not clear, but they probably had to do with internal conflicts and the end of the relatively cordial relations between the Communist Party and the Perón regime.[21] In the same year that Bermann's journal died, another appeared to take its place. The *Acta Neuropsiquiátrica Argentina* declared from its first issue that it was a rigorously scientific journal without political or theoretical commitments.[22] Its founder and director, Guillermo Vidal, was an Argentine-born psychiatrist who had studied medicine in Paraguay but trained as a psychiatrist at the Universidad de Buenos Aires and as a psychoanalyst at the APA. Early in his career, Vidal had been interested in biologically based psychiatry and he later returned to it. He described himself, however, as a "frustrated psychoanalyst." His final presentation at the APA had not been approved because, he was sure, its Jungian slant did not fit the APA's rigid theoretical orthodoxy.[23] According to Vidal, the purpose of *Acta* was to provide a place for discussion of scientific psychiatry. In other words, he wanted to remove ideology from psychiatry. Vidal was a friend of Bermann's; he had contributed to the last issues of the *Revista,* and Bermann served on *Acta*'s advisory committee until 1968, when he resigned over political disagreements. *Acta*'s original board of editors included such progressive psychiatrists as Mauricio Goldenberg, who was its co-founder, and at least one Catholic analyst, Raúl Usandivaras, a disciple of Celes Cárcamo. With the second issue Cárcamo himself joined the editorial board. In the 1960s a large number of APA-trained psychoanalysts became board members, and for a time the journal was more psychoanalytically oriented.

From the beginning the new journal was much more open to a variety of orientations than its predecessor. Pavlovians argued with psychoanalysts, neurologists argued with drug therapists. In accord with the mental health philosophy, *Acta* published numerous articles by sociologists, anthropologists, and other social scientists.[24] In a sense, *Acta* carried out the program that Bermann had set for his *Revista* but was unable to follow because of his political commitment. Psychoanalysts were much more in evidence in *Acta* than they had been in the *Revista,* and not only orthodox analysts in the mold of Angel Garma. Emilio Rodrigué published a paper on Bion's theory of group therapy in the first issue.[25] Later *Acta* opened its pages to therapists who combined LSD with psychoanalysis.[26]

Both *Revista* and *Acta* promoted a more autonomous and "scientific" psychiatry. New therapeutic methods with more solid theoretical bases were now available for discussion and challenge, and advertising revenue poured in from pharmaceutical firms. *Acta,* which became the most prestigious psychiatric journal in Latin America, was instrumental in the consolidation of a psychoanalytically grounded psychiatry that could claim scientific autonomy. In 1962 it changed its name to *Acta Psiquiátrica y Psicológica Argentina,* then a year later to *Acta Psiquiátrica y Psicológica Latinoamericana.* The name change clearly recognized psychiatry's growing independence from neurology. In 1966 Vidal established the Acta Foundation for Mental Health, which until the late 1970s was a major center for psychiatric research, services, and teaching.

Although *Acta* became increasingly psychoanalytically oriented through the years (more and more APA analysts joined its editorial and advisory boards), the journal never lost its identity as a *psychiatric* journal. Thus *Acta,* unlike the *Revista de Psicoanálisis,* located psychoanalysis in the psychiatric field, thus legitimizing the participation of psychoanalysts in psychiatric forums. At the same time, psychiatrists who took other theoretical and clinical approaches also found its pages open, so psychoanalysts' findings were forced to share the stage with theirs.[27]

The actual number of *Acta*'s readers is impossible to establish, but specialists of all persuasions overwhelmingly agree that it certainly was the most prestigious psychiatric forum in Argentina and throughout Latin America. It is doubtful that psychoanalysis would have been so readily accepted by the progressive sectors of the psychiatric community without its influence.

Psychiatry and Ideology in the Late 1960s

Acta and the several conferences on psychiatry that were held in the early 1960s were expressions of the growing autonomy of the psychiatric field. Here scientific discussion took precedence over political and ideological considerations. Arguments were not presented in political terms; they might be influenced by political considerations, but those considerations were not allowed to get in the way of theoretical reasoning. Psychiatrists were able to establish relatively independent mechanisms of professional recognition and scientific debate that functioned largely according to rules established within the psychiatric field.

In the 1960s the mental health community was divided into several groups, with some overlap. The main distinction was between psychiatrists linked to the asylum system and those who rejected it. Among the latter group (we can call them the progressives) there were various points of disagreement. How important were social factors in the etiology of neurosis, and should consideration be given to the social impact of psychotherapy? For the orthodox analysts, the only appropriate setting for psychotherapy was the analyst's private office. Opposing them were others who emphasized the centrality of social interactions in the etiology of neurosis, and therefore the need for interactive therapies outside the therapist's office.[28] Even this group could not agree on the nature of the psychotherapeutic process. José Bleger, for instance, tried to construct a system of "psychohygiene" by applying concepts and theories derived from psychoanalysis to institutional, group, and preventive therapies. According to him,

> [psychoanalysis'] social reach is determined not by the number of patients who can be cured with this procedure but by the advances [it provides] in our knowledge of the normal and pathological development processes and by the possibility of using that knowledge to promote short-term techniques and procedures (narcoanalysis, hypnoanalysis, lysergic acid, etc.), and above all by the creation of instruments for psychohygiene.[29]

Others, such as José Itzigsohn and Jorge Thénon, rejected psychoanalysis in favor of Pavlovian reflexology. For them human behavior was a result of conditioned reflexes, there was no universal "human nature," and appropriate psychotherapy could create a "new man," properly "conditioned" to learn new ways of life. To Jorge Thénon and some of his colleagues, psychotherapy was essentially a kind of teaching process by which the therapist should rationally try to destroy all that was negative in the patient and "correct errors."[30] For this purpose the therapist's ideology had to be clearly stated from the beginning.

The various psychotherapeutic schools managed to permeate one another more than some of their adherents were willing to admit. Some Pavlovian reflexologists approached the Freudian technique. Reflexologists taught in the psychoanalytically oriented psychology program at the university and were invited to lecture at the medical school together with psychoanalysts. Some of them also worked with psychoanalytically oriented psychiatric services at general hospitals. In 1958 a group of psychiatrists of various persuasions, psychoanalysts and reflexologists among them, founded the influential Ateneo Psiquiátrico de Buenos Aires. Moreover, according to Marie Langer, reflexologists frequently referred patients to psychoanalysts when their clinical approach failed to obtain the hoped-for results. Other schools, such as phenomenology, also attracted some Catholic psychoanalysts, such as Jorge Saurí. For reasons that went far beyond intramural discussions, however, psychoanalysis was becoming a climate of opinion that affected the relationship between psychoanalysts and other psychiatrists.

Gradually, however, the terms of the debate changed, particularly after the coup of 1966 and more dramatically after the social movements that emerged after 1969, which were both cause and consequence of the deep politicization of society. The new debates took place in the Federación Argentina de Psiquiatras (FAP), founded in 1960. The original group represented a mix of psychiatric schools, among them psychoanalysts who, like Enrique Pichon Rivière, Horacio Etchegoyen, and José Bleger, combined psychoanalysis with institutional psychiatric practice.[31] When conflicts intensified between practitioners of different schools on the one hand and between provincial and porteño psychiatrists on the other, the FAP gradually lost relevance. After 1967, however, it was reorganized and became an actively political organization. Now it attracted increasing numbers of psychoanalysts who had lost patience with the APA's elitism in this time of growing political ferment. In the late 1960s Emilio Rodrigué, who had been president of the APA until shortly before, was elected president of the Asociación de Psiquiatras de la Capital Federal, a branch of the FAP. The mere fact of becoming members of the FAP forced psychoanalysts to redefine their professional identity. Now they recognized themselves as members of the psychiatric community. Thus Rodrigué referred to "us psychiatrists" in an address to the FAP in 1969.

By the late 1960s the axis of the debate among psychiatrists had shifted. Now it was focused less on therapeutic approaches and theories than on two interconnected issues: (a) politics at a time when psychiatrists were being persecuted by the military government and (b) the social role of the psychiatrist. This explains why Rodrigué, a charismatic and by then Marxist psychoanalyst, was elected in absentia to the presidency of the Buenos Aires FAP by a commission dominated by Communist psychiatrists who had no sympathy for psychoanalysis. Rodrigué shared their Marxist ideology and had the ability, according to Jorge Balán, to attract young leftist analysts to "transform the FAP into an instrument of professional and political struggle."[32] His commitment to psychoanalysis was considered irrelevant. In contrast, Mauricio Goldenberg, who had been one of the progressives but accepted appointment by the military government to a post at the Instituto Nacional de Salud Mental, was forced to resign from the FAP when he tried to invite the INSM director to speak at a psychiatric conference. As a progressive Buenos Aires psychiatrist argued in 1969, the time when psychiatrists could debate the usefulness of psychoanalysis or the merits of dynamic psychiatry versus the somatic approach was over. Now the dichotomy was between those psychiatrists who understood that their role did not end with helping the sick and were committed to changing the social and economic conditions that made them sick, on the one hand, and those who limited themselves to practicing traditional psychiatry (including orthodox psychoanalysis), on the other. Only the first group should be welcomed as members of the FAP.[33] This position had considerable support. José Bleger in particular believed that "as psychiatrists and as doctors we must be deeply involved [*hasta la coronilla*] in social and economic problems." Conservative psychiatrists threatened to resign. The *Boletín Informativo*, the publication of the Asociación de Psiquiatras de la Capital, made its position clear in 1971:

> There are psychiatrists who collaborate with the regime and put their science at the service of those sectors that dominate and harm the people. There are those who try to isolate themselves from the social reality in which they live, and finally, there are those who question their raison d'être as psychiatrists and take for granted the contradiction inherent in their class position.[34]

In the early 1970s the FAP became the operation center of those leftist psychoanalysts who attacked the APA's elitism and eventually resigned from the organization. The new debates redefined identities within the psychiatric community. At a time when all Argentine society was politically polarized, theoretical differences were much less important than political commitment. When the debate over the social impact of psychiatry had started in the 1960s, for Bermann and the others the social dimension of psychiatry had consisted mainly of a broader understanding of the individual's place in society; for the younger generation of activists one decade later, psychiatry was an instrument for social and political struggle. The theoretical debates promoted by *Acta* in the early 1960s was more difficult to maintain now. As positions hardened, psychoanalysis was pushed to the fore because it was perceived as a science that developed in opposition to traditional repressive psychiatry and against purely somatic therapies, which were now seen as mechanisms of social control. Moreover, the existence of a group of progressive psychoanalysts trained under Pichon Rivière, Rodrigué, Bleger, and Langer could attract large numbers of young leftists and progressive psychiatrists who by then believed that some kind of psychoanalytic training was an indispensable part of psychiatric training. More important, by the early 1970s psychoanalysis was firmly rooted in Argentine culture. Later psychiatrists and psychoanalysts in the FAP would redefine themselves as "mental health workers," thus placing themselves on an equal footing with psychologists, nurses, and other "workers."

Mental Health and Psychiatry at the General Hospital

With some exceptions, the integration of psychoanalytic therapy into the system of psychiatric care took place not in the mental hospitals but in the psychiatric services established in general hospitals after the fall of Perón. Those services were offered as components of the mental health system. The most important of those services, the one that became surrounded by myth after it was closed by the military authorities in the 1970s, was the one headed by Dr. Mauricio Goldenberg at the Hospital Gregorio Aráoz Alfaro in the industrial suburb of Lanús in Buenos Aires Province. In the collective memory and in the history of the Argentine psychoanalytic movement, Goldenberg's service represents a golden age. Goldenberg left Argentina in the 1970s, after two of his children were killed by the military, and settled in Venezuela. After democracy was restored in 1983, several official functions were organized to honor him and his closest colleagues.[35] Goldenberg is credited with modernizing the Argentine mental health system and, more important in a country such as Argentina, with introducing psychoanalysis in public hospitals.

In 1956 Mauricio Goldenberg, then a young psychiatrist who had spent some years in France after training under Gonzalo Bosch at the Hospicio, was appointed head of the psychopathology service at the Hospital Gregorio

Aráoz Alfaro, one of the big hospitals built during the Perón government in the province of Buenos Aires. Goldenberg introduced an interdisciplinary approach in which psychoanalysis gradually played an increasing role. Despite his recent claims, however, psychoanalysis was not at the center of his early theoretical concerns. Like Langer, Goldenberg has reconstructed his history to accord with his current outlook.[36]

The fact is that during his stay at the Hospicio and at the Liga Argentina de Higiene Mental (in the 1940s he was on its board of directors), Goldenberg's orientation was closer to traditional eugenics than to anything having to do with psychoanalysis. His early publications dealt with such topics as alcoholism and the relationship between immigration and madness. In those works Goldenberg proposed classic eugenic measures such as immigration control and the imprisonment of alcoholics. At that point he was also interested in somatic treatments, and with Mario Sbarbi, a fierce opponent of psychoanalysis, he wrote articles on the use of electroconvulsive therapy (ECT) and psychotherapy. At that time Goldenberg's idea of psychotherapy was a far remove from psychoanalysis: after administering ECT to patients, his "intensive psychotherapy" consisted of playing a phonograph record to plant suggestions in their minds.[37] After assuming his post at the Aráoz Alfaro, however, Goldenberg did become one of the leaders of the movement to modernize psychiatry. In 1958 he was appointed president of the INSM, and in the mid-1960s he became a member of a city commission organized to formulate a plan for overhauling Buenos Aires' mental health system.

Goldenberg presented his proposals in a series of publications and conferences. In a paper delivered at the Segunda Conferencia Argentina de Asistencia Psiquiátrica, in 1958, he summarized some of his most important ideas. A good portion of his proposals at that time was an update of the old program of the Liga Argentina de Higiene Mental. Goldenberg concentrated on one problem: the impact of social conditions on mental health. This concern placed him within the group of progressive psychiatrists, along with Gregorio Bermann and Enrique Pichon Rivière. He spoke of the need for early detection of mental disorders and the importance of proper treatment of the neuroses. Although he emphasized the importance of psychotherapy, he had nothing to say about psychoanalysis. For the more serious cases he recommended shock treatments of various kinds. More important, he stressed the importance of providing mental health services in general hospitals and day hospitals, limiting the traditional asylum and colonies to chronic cases. These were the old mental hygiene themes in modern dress. Influenced by the mental health approach, however, Goldenberg did extend the Liga's program, and he pointed out that most patients could be treated on an outpatient basis. His model was clearly based on the postwar system of community care in the United States, and soon he became a promoter of the mental health movement.[38]

Goldenberg had many friends in the psychoanalytic community. From the beginning of his tenure at the Aráoz Alfaro he hired capable young psychiatrists without regard to their orientations, many psychoanalysts among them. Moreover, he promoted interdisciplinary groups; his service was one of the first to include psychologists, and later he added sociologists, anthropologists, and other social scientists.[39]

The Aráoz Alfaro was not the first general hospital to offer a mental health service—the Rawson Hospital in Buenos Aires had had a psychiatric service since 1950—but Goldenberg's was the first to provide the full range of psychiatric care, with facilities for hospitalized patients and for outpatients. Gradually Goldenberg's service became a major center of psychiatric care, research, and teaching, and its integration with the hospital's other services made it a model for other general hospitals. It provided advice and psychological assistance to patients whose presenting problems were medical. The Aráoz Alfaro was the first to integrate psychiatry and psychology with general medicine. Gradually Goldenberg's service expanded. In 1960 it assisted 6,767 patients. By 1964 that figure rose to 14,222 (more than 10 percent of all the hospital's patients).[40]

As in the United States, the psychiatric services established in general hospitals played a very large role in the diffusion of psychoanalysis, primarily because they brought psychotherapy to low-income patients who otherwise have had no access to it. Of the patients aided by Goldenberg's service, those suffering from neuroses accounted for 39.5 percent in 1960 and 54 percent in 1964.[41] Since most of the psychotherapy offered was psychoanalytically oriented, either individually or in groups, the service spread a certain psychoanalytic culture to the mostly working-class patients.[42] Of fifty doctors working in Goldenberg's service in 1962, thirty-two were in analytic training or had finished it—and this figure does not include a group who followed Harry Stack Sullivan and Erich Fromm.[43]

The psychiatric services achieved an old goal of the mental hygienists: they removed the moral stigma from mental patients. Now those patients were treated like any other patients. With this change, popular attitudes toward mental disorders began to change, and so did the culture of the hospital. Doctors started paying more attention to the psychological dimension of diseases, and psy terminology crept into their language. The presence of psychiatrists on a hospital staff was taken for granted and their profession gained in acceptance and prestige.[44]

A service such as Goldenberg's provided an alternative place for psychiatric training for young psychiatrists with progressive ideas and an interest in social conditions; the presence of psychoanalysts also helped to end the decades-old quarrel between supporters of the institutional approach and those who insisted on the centrality of the analyst's couch. Goldenberg's experience in Lanús changed the ways psychiatry was practiced and perceived, and it had an impact on psychoanalysis as well. As Hugo Vezzetti points out, if Goldenberg's service was presented as an alternative to traditional asylum-centered psychiatry, it was also an alternative to the APA's couch-centered psychoanalysis. What his service was offering was not psychoanalysis in the traditional sense but a broader psychoanalytic approach to mental disorders.[45]

The spread of psychoanalysis was also encouraged by the establishment of the Department of Psychiatry and Psychology in Dr. Florencio Escardó's service at the Children's Hospital. Escardó was the mentor of a whole generation of pediatricians who introduced the use of psychoanalytically oriented techniques in their practices. The service's Department of Psychiatry and Psychology was headed by three APA members who specialized in child psychoanalysis and was the home of Eva Giberti's School for Parents. Escardó's service assisted over 1,000 inpatients between 1965 to 1968 and over 9,000 outpatients in 1968 alone. Psychologists and doctors worked as equals to provide psychological support to their young patients. Each professional attended to three or four beds plus outpatients. The psychologists' responsibilities were not limited to children with identified psychological disorders; their services were part of the general assistance offered to all patients. Psychologists and doctors formed a therapeutic team. Escardó's service put strong emphasis on the psychological welfare of patients. Mothers were required to stay with their children day and night as long as they were in the hospital.

Psychologists trained in psychoanalysis had to adapt the psychoanalytic theory and technique they had learned to the working conditions of a public hospital. "Because of our psychoanalytic training, at the beginning it was difficult for us to forget the ambitious goals of psychoanalysis and be satisfied with more limited ones," wrote Giberti and her colleagues. When possible, psychoanalytic interpretations were offered liberally. "In general [when a traumatic medical procedure was imminent] mother and child are duly informed, in simple language, about how the procedure will be carried out. Afterward the fantasies and anxieties generated by the traumatic situation are interpreted." Since many patients had little formal education, however, communication was not always easy. "After many failures we discovered the efficacy of the language of action." Sometimes the urgency of a situation forced psychologists to redefine basic technical issues, such as the handling of transference. When a traumatic procedure had to be performed on a child and the mother was not available, the psychologist, rather than trying to interpret the transference relationship thus generated, took on the role of omnipotent mother and even played it out.[46] The psychiatric services established in some general hospitals constituted a privileged space for the diffusion of a psychoanalytic way of thinking about problems and human relationships. At Escardó's service psychoanalytically oriented psychological support was not provided upon demand but was an integral part of the general medical assistance. In that context the psychologist shared with the clinical doctor the aura of authority provided by the hospital environment.

The renovation of the mental health system fostered the entrance of psychoanalysts to at least some areas of the psychiatric establishment. In the mid-1960s Goldenberg, then an official of the city mental health system, signed an agreement with the APA for the training of municipal doctors. Some of the doctors in charge of the reforms had completed psychoanalytic training. Psychoanalysis was by then the most firmly established nonsomatic approach to psychiatry. These experiences, like the earlier ones at the Aráoz Alfaro, had an impact on the analytic profession. Progressive analysts who had to adapt their technique to conditions and patients they had never encountered before began to see psychoanalysis as a tool for social change.

THERAPEUTIC COMMUNITIES

Ironically enough, some innovations of the 1960s, such as therapeutic communities patterned on British and U.S. models, whose goal was precisely to democratize the psychiatric environment, were promoted by the otherwise repressive military government established in 1966. The modernizing rhetoric of the military regime attracted a few capable young technicians in many areas, including psychiatry, particularly at the beginning. The new authorities appointed Col. Dr. Julio Ricardo Esteves, a military doctor with progressive ideas, as intervenor of the INSM. Esteves appointed other progressive psychiatrists, such as Mauricio Goldenberg and Wilbur Ricardo Grimson, to key positions in the area of mental health.

The renovation of the psychiatric services during the so-called Revolución Argentina was part of the military government's general emphasis on modernization and efficiency imposed from the top down. Mental health policies that emphasized democratization, however, were in open conflict with the government's authoritarian corporative model. As Dr. Grimson, who headed one of the therapeutic communities established after 1966, points out, "in 1972 you couldn't vote anywhere in Argentina, yet people were voting at the mental hospital."[47] The mental health system was modernized not only at the national level but at the municipal level as well (although later most of the reforms were dismantled). Its budget was increased and new experiments were carried out. The central themes of mental health were explicitly introduced in state plans. Buenos Aires' mental health plan for 1969, formulated with the advice of Goldenberg, among others, stressed the influence of social conditions on the development of mental disorders. "Mental health is not only the absence of disease but a state of complete physical, mental, and social welfare. . . . Health care is carried out with a comprehensive conception of the individual in relation to the family, the work environment, and the community, under their geographical and cultural conditions."[48] The plan, modeled on John F. Kennedy's Mental Health Act of 1963, provided for a system of psychiatric services divorced from the Hospicio and provided by general hospitals and community mental health centers. Emphasis was put on care at the community level, on group as well as individual psychotherapy, on interdisciplinary teams composed of psychiatrists, psychologists, social workers, sociologists, and educators, and on the training of so-called mental health agents. The last group would consist of teachers and community workers who would promote mental health in their own areas of competence.

The INSM formulated a national mental health plan that called for a network of centers that would provide psychiatric care outside the old mental hospitals. The plan also proposed reform of the old asylums, the establishment of day hospitals, and experiments with therapeutic communities in public hospitals.[49] The best-known therapeutic communities were those established at the A. L. Roballos Hospital in the province of Entre Ríos; at a new clinic in Federal, also in Entre Ríos; and at the José E. Esteves Hospital in Lomas de Zamora, an industrial suburb of Buenos Aires, not far from Lanús.

The concept of a therapeutic community had been introduced in Great Britain by Maxwell Jones, a Scottish physician born in South Africa, at the Mill Hill Emergency Hospital, north of London, in the 1940s. The idea was later developed with a clearer psychoanalytic bias in Britain and especially in the United States.[50] In a therapeutic community all facets of the institution, including the relationships between patients and staff and among patients themselves, became therapeutic tools. This project implied a drastic democratization of the hospital's structure. In the most radical version, under the influence of the antipsychiatry movement, each patient was to have a voice in matters of general policy (in some cases even in the admission or discharge of other patients), which were decided in general assemblies of representatives of staff and patients.[51] The therapeutic community represented a complete break with traditional psychiatry and with orthodox psychoanalytic practice. It challenged the very authority of psychiatrists. In a therapeutic community patients were not passive recipients of therapeutic manipulations but active participants in the therapeutic process.

Paradoxically, working in this new environment was sometimes easier for psychiatrists educated in the traditional school than for some young analysts. Grimson recalls that

> people who had done their training at hospices or colonies—within traditional psychiatry, that is—were turned into therapeutic community professionals more easily than young psychoanalysts interested in professional psychoanalysis. That is, it was easier to convince someone who was used to seeing psychiatric drugs and administering ECT that now he had to organize a soccer team and go out in the field and play. Meanwhile the psychoanalyst stood on the sidelines in his light coat with an identification badge on it so he wouldn't lose his identity. He looked at the soccer match and said, "This is interesting," but he was wondering what was going to happen with transference. The only transference that mattered there was the transference of the ball to the goal. We played a soccer match, staff against patients, and the patients won.[52]

All the same, Grimson himself admits that most of the therapy carried out at Lomas de Zamora—music therapy, psychodrama, and so on—was based on psychoanalytic concepts.[53]

These efforts to revitalize the psychiatric system failed after a few years. The failure was due in part to the resistance of the powerful clique of old-school psychiatrists who still controlled psychiatry at the medical school and in the big mental hospitals, and who had powerful connections with the military government. They set out to persuade the generals that therapeutic communities were communist, ignoring the fact that they had been introduced from the United States and would have horrified the Soviets.[54] Although some progressives were invited occasionally to lecture at the medical school, no new development outside of the traditional psychiatric establishment could gain a foothold there.[55] This resistance to innovation became clear when in 1965 the chair in psychiatry became vacant and Goldenberg, then an associate professor, applied for the position. Horacio Etchegoyen, a psychoanalyst who held the chair of psychiatry at the University of Mendoza, was appointed to the search committee with the support of Florencio Escardó. Etchegoyen perhaps too clearly favored Goldenberg. The powerful machinery linked to the Hospicio fought back, and finally succeeded in having Etchegoyen removed from the committee on the grounds that he had presented a pornographic paper at the APA. Without Etchegoyen, who finally lost his position at Mendoza, too, as a result of pressure brought by his political enemies in Buenos Aires, Goldenberg was rejected in favor of a psychiatrist of the old school.[56]

The most important reason for the failure of these experiments, however, was that they attempted the impossible, as the FAP pointed out: to impose democracy on psychiatry by military fiat. The therapeutic communities were imposed from above in hospitals where doctors were being persecuted for political reasons.[57] Moreover, while the mental health plan called for interdisciplinary teams, the government passed a law that specifically restricted the legal competence of psychologists to research and testing. Furthermore, while the INSM was promoting democracy in mental hospitals, it was proposing at the same time to increase the number of circumstances in which an individual could be forcibly committed to a mental institution, without even a judicial finding of mental incompetence.[58]

In 1970, after Esteves was removed from the INSM and replaced by a doctor from the Federal Police Department, the therapeutic communities were formally terminated and the patients returned to traditional hospitals. Grimson and other doctors who had participated in the experiments were dismissed.[59] Some of them were persecuted by the military government established in 1976 and had to go into exile. A few lost their lives. Much energy went into the effort to revitalize the system of psychiatric care, but in the end nothing really changed. To this day that system is still based on the asylum, and nothing much has changed there, either. Yet these experiments had one important consequence: they reinforced the hold that psychoanalysis already had on Argentine society.

Psychologists Take the Stage

One factor that contributed greatly to the diffusion of psychoanalysis in the 1960s and 1970s was the introduction of psychology programs at various universities, particularly at the University of Buenos Aires (UBA), in the late 1950s. Most of those programs sooner or later (and more sooner than later) acquired a clear psychoanalytic orientation. A survey of Argentine psychologists in the early 1970s showed that 92 percent worked as clinical psychologists, meaning that they practiced some kind of psychoanalysis.[1]

In Argentina psychology had been closely tied to psychoanalysis from the beginning. In other countries "scientific [experimental] psychology" was already an established discipline when psychoanalysis made its appearance. In the United States in particular, for decades psychology was defined in opposition to psychoanalysis, which was considered to lack a firm scientific foundation. Experimental psychologists viewed psychoanalytic interpretation as just a new name for suggestion. In the 1940s and 1950s, U.S. psychologists were busy using their own methods to test psychoanalytic theories in an effort to expose their lack of a scientific basis.[2] Only in the 1960s, with the emergence of clinical psychology as a widely accepted specialty, did psychologists start to absorb Freudian concepts. Even then, however, psychology preserved its autonomy as a scientific and professional field. In Argentina, on the contrary, psychology's standing as a science was perceived as based on its close relationship with psychoanalysis. It was only through psychoanalysis that "psychology became a science." All other psychological theories were seen as mere techniques, with the possible exception of Jean Piaget's developmental psychology.[3]

By the mid-1960s, new private and public universities expanded the supply of psychological training.[4] In 1968 there were 2,787 psychology students at the University of Buenos Aires alone.[5] By 1995 there were 38,825 graduates in psychology in Argentina, most of them practicing some form of psychoanalysis.[6] More than 50 percent of them were concentrated in the city of Buenos Aires. In that year there were 506 psychologists for every 100,000 inhabitants of the city; in other words, one of every 198 porteños was a psychologist. In proportion to population, Argentina has many more psychologists than any other country in the Americas, and probably in the world.[7]

In the 1960s and 1970s the proliferation of clinical psychologists dramatically expanded the supply of psychoanalytic therapy. Their fees were usually much lower than those of APA-trained psychoanalysts. The APA was still a relatively small institution, and the presence of so many psychologists thus made psychoanalysis available to many more people at substantially lower cost. In addition to their private practices, psychologists tended to work in public institutions (usually for very low pay or none at all), particularly at the beginning of their careers, in order to get the practical experience the university did not provide. By the early 1970s, 49 percent of a representative group of psychologists surveyed worked in some kind of public institution, generally part-time and without pay. The consequence was that psychologists were also instrumental in disseminating psychoanalytically oriented psychology in public hospitals. However, the fact that most of the psychoanalytic therapy offered was provided by psychologists rather than M.D.'s reinforced psychoanalysts' tendency to differentiate their field from psychiatry. Psychoanalysis in Argentina, in contrast to the United States, became gradually divorced from medicine.

The universities' psychology programs (housed in the schools of humanities or, in Buenos Aires, in the School of Philosophy and Literature) promoted the diffusion of psychoanalysis throughout their institutions. Students in other programs took courses in psychoanalysis, and psychology professors also taught in other programs. For years the philosopher León Rozitchner, a popular teacher, led a seminar on Freud and Marx that attracted a large number of students from a variety of programs. The result was a rapid spread of psy knowledge and additional opportunities for combining psychoanalysis with the social sciences. In 1964, for instance, the Instituto de Desarrollo Económico y Social, a prestigious private research institute devoted to the social sciences, organized a conference on the links between psychology and sociology attended by psychiatrists, psychologists, sociologists, and a few APA psychoanalysts.

After the coup of 1966 with its devastating consequences for the university, students sought to satisfy their intellectual demands in private study groups led by fashionable intellectuals. These study groups became a tradition, a kind of underground university. This mechanism put psychology students in contact with philosophers and social scientists who had been banned from the university by the military authorities, thus generating additional points of contact between psy thought and the social sciences.

Psychologists expanded not only the supply of psychoanalysis but also the demand for it. Since they were not admitted to the APA until the early 1980s, for two decades psychologists tried to reproduce the APA's training model for themselves. They supplemented their university academic training—provided in large part by APA analysts—with unofficial training analysis provided by junior APA psychoanalysts and supervision by APA members on a private basis. In the early 1970s 95 percent of a representative sample of psychologists either were in or had undergone psychoanalytic therapy. Of that group 82 percent had been or were in therapy with APA-trained psychoanalysts, while only 11 percent chose other psychologists as therapists.[8] In 1986, in the midst of a deep economic depression, 68 percent of psychology students were still in some kind of psychotherapy.[9] Moreover, psychologists became the largest group of consumers for literature produced by APA psychoanalysts. Psychologists were the main agents for the dissemination of psychoanalytic practice outside the APA.

Despite the popularity of their profession, psychologists' position in the psy community was problematic. The professionalization of psychology was a complex issue from the beginning. From the early 1960s on, psychology students were trained in psychoanalysis by psychoanalysts, but they were not allowed to join the APA, which alone could provide legitimate analytic training. Moreover, in many parts of the country, most notably in Buenos Aires, where most of them lived and practiced, psychologists were legally forbidden to practice any kind of psychotherapy. Law 17,132, passed in 1967 by the military government, reduced the professional status of psychologists to mere *auxiliares de psiquiatría*, on a par with nurses, and specifically prohibited them from practicing psychoanalysis. This law reaffirmed a Ministry of Public Health resolution of 1954, which had limited the practice of psychotherapy and specifically of psychoanalysis to physicians. Psychologists could only perform tests and do research, under the direct supervision of a medical doctor.[10] Nevertheless, most psychologists *did* practice psychoanalysis in Buenos Aires, and some even practiced psychotherapy in the psychiatric services of public hospitals. The law was rarely (if ever) enforced, yet from the beginning psychologists bore a stigma of illegality that in practical terms meant charging much lower fees than "real" analysts.

Another roadblock in the way of professional status was psychologists' relationship with the medical (particularly the psychiatric) establishment. Psychologists who practiced psychoanalytically oriented therapies were seen as a serious threat to doctors' monopoly on the art of healing. Psychologists who practiced psychotherapy were perceived as stepping over the line. Psychologists, however, were dependent on psychiatrists for residencies in psychiatric institutions, a crucial component of their professional training.

To understand the professionalization and development of psychology in Argentina, then, we have to understand its complex relationship with the state and the state-supported medical profession on the one hand and with the analytic community on the other, at a time when no alternative model for professional identity was available to psychologists and the very domain of the discipline was not well defined.

One other factor made the development of a professional identity even more complicated: gender. Whereas medicine was perceived as a male profession, psychology has been perceived as an essentially female profession. Most members of the first generation of graduates in psychology were women, and in 1986 74 percent of the UBA's psychology students were still women.[11] The membership of the Asociación de Psicólogos de Buenos Aires (APBA), founded in 1962 to defend the professional interests of psychologists, was composed almost entirely of women in its early years. Psychologists therefore had to fight for professional recognition from a position defined as weak: from a female position. This gender component would have a crucial impact in their relationship with the (mostly male) psychoanalytic community.[12]

Psychology Before the Psychology Program

Until the creation of the psychology programs at the universities, the scientific status and domain of psychology were never clearly defined. Whereas academic training in psychology in the United States had always put strong emphasis on experimentation, in Argentina psychology occupied an unspecified space somewhere between philosophy, biology, and the social sciences. Since the first chair in psychology was established at the University of Buenos Aires late in the nineteenth century, however, psychological teaching there had had a clear clinical-psychopathological bias that opened the door to psychoanalysis. The inability of psychology to define its own domain also goes far toward explaining the theoretical vacuum that psychoanalysis filled after the program was introduced in 1957.

Among the Latin American countries, Argentina enjoyed some prestige in the teaching of psychology and to a lesser extent in psychological research. The first laboratory of experimental psychology in Latin America, patterned after Wilhelm Wundt's laboratory in Leipzig, was established in Buenos Aires by Horacio Piñero, a psychiatrist, in 1898.[13] As we saw earlier, however, Wundt's works were known in Argentina mostly through French translations and read through the lens of positivism. Only the physiological aspects of his work were appreciated.[14] Although psychology had been taught at various times in the law and medical schools, it was in the School of Philosophy and Literature that it finally settled.[15] Originally the teaching of psychology was not psychoanalytically oriented; it was organized around other academic and theoretical traditions that in some respects were incompatible with psychoanalysis. Yet there were nuances that opened some spaces for psychoanalysis, and since the 1920s it gradually occupied a larger space in the teaching of psychology at the University of Buenos Aires.[16] The ambiguity of psychology's domain was recognized and discussed by the men who taught the courses and was reflected in their syllabi. Physiological, experimental, clinical, and philosophical orientations coexisted uneasily. It is worth noting that when Horacio Piñero, a positivist medical doctor who had held the chair in psychology since 1901, traced the genealogy of the discipline he taught, he named as its three critical events the establishment of Wilhelm Wundt's laboratory of experimental psychology in Leipzig, Jean-Marie Charcot's studies on hysteria and hypnosis at the Salpêtrière in Paris, and the launching of Théodule Ribot's *Revue Philosophique*.[17]

The early clinical-psychopathological bias of the teaching of psychology originated in the popularity of Charcot and particularly Ribot, and in the fact that most holders of the chair in psychology were medical doctors. Piñero's psychopathological approach is evident in the topics he covered in his courses and in his requirement that students attend lectures and demonstrations at his psychiatric service in the Hospital Nacional de Alienadas. A second course introduced in 1907 was intended to have a more philosophical orientation. The first course (called originally "Normal and Pathological Psychology," later "Experimental and Physiological Psychology") concentrated on clinical and experimental aspects of psychology; the second focused on the superior mental functions, consciousness, and the relationship between psychology and philosophy.

Another factor that contributed to the introduction of psychoanalysis in the teaching of psychology was the general decline of the positivist paradigm in the early 1920s and the consequent antipositivist reaction that promoted a "spiritual" approach to psychology. One of the leading antipositivist philosophers of the time, Coroliano Alberini, taught the second course for almost twenty years. Although he did not specifically discuss psychoanalysis, he was open to it, and a few of his students developed an interest in Freud while taking his course.[18]

Gradually the experimental aspects of the first course were deemphasized until many of the laboratories established in the 1920s were finally closed by the Perón government in 1949.[19] A more humanistic approach to psychology, influenced by phenomenological philosophy but still with room for Freud, gained ground during those years.

The teaching of psychology at the University of Buenos Aires thus took two seemingly different paths that nonetheless converged in psychoanalysis. On the one hand, the psychopathological-clinical tradition, which was rooted in positivism but survived its crisis, opened a space for the discussion of psychotherapeutic techniques. On the other hand, the decline of positivism led to psychological orientations less tied to the biological-physiological tradition.

Freud was mentioned for the first time in Horacio Piñero's course in 1914. Thereafter psychoanalysis gradually increased its presence, particularly after Enrique Mouchet was appointed to the chair in the 1920s. The syllabus of 1930 makes several references to psychoanalysis, including a discussion of the relationship between psychoanalysis and psychology. Thus by 1930 psychoanalysis was considered an autonomous science whose relations with psychology needed to be established and discussed. From then on, Mouchet discussed not only psychoanalysis in general but specific aspects of psychoanalytic theory. He introduced discussions on "the Freudian unconscious and psychoanalytic theory" in 1931 and "What is true in psychoanalysis?" in 1936. Although the question suggests some skepticism, the fact that it was asked presumes that students were familiar with the subject. In 1942 Mouchet devoted a substantial part of his course not only to psychoanalysis but to Freud's life and works.

After Mouchet left in 1943, psychoanalysis continued to gain space in the psychology courses. During the Perón regime, the teaching of psychology became more oriented toward philosophy, with emphasis on phenomenology. The new professor of psychology, Luis Felipe García de Onrubia, a graduate of the School of Philosophy with no medical degree, was particularly interested in defining the domain of the discipline he was teaching. Like his predecessors, he was unable to anchor psychology in any particular academic tradition. In 1950 García de Onrubia edited the first of a series of monographs on psychology published by the School of Philosophy. The topics covered reveal the competition between theoretical traditions, with none gaining dominance. The first monograph was *Introduction to Psychopathology*, by the Peruvian Honorio Delgado. The second, on the experimental tradition, was August Riekel's *Eidetics: Sensory Memory and Its Research*. The third, seventh, and eighth monographs dealt with philosophical issues; García de Onrubia's own contribution, *Intentional Psychology*, shows the strong influence of phenomenology and Sartre's existentialism. The fourth monograph was Emil Utitz's *Characterology*, the fifth a discussion of Gestalt theory by Oscar Oñativia. Finally, the sixth monograph was a summary of an M.A. thesis in which the author used psychometric techniques. Nothing on psychoanalysis in any of them, yet Gestalt theory and psychoanalysis occupied a prominent place in García de Onrubia's own teaching.

Thus the centrality of psychoanalysis at the School of Philosophy even before the psychology program was launched was the result of several factors. First was the old clinical-psychopathological tradition in the teaching of psychology, which facilitated the discussion of psychotherapy. Second was the decline of experimental psychology that followed the decline of positivism, which made room for "spiritual" theories. Third was the lack of a specific, valid, and autonomous domain for psychology, which made it difficult for a dominant specifically "psychological" paradigm to emerge; psychoanalysis filled the theoretical vacuum and provided psychologists with a professional model. Finally, there was students' obvious interest in psychoanalysis.

The Launching of the Psychology Program

Since the beginning of the 1950s, the perception had grown in academic and professional circles that the time was ripe for a professional program in psychology. As early as the 1920s the armed forces and some provincial educational systems had established psychological bureaus to evaluate staff and candidates. In 1925 the government established the Instituto de Psicotecnia y Orientación Profesional under the direction of Carlos Jesinghaus, a German doctor who was interested in testing for occupational aptitude. The need for specialized professionals, properly trained to carry out these activities, soon became clear.[20] In 1953 a program in psychometry was launched in Rosario and in 1954 the need for a psychology program at the university level was discussed at an international conference on psychology in Tucumán, attended by psychology teachers and some psychoanalysts from the APA.[21] However, no such programs materialized until after the fall of Perón, when the rush to modernize encouraged the universities to satisfy the demand for them.[22] When the first program was launched in Rosario in 1956, 200 students were already enrolled in a psychometry program that had been introduced three years before. When in 1956 the Instituto de Rehabilitación del Lisiado in Buenos Aires offered a three-year course, mostly taught by psychoanalysts, to train assistants in child psychiatry, ten candidates (mostly women) applied for every vacancy.[23]

At the beginning, the psychology programs offered in Rosario and in Buenos Aires reflected the survival of older traditions in the teaching of psychology as well as the perennial vagueness of its scientific status. In Buenos Aires the placement of the program in the School of Philosophy (as opposed to the School of Medicine, say) bespoke the older tradition of placing psychology within the realm of philosophy. Yet the first director appointed was a medical doctor, Marcos Victoria, who himself was a product of the convergence of the two traditions. Victoria had been a collaborator and disciple of both Christofredo Jakob, the father of Argentine neurology and an extreme positivist, and Coriolano Alberini, the antipositivist philosopher. The professional profile of the psychology program in neither Rosario nor Buenos Aires was well defined; both programs were originally designed to provide training in academic psychology, with no indication where their graduates might work or what they might do there.[24] It was quite clear to the faculty what they were *not* to do: therapy, which was exactly what most students expected to be trained for. Dr. Marcos Victoria was adamantly against any kind of clinical practice by psychologists.[25]

Psychoanalysis and the Psychology Program

From the beginning the professional identity of the future graduates in psychology was at least as problematic as the domain of the science they were studying. No psychologists were available to teach them and serve as role models. Most faculty members were medical doctors, with an interest in defending the medical profession's monopoly on the art of healing. The future psychologists were taught by teachers who did not want to serve as their professional role models. Although the original orientation of the program was academic, most students were interested in learning psychoanalysis, which not only was popular but was seen as a potential source of income, and which had been an important component in the teaching of psychology for decades. The demand for psychoanalysis already existed in Argentine society, and modern psychology was seen as synonymous with psychoanalysis. And since the Argentine academic world did not offer a valid professional alternative, future psychologists were forced to look for professional options elsewhere. The obvious one was the clinical model. Other areas of specialization were offered—educational and industrial psychology, for instance—but most students specialized in clinical psychology; that is, in psychoanalysis.

It soon became clear that students' expectations were in conflict with the programs' orientation (or lack of it). The student body that had recovered its power and voice after 1955 demanded curriculum reform and changes in the faculty. In Rosario, under the leadership of Jaime Bernstein, co-founder of Paidós, a publishing house that specializes in psychoanalytic works, students and some professors invited psychoanalysts from Buenos Aires to teach courses on clinical psychology. The students in Buenos Aires, with some faculty support, secured the substitution of Enrique Butelman, a professor of social psychology and Bernstein's associate in Paidós, for Marcos Victoria as program director, and the hiring of psychoanalysts as teachers. Among the first psychoanalysts hired in both Rosario and Buenos Aires was José Bleger. As early as 1959 students could take a course specifically on psychoanalysis taught by León Ostrov (a nonmedical member of the APA), and introductory courses on psychology and psychopathology offered by Bleger and Jorge García Badaracco. By 1964, psychology students in Buenos Aires were taking eleven mandatory psychoanalytically oriented courses, seven of them taught by APA members.

Students' interest in psychoanalysis, however, was not unqualified. The psychology programs were introduced in part in response to the modernizing anxieties of some sectors of society, including large portions of the university community. Students of psychology, sociology, and other "new" social sciences saw themselves as agents of this modernization. They were interested in psychoanalysis because it incarnated "modern" psychology: "We consider that it is only through psychoanalysis that psychology became a science," announced a student publication.[26] Thus students were not interested in being taught by "conservative" APA psychoanalysts. Angel Garma, who applied for the chair in psychoanalysis and who was very popular in the more conservative medical school, was rejected by the students; they were more interested in the likes of José Bleger and Fernando Ulloa, who could add leftist political leanings to their psychoanalytic credentials. Bleger, in particular, had theorized on the compatibility of Freud and Marx. His students saw him as a Marxist psychoanalyst with an interest in the other social sciences. Students were even willing to accept the teaching of Telma

Reca, a child psychiatrist who, although not a psychoanalyst, was politically leftist and was identified with modern trends in psychiatry. The faculty also included such professors as Dr. José Itzigsohn, a Communist reflexologist who was nonetheless on good terms with the progressives of the psychoanalytic community, and his assistant, Antonio Caparrós, of similar political and theoretical persuasions.

The psychoanalytic orientation of the programs was thus the result of a combination of complex factors. First, a tradition of psychoanalytic teaching was already in place when the programs were launched. Second, there was a powerful body of students who were already interested in psychoanalysis and who were dissatisfied with the original orientation of the programs. Third, by the time the programs were introduced, no alternative psychological paradigm was in place, only a combination of old and new traditions. Psychoanalysis, a well-established discipline that enjoyed legitimacy and increasing popularity and prestige, represented the new in psychology and provided a professional model.[27]

The Professionalization of Psychology

PSYCHOLOGISTS AND THE MEDICAL CORPORATION

Like their counterparts in the United States, Argentine psychiatrists opposed the development of a separate, legally protected profession of clinical psychologists. In the United States, however, clinical psychologists emerged as a strong minority group within a well-established profession. Their guild, the American Psychological Association, had the ability and power to negotiate with the American Medical Association. When psychiatrists claimed that "the lay psychotherapist is a quack," psychologists could respond that a psychiatrist "is a person who practices psychotherapy without even a Ph.D."[28] It was a very different situation from the one in Argentina, where professional psychology was born when psychoanalysis was already a well-established and prestigious profession. Furthermore, psychology occupied the weakest position among the psy professions. Psychology acquired professional status in Argentina in the framework of its turbulent relations with psychiatry and psychoanalysis.

The conflict between psychiatrists and psychologists originated in part in the fact that psychologists graduated with the kind of training that most M.D.'s lacked. The training in psychology that most medical students received was perfunctory, only a few courses on classic somatic psychiatry.

Psychotherapy and psychoanalysis were conspicuously absent from the curricula of most medical schools.[29] Hence the success of extracurricular courses on psychoanalysis taught by APA members in the late 1950s. Until fairly recently the medical school of the UBA, whose psychiatric department was headed by psychiatrists trained in the somatic tradition, offered no training in psychotherapeutic techniques, let alone in psychoanalysis.[30]

As long as psychoanalysis was practiced by APA-affiliated analysts, most of them M.D.'s, conservative psychiatrists objected to it on the grounds that it was poor medicine or outright quackery, but they did not see it as a direct threat to the medical profession. The psychology programs changed the terms of the doctors' resistance. Now they saw psychologists as a new breed of nonmedical professionals, who also happened to be mostly women, and who were disputing the male doctors' monopoly on healing. The doctors' opposition was immediate and crossed ideological and theoretical lines. Marcos Victoria peremptorily declared, "No one who is not a doctor has the right to cure by either physical or psychological means."[31] This opinion was shared by Gregorio Bermann, who expressed his horror when the first chair in psychopathology at the University of Córdoba was established in the School of Philosophy and Humanities, in company with the psychology program, and not in the medical school. Worse, the professor who held the chair did not have a medical degree. "The psychiatrist," Bermann declared, "is a physician who specializes in mental disorders. The psychologist . . . is a technician who sometimes is involved in problems related to mental pathology. . . . The psychologist is a technician whose help is required by the psychiatrist, but he does not have to conjecture about the sick person and much less to diagnose and prescribe."[32]

Marcos Victoria was politically a liberal, Bermann a fellow traveler of the Communist Party. They also differed in their theoretical orientation. They joined forces, however, in their determination to keep psychologists out of the business of curing people. Similar ideas were expressed by the four M.D.'s who published "Education and Training of the Psychologist" in *Humanidades,* the journal of the University of La Plata, in 1961. Although the program offered at La Plata trained future psychologists to "carry out clinical, educational, and labor tasks," they made it clear that performing diagnosis or treatment did not fall within psychologists' competence. Psychologists should limit themselves to administering tests, taking measurements, and formulating suggestions and recommendations for the "best adaptation of the individual." The clinical psychologist "is not in a position to treat on his own responsibility the so-called personality functional disorders such as neurosis or psychoneurosis or to make diagnoses." Psychologists should be well educated in biology and physiology, however, so they could better assist psychiatrists.

The Argentine medical corporation perceived the new profession as a threat at a time when the medical profession had finally achieved undisputed hegemony in the health sector and was reformulating its relationship with the state and its own professional identity.[33] The gray area where psychotherapy had allowed people without a medical degree to enjoy some prestige and legitimacy in medical circles was gone. Psychologists, with five years of study in psychology and psychotherapeutic methods, claimed with some justice that they were in fact better equipped than most graduates in medicine to administer psychotherapy at a time when that technique, particularly psychoanalysis, was becoming very popular and profitable.

The refusal of psychiatrists to accept psychologists as psychotherapists had important consequences in the development of psychoanalysis as a discipline. As Mauricio Knobel, a psychoanalyst with high visibility in the media, complained, "Some psychologists, in their zeal to avoid 'submitting' to the medical model, seek techniques for approaching the mentally ill that are openly nonmedical."[34] Psychologists developed a professional identity as "intellectuals" more than as members of the medical community. This may help to explain their receptivity to the highly theoretical and nonmedical French model of psychoanalysis, which has become the mainstream of Argentine psychoanalysis.

PSYCHOLOGISTS AND PSYCHOANALYSTS

The conflict between psychologists and psychiatrists was sometimes brutally confrontational. The complex relationship between psychologists and psychoanalysts was subtler. While psychiatrists simply wanted to keep psychologists out of the business of curing people, psychoanalysis' intentions were far more intricate because their vested interests were more complex. Psychoanalysts taught aspects of psychoanalytic theory to students who were eager to learn them but who knew that the doors of the APA, and therefore of "real" psychoanalytic training, were closed to them. Although the APA still occasionally admitted some nonmedical members, it refused to admit psychologists, pointing to the ministerial regulation of 1954 limiting the practice of psychotherapy and psychoanalysis to doctors. It is interesting to note, however, that that regulation and the law passed in 1967 (which apparently was revised upon the APA's advice)[35] did not forbid the APA to accept nonmedical members. As the regulation of 1954 explicitly established, the diplomas granted by the APA had no official standing and therefore did not entitle its graduates to practice any kind of therapy. As far as the law was concerned, APA graduates who were M.D.'s could practice psychoanalysis because they were M.D.'s, not because they had undergone psychoanalytic training at the APA. Legally, all physicians were entitled to style themselves psychoanalysts, regardless of whether they had ever set foot in the APA. Accepting psychologists for analytic training, then, would not have changed the legal status of psychologists; they still could not have legally practiced psychotherapy in the city of Buenos Aires or in most provinces of the country. But since psychologists were practicing psychoanalysis anyway, the APA's refusal to admit psychologists seems to have been prompted more by a determination to restrict the supply of properly trained analysts than by deference to the law.

If the APA did not accept psychologists, however, individual psychoanalysts did accept them in private study groups, for supervision, and for unofficial training analysis. Some of them were their teachers at the university or at private institutions they organized.[36] The psychoanalytic community, however, did not recognize this training.

Even the most progressive APA members were as eager as the conservatives to keep psychoanalysis for themselves. José Bleger made this clear in the first lecture of his course on psychoanalysis at the university. Lay analysis, he said, is "carried out by people who have correct and complete training but are outside the medical profession. This is not solely a legal problem, but its discussion has nothing to do with the teaching offered by the university, because we have made it quite clear that so far, and surely for a long time to come, psychoanalysts can be trained only in psychoanalytic institutes."[37]

In Bleger's view, psychologists had a crucial role to play in the promotion of mental health. He wanted to socialize psychological and psychiatric care.[38] His "psychohygiene" was another version of "mental health"; he defined it as dealing not with the treatment of people with mental disorders but with the promotion of mental health, by assisting healthy people in stressful everyday-life situations. Psychohygiene, a nonmedical field but based on psychoanalytic theory, was the appropriate realm of psychologists' professional activity. Psychologists should disseminate psychoanalytic knowledge without practicing psychoanalysis themselves. That was Bleger's reason for wanting to keep psychology clearly separated from medicine. "*Psychologists should not be encouraged to become therapists.* . . . Psychologists must be led to the field of psychohygiene, they should have the necessary tools to act *before people develop mental disorders,* in group activities, in institutions, and by working in the community."[39]

What was needed, according to Bleger, was not to train more psychoanalysts, whose social impact would be limited, but rather to create a large army of mental health agents, psychologists educated in psychoanalytic theory who would reach out to broader sectors of the population to prevent mental illness. Psychoanalysts were still necessary, however. The practical consequence of his proposal was to make psychologists permanently subordinate to psychoanalysts. Let us follow his reasoning.

According to Bleger (and to Freud), psychoanalytic therapy and research cannot be separated. Bleger narrowly defines psychoanalysis as "the process of investigation and therapy that is carried out by using the systematic interpretation of transference, by analyzing the neurosis of transference, and by using countertransference."[40] Moreover, he claimed that psychoanalytic theory was the foundation of scientific psychology. Psychologists, therefore, should be educated in psychoanalysis and encouraged to use its theory in their work. Nonetheless, since psychologists were not admitted to the APA's psychoanalytic institute, they could not become psychoanalysts, and in fact they should not be encouraged to do so. "We should not teach psychologists how to handle clinical psychoanalysis, although they should have full and correct information on it."[41] He goes so far as to propose that the APA create an institute specifically for the education of psychologists, making clear that its goal was not to turn them into psychoanalysts. He even acknowledges the importance of private schools of psychoanalysis outside of the APA, as long as those schools "limit themselves to the teaching of psychoanalytic theory [and not its actual practice]." He does not address the problem of how to distinguish psychoanalytic theory from psychoanalytic therapy if, as we saw, therapy and theory cannot be separated. Psychologists should, therefore, become diffusers of psychoanalytic knowledge, which by definition could not be produced or theorized by them.

Although the role that Bleger assigned to psychologists originated in his ideas on how a mental health system should be organized, it was certainly consistent with psychoanalysts' professional interests. Psychologists constituted an important segment of the market for analytic therapy. They had to seek substitute training in private groups and in private analysis at substantial financial sacrifice. Thus a rigid hierarchy was maintained. While the very few certified APA training analysts worked only with APA members, other members (most of them associates or even candidates) built up a clientele of psychologists. The portion of the market left to psychologists consisted of everyone who could not afford the APA psychoanalysts' stratospheric fees.[42] This fragmentation of the market and the prestige enjoyed by psychoanalysts explain why their income did not suffer significantly from the competition of the new professionals. Moreover, because psychologists were now so numerous, they also constituted the most important segment of the market for the psychoanalysts' books and other writings, as the prefaces of most of them make clear.

For this situation to persist, however, two conditions were needed: psychologists had to continue to be educated in psychoanalysis and in the use of its theory and technique; and they must produce no psychoanalytic theory themselves and continue to be deprived of legitimacy as practitioners of psychoanalysis.[43] The latter point was particularly important because it was the psychologists' theoretical dependency that forced them to become clients of APA psychoanalysts. Bleger himself suggested this ideal:

> The problem is . . . to find the means for psychologists to receive the benefit of psychoanalysis without stopping them from being psychologists and without turning them into wild analysts or into therapists. . . . We must teach psychoanalysis in such a way that they absorb psychoanalytic thought . . . and can operate according to that theory but with psychological techniques and procedures.[44]

Note the expression "wild analysts" for psychologists who practice psychoanalysis. That was Freud's term for people who practiced psychoanalysis without proper training; people who had undergone proper psychoanalytic training but lacked a medical degree were "lay analysts."

Mauricio Knobel was less interested than Bleger in assigning psychologists a specific role as social disseminators of psychoanalytic knowledge. For him psychologists should be allowed to practice psychotherapy, but only under the strict supervision of a physician. This restriction, he thought, would ensure that psychologists could not invade the psychiatrists' domain. Knobel, like other psychoanalysts, psychoanalyzed the professional conflict between psychologists and psychoanalysts: "For the psychologist the struggle can be arduous and distressing. Depressive-melancholic anxieties can mobilize truly manic reactions. An example can be seen in the omnipotent feeling that leads them to suppose that *all* human pathology is accessible and controllable through psychic manipulation." Knobel is thus accusing psychologists of his own sin: "psychic omnipotence." According to Knobel, psychologists could perform psychotherapy only in those cases in which the "strictly anatomopathological" dimension of the disorder was not considered relevant. How this distinction could be made he does not say.[45] What is clear is that any conception of the human being as a "psychobiological unity" precluded the practice of psychotherapy by psychologists, who lacked training in the "biological aspect" of diseases.

Psychologists, therefore, were placed by their own teachers in the middle of a self-reproducing system that subordinated them to psychoanalysts. Although they did treat large numbers of patients, both in private practice and in institutions, they knew the social and professional prestige enjoyed by APA analysts was closed to them.[46]

GENDER AND PROFESSION

From the beginning psychologists were forced not only to find a professional identity different from that of their teachers but also to deal with their subordinate position with respect to their intellectual mentors. The latter issue led to particularly complicated situations when a transferential relationship developed between teacher and student. The gender issue complicated the relationship further. There were some female physicians, but doctors and psychiatrists in particular were overwhelmingly male. So were psychoanalysts. True, a relatively large number of women were affiliated with the APA, but they were still a minority. As late as 1971 only 22 of 72 full members and 37 of 108 associate members were women. Almost all the psychoanalysts teaching at the university in the early years were men.[47]

Psychology students, particularly in the early years of the program, were overwhelmingly female. Rubén Ardila described the typical Argentine psychologist in the early 1970s as a woman under 31 years of age who worked in psychoanalysis and was married either to a doctor or to another psychologist. She started her career in a public institution, working without pay to obtain experience, and later opened a private practice. Her income was not very high, and she read only professional journals published in Spanish, mostly in Argentina. She was in personal (informal training) analysis.[48]

From the beginning, then, psychology (like teaching) was considered a female career. The program attracted women for at least three reasons. First, the program was housed in the School of Philosophy, which had traditionally been a "women's school." Second, since psychology was less prestigious and less demanding than medicine, it was seen as appropriate for modern women in this conservative society. Third, psychology (particularly clinical psychology) could be practiced at home, and so would interfere less with "women's duties" than other professions. The feminization of the profession reinforced the subordination of psychologists to psychiatrists and psychoanalysts. In the 1960s psychology joined teaching in a primary school as a "natural" career for a woman. In 1962 a group of recent graduates in psychology formed the Asociación de Psicólogos de Buenos Aires (APBA), with the goal of protecting and improving their professional status and to lobby for the reform of the law that limited their professional activities. All of its founding members but one were women.

Gender perceptions and corporative interests were sometimes difficult to distinguish. Adela Duarte, a member of the APBA since its early days, remembers the response of the national director of mental health (a psychiatrist) when the APBA petitioned for a new regulation that would allow psychologists to practice psychotherapy: "How many are you? Two hundred girls? We are twenty-eight thousand medical doctors, and you really think we're going to give away resources like this, so you can take our patients away from us?"[49] What bothered the physician so much was not only the thought of competition but the fact that the psychologists were "girls."

Gradually, however, more men enrolled in the psychology programs, and immediately they moved into leadership positions in the APBA. The first board of directors had only one male member. The board that served between 1967 and 1968 had five. In 1968 the first male president took office. From then until 1986, although a large majority of the members were still women, only three women served as president. One of them, Beatriz Perossio, was "disappeared" by the military regime in 1977, during her term in office, and was succeeded by the vice president, Hugo Vezzetti. As more men became psychologists and were overrepresented in the elective offices of their professional organization, the profession came to be perceived (and to perceive itself) as more "masculine." Psychologists now became more active in challenging their subordinate status. As a female APBA member points out, 1968 was a turning point for the APBA and for the profession: "Perhaps it's not by chance that he [Osvaldo Devries]—*our first male president*—was the one to take on the task of reorganizing."[50]

The masculinization of the profession and the political effervescence of the late 1960s encouraged professionals in general to question traditional models. The APBA became more politically active. In 1967 the Confederación General del Trabajo de los Argentinos, the most radical of the umbrella labor organizations at the time, invited the APBA to work with the residents of shantytowns. In the late 1960s the APBA organized strikes in hospitals, usually in response to abuses of psychologists by doctors.[51]

Some politically active psychologists started to see their profession as a tool for revolution, and that vision led to criticism of the model of psychology as a liberal profession. According to the APBA, a majority of psychologists saw themselves as professionals with a high level of scientific preparation, in possession of "conceptual instruments that allow them to modify human reality."[52] Similarly, 40 percent of a group of psychologists surveyed in the early 1970s said their "ideal kind of work" was "planning, psychohygiene, community-based psychology, and institutional psychology."[53] This perception of the psychologist's role, so close to Bleger's, coexisted uneasily with continued complaints against Bleger and others' intention to subordinate psychologists to psychiatrists and psychoanalysts.[54] Despite its increasingly revolutionary rhetoric, the APBA's professional activity continued to center on securing a place for psychology among the liberal professions, since the only source of income for most of its members was their private practice. Paradoxically, as soon as psychologists felt that their efforts were succeeding, they took steps to exclude potential competitors. According to a psychoanalyst who worked closely with psychologists, the psychologists objected to the inclusion of social workers in his psychiatric service with arguments that sounded very much like those the M.D.'s used to oppose the inclusion of psychologists.[55]

Despite the continued tensions and contradictions in the psychologists' professional identity, the most critical sectors of the profession concentrated on freeing psychology from the APA model. To its traditional union activities the APBA gradually added others that it characterized as "scientific or educational." In the late 1960s, under its first male president, it organized courses and seminars, some taught by "progressive" psychoanalysts, others by psychologists. Soon the APBA passed a regulation establishing that only psychologists could teach the courses it offered. The idea was to create an alternative place for training outside of the APA, and thus to achieve independence from psychoanalysts—in their own words, to "cut the umbilical cord" that tied psychologists to the psychoanalytic establishment. Moreover, as more generations of psychologists graduated from various schools (including the private universities that proliferated in the 1960s, and whose graduates were admitted to the APBA after 1972), more university professors were psychologists themselves. Nonetheless, the psychologists continued to be ambivalent about psychoanalysis. A majority of psychologists still considered APA-trained psychoanalysts their intellectual parents. That is why a large majority of the psychologists in treatment surveyed in the early 1970s were in therapy with psychoanalysts.[56]

In the politicized environment of the late 1960s, however, attitudes toward traditional psychoanalysis turned more critical. The APA increasingly came to be seen as an oppressive institution, and when it found itself in crisis in 1971, as we shall see, psychologists were quick to ally themselves with the radicals who decamped. Bleger, who stayed, was openly criticized in spite of the role he had played as "spiritual father" to several generations of psychologists. A series of documents published by students and professionals, some of them collected in a volume published in 1973 under the title *El rol del psicólogo,* clearly acknowledged the contradiction between "professional identification with the professional praxis of our teachers (psychoanalysts), which besides offered a comfortable place within the system (liberal professional who works in his private office) and, on the other hand, the need to achieve a professional identity that included a social dimension. . . . [Psychologists felt that they had to be] social 'change agents.' "[57]

The tensions were reflected in the pages of the *Revista Argentina de Psicología (RAP),* the APBA's journal, founded in 1969.[58] Although the journal was much more interdisciplinary than the APA's *Revista de Psicoanálisis* and openly criticized the APA, prominent APA analysts were invited to submit articles and to participate in roundtables. The APBA also asked for the APA's support (without success) in its struggle to improve psychologists' professional status.[59]

In the first issue of *RAP* the Lacanian analyst Oscar Masotta savaged Emilio Rodrigué's ideas on psychoanalysis with acid irony.[60] Rodrigué had been president of the APA until the previous year. Masotta's criticisms were directed not against Rodrigué alone but against the whole psychoanalytic establishment. His main argument was that APA psychoanalysts did not and could not understand Freud. Rodrigué responded with equal irony in a later issue. Masotta was not a member of the APBA; he was not even a psychologist. The fact that the first harsh criticism of the APA to appear in the pages of *RAP* was administered by an outsider, and that Rodrigué was immediately given the chance to respond and to have the last word (Masotta was not allowed to respond to Rodrigué's response), gives us a hint of the psychologists' contradictory feelings toward the psychoanalytic establishment.

The tensions surrounding the gender identity of the profession were also present in *RAP's* pages. In the first issue Juana Danis agreed with Bleger that psychologists should know psychoanalytic theories but should assume an essentially social rather than therapeutic role. Psychologists ought to be "midwives of changes" in their communities. It was not their task to cure or to delve into the unconscious aspects of social behaviors. In psychologists' hands psychoanalytic knowledge "perhaps has lost some of its purity, but it is well enough established now to be able to tolerate its amalgamation with social reality."[61]

Roberto Harari, later president of the APBA and one of the first psychologists to publish works on Lacanian psychoanalytic theory, responded to Danis in acrid tones.[62] For Harari the differences between psychologists and psychoanalysts were superficial. Psychologists should practice psychoanalysis on an equal footing with APA-trained analysts. He distinguished between science and profession. Since psychoanalysis was a science and not a profession, Harari concluded, there was no point in using a characterization of psychology and psychoanalysis as the basis for a discussion of professional identity.[63]

It is worth noting that the participants in this debate took positions that accorded with their gender-defined roles. Danis agreed with (male) psychoanalysts that (mostly female) psychologists should have a different identity from psychoanalysts and should be subordinate to them. She was "feminizing" the profession. Harari recognized no difference between psychologists and psychoanalysts. For him the issue was not the status of a feminized profession but rather the epistemological status of a science that psychologists were as well equipped as medical doctors to practice and theorize about.

IN SEARCH OF A PLACE UNDER THE SUN

Unlike the APA, the APBA quickly became involved in political issues. The APBA functioned more as a union than as an educational or scientific organization, and it maintained close ties with the university, whereas APA psychoanalysts in general severed their ties with the medical establishment, except when it suited them to boast of their credentials as M.D.'s.[64] Psychologists also had a larger presence than psychoanalysts in the public health system, where they worked with working-class patients. Psychologists in general were also more open to such alternative techniques as group therapy than most orthodox APA analysts. The repressive policies of the successive military regimes also had a great deal to do with the politicization of the psychologists. The military perceived the School of Philosophy in general and the psychology and sociology programs in particular as fertile ground for subversion. In the 1970s one general branded both Marx and Freud as intellectual criminals.[65]

After the coup of 1966 the psychology program was virtually closed, and many teachers were forced to resign. The military government installed in 1976 damaged the program further by placing it under the direct supervision of the president of the university and appointing as program directors people whose professional background was not psychology.[66] The military governments that ruled the country in the 1960s and 1970s left the APA largely alone, but the psychology program was usually the first to feel their wrath. The APBA, too, suffered the consequences of military policies, particularly after 1976. As we have seen, one of its presidents was "disappeared," brutally tortured before she was murdered by the military authorities, and many others were arrested and tortured. The APBA's offices were raided many times. Psychologists were seen as agents of resistance to military rule, and that was how they came to see themselves.

The politicization of the profession and the subordinate position of psychologists in the psy hierarchy explain their association with the radical APA dissidents in 1971. Psychologists had traditionally been reluctant to seek the support of medical doctors. As late as 1970 some APBA members objected to appealing for the support of the FAP when they came into conflict with the director of a hospital. Psychologists, they argued, should be able to fight their own battles; in any case, little help could be expected from doctors. Yet two years later the APBA joined the FAP in sponsoring the openly Marxist Centro de Docencia e Investigación (CDI), an umbrella organization that provided psychoanalytic training to the newly defined "mental health workers."[67] Like most of the Argentine leftist intelligentsia, in the early 1970s many politically active psychologists moved toward left-wing Peronism.

Psychologists' participation in the CDI and their association with the FAP and with dissident analysts opened a new door to higher professional status. They could count now on the support of the progressive wing of the medical profession in working toward their long-term goal of legal status as psychotherapists. The new alliance in fact eliminated professional distinctions. FAP, APBA, and other professional associations now formed the openly leftist Coordinadora de Trabajadores de Salud Mental. All professionals who dealt with mental patients, from psychiatrists to nurses, were now "mental health workers," without distinction of rank. It was taken for granted that a substantial portion of their training should consist of psychoanalytic theory. The APA had lost its monopoly. Between 1973 and 1976, under the democratic government led by Perón and by his third wife after his death, new progressive mental health services were opened, services more hospitable to psychologists. Though legally they were still barred from practicing psychotherapy, they had in fact expanded the psy realm.

★ ★ ★

Psychologists fitted better into the model of the politicized intellectual of the period than most APA analysts did. Moreover, psychologists helped to demedicalize their discipline in their quest for alternative sources of legitimacy. They were therefore very receptive to the French Lacanian school of psychoanalysis, which is closer to linguistics and philosophy than to medicine. Orthodox psychoanalysts derived their professional standing from their membership in an international organization, the IPA. Jacques Lacan was expelled from the IPA in the 1950s, became its harshest critic, and founded his own psychoanalytic school, which offered a source of legitimacy not only outside but against the IPA. Argentine psychologists' increasing allegiance to Lacan was reflected in the pages of *RAP,* where articles on Louis Althusser, linguistics, semiotics, and anthropology ran alongside others dealing with psychoanalytic theory or specific problems of the profession. Lacanianism was at home in *RAP* long before Lacan's name appeared for the first time in the *Revista de Psicoanálisis.* The table of contents of a single issue of *RAP* in 1971 is representative of the vast scope of its sponsors' intellectual interests: "Paternal Function and Cultural Creations" by the French analyst Guy Rosolato; "Action and Structure" by Jacques-Alain Miller, Lacan's son-in-law and intellectual heir; "Conditions of Production and of Ideologizing in the Social Sciences in Dependent Countries" by Mario Margulis; "Parental Responsibility and the Mass Media" by Eva Giberti; and "The Problematics of Louis Althusser and the Epistemology of the Social Sciences" by Eliseo Verón (a linguist and sociologist) and Raúl Sciarreta (a Marxist philosopher).

The expansion of Lacanianism cannot be separated from the intellectual environment of the 1970s and the embrace of structuralism. For those psychologists who were ready for a definitive break with the APA, however, Lacanianism offered an additional source of professional identity.[68] The difficult process of achieving that identity led psychologists to look for models in nonmedical versions of psychoanalysis. As two prominent psychologists pointed out, Lacanianism was the first new psychoanalytic theory ever to gain widespread acceptance without being introduced by the APA.[69] In the end, M.D.'s lost control over psychoanalytic therapy and theory.

The tensions produced by psychologists' quest for a professional identity relaxed only when, in the early 1980s, the ban on their practice of psychotherapy was finally lifted after intense lobbying by a wide range of people under the slogan "Make legal what is legitimate." When the prohibition was lifted, the APA and the Asociación Psicoanalítica de Buenos Aires (APdeBA, which had split from the APA in 1976) opened their doors to psychologists for analytic training. Moreover, psychoanalytic institutions not affiliated with the IPA, most of them associated with the doctrines of Lacan, proliferated in Buenos Aires. Some of them offered analytic training under the Lacanian standards, which in general are much less rigid and demanding than the IPA's. Since Lacanianism had achieved broad acceptance in porteño society, psychologists no longer needed the IPA for professional legitimacy as psychoanalysts. After playing a leading role in the dissemination of psychoanalysis in Argentine culture for twenty years, psychologists could at last claim it as their own.

SEVEN

When Marx Meets Freud

So far we have only glanced at one of the cultural changes that contributed to the emergence of a psy culture in Argentina: the relationship between psychoanalysis and politics, and particularly the embrace of psychoanalysis by the intellectual left. In the 1960s critical sectors of the left gradually seized on psychoanalysis both as a therapeutic technique and as a theoretical instrument to analyze society. This was a crucial boost for psychoanalysis because of the enormous influence wielded by the New Left in Argentine culture in those years.[1] In the decade and a half that followed the Cuban Revolution, leftist intellectuals dominated the field of cultural production in Latin America as never before. New Left intellectuals, many of them without formal political allegiance, were influential from Mexico to Argentina. What makes the Argentine case unique is the central place that the Perón experience played in the definition of the New Left's identity, and the incorporation of psychoanalysis in its conceptual artillery.

Psychoanalysis, Politics, and the Left

The divergence between the traditional Communist left and psychoanalysis is an old story that goes back to the 1930s. After the Bolshevik Revolution the Soviet state not only allowed psychoanalysis to flourish but established several institutions for psychoanalytic research and practice. The driving force behind this interest in the discipline was Lev Trotsky and a group of intellectuals and doctors gathered around him. After Trotsky's fall and in part as a consequence of it, all psychoanalysts were dismissed, the institutions were closed, and by the beginning of the 1930s psychoanalysis was all but banned from the Soviet Union.[2]

In the 1930s the Argentine Communist Party, following the Soviet line, openly rejected psychoanalysis and promoted Pavlov's reflexology in its place. Reflexology became the Party's approved psychiatric theory and psychoanalysis was condemned as a bourgeois-idealist doctrine.[3] In the 1940s and 1950s members of the traditional left, whose point of reference was the Communist Party (whether they were affiliated with it or not), had difficulty in approaching psychoanalysis, at least openly, since it was denounced by the Party.

The place of psychoanalysis in the theoretical discussions of the traditional left in the 1960s was marginal. It was perceived as a frivolous fashion. Some of the references to psychoanalysis in leftist publications, however, constitute evidence that it did enjoy some level of adherence among independent sectors of the left. As early as 1960, Héctor Agosti, head of the Communist Party, complained publicly against "neo-Marxists" who "feed on an eclectic soup: Marxism mixed with psychoanalysis."[4] In 1961 the independent leftist cultural magazine *El Escarabajo de Oro* distinguished between a revolutionary left and a "snobbish pseudo-left" that was more interested in psychoanalysis, mescaline, and rock music than in the Cuban Revolution.[5] For the traditional left, psychoanalysis was an opiate, a frivolous luxury, like the avant-garde art promoted by the Instituto Torcuato Di Tella.[6] To the delight of psychoanalysts, however, some Communists did secretly undergo psychoanalytic therapy after disappointing experiences with reflexology.[7] Even some Communist psychiatrists were finding reflexology less useful than they had been led to expect and were turning to psychoanalytically oriented techniques.[8] Some of them approached Pichon Rivière for informal training. They may have rejected psychoanalytic theory, but they accepted psychoanalysis as a therapeutic technique.

Meanwhile some independent leftists made serious attempts to reconcile psychoanalysis with Marxism. Their acceptance of Freud's doctrine, both as a therapy and as a theory, was made possible in part by the rapid weakening of the Party's hold on Argentine leftist culture and the rise of a heterogeneous and critical New Left that was more open to the "modern" social sciences and to new analytical instruments. Psychoanalysis entered the left by two paths, one therapeutic, one theoretical. These patterns did not necessarily respond to the same logic, but in most cases they converged. Many intellectuals who tried to use psychoanalysis as a theoretical tool had previously undergone psychoanalytic therapy themselves, and vice versa.[9]

Perón, Frondizi, and the New Critical Left

The anti-Perón coalition that had put Communists, conservatives, and liberals on the same side did not survive the fall of Perón.[10] A combination of factors turned the left against liberalism after 1955. These factors ranged from the brutality of the so-called Revolución Libertadora, the military regime that ousted Perón and harshly repressed his sympathizers in the name of a democratic restoration, to a general feeling that bourgeois society and values were disintegrating.[11] Furthermore, since the large Peronist faction was not permitted to run candidates until 1972, the post-Perón order bore the mark of illegitimacy from its birth.

The Perón experience posed serious problems for the most critical sectors of the left, in and outside of the Communist Party. The liberals' tendency to explain the Perón phenomenon as an aberration was not satisfactory.[12] After all, despite the expectations of *Libertadores* and Communists alike, the working class remained Peronist to the core, even after Perón was gone. Since 1945 Perón, by virtually monopolizing the support of the working class, had usurped the left's "natural constituency." Perón had also created a seemingly unbridgeable gap between intellectuals and workers. After 1955, however, the pro- and anti-Perón dichotomy that had organized political identities for a decade vanished. Thus the generation of leftists that came of age during the Perón decade found itself in a quandary. It was clear that there was a huge gap between the left and the proletariat, the class that was supposed to carry out the revolutionary design. In the aftermath of the Perón decade, then, independent leftist intellectuals were forced not only to revise current liberal interpretations of Peronism but to redefine their own political identity.

Although the centrality of Peronism in the debates of the left cannot be overemphasized, it was not the only factor that muddled the identity of the left. As elsewhere in Latin America, leftist intellectuals had to deal with Khrushchev's revelations at the Twentieth Congress of the Communist Party of the Soviet Union; the crushing of the Hungarian uprising in 1956; the Cuban Revolution; and the decolonization of Africa, especially Algeria's struggle for independence. The events in Cuba and Algeria were of particular importance. They challenged the Communist Party's claim to the "leading role" in the revolutionary process, and by demonstrating that violence could be a useful instrument for social and political change they challenged the traditional moderation of Latin American Communist parties, which in general opposed violence for political purposes. Besides, the events in both Cuba and Algeria added a nationalist tone to the abstract idea of revolution. They were social revolutions but also national revolutions. All these factors shook up the rigid ideological structures of the traditional left and fostered the emergence of new critical groups that disputed the Party's claim to the only correct interpretation of Marx. These groups had three important things in common: their search for independence from the rigidity of the Party, their acceptance of new instruments to analyze the complex Argentine reality, and their self-definition as intellectuals.

Since the last years of Perón's rule a group of young leftist intellectuals, most of them students or recent graduates of the UBA's School of Philosophy and Literature, had published a literary journal, *Contorno,* which later turned to politics.[13] In its heyday, when it claimed a circulation of 10,000 copies, *Contorno* served as an ideological guide for many young people.[14] The journal represented a new generation of intellectuals eager to distance themselves from the liberal writers of *Sur,* the most prestigious literary journal until the fall of Perón. Politically, *Contorno*'s position could be characterized as anti-anti-Peronism. *Contorno* was not Peronist, but it recognized the importance of Peronism's relationship with the working class. *Contorno* tried to fashion an alternative interpretation of Peronism.

Most *contornistas,* like many other Argentine leftist intellectuals of the period, were deeply influenced by French existentialism. For them politics was lived as ethics. They placed themselves "in history," as committed intellectuals. After the fall of Perón they tried to understand the events of the previous ten years and their own responsibility for them as middle-class intellectuals who had been alienated from the masses. At the same time they tried to define their own identity in post-Perón Argentina. In 1956 a whole issue of *Contorno* was devoted to an analysis and interpretation of Peronism. The fall of Perón provided *contornistas* with a unique opportunity to end their isolation from the working class. They recognized that the process was going to be painful. As one of the group's leaders, Ismael Viñas, put it,

> We have to rid ourselves of that . . . tendency we have as children of the middle class to renounce our economic privileges, but only on condition that the proletarians bow to our leadership; that is, if they accept our supposed superiority based on our *culture,* which is the result of precisely the privileges we now have. . . .
>
> Only when we can recognize, not only with our minds but in our hearts, that we belong to the middle class, and that that fact separates us

from the proletariat, will we be in a position to overcome that separation.
... It is not enough to be active in a certain political party, it is not enough
to read Marx ... we have to turn ourselves inside out like a glove, and that
is a painful and profound operation.[15]

Such feelings spawned a whole literature of self-mortification. Progressive
members of the middle class blamed themselves for abandoning the working class after 1945.[16] The identity crisis that struck intellectual leftists when
they realized that since 1945 they had been on the "wrong side of history"
opened up what Silvia Sigal calls "intellectual availability." "The identity
crisis is followed by a *'puesta en disponibilidad,'* an opening that led them to
search for a new ideological mix that could provide them a place, as intellectuals, in society, and in politics."[17]

Another important episode that redefined the identity of the left was the
so-called Frondizi betrayal. In 1958 Arturo Frondizi was elected president of
Argentina with the strong support of the New Left (including members of
the *Contorno* group). Frondizi's program appealed to leftist intellectuals because it represented the opposite of the Revolución Libertadora that had
overthrown Perón. Frondizi's plan included an approach to the Peronist
masses (his triumph was the result of a secret pact with Perón, who urged his
followers to vote for Frondizi). His leftist followers saw him as the first step
toward a "national revolution": rapid economic and social modernization
within the framework of economic nationalism. Frondizi, a politician with a
strong intellectual background and leftist sympathies, was seen as an alternative to both Peronism and the anti-Peronism of the heirs of the Revolución
Libertadora. In the eyes of some sectors of the New Left, he was offering a
bourgeois democracy that would carry out the structural changes necessary
for a successful revolution.[18] For his leftist supporters, Frondizi was a kind of
Lenin playing the role of Kerensky.[19]

Frondizi provided the progressive left a new (and ephemeral) political
identity. In Frondizi, Silvia Sigal writes, "the numerous intellectuals—and
portions of the middle class—that could not make complete political sense
of mere rejection of the Revolución Libertadora or of their double position
as non-Peronists and non-anti-Peronists found the solution they were looking for in a project that promised to bring people together in a development
program with nationalist accents."[20]

These expectations were soon disappointed. Frondizi made a full 180-
degree turn from the positions he had held for decades of political activity.
Under pressure from the military, who were suspicious of his connections to

Perón and to the left, Frondizi took harsh measures against the combative Peronist working class and instituted economic policies that diverged widely from the nationalist ideology he had long preached. He signed contracts with foreign (mostly U.S.) companies for the exploitation of oil deposits in Patagonia. Adding insult to injury, in what was perceived as a surrender to the Catholic Church, Frondizi legalized the establishment of private universities on an equal footing with public universities. Within a year of his election, Frondizi had alienated his supporters on both the right and the left. They felt betrayed. In 1962 he was removed from office by a military coup.

The feeling of betrayal had important consequences for the New Left. It was not only their political expectations that had been betrayed. It was not enough that after the Perón decade they were forced to redefine their identity in relation to the working class; after the Frondizi experience they felt forced to redefine their role as intellectuals in relation to the state. Once again they had been caught on the wrong side of history. The Frondizi affair and its aftermath led to a more general lack of faith in the ability of the democratic political system to channel social and political demands. As León Rozitchner put it as early as 1959, when the left was already withdrawing its support from Frondizi, "democracy is a fiction and a formal concession."[21]

Frondizi was succeeded by a series of civilian and military regimes. The political game was carried out outside the political parties and the formal political system. Politics was controlled by the so-called pressure groups, the special interests. The general distrust of the political system was evident in the cautious, almost benevolent reaction to the military coup of 1966 in almost all sectors of society, even some of the New Left.[22] By then the political system was so lacking in legitimacy that when Gen. Juan Carlos Onganía overthrew the constitutional president Arturo Illía, the writer Ernesto Sábato went on the record saying:

> I think this is the end of an era. The time has come to get rid of preconceptions and apocryphal values that have no relation to reality. We must have the courage to understand (and to say) that this is the end of institutions in which nobody seriously believes any longer. Do you believe in the Chamber of Deputies? Do you know many people who believe in that kind of farce? This is why ordinary people on the streets have felt deep relief.[23]

As the sociologist Juan Carlos Torre has said, the repressions carried out by the government established in 1966 "annulled the public sphere as a space for the arbitration of demands and political exchange" and dealt another blow to the battered working class and progressive young people.[24] Shortly after taking power, the government took over the universities, expelled professors, and repressed students, thus ending what is now perceived as a golden age in the life of the University of Buenos Aires.

Political Disappointment and Psychoanalytic Therapy

The Frondizi affair not only contributed to the radicalization of the left; the identity problems it caused encouraged some leftists to seek in psychoanalysis not only a therapy but a tool to help them understand reality and their own place in it. For people who lived politics as an ethic, who were deeply and personally committed to it, finding themselves without a clear political identity and once again on the wrong side of history was felt as a personal failure. "I'm retiring from politics because I'm tired of suffering," said the former *contornista* Ramón Alcalde to Ismael Viñas sometime during the 1960s.

For some members of the *Contorno* generation political disappointments had more serious consequences. Viñas recalls experiencing a psychotic episode after an interview with Frondizi. Shortly afterward he sought psychoanalytic therapy at the clinic of Dr. Alberto Fontana. "I went to a meeting with Frondizi at the government palace. He was lying to me, and I knew he was lying. When I left the meeting, I had a psychotic episode. I saw myself flying over the Plaza de Mayo."[25] Of course it would be too simplistic to believe that Viñas's hallucination was a direct consequence of his meeting with Frondizi. In fact, he acknowledges that he was going through a particularly difficult time in his personal life. Nonetheless, it is significant that when I asked him what had led him to psychoanalysis, the Frondizi betrayal was the first thing that came to his mind. Politics seems to have played a role in leading some young intellectuals to psychoanalysis.

In the early 1960s a group of former *contornistas*, led by Ismael Viñas, Ramón Alcalde, and Susana Fiorito, formed a new political party, the Movimiento de Liberación Nacional (MLN). Other former *contornistas*, such as León Rozitchner, were close to the party without becoming members of it. Ideologically the MLN was a radical version of Frondizi's original program: it stood for national liberation from imperialism and for an approach to the Peronist masses. The MLN appealed to the New Left because its leaders were highly visible and influential intellectuals and particularly because, unlike most leftist political parties, it was able to attract some support from labor unions.

The interesting thing about the MLN is that almost all members of its directorate underwent therapy as a group at the clinic of Dr. Alberto Fontana. Some members of the party joked that MLN stood for Movimiento Lisergístico Nacional.[26] MLN members' flirtation with psychoanalysis cum psychedelic drugs should not be confused with the convergence of the New Left and the counterculture in the United States.[27] MLNers, as one of its former members remembers, generally took a dim view of the counterculture and considered it nothing but the whims of spoiled bourgeois children. For members of the MLN directorate Fontana's therapy was a radical way to explore the self and gain insight into their own revolutionary subjectivity and their group identity. For some Fontana's therapy was also a kind of existential experience: "to put the body forward," as one former MLN leader remembers.[28] Political issues were sometimes brought up in Fontana's group meetings and they turned into political and philosophical discussions. In the end the *Contorno*-MLN group at Fontana's dissolved because Fontana did not share their formal commitment to Marxism. That was not the end of their therapy, though: each member sought another group or went into private analysis.[29]

I am not suggesting that political frustration led in a straight line to psychoanalysis. I do think it reasonable to conclude that for some members of the *Contorno* generation, politics was a traumatic experience that forced them to rethink their political and personal identity. Some of them sought in psychoanalysis an instrument for self-understanding. This approach to psychoanalysis as therapy converged with an interest in it as theory.

By the mid-1960s psychoanalysis was becoming an important element of the culture of the left, at least in Buenos Aires. A former political activist remembers his amazement when he arrived in Buenos Aires from his native Corrientes province in the mid-1960s. As a young man of the traditional left from the provinces, he had never known anyone who had been in psychoanalysis. He was attending a meeting of a radical leftist group one day when one of the group asked if future meetings could be shifted to another day, because otherwise they would conflict with his psychoanalysis. Nobody objected. It was not long after that that he himself started psychoanalytic therapy, because "everybody else did it, and if you didn't, you were looked down on." Psychoanalysis and militancy fed each other: psychoanalysis "didn't keep you from militancy. It didn't shift the direction of your militancy. On the contrary, it may have clarified it."[30]

POLITICS, PSYCHOANALYSIS, AND THE NEW SOCIAL SCIENCES

If New Leftists gradually accepted political violence as an instrument of social change, they also insisted on preserving the autonomy of the intellectual sphere, despite the increasing politicization of intellectual pursuits.[31] They saw themselves as the "critical conscience of society." This position was expressed in the pages of the short-lived but influential journal *Cuestiones de Filosofía,* published in the early 1960s by a group of students, graduates, and faculty of the School of Philosophy:

> Until historical conditions are transformed, we will not be able to achieve a totally autonomous culture; but we need to work on it in order to think about ourselves, to think about political practice and work out the firmest and broadest possible knowledge of its conditions. This circle, therefore, requires that cultural work not be abandoned, that it be mixed with the aims of political action but kept separate from it.[32]

The publishers of *Cuestiones de Filosofía* did not reject political action, but they saw their role in it as defined by their position as *intellectuals.* This autonomy gave them room for the incorporation of divergent views. While they defended Sartre's humanist vision of Marxism, they also introduced structuralism as a means to analyze society. The New Left, disappointed by liberal democracy and intent on clarifying its own identity, was much more open to new analytical tools than the traditional left. These new tools included the discourse of the new social sciences, which had spread rapidly since the University of Buenos Aires launched its sociology and psychology programs.[33] An issue of *Cuestiones de Filosofía* devoted to the human sciences included an article by José Bleger on psychoanalysis and Marxism; by placing psychoanalysis among the social sciences, they made it available as one of the new instruments for a better understanding of society.

The people who published *Pasado y Presente* had more ambitious goals. That journal, established in Córdoba by a group of former members of the Communist Party, played a central role in the spread of Antonio Gramsci's thought in Latin America. Its editors took upon themselves the task of working out a revolutionary theory for Argentina. In carrying out this task, they did not hesitate to seek the aid of the new "bourgeois" social sciences. Marxism could and should enrich itself with other social theories: "Marxism triumphs by using the weapons of its adversary and enriching itself with its treasures, not as spoils of war but as a prize for its recognized victory."[34] This view of their place in the intellectual world allowed them to include discussions of Sartre's existentialism, Edmund Husserl's phenomenology, Claude Lévi-Strauss's structuralism, and Lacanian psychoanalysis. It was in this journal that Oscar Masotta published his first article on Lacan in 1965.[35] (More on this below.) By the mid-1960s, the New Left was finding a place for psychoanalysis among the social sciences.

The merger of the social sciences and psychoanalysis proceeded along various fronts. In the late 1950s Pichon Rivière founded his Escuela de Psiquiatría Social, devoted to social psychology. Since the 1940s the sociologist Gino Germani, under the influence of the cultural approach to psychoanalysis developing in the United States, had advocated an alliance between the social sciences and a psychoanalysis freed from the constraints imposed by psychoanalytic institutions.[36] The works of Bleger, Masotta, and Rozitchner discussed below, then, combining Marxism, the social sciences, and psychoanalysis, have to be seen in the context of an increasing acceptance of psychoanalytic thought among the social sciences, outside the therapeutic practice promoted by the APA.

Politics tended to be psychologized in the 1960s, in Argentina as elsewhere. When "the personal is political," the political becomes personal. Enter psychoanalysis, at least in Argentina. In the United States the left embraced a humanistic psychology that had been born as an optimistic alternative to psychoanalysis, which had become the core of mainstream psychiatry since World War II.[37] Humanistic psychology had arisen in response to concerns about how to create the individual conditions for true democracy in the postwar world. In the 1960s humanistic psychology was appropriated by the New Left and the counterculture. Psychoanalysis provided a pessimistic picture of human beings in eternal conflict; humanistic psychologists exhorted their colleagues to shift their attention from psychoanalysis' demolition of "the dream of self-determination to shoring it up."[38] This approach was compatible with the utopian spirit of the New Left in the United States.

In Argentina, as we saw, the situation was rather different. There the New Left was born of a traumatic soul-searching. Argentine leftist intellectuals were more interested in preparing the conditions for revolution and in understanding why and how they always seemed to be caught on the wrong side of history than in focusing on such immediate goals as civil rights and stopping the war in Vietnam. Psychoanalysis was a more suitable tool than humanistic psychology for self-understanding at a time when the left had very few reasons to feel optimistic.

Although some areas of psychoanalytic theory were important elements of the thought of such leftist thinkers in the United States as Herbert Marcuse and Erich Fromm, psychoanalysis could not be used as a weapon against the establishment because it was a part of it. Psychoanalysis was taught in the top medical schools and most psychiatrists were trained in it. The social conservatism of the U.S. psychoanalytic community certainly contributed to this perception of psychoanalysis as a mainstream doctrine.[39] In Argentina, although psychoanalysis did enter into progressive areas of the public mental health system, it was still perceived as a discipline going against the grain of traditional psychiatry, still based on the asylum. The Argentine leftist political movements could absorb psychoanalysis more easily than their U.S. counterparts.

Freud Among the Marxists

Three intellectuals played important roles in placing psychoanalysis among the left's theoretical artillery. Despite their differences, all three read psychoanalysis from a nonmedical perspective.

JOSÉ BLEGER, READER OF GEORGES POLITZER

José Bleger was in a unique position to join psychoanalysis and Marxism, since he was both a practicing psychoanalyst affiliated with the APA and a member of the Communist Party. His position, having to pledge allegiance to two apparently incompatible systems of thought, was similar to the one in which such Freudian Marxists as Wilhelm Reich had found themselves in the early 1930s.[40] Like the earlier Freudian Marxists, Bleger set out to reconcile psychoanalysis and dialectical materialism. He turned for guidance not to the German Freudian Marxists, however, but to the Hungarian-born French philosopher Georges Politzer.[41]

Like his mentor, Enrique Pichon Rivière, Bleger was a popular teacher at the university and a bridge between psychoanalysis and Communist psychiatrists disenchanted with reflexology and the Party. Bleger became an associate member of the APA in 1958, but he never accepted some of the theoretical foundations of psychoanalysis, such as the instinct theory. Technically, however, he was an orthodox follower of Melanie Klein. In 1958 Bleger published a book titled *Psicoanálisis y materialismo dialéctico,* which so displeased the Party that he was expelled. There and throughout most of his career, Bleger took upon himself the task of continuing the work that Politzer had started in France over three decades earlier: formulating a "concrete psychology" based on the "recoverable" or nonidealistic elements of psychoanalysis. This concrete psychology would supersede traditional experimental and introspective psychology and would make psychology "more psychological"; in other words, less allied with biology and neurology.[42]

According to Bleger, the Marxists' denunciation of psychoanalysis as an idealistic science was valid, but only if it were directed against the right target: the ideological contents of Freud's theory. In its conceptual structure, psychoanalysis was a major breakthrough in psychological thought because it incorporated dialectical thought. Following Politzer, Bleger made a distinction between psychoanalytic discoveries and practice, which constituted the true Freudian revolution, and psychoanalytic theory, which was based on idealistic and mechanistic concepts. He focused on Freud's early works, the ones in which he had introduced drama in psychology. Bleger rejected Freud's return to what he called "animistic and idealistic psychology," however, particularly through the instinct theory and a *reified* notion of libido. Bleger discerned a gradual divergence between psychoanalytic practice, which uses drama, and theory, formulated in dynamic terms. By a dynamic theory Bleger understood a theory that explains facts in terms of reified drives.[43] Whereas the German Freudian Marxists considered the instinct and libido theories the most revolutionary aspects of psychoanalysis, its link to psychological materialism, Bleger wanted to strip psychoanalysis of both concepts.

Bleger's book consists of eight essays written over seven years. Four of those essays had been previously published or presented at psychoanalytic conferences. Bleger was pulled between his loyalty to Communist orthodoxy and his no less orthodox psychoanalytic education. Forced to acknowledge the scientific validity of reflexology, he felt compelled to show that it was compatible with psychoanalysis and psychotherapy in general.[44]

In his attempt to stress Freud's originality, Bleger committed what can be considered a Freudian slip. He credited Freud with discovering the dialectics of facts. This discovery, Bleger suggested, was truly original and difficult to trace to earlier sources. "Freud was born in 1846," Bleger continued, "fifteen years after Hegel's death and two before the publication of Marx and Engels' *Communist Manifesto.*"[45] In fact, as Bleger knew very well, Freud was born in 1856, twenty-five years after Hegel's death and eight years after the *Communist Manifesto.* By moving Freud's birth back ten years, he was attempting (unconsciously?) to emphasize the originality of the positive aspect of Freud's thought. Yet he took pains to show that the "idealistic" (that is, negative) aspects of Freud's theory could be easily traced to the scientific thought current at the time Freud was writing, and therefore were historically determined. Thus, according to Bleger, while the positive (dialectical-materialist) parts of Freud's theory were totally original and attributable solely of its author's genius, its negative aspects were nothing but the necessary result of the influence on Freud of contemporary science.

Bleger addressed his book to three audiences. To psychoanalysts he showed that Freud's theory must not be read naively, and that its ideological content had to be made explicit. To Marxists he showed that their criticism of psychoanalysis was valid although misdirected. Instead of focusing only on its ideological aspects, they should direct their critical efforts at its epistemological foundations. Such an analysis would show that psychoanalysis contained the elements necessary to form the basis of a dialectical-materialist psychological theory (thus superseding reflexology), but only after it was shorn of its idealistic components. The third audience consisted of young students and professionals, his students. They did the most to disseminate Bleger's views.

One problem that Bleger confronted in following Politzer was the fact that Politzer's ideas changed after he joined the French Communist Party. When Politzer was trying to use psychoanalysis as the basis for his concrete psychology, he was a Marxist (influenced by existentialism) but not yet a Communist. When he joined the Party, he openly denounced psychoanalysis. In order to use Politzer to legitimize his intellectual enterprise, Bleger needed to construct a Politzer who was both a Communist and a supporter of psychoanalysis. Bleger tried to resolve this dilemma by claiming to find continuity in Politzer's thought: the precommunist Politzer was trying to base his concrete psychology on psychoanalysis' acceptable elements, and the Communist Politzer was simply following that line of thought, exposing the unacceptable parts of the Freudian system. As we shall see, Bleger's views later changed in this regard.

Psicoanálisis y dialéctica materialista was harshly criticized by Communist doctors as well as by the Party.[46] The Party's Cultural Commission organized a debate on the book and published it in its journal, *Cuadernos de Cultura*.[47] The Party line was that Bleger's distinction between the psychoanalytic method (good) and Freudian theory (bad) was not sustainable. Psychoanalysis was an imperialist war tactic. The debate ended with ritual self-criticism. "As a corollary of the meeting, it became clear—and was acknowledged by Bleger himself—that a more active militancy in the Party will help the author to overcome ideological weaknesses and find a correct solution in the concrete field of psychology."

Despite the negative publicity the book received from the Party, it was not discussed within the APA.[48] The *Revista de Psicoanálisis* reviewed all works by APA members, but it made an exception in this case. The only review of the book written by an APA member (Fernando Ulloa) was published in the *Acta Neuropsiquiátrica Argentina*.[49] This omission shows both the limits and the flexibility of the APA's acceptance of deviations. The association turned a blind eye to theoretical deviations as long as the psychoanalytic technical framework was preserved. In those years other APA members who did not question the basic theoretical ideas of psychoanalysis as Bleger was doing were nonetheless expelled for technical deviations.

Bleger's book was reissued in 1963 and 1973 and was widely read by students and progressive psychiatrists. His attempt to create a new psychology, however, was no more successful than Politzer's had been. Yet his *Psicoanálisis* opened a door for the acceptance of psychoanalysis by left-wing students and intellectuals at a time when psychoanalysis was becoming widely popular as a therapy and as a cultural artifact and the noncommunist left was gradually becoming more open to different theoretical approaches.

In an effort to sort out the kind of relationship that could be established between Freud and Marx, Bleger expanded his ideas in an article called "Psicoanálisis y marxismo." Since Marxism and psychoanalysis had different epistemological status, Bleger concluded that the only possible relationship between them could be established by an evaluation of the methods, hypotheses, and theories of psychoanalysis within the Marxist framework. An application of "the general laws of dialectics to find the particular and specific form that they have in [psychoanalysis]" would enrich both dialectics and science. Thus Bleger opened a space in which psychoanalysis and Marxism could be complementary.

In spite of his strong political commitments,[50] Bleger continued to defend the autonomy of science. He insisted that psychoanalysts could and should be committed to politics, but psychoanalysis as a science had to be kept separate from politics: "Scientific inquiry and discussion have to be carried out as problems and fields that are worthwhile in their own right."[51] In accord with his ideas on the autonomy of science, Bleger refused to join those who resigned from the APA in 1971 for political reasons.

Bleger's book was the first serious attempt in Argentina to reconcile dialectical materialism and psychoanalysis. For that purpose, however, Bleger read psychoanalysis through Politzer and was forced to reject some of the most basic concepts of Freudian psychoanalysis, such as instinct and libido— the very concepts that such Freudian Marxists as Wilhelm Reich, Herbert Marcuse, and the early Erich Fromm had considered the most revolutionary parts of Freud's doctrine.

While Bleger set out to show that the left should be more careful in its assessments of psychoanalysis, others were trying to use psychoanalysis as an analytical tool to throw light on Marxist theory. León Rozitchner was one of them.

LEÓN ROZITCHNER AND THE SUBJECTIVITY PROBLEM

Oscar Masotta called León Rozitchner one of the leading "sophists" of the 1960s.[52] Those "sophists" were intellectuals who "sold" their knowledge in private study groups, thus originating a kind of parallel university. Rozitchner was also a popular teacher at the university and his seminars on Freud and Marx enjoyed large enrollments.[53] Rozitchner started his intellectual journey in the early 1950s as a member of the *Contorno* group. Ever since then he has had little patience with the traditional Argentine left, which he considers not up to its revolutionary task.[54] In the early 1970s, Rozitchner was close to one of the groups that split from the APA and taught classes on Marx and Freud at the school they organized.

Rozitchner studied philosophy under Jean Wahl in Paris. Back in Argentina he joined the group that published *Contorno,* and later developed close links with the MLN. He had become interested in psychoanalysis while he was still a student in France, probably under the influence of the philosopher Maurice Merleau-Ponty, who was interested in it and was a friend of Jacques Lacan. In the late 1950s Rozitchner translated Jean-Baptiste Pontalis's book *Vigencia de Sigmund Freud.* Later he used psychoanalysis as a tool to address what he and the French existentialists considered one of the most serious blind spots in Marxist theory: the problem of subjectivity.

Like Bleger, Rozitchner had a humanistic conception of Marxism, so he opposed the structuralist-Althusserian-Lacanian wave of the 1970s.[55] Bleger's and Rozitchner's projects, however, were radically different. Rozitchner had no interest in identifying dialectical-materialist elements in psychoanalysis or in founding a new psychology; he sought in psychoanalysis an analytical tool for understanding revolutionary rationality, intersubjectivity, and the making of a revolutionary subject. Like other intellectuals of the time, Rozitchner was looking for a theoretical instrument that would help him understand the failure of the left to persuade the working class to carry out its revolutionary design. That problem was linked to the other big puzzle in Argentine politics: the persistence of Peronism. According to Rozitchner, Freud's theory was perfectly compatible with Marx's ideas, and so was uniquely suited to address both problems. If Freud himself had not been a political revolutionary, his works could be read as revolutionary. Like the German Freudian Marxists, Rozitchner considered that both the libido and the unconscious, far from being problematic concepts, were at the core of psychoanalytic revolutionary theory.

In an article titled "La izquierda sin sujeto," published in September 1966 in the leftist journal *La Rosa Blindada,* Rozitchner anticipated many of the themes he was to address in his book on Freud, which he was already working on. *La Rosa Blindada* was a cultural and literary magazine of the radical New Left. Many members of its editorial board were disenchanted former Communists, among them Antonio Caparrós, a psychiatrist who at some point drew close to psychoanalytic circles. In 1966 *La Rosa Blindada* published a review of an article by Jacques Lacan on female sexuality.[56]

In "La izquierda sin sujeto," Rozitchner analyzed the conditions for the development of revolutionary rational framework. At the same time he showed that Peronism could not be the basis for a revolutionary process. The article can be read as sharp criticism of the intellectual and political rigidities of the traditional left and of its inability to reach out to the working class. If revolution did not happen when and how the analytic categories used by the left predicted, Rozitchner argued, it was because the left's logic was faulty. What was needed was a new revolutionary logic that could emerge only from a new revolutionary subject, free of all taint of the bourgeois.[57] Therefore, the transition from the bourgeois culture to a true revolutionary culture needed to uncover not only the contradictions of the bourgeois system at the social, economic, and political levels but, more important, the contradictions within the individual leftist militant. Psychoanalysis would provide the instrument for overcoming these contradictions.

These problems were taken up again in Rozitchner's *Freud y los límites del individualismo burgués* of 1972. *Freud* is a dense text of over five hundred pages. It consists largely of commentary on two of Freud's most "social" texts, the ones Bleger had dismissed as products of Freud's "pseudo-sociological thought": *Civilization and Its Discontents* and *Group Psychology and the Analysis of the Ego*.[58] For Bleger, Freud's "social" writings were unwarranted detours into sociology; for Rozitchner they were a step toward including the subject in the analysis of collective process. According to Rozitchner's reading of Freud, individual psychology and social psychology could not be separated; the one depended on the other.[59]

Unlike Politzer and Bleger, Rozitchner assigns the unconscious a particularly important role in freeing the subject from the repression imposed by culture. Giving primacy to instincts, Rozitchner identifies the unconscious with the id of Freud's late works. If for Bleger the theory of libido was an idealist atavism in Freud's theory, for Rozitchner it was at the core of Freud's dialectical and materialist theory. Thus Freud's discovery of the body as

libidinously determined by others parallels Marx's discovery of human beings as necessarily linked to nature.[60] While Bleger found the most revolutionary elements of psychoanalysis in Freud's early works, such as *The Interpretation of Dreams,* for Rozitchner it was in Freud's later works, *The Ego and
the Id* and *Beyond the Pleasure Principle,* where Freud developed the instinct
theory, that psychoanalysis became dialectical.

Bleger had made a clear distinction between psychoanalytic practice, the
realm of dialectics and drama, and psychoanalytic theory, still tainted with
idealistic and mechanistic elements.[61] Rozitchner valued psychoanalytic
theory and identified its practice with the therapy carried out by APA analysts, in alliance with the bourgeoisie. In Rozitchner's view, the only social
framework a conventional APA-affiliated analyst could take into consideration was the bourgeois family. By focusing only on sexual repression, the
bourgeois analyst got only a partial view of the problem, since sexual repression was only one aspect of the broader repression imposed by the capitalist
system.[62] For Rozitchner the *real* analysis of the individual, consisting of
freeing him from the paternal superego, would necessarily result in a "collective cure," freeing society from the bourgeois-imposed collective superego. In other words, analysis would lead to revolution.

To show what *real* psychoanalysis is about, Rozitchner reads Freud in his
own idiosyncratic way. To begin with, Rozitchner attributes to Freud an
idea of historicity that is not easy to find in Freud's own writings. Freud
never analyzes the problem of culture in terms of "modes of production,"
as Rozitchner claims. Freud sees "culture" or "civilization" as a painful but
necessary process derived from instinctual needs. He makes it clear that a
radical change in the structure of property would do little to change the repressive effects of culture.[63] According to Rozitchner, Freud knew that "social neuroses" (such as alienation) had to be dealt with in the same way psychoanalysis deals with individual neuroses. Freud just failed to understand
the role of the revolutionary leader in administering the social "therapy."
But Freud was much more cautious than Rozitchner admits in establishing
analogies between social and individual neuroses. In *The Future of an Illusion*
he wrote:

> But we should be very cautious and not forget that, after all, we are only
> dealing with analogies and that it is dangerous, not only with men, but also
> with concepts, to tear them from the sphere in which they have originated
> and been evolved. Moreover, the diagnosis of communal neuroses is faced
> with a special difficulty. In an individual neurosis we take as our starting

point the contrast that distinguishes the patient from his environment, which is assumed to be "normal." For a group all of whose members are affected by one and the same disorder no such background could exist: it would have to be found elsewhere.[64]

For Freud, therefore, the problem was not to find a revolutionary "therapist" able and willing to carry out the appropriate "therapy" (i.e., revolution) on a social group but to recognize that the analogy between individual neuroses and social neurosis could be carried too far.[65]

More idiosyncratic was Rozitchner's reading of Freud's *Group Psychology,* which was based in part on what Freud did not say. In order to emphasize the revolutionary character of Freud's book, Rozitchner focused on what Freud omitted. Freud based the first part of *Group Psychology* on his critical reading of Gustave Le Bon's *Psychologie des foules,* but he said nothing about Le Bon's explicitly political references. Rozitchner considers that, since Freud's *Group Psychology* achieves the "scientific destruction of bourgeois social psychology and of the bourgeois individuality integrated in its institutions," then its point of departure must have been Le Bon's complete text, particularly those portions of it that Freud did not include in his discussion; "the excluded text is present in his theoretical struggle, which is thus political."[66] Rozitchner does not seem to be interested in *why* Freud decided to exclude those portions of *Psychologie des foules;* instead he explains why Freud *should have been* interested in what he omitted. In other words, he explains Freud's work by examining what is not there.

Rozitchner's peculiar reading of Freud's text surfaces again when he analyzes Freud's characterization of one of the "artificial" groups he discussed: the army. Here Rozitchner attributes to Freud's ideas a historical dimension that is difficult to find in the original text. In explaining his theory that groups are held together by libidinous bonds, Freud claimed that an army is held together by the illusion that the commanding general, like Christ for the Catholic Church, "is a father who loves all soldiers equally." Freud anticipated an objection, however. This is the way he met it, as Rozitchner quotes it: "An objection will justly be raised against this conception of the libidinal structure of an army on the ground that no place has been found in it for such ideas as those of one's country, of national glory, etc. which are of such importance in holding an army together.... Such ideas are not indispensable to the existence of an army." Rozitchner concludes that Freud's dismissal of the objection was justified because he was referring to a "bourgeois" army. Rozitchner explains: "And we say bourgeois army because it is the kind of army in which the men who belong to it do not integrate the rational *knowledge* of that army and of the violence generated by such a warrior-like community." In a bourgeois army, Rozitchner claims, such concepts as fatherland and national pride are abstractions that only hide the fact that a bourgeois army is merely a class army. But was a bourgeois army really the one Freud had in mind? If we supply the part that Rozitchner omits from his quotation of Freud's text (in italics in the passage below), things may look different:

> An objection will justly be raised against this conception of the libidinal structure of an army on the ground that no place has been found in it for such ideas as those of one's country, of national glory, etc. which are of such importance in holding an army together. *The answer is that that is a different instance of a group tie, and no longer such a simple one; for the examples of great generals, like Caesar, Wallenstein, or Napoleon, show that* such ideas are not indispensable to the existence of an army.

The armies of Caesar, Wallenstein, and Napoleon (with the debatable exception of Napoleon's) could hardly be characterized as bourgeois. Freud was referring to prebourgeois armies. Thus any libidinal links between the ranks and the commanding general—necessary only in a bourgeois army, given the abstract character of such notions as "fatherland," according to Rozitchner—seem to be ahistorical. In fact, when Freud gave an example of a bourgeois army—the German army in World War I—he justified his focus on libidinal bonding on practical rather than theoretical grounds. Most cases of war neurosis, Freud claimed, were due to the bad treatment that soldiers received from their superiors.[67] Therefore, Rozitchner turns Freud's universal category into historical ones in order to stress the revolutionary character of Freud's theory.

Rozitchner's attempt to make Freud and Marx compatible differed from Bleger's. Bleger's effort to find dialectical elements in psychoanalysis forced him to reject Freud's theory of instincts. His refusal to accept libidinal theory put him paradoxically close to Freud's critics on the right. Rozitchner tried to show that Freud's theoretical structure was revolutionary and could be used as an analytical tool to understand (and change) society. According to Rozitchner, Freud, by showing the necessary connection between social psychology and individual psychology, historicized both subject and society. This operation, however, required a reading of Freud that introduced historicity from the outside.

OSCAR MASOTTA: FROM SARTRE TO LACAN

Oscar Masotta was probably more influential than either Bleger or Rozitch-ner. Beatriz Sarlo characterized him as an intellectual beacon for many young people in the 1960s. Masotta was a self-taught intellectual who developed formal contacts with the University of Buenos Aires without ever having acquired a degree. In the late 1950s he worked for (and published in) the *Revista de la Universidad de Buenos Aires*. In the early 1960s he was a full-time researcher at the university's Centro de Estudios Superiores de Arte until he was dismissed by the military authorities who took power in 1966. Masotta's intellectual career, like Rozitchner's, started in *Contorno* in the 1950s. He belonged to a somewhat marginal group among the people who published the journal. What distinguished Masotta's group was its almost fanatic allegiance to Jean-Paul Sartre's existentialism, their open sympathy for Peronism, and their open homosexuality (in Masotta's case more a kind of "theoretical sympathy" than an actual lifestyle).[68] At that time Masotta was interested in literature and philosophy. Although he did not belong to any political party, he identified himself as a Marxist and published in the left's political journals.[69] Masotta developed close ties with avant-garde circles at the Instituto Di Tella, and he organized private study groups on topics as diverse as philosophy, Marxism, art, and later Lacanian psychoanalysis. At one point he had more than four hundred private students.

Masotta's broad influence was the result of two factors: his multifaceted personality and the wide range of his intellectual interests. Throughout his life he was influential as a writer on philosophy, literary criticism, pop art, and Lacan's psychoanalytic theories. In 1974 Masotta founded the first Lacanian psychoanalytic institute in Argentina and probably in the Spanish-speaking world, the Escuela Freudiana de Buenos Aires. Once the school was established, Masotta left for Europe. He died there in 1979, after introducing Lacanian psychoanalysis in Spain. Today Masotta is almost a cult figure in Argentina. In the 1990s four books dealing with various aspects of his personality and intellectual career were published. As one of the books, written by Masotta's old friend Carlos Correas, is titled, there has been an "operation Masotta."[70]

Masotta's transition from Sartre's existentialism to Lévi-Strauss's structuralism and to Lacan's psychoanalysis was more a matter of adding new elements that gradually displaced the older ones than of substituting whole new systems of thought for previous ones. As Masotta himself wrote in 1968, in the preface to a collection of previously published essays:

I have not evolved from Marxism to pop art, nor by concentrating on the works of pop artists am I betraying or denying yesterday's Marxism. Quite the contrary, when I focus on the vitality of contemporary artistic production, I consider that I am remaining faithful to . . . the demands and the needs of Marxist theory. . . . My general points of view—the basic ones with respect to class struggle, the role of the proletariat in history, the need for revolution—are the same today as they were fifteen years ago.[71]

The very title of the collection, *Conciencia y estructura,* even if by then Masotta openly opted for structure over conscience, still shows that he was not ready to dismiss conscience altogether.

Masotta's project differed from Rozitchner's and Bleger's. For Masotta, psychoanalysis was one of the new social sciences that would update Marxist theory. I focus here on the early Masotta, the young man who was still making his transition from existentialism and Marxism to structuralism and psychoanalysis, a transition that was probably smoother than some of his former followers are willing to admit. Throughout this transition, Masotta introduced psychoanalysis as a tool that would complement and throw light on traditional Marxist theory. The next chapter discusses Masotta's later career. Since the mid-1950s Masotta had been interested in the developments of French psychoanalysis, particularly after Lacan's break with the International Psychoanalytic Association in 1953.[72] The channel through which Masotta was introduced to psychoanalysis was not Lacan, however, but his readings of Sartre and Merleau-Ponty. Lacan was a later discovery that he tried to integrate into existential philosophy.

In 1957 Sartre published "Questions de méthode" in *Les Temps Modernes.*[73] In this piece, later included as the first part of his *Critique de la raison dialectique* (the only part that Masotta ever understood, according to Carlos Correas, or even read), Sartre criticized the antihumanism of Communist Marxism and its claim to universality. As a corrective, Sartre proposed the introduction of the social sciences, chief among them psychoanalysis. His goal was to put the human being back into Marxism. Psychoanalysis would play a prominent role in this program as the science that "enables us to recover the complete human being in the adult, that is, not only what he is now but also the weight of his history."[74] According to Sartre, dialectical materialism could no longer afford to deprive itself of an instrument that would allow it to find the individual in the mass.

It was Sartre, therefore, who insisted on the need to introduce psychoanalysis into Marxism in order to fill in one of its most troublesome blind spots. The message, as we saw, was faithfully received by Rozitchner, and by Masotta too, at a time when the subjectivity problem was preoccupying the intellectual left. In 1960 Masotta agreed on the need for psychoanalysis as an analytic device: "The question, then, is to restore [to Marxism], through the use of appropriate interpretive techniques, the possibility of giving an account of the emergence of individual history in the dialectical perspective of a relationship with the totality of the current history. In first place among those instruments that Marxism has to assimilate is psychoanalysis."[75]

The year 1960 was particularly important in Masotta's life. That was the year his theoretical interest in psychoanalysis converged with his discovery of it as a therapy. After the death of his father, Masotta sank into a deep depression.[76] This period had two important consequences. The first, as he himself put it years later, was his discovery of psychoanalysis: "Suddenly I had to forget Merleau-Ponty and Sartre, ideas and politics, 'commitment,' and the ideas I had invented about myself. I had to look for an analyst."[77] This was his first approach to psychoanalysis as therapy. What Masotta describes as a substitution was in fact a convergence. It had been through Sartre that he had arrived at psychoanalytic theory in the first place. By the time Masotta wrote that piece, he was already constructing his identity as a pioneering Lacanian analyst and was more interested in emphasizing ruptures than continuities in his intellectual journey.

The other consequence of Masotta's depression was that during the crisis Enrique Pichon Rivière took him into his home.[78] There Masotta had access to the writings of Lacan and had the time to study them carefully. "In reference to Knowledge," he wrote, "in those years I 'discovered' Lévi-Strauss, structural linguistics, and Jacques Lacan."[79] Masotta maintained a close relationship with Pichon Rivière, who later lent his expertise to the "happenings" that Masotta organized at the Instituto Di Tella, providing psychoanalytic interpretations for the media.

Gradually Masotta's passion for existentialism dwindled (although Sartre continued to be an important influence for some time), and into its place stepped pop art and Lacan. A result of his studies on Lacan was a paper he presented in 1964 at Pichon Rivière's Escuela de Psiquiatría Social and published in 1965 in *Pasado y Presente,* the first discussion of Lacan in Argentina and, some say, in the Spanish language. As interesting as the article itself is the fact that it was published in *Pasado y Presente.* Remember that the journal was published by a sector of the New Left that was particularly open to new ideas. The publication of Masotta's paper there amounted to legitimation of psychoanalytic thought by leftist culture.

From the beginning of the article it is clear that Masotta was seeking to establish connections between Lacan and his own current philosophical interests. At the center of Lacan's position, according to Masotta's reading, was the concept of the "radical opacity of the subject." "Jacques Lacan" was an attempt to understand Lacan in terms of what Masotta still considered the most relevant form of thought, French existential phenomenology. The last part of the article is a discussion of how to reconcile Lacan's theory with Marxism. Unlike Rozitchner, however, Masotta did not focus on Freud's social theory. He concluded that it was in Lacan's thought that the link between the two systems had to be sought. According to Masotta, it was Lacan that established the connection between the individual on the one hand and the social and historical on the other.

Lacan's emphasis on language and on the unconscious as a structure opened a new set of problems related to the compatibility of psychoanalysis, Marxism, and structuralism at a time when Louis Althusser's writings were barely known in Argentina. The very idea of structure was still problematic for Masotta: "But how much is this ontology worth without cogito, this philosophy of the unconscious and of structures, which at times seems to become a generalized formalism where man has less density than symbols and models preexist the individual?" Although Masotta found no satisfactory answer, he concluded that "phenomenology, structuralism, Marxism, psychoanalysis, all converge in Lacan, and this happens at the most immanent level of his work and his teaching."[80] Masotta lamented, however, Lacan's silence on concrete ideological issues. Unlike Sartre, Lacan did not connect his description of the subject to the "material" need for class struggle.

In "Jacques Lacan" Masotta was suggesting that it was time for a transition from a Sartrean understanding of Marxism to a Marxism illuminated by the new social sciences, structuralism, and Lacanian psychoanalysis. Thus Masotta wrote in "Roberto Arlt, yo mismo," an autobiographical essay:

> Only today I begin to understand that Marxism is not at all a philosophy of consciousness, because it radically excludes phenomenology. Marxism's philosophy must be rediscovered and specified in the modern doctrines (or "sciences") of language, of structure, and of the unconscious. In the linguistic models and in the unconscious of the Freudians. To the alternative "consciousness or structure" we must answer, I think, by choosing structure.[81]

Masotta's early efforts to reconcile Marxism and psychoanalysis are reminiscent of Rozitchner's. Both arrived at psychoanalysis under the influence of French existentialism; both saw it as a way to resolve problems that Marx could not address. In the end, however, their paths diverged. Whereas Masotta's existentialism took him to Lacan via structuralism, Rozitchner remained faithful to a humanist Marxism and continued to seek in psychoanalysis what was missing in Marxism. In a sense, Masotta's intellectual trajectory was quite typical, for many Latin American intellectuals moved to structuralism in the late 1960s, when Marx's thought came to seem synonymous with Althusser's. Yet we should not overemphasize the typicalness of Masotta's intellectual journey. In the early 1970s, when politics permeated everything, Masotta and his followers tried to keep psychoanalysis away from politics. In the preface to his *Ensayos lacanianos* of 1976, Masotta wrote that his 1965 article on Lacan

> was based on concepts that today are, if not superseded, which would be improbable, at least abandoned: a certain globalism, the need to connect, to seal, the "union" between psychoanalysis and Marxism. There was also a certain language that was fashionable at that time that allowed us to compare fields that were, if not incompatible and remote, at least difficult to handle (existentialism, structuralism, phenomenology).

The final approach between psychoanalysis and the revolutionary left took place in the early 1970s, when Althusser's structuralist reading of Marx and psychoanalysis made its way to Argentina.[82] Yet psychoanalysis and Marxism were already moving closer together in the 1960s, as we have seen. In view of the large role played by the intellectual left in Argentine culture in the 1960s, this acceptance of psychoanalysis made it interesting and attractive to broad sectors of society. Bleger, Rozitchner, and Masotta, each in his own way, tried to carve out a space for psychoanalysis in the culture of the left. Whatever the merits of their logic, in that project, at least, they succeeded.

Later in the decade, when leftist groups turned to guerrilla warfare and violence became a part of Argentine political culture, psychoanalysis would play still another important role in the life of political militants. Being part of an armed group erased the boundaries between public and private life. Family and personal life were subordinated to politics. Living a clandestine life under constant threat was a highly stressful experience. Many leftist militants interviewed by the historian María Matilde Ollier said they had started psychoanalysis in the hope of resolving the internal conflicts that arose from their political activities. For many militants, psychoanalysis was a way of articulating the relationship between their private world and their all-absorbing militancy. For others the hour with the analyst was the only opportunity to speak candidly in safety. One former militant remembers that "in the political group you had to talk about all kinds of topics, private, personal issues. For me that was a bluff and I started to think at that time that [analytic therapy] was good for [dealing with] private issues." Another former member of a guerrilla group said: "I started my analysis when I was twenty-eight years old. I was wondering how to connect the individual and the socialist self."[83] For others, particularly psychoanalysts who were involved in politics, when political activity became dangerous in the increasingly repressive mid-1970s, psychoanalysis became a substitute for militancy. A prominent Lacanian analyst remembers that after he came close to being killed by a right-wing death squad and realized that he himself would be unable to kill another human being, he left politics and devoted himself to psychoanalytic research and practice.[84] Thus, while for some leftists psychoanalysis shed light on their political militancy, for others it became a substitute for it.

EIGHT

Politics, Lacanianism,
and the Intellectual Left

Psychoanalysis' entrance into the discourse of the left was an important factor in its widespread acceptance in Argentina. By the mid-1970s leftist intellectuals of all persuasions recognized psychoanalysis as an appropriate subject to think and talk about. The 1960s had been the decade when psychoanalysis was accepted by the left. The early 1970s was the time when intellectual leftists became agents for its diffusion. When in 1979 Noé Jitrik, a literary critic and former *contornista,* reviewed the Argentine artistic and scientific achievements of the early 1970s, he found it natural to include psychoanalysis among the areas of "cultural production" worth discussing.[1] In the early 1970s important cultural journals devoted entire issues to psychoanalysis, and its language permeated fiction and literary criticism. Psychoanalysis had become part of "the world taken for granted" for the intellectual left.[2]

Psychoanalysis' integration with the culture of the left resulted from a combination of factors. First, since the late 1960s psychoanalysis had become highly politicized. In 1971 a group of leftist members of the APA, among them a founding member and a past president, broke with the institution and with the IPA. This was the first time in the history of the international psychoanalytic movement that a group had split from the IPA *as a group* for purely political reasons. The secessionists not only defied the APA's rigid institutional framework but opened a broader debate whose impact was felt far beyond the psy community.

The second factor was the growing number of Lacan's followers. Whereas orthodox APA psychoanalysis had a clear clinical orientation, Lacanian psychoanalysis was seen as a cultural phenomenon. Many Lacanians had backgrounds in philosophy, literature, or psychology, only very few in medicine. By the time they approached psychoanalysis, some of them had already established reputations as writers or critics. This was a distinct advantage in a country such as Argentina, where the intellectual elite has traditionally been small and fluid, so that symbolic capital gathered in one field can readily be transferred to another. Lacanians carried psychoanalytic views and language into literature and criticism. Moreover, the reception of Lacanian psychoanalysis helped to establish the professional status of psychologists.

A third factor was the identification of mental patients as an oppressed group and of mental institutions as mechanisms of social control. This view of the mental health problem was related to the translation of works by representatives of the British and French antipsychiatry movement and to the growing perception of the world as divided between oppressors and oppressed.

When "All Is Politics"

As we have seen, many leftist intellectuals turned to the social sciences in their efforts to understand the hold of Peronism on the working class and their own failure to reach the workers, but the general feeling among them was pessimistic. "We have to turn ourselves inside out like a glove," Ismael Viñas had said in the late 1950s. "In Argentina, in 1965, we leftist intellectuals are harmless. . . . We are met with the justified indifference of the only class to which we trust our liberation," wrote Ricardo Piglia years later.[3] Perón had wooed the working class too well.

The period that began with the coup of 1966 had unexpected consequences for the military regime and for the relationship between intellectuals and workers. One of the generals' obsessions was to depoliticize society and eliminate all vestiges of "leftist subversion." Their repressions only fanned the flames for the leftists and made radicals of the middle-class young.[4] The regime's attempt to eliminate (liberal) politics pushed groups of politicized young men and women to seek violent solutions. The Cuban experience had shown that violence could be effective. As elsewhere, the works of Frantz Fanon and Che Guevara became required reading for radicalized young people.[5] Since the early 1960s, Cuba had been a land of pilgrimage and training for aspiring emulators of Che Guevara and a cultural icon for progressive intellectuals. In the words of Tulio Halperín, Cuba became the "Antillean Rome." Later the French Mai '68 and the Chinese Cultural Revolution would also have an important impact on the radicalization of youth.

The repressive policies of the government of 1966 put university students and workers on the same side for the first time: both groups became victims of the official repression. Now stirrings of progressivism began to be felt in the organized working class, even among some people who still proclaimed allegiance to Perón. The old Peronist union leadership had lost its aggressiveness and cultivated ties with the military regime. Progressive workers in the militant unions in Córdoba and in the Confederación General del Trabajo de los Argentinos (CGTA) were much more receptive to what intellectuals had to say than the orthodox Peronist unions.[6] "No single sector of society alone could defeat the dictatorship," claimed Raimundo Ongaro, head of the CGTA in 1970. According to Ongaro, the working class needed the support of all other oppressed groups—students, intellectuals, priests who rebelled against the church hierarchy, even officers and NCOs of the armed forces who rebelled against the oppression of generals and admirals, with their links to international monopolies.[7]

The Cordobazo marked the beginning of the end of the military regime of 1966. In the Argentine version of the episodes that had shaken Paris exactly one year before, students and workers mobilized together in the city of Córdoba in a violent rebellion that shook the regime apart. The old dream of intellectuals shoulder to shoulder with workers finally came true. "The Cordobazo changed the way intellectuals looked at themselves and at their role in the Argentine scheme of things," claimed Ricardo Piglia in 1973.[8] Similarly, Marie Langer, then a leader of one of the leftist groups that split from the APA, said in 1971: "We, as an institution, were waked up by the Cordobazo."[9] Intellectuals finally found a place for themselves in the revolutionary process. The Cordobazo also launched a period of unprecedented political violence in twentieth-century Argentina. The Cordobazo demonstrated that in the short run, at least, "the people" could rise violently against the regime and shake it. During those years, political groups of many persuasions, from Guevarists and Trotskyites to Peronists, started organizing for armed struggle to topple the regime and establish some kind of socialism. In 1968 the Peronists attempted to organize a guerrilla movement in Taco Ralo, in the province of Tucumán; and in 1969 the first urban guerrillas emerged when the self-styled Fuerzas Armadas de Liberación (FAL) attacked a military garrison. Other military garrisons and police headquarters were attacked; banks were robbed; whole towns were taken over; executives of foreign companies and military officers were kidnapped and executed (the most notorious case was the killing of former president Pedro Aramburu). These leftist actions were matched by systematic torture, illegal executions, and gradually the "disappearance" of leftist militants by right-wing groups that enjoyed total impunity. By the early 1970s violence had become the central feature of Argentine politics.[10]

Urban guerrillas were hardly unique to Argentina. In his film *That Ob-scure Object of Desire* Luis Buñuel parodied the alphabet soup of European guerrilla movements known by their initials. A similar phenomenon was developing elsewhere in Latin America. In those years revolutionary groups shifted from Cuban-style incursions in the countryside to attacks in the cities, particularly in the most developed countries of South America. In Argentina violence became a way of life without parallel elsewhere in Latin America. Some armed insurgents achieved a unique level of sophistication and milita-rization. The Montoneros, the Peronist revolutionaries, were by far the largest and most active urban guerrilla organization in Latin America.

Meanwhile other avenues to political action were opening for middle-class youth. Radical sectors emerged at the fringes of the traditionally con-servative Argentine Catholic Church in the wake of Vatican II and the Latin American Bishops' Conference in Medellín in 1968. Liberation theology attracted many Catholic high school and university students. In this po-liticized version of Catholic doctrine they found a justification for violent political struggle. They rejected liberal party politics, as well as the liberal principle of separation of the political and religious spheres. For some of them Peronism was the natural choice, since it cultivated the image of a na-tional movement in opposition to traditional politics and the liberal party system. The Catholic left converged with the radical left in the conviction that only revolutionary changes (by whatever means) could solve Argentina's problems. The example of Camilo Torres, a Colombian priest who joined the guerrillas and was killed in action, provided inspiration.[11] In 1968 the largely Peronist and leftist Movement of Priests for the Third World was of-ficially born.

Peronism enjoyed a massive revival with the politicization of the middle class. Until late in the 1960s, intellectuals found no common ground with the Peronists. Now Peronism came to symbolize rebellion against the anti-Peronist older generation, resistance to the dictatorship, and above all the object of the loyalty of the working class. Peronism was seen as the only movement that could lead Argentina to a nationalized version of socialism. For leftist Catholics, moreover, Peronism was a way to approach socialism without Marx. All these interpretations were encouraged by Perón, who adapted his discourse (although not his ideology) to the new conditions of the 1960s.[12] By 1970 few radical young people doubted the revolutionary potential of Peronism. By the early 1970s the return of Perón, then living in exile in Spain, had become an obsession. The establishment of Salvador Allende's Unidad Popular government in Chile in 1970 gave young Argentines reason to feel optimistic about establishing socialism in their own country. Finally in 1973 Perón returned and assumed the presidency for the third time, only to die in July 1974. During Perón's short term in office and its aftermath, the Peronist left painfully came to realize how misplaced their expectations had been.

The Politicization of the Intellectual Sphere

The radicalization of society had important consequences for the intellectual left. Revolution, which in the early 1960s had been seen as necessary but remote, now seemed not only possible but imminent. The line between political activism and intellectual activity became less clear. Intellectual activity became just another way of doing politics. "Today more than ever, when Latin America is heading toward revolutionary changes—witness the Cuban Revolution and the events in Chile . . . —literature cannot—should not—be separated from politics," declared a literary critic; "more than that, it should be subordinated to it."[13] The Sartrean model of the socially and politically "committed" intellectual was being displaced by a new model inspired by Fanon, the militant intellectual.[14]

A euphoric optimism displaced the collective guilt of the early 1960s. Then the problem had been to understand if and how intellectuals had a part to play in the revolutionary process, and if not, why not. By 1970 the problem was to define exactly what role the intellectual would play during and after the imminent establishment of the socialist order.[15] Defining just how far intellectuals could go in preserving their independence from politics, however, continued to be a preoccupation of some leftist intellectuals, especially after the Padilla affair. In 1971 the Cuban poet Heriberto Padilla was imprisoned by the Castro regime and forced to perform humiliating self-criticism in public. This was a turning point in the relationship between the revolutionary government of Cuba and progressive intellectuals. Many European and Latin American intellectuals, including Rossana Rossanda, Jean-Paul Sartre, and Mario Vargas Llosa, published a letter denouncing the treatment of Padilla. Reactions in Argentina were mixed. Many intellectuals agreed with the letter writers; the journal *Los Libros* denounced Padilla and his supporters and defended the Castro regime.[16]

When the line between the political and the intellectual spheres of activity became blurred and many leftist intellectuals turned to Perón, the world came to be seen as a set of dichotomies, the most important of which was dependency / liberation. The discourse of liberation had been common since

the 1960s, when dependency theory was first formulated in academic circles; but what had then been seen as a problem was now taken for granted as
a central fact of life to be dealt with in the analysis of society and politics.[17]
The writings of nationalist writers such as Juan José Hernández Arregui
and Arturo Jauretche, who also absorbed Marxist concepts, became required
reading, as did the works of revisionist historians who questioned the country's liberal heritage. The idea of liberation was so powerful that even a
right-wing neo-liberal party adopted the word for its election campaign in
1973.[18] The discourse of liberation of course had a personal, subjective dimension that made its adherents even more receptive to psychoanalysis.

In the environment of the late 1960s there was little room for the kind of
avant-garde experiences promoted by the Instituto Torcuato Di Tella. The
financial difficulties of the industrial firm that supported it and government
censorship might have killed the Di Tella in any case, but the defection of
artists was the death blow. Many artists who had been active in the institution broke their ties with it in the late 1960s on the ground that the activities it promoted were elitist and had nothing to do with the cultural needs
of "the people." The relationship between cultural and political avant-
gardism became more complex than ever before.[19]

In those turbulent years some popular theories found themselves with
strange bedfellows. Structuralism, which in the early 1960s had been of interest mostly to sociologists and some literary critics (curiously, less to anthropologists), became in the late 1960s a fashion that transcended the academic audience. Leftists who were most receptive to the structuralist fashion
became caught up in the works of Louis Althusser, usually through commentators.[20] The first issue of Cuadernos de Psicología Concreta freely mixed
Althusser's name with the discourse of anti-imperialism and dependency,
with generous references to Frantz Fanon.[21]

The tension between the rapid politicization of intellectual activity and
the specificity of discourses implicitly demanded by the "new knowledge"
was reflected in some of the most widely read cultural journals of the time.
The most prestigious of them, Los Libros ("a month of publications in Latin
America"), was devoted to the critical review of both fiction and nonfic-
tion. Here Althusser rubbed shoulders with Lacan, Noam Chomsky, and
Umberto Eco. The "specific discourse and rigorous method" the editors
promised to introduce to book criticism gradually gave way to the discourse
of dependency. In 1971 the slogan became "For a political criticism of culture"; in 1975 it became simply "Politics in culture." Emphasis on the specificity of discourses continued to be an important element of Los Libros'

project (despite charges of elitism), but the journal's position in the Padilla affair suggests that its commitment to intellectual autonomy was less than solid. After a series of changes in its editorial board, *Los Libros* became totally politicized. Book reviews gave way to political discussions. In 1975 Ricardo Piglia, one of the three members of the editorial board at the time, resigned over disagreement with the other two on the nature of Isabel Perón's government.

Psychoanalysis made its way into the political debates of the intellectual left on at least three levels, which were interconnected but for the sake of clarity will be discussed separately: (a) the politicization of psychoanalysis; (b) the acceptance of Lacanian psychoanalysis by people who had already accumulated symbolic capital in some other field and transferred that capital to psychoanalysis; and (c) the spread of the discourse of oppression and liberation beyond social classes to all victims of the capitalist order, such as inmates of madhouses. Psychoanalysts who made names for themselves in other fields helped the process along. Eduardo Pavlovsky, well known as a playwright, became notorious when he explored the psychology of torturers in *Señor Galíndez* in the early 1970s. The military, provoked to fury, put Pavlovsky on its death list after the coup of 1976. Another psychoanalyst who turned to writing was Emilio Rodrigué, whose novel *Heroína* (1969), a satirical treatment of the psychoanalytic establishment, was turned into a feature film.[22] *Heroína* put Rodrigué in the authors' guild, and literary journals interviewed him on literary matters.

The Politicization of Psychoanalysis

THE DEBATES OF 1965

In 1965 a group of psychologists organized a debate at the School of Philosophy on the relationship of ideology, psychology, and science. The discussions also addressed the limits of political commitment by psychologists and, by extension, by intellectuals in general. Among the invited debaters were José Bleger, León Rozitchner, Antonio Caparrós, Enrique Pichon Rivière, and Armando Bauleo. The debate of 1965 was a turning point. Positions that would be central to the later politicization of psychoanalysis were marked out there. Throughout the debate, unless I indicate otherwise, the term "psychology" is synonymous with "psychoanalysis."

Two positions became clear immediately. One was put forward by two of the APA members, Bleger and Pichon Rivière. The other position, with different nuances, was offered by Rozitchner, Antonio Caparrós, and Armando Bauleo (an APA member with strong ties to the left). Bleger emphasized the importance of maintaining the autonomy of the scientific fields and defended a humanistic conception of psychology. According to him, "there is a praxis of the scientific field that has to be respected, otherwise we will have 'self-mutilated' psychologists, deteriorated psychologists who, in other words, are neither psychologists nor ideologists." Psychologists with political commitments should work on two levels: the level of ideological and political commitment on the one hand and the level of scientific practice on the other. The two had to be clearly distinguished. Bleger's use of the term "self-mutilated" was not innocent. He was referring to Henri Lefevbre's characterization of Georges Politzer when he abandoned psychology after joining the Communist Party in 1929. The opposite of Politzer's self-mutilation was the case of Henri Wallon, the French psychologist who is credited with inspiring Lacan's theory of the mirror stage. Wallon shared Politzer's political commitment (like Politzer, he fought in the French Resistance) but he continued to do research and to publish on psychology. Bleger did not advocate total compartmentalization of ideology and scientific practice, but rather a distinction that would protect the autonomy of science. Psychologists had to establish links between science and the wider world, but they had to make sure their psychological practice was not tainted by their political ideology.

From a slightly different perspective, Pichon Rivière expressed a position that was compatible with his disciple's. For Pichon the basis for any therapeutic practice was what he called ECRO (*esquema conceptual, referencial, y operativo*), which provided the referential framework that included the psychologist's own ideology. Psychological practice, however, could take place only within the analytic framework. Political ideology had no part in actual psychological practice. For Pichon the criterion of the practicing psychologist should be effectiveness.

León Rozitchner and Antonio Caparrós could not have disagreed more. According to Rozitchner, a psychologist could link ideology and scientific practice in one of two ways: one could determine whether a particular behavior was or was not coherent with the ideology of the actor, without considering the truth of that ideology, or one could try to determine the level of truth involved in the particular ideology. For Rozitchner, the psychologist's task was to investigate the ideology to determine its truth. For Rozitchner, therefore, the practice of concrete psychology could not be restricted to the scientific field and had to address philosophical issues of truth, taking into account, in the Marxist sense, the multiple determinants of psychological developments. Otherwise, psychology would remain a prisoner of a bourgeois abstraction.

Antonio Caparrós agreed with Rozitchner in general but took a more radical view. For Caparrós, there was no possible distinction between the psychologist as a scientist and the psychologist as a political militant. "It is not enough to be a psychologist, one must be a man, [and] as a man he must seize his moment, his time, and act in accordance with certain goals. And as a psychologist he must be a militant who does psychology."[23] Thus psychology, which for Caparrós was not the same as psychoanalysis, could not be dissociated from ideology, and ideology had to be put into practice in political militancy. If for any reason militancy could not be reconciled with professional activity, it was clear that for Caparrós militancy always took precedence.

These debates delineated two kinds of intellectual. The one supported by Bleger, in the tradition of Sartre, was committed to political activity but as an intellectual. The other, which in its most radical form was promoted by Caparrós, was the militant intellectual who would be triumphant in the early 1970s. Science could make sense only as a subordinate part of political militancy.

The debates of 1965 proposed a general examination of the philosophical bases of psychology (meaning psychoanalysis). Should it be concerned with truth or be restricted to the working out and application of practical measures? What was the basis of such ideas as normality and disorder? This debate took the discussion of psychoanalysis much further than the APA was ready to go, and questioned the very basis of the psychoanalysis practiced and promoted in the official institution.

THE APA'S 'ANNUS HORRIBILIS':
THE PLATAFORMA–DOCUMENTO SECESSION

Since the mid-1960s psychologists had been much more open to politicization than most APA-affiliated analysts. Theoretically, the APA remained politically neutral; yet the earthquake that shook the analytic community in the early 1970s came from within the APA. Friction had riven the APA throughout the 1960s. Young candidates and associate members chafed against the APA's hierarchical structure and its training system. Many of these young members also worked in public hospitals, some in Mauricio Goldenberg's service in Lanús. Their experiences there put them in contact with a social and political world that was alien to the APA. Many of the young analysts were followers of Pichon Rivière and Bleger, who, within the limits imposed by their allegiance to the IPA, promoted a psychoanalysis committed to social and political goals.

The most progressive APA members absorbed the highly charged atmosphere of the 1960s. In 1969 some APA analysts went on strike to mourn the victims of political repression in Córdoba and bought space in major newspapers to publicize the issue. The APA's conservative leadership reacted with outrage.[24] The final crisis came as a result of a combination of local and international events. In 1969 the annual international psychoanalytic congress was convened in Rome. Still under the influence of the "spirit of '68," a group of young European analysts shunned the congress at the Rome Hilton and organized their own congress at a trattoria. There they debated the foundations of analytic training, the hierarchical structure of psychoanalytic institutions, the bourgeois ideology of psychoanalysis. The group wrote a political platform and henceforth was known as the International Platform. Some Argentines joined the movement and upon their return founded a local branch, Plataforma, led by Armando Bauleo and Hernán Kesselman, both junior members of the APA and both patients of Marie Langer. They were joined by a large group of junior and a few senior members, including Rodrigué, Langer, and Pavlovsky.

Plataforma set out to mobilize other members and politicize the APA, and some dissidents began to agitate openly in radical political groups and to participate actively in the FAP. Some of them approached Peronist revolutionary groups and developed ties with other leftist organizations. Broad political concerns were mixed with diatribes against the elitism of the APA. Soon another group emerged to demand the democratization of the institution. This group, called Documento, joined Plataforma in pressing for reform and radicalization.[25] At the International Psychoanalytic Congress of 1971, in Vienna, in a paper titled "Psychoanalysis and/or Social Revolution," Marie Langer recalled that in the 1930s she had given up Marxism for psychoanalysis; this time, she vowed, she would give up neither. When the APA's leadership refused to publish Langer's paper in the *Revista de Psicoanálisis,* the Plataforma and Documento groups resigned, thus giving up their affiliation with the IPA. Plataforma and Documento were soon joined by two philosophers who, from different points of view, were interested in psychoanalysis, León Rozitchner and Raúl Sciarreta, and by a large number of other high-profile intellectuals. Pichon Rivière and Bleger, considered the spiritual leaders of the two dissident groups, remained in the APA.

The secession of Plataforma and Documento produced some effect in the APA, although no official notice was taken of it. The APA's structure was eventually democratized. All full members could be training analysts, and associate members could now vote in the general assemblies and participate in the governance of the institution. Nonetheless, the organization that gathered all the politically committed (and now self-styled revolutionary) analysts was the FAP. Soon after the split, Marie Langer was elected to the FAP's presidency. The FAP, the APBA, and the Association of Psychopedagogues joined forces to found the Coordinadora de Trabajadores de Salud Mental, which gathered all "mental health workers" under equal conditions. Psychoanalysts, psychologists, psychiatrists, and nurses were all now "mental health workers," without distinction of rank. At the same time the Coordinadora created the Centro de Docencia e Investigación (CDI), led by analysts from Plataforma and Documento, which offered courses on psychoanalysis, Marxist philosophy, and a wide variety of other subjects to mental health workers. In a fashion typical of those times of political communion, the CDI operated for a time in an office provided without charge by the union of graphic workers, led by Raimundo Ongaro, leader of the CGTA. The FAP and CDI became by far the most radical professional organizations of the period.[26]

The CDI and the Coordinadora offered psychologists an opportunity to obtain analytic training outside of the APA, as well as professional recognition by prominent analysts. It is not surprising, therefore, that a large number of psychologists and radical psychiatrists joined the Coordinadora and took courses there. For leftist psychologists the CDI resolved two pressing issues: it offered professional recognition, since now psychoanalysts outside of the APA considered them colleagues, and they could make their political commitment compatible with their psychoanalytic practice. Both areas of activity were now perceived as two sides of the same coin.

Plataforma explained its split from the APA in an open letter addressed to "all mental health workers": the APA had distorted "real psychoanalysis." As the true representatives of "real psychoanalysis" they wanted to put their science "at the service of those ideologies that challenge, without compromise, the system that in our country is characterized by favoring the exploitation of the oppressed classes, by giving away our wealth to big monopolies, and by repressing all political manifestations that try to rebel against it."[27] Plataforma committed itself to joining the fight for national liberation and a socialist society. After this general statement, the communiqué turned into a detailed criticism of the hierarchical and elitist structure of the

APA and of its ideology. To the members of Plataforma the establishment of socialism seemed to be connected to the way the APA was organized. The Documento group issued a similar statement. They, too, linked their denunciation of the APA to their broader political project.

At the theoretical level, to place psychoanalysis at the service of the imminent revolution meant to expose the ideology behind the supposedly value-free official psychoanalysis and to explore ways of joining Marxism and psychoanalysis.[28] In this project the discovery of Wilhelm Reich's early works played a crucial role. In a way typical of the times, however, Reich's theories were combined in a kind of theoretical salad with citations from Althusser. At the practical level, the implications of the attempt at placing psychoanalysis at the service of the revolution were less clear. "We do not propose the elimination of individual treatment," said one member of Plataforma, "but we believe we should not ignore any theory or technique that reinforces our ideological positions." Another member of Plataforma said that the question "is not to offer cheap psychoanalysis. . . . We are also part of the system of production. As long as we act in this society . . . the relationship between analyst and patient is a commercial relationship, psychoanalysis is a consumer product."[29] Some analysts offered their services in shantytowns; others worked in public hospitals, in many cases without giving up their private practices.[30] A few were active in leftist political and armed organizations. Eduardo Pavlovsky, for instance, ran unsuccessfully for Congress as the candidate of the Partido Socialista de los Trabajadores (PST), a Trotskyite party. During the dictatorship established in 1976 some *plataformistas* who remained in the country became active in human rights organizations. Many had to go into exile and at least one of them disappeared.

The secession of Plataforma and Documento had vast repercussions in the media and in society at large. The episode certainly had important consequences for the development and diffusion of psychoanalysis in Argentina. It broke the APA's hegemony over the practice of psychoanalysis. More important, it put into question the need for an institutional framework for the practice of psychoanalysis. The dissidents' work in hospitals and shantytowns made psychoanalysis available and widely known as a leftist psychiatric theory. Their well-publicized split from the APA made psychoanalysis a topic of discussion and debate among leftist intellectuals and won it further publicity when debates on its politicization were published in such journals as *Nuevo Hombre* and *Los Libros*.

In those journals the debates on psychoanalysis were part of general discussions about the autonomy of intellectual work. "The conflict that agitates the psychoanalytic institution . . . seems to be a sign of a general situation that includes us all, since the problems it exposes are linked to the future of culture, that is, with the political future of the whole country," proclaimed *Los Libros*.[31] The conflict within the APA was just one more piece of evidence that the liberal distinction between professional life and political life was no longer workable in the supposedly prerevolutionary 1970s. Psychoanalysis, like literature, was just one of the areas in which the relationship between intellectual and political activities had to be specified. Like literary critics, filmmakers, and writers, radical analysts claimed for their field a place in antiestablishment and revolutionary intellectual activities.

The secession of Plataforma and Documento drew critical comments from various sectors of the intellectual left.[32] The Marxist Raúl Sciarreta, for instance, resigned from Plataforma only a month after the separation from the APA. A philosopher, he had been educating psychologists and other members of the psy community on the works of Marx, Althusser, and Lacan in private seminars for years. His letter of resignation pointed to what he saw as some of the most serious problems affecting the Plataforma project. Plataforma assigned itself a leading role in the organization of mental health workers, thus reproducing the hierarchical structure it claimed to be fighting against. Sciarreta also took issue with Plataforma's ideological rigidity and intolerance. He criticized what he considered to be Plataforma's empty revolutionary rhetoric, its populism, and its antitheoretical stand. Sciarreta characterized Plataforma's ideology as infantile. What he was demanding was the autonomy of the intellectual without denying the importance of political commitment.[33]

Another problem that Plataforma and Documento had to face was the political heterogeneity of its members. Some were leftist Peronist militants; others belonged to various Marxist groups; at least one was a Communist. Many of them, however, had had no previous political experience and tried to learn everything, from Marxist theory to versions of psychoanalysis not endorsed by the APA, as quickly as possible. "We were not street-wise enough," Emilio Rodrigué acknowledges today. Moreover, for some of the Plataforma leaders (particularly the more senior ones, who were in general the ones with the least political experience), the whole movement was part of a broader existential experience that included a ludic element and some frivolity.[34] Rodrigué admits now that among the contributors to the turmoil of the Plataforma project "I would add, believe it or not, La Casona." La Casona was a house Rodrigué rented with Pavlovsky, Bauleo, and Kesselman, a sort of fraternity house cum New Age commune. The ludic spirit that permeated the experience is made clear in Rodrigué's *Anti-yoyo,* a slightly fictionalized account of the whole period.[35] This frivolous dimension of the experience alienated some of the veteran leftists. Unable to overcome its internal contradictions (and the narcissism of its members, according to Rodrigué), Plataforma dissolved only a year after the secession.[36] Despite the group's short life, however, the Plataforma-Documento episode had long-term consequences for both the psy community and the intellectual left.

Although the theoretical and political limitations of the Plataforma-Documento project were quickly noted, the break with the APA made psychoanalysis a subject of lively interest among the intellectual left. For the first time cultural and literary journals discussed it seriously.

In August 1971 Hernán Kesselman, one of the founding members of Plataforma, published an article in the leftist journal *Nuevo Hombre* (he was on its editorial board). It was the first time the journal had published anything related to psychoanalysis.[37] Kesselman's article was a short discussion of the history of the International Platform movement and of its main ideological thrust. His general line of argument echoed Plataforma's manifesto: "Intellectualism will be overcome only to the extent that psychoanalysts are able not only to integrate themselves with the other militant intellectuals but to blend with the most exploited sectors of the population in order to carry out together the fight to the finish."[38]

How this integration and this "blending" would take place was never made explicit. Kesselman's paper incorporated some populist themes. A new social order, national liberation, and some Peronist slogans ("economic freedom, social justice, and political sovereignty") were presented as prerequisites for a general ideological revision of psychoanalysis, which in turn would help to achieve national liberation in a kind of dialectical process.

A few months later Antonio Caparrós responded to Kesselman in a critical article.[39] Caparrós started by denying the possibility of an alliance between psychoanalysis, whose aim was to adapt and adjust patients to the system, and anti-imperialist revolution. Psychoanalysts could ally themselves with the most exploited sectors of the population only as militants, never as psychoanalysts, since psychoanalysis was ideologically tainted. According to Caparrós, the incompatibility of psychoanalysis and revolution had been proved in Cuba, where he had been invited by Che Guevara in the mid-1960s to carry out an experiment on the use of "moral incentives."[40] That experiment was possible, Caparrós claimed, only after he had completely abandoned all psychoanalytic theoretical formulations. Note that Caparrós could not have "abandoned" psychoanalytic formulations unless he had embraced them in the first place; psychoanalysis had managed to penetrate the thought even of its critics. For Caparrós, then, Plataforma's intention to blend Marxism and psychoanalysis and put psychoanalysis at the service of the revolution was a fool's errand because psychoanalysis, as a bourgeois and ideologically reactionary practice, was essentially antirevolutionary. Plataforma's project was therefore wrong in its very foundations.

The psychologist Miriam Chorne and the sociologist Juan Carlos Torre offered another line of criticism in *Los Libros*. They concentrated on the ideological and theoretical limitations of the psychoanalytic rebels. According to them, the APA's claim of political and ideological neutrality was in fact an alibi for a practice that was highly ideologized and that thus required a complete overhaul. The problems confronted by psychoanalysts who questioned not only the institution but also the foundations of their own science were not very different from the problems confronted by other intellectuals and professionals. The issue, in Chorne and Torre's view, was that Plataforma and Documento had little to offer in exchange. Their programmatic poverty was the result of the political and social isolation that the psychoanalytic institution imposed on its members, which affected even the dissidents. Plataforma and Documento gave up the canonical responses to reality provided by the APA, but to meet the new challenges they had available only "the deficiencies of the world they are now abandoning."[41] Their lack of analytical tools and political contacts forced psychoanalysts to a desperate and somehow uncritical search for them. This desperate search resulted in a bland theoretical eclecticism evident in the list of courses offered by the Centro de Docencia e Investigación, which ranged from Marxist economics to psychoanalysis to cybernetics, in no particular order.

Moreover, if Marxism worked as a "unifying myth" for the rebels, the concrete relationship between Marxism and psychoanalysis was never specified. "What is the specific practice of psychoanalysis in which contact between Marxism and psychoanalysis could take place?" ask Chorne and Torre. Plataforma and Documento had no answer to this crucial question. For Chorne and Torre, the main limitation of the Plataforma-Documento project was the theoretical and political limitations of the people involved in it. Psychoanalysis did have a revolutionary potential, but more theoretical precision was needed to uncover it, and Torre and Chorne doubted that the dissident psychoanalysts were able to provide it.

Roberto Harari, a former president of the APBA, and the writer Germán García offered another line of debate. Both were studying Lacan's theories but not in the same group. García was a friend and disciple of Oscar Masotta; Harari approached Lacan independently. Although the targets of their criticisms were not the same, their opinions had similar theoretical bases.

Roberto Harari stepped into the debate in response to Caparrós and Kesselman.[42] While Kesselman and Caparrós assumed that there could be a relationship (positive for Kesselman, negative for Caparrós) between psychoanalysis and revolution, Harari shifted the debate to a totally different level. Basing his argument on Althusser's work, Harari contended that there could be no conceivable link between the two terms. Psychoanalysis is a science and has to be understood as such. Thus it has nothing to do either with ideology (which by definition is not scientific) or with any political discourse. According to Caparrós, psychoanalysts reinforced the system and therefore could not be agents of its destruction. Harari refuted this argument by reminding readers that, according to Marx, workers also reinforced the system through their work in factories, yet it was up to them as revolutionary militants to fight for the destruction of the system that exploited them. In other words, for Harari it made no sense to use the profession as a base for political activism; there was (and should be) a clear distinction between scientific activity and political militancy. This sharp distinction between the intellectual and the political contradicted not only the recent tendency to subordinate intellectual activity to politics but also Sartre's old model of the "committed intellectual."

Harari was more radical than Bleger in insisting on the autonomy of the scientific sphere. Although Bleger had never abandoned psychoanalysis, he believed it was possible to strip the Freudian system of its ideological contents and create a "concrete psychology" based on its valid elements. For Harari the discourse of science and the discourse of ideology were totally independent. Science is revolutionary in itself because it "decenters the recognition / ignorance" axis to which people are bound before new scientific territory is opened. Science should not be considered a mere "superstructural reflex" of a given mode of production.[43] For Harari, then, it made absolutely no sense to politicize psychoanalysis.

Harari also took issue with Caparrós's claim that a nonpsychoanalytic psychological theory could be revolutionary. Harari's response was (again) that anyone working within the current system of domination (whatever the theoretical foundation of the practice in question) was, *as a professional,* reproducing the system. More important, "it is impossible to understand how any theoretical scheme can provide an explanation for the individual's deep motivations without using the formal and abstract concept of the unconscious. An unconscious that is neither bourgeois nor proletarian." Psychoanalysis, the science of the unconscious, was the only psychological theory that could offer such an explanation.

Germán García's criticism was based on similar premises. According to García, the problem was less the relations between politics and psychoanalysis, which for him, as for Harari, belonged to different realms, than the theoretical poverty of the rebels. Whereas Torre and Chorne had emphasized Plataforma and Documento's lack of political sophistication, García pointed out their lack of psychoanalytic refinement. A "right" approach to psychoanalysis could not be obtained through political activism, as the dissidents argued, but by way of a "return to Freud" through the reading of Lacan. "Psychoanalysts' political declarations and practices run the risk of becoming an alibi for theoretical blindness in their scientific practice."[44] The explosion of the psy realm in the 1960s and particularly the emergence of a nonmedical Lacanian movement made possible paradoxical situations like this. García, who had no formal analytic training or even a university degree, felt no qualms about lecturing on psychoanalysis to people who until very recently had been at the top of the hierarchy of the institution that claimed a monopoly on its legitimate practice.

Against Plataforma's voluntarism and humanism García opposed a vision of reality based on Lacanian structuralism in which human actions and beliefs were predetermined by the structure of desire; deciphering that structure was the task of psychoanalysis. The issue was not to ignore psychoanalysis in order to do politics, since political activity and ideas were also determined by "the anguish put in play in relation to the risk of pain and death."

Harari and García, despite their difference in focus, agreed on one crucial point. Psychoanalysis was essentially revolutionary not because it could be joined with Marxism or because it could be used for revolutionary purposes but because of its very nature, as the science of the unconscious and of desire. García warned *plataformistas* not to "drown in political rhetoric—or practice—the other part of the psychoanalytic revolution: the analysis of desire. . . ."[45]

The debates that followed the politicization of psychoanalysis went beyond the psy community. Debates on the possible relationship between psychoanalysis and revolution were not new in Argentina, but they had been limited to insiders. When psychoanalysis became politicized, it became a concern far beyond psychoanalytic circles. Now it became part of the general discussion of the relationship between intellectuals and politics.

Paradoxically, it entered those discussions also through a movement that eventually took it back out of politics—Lacanianism.

Lacanianism: The Emergence of the Psychoanalyst Intellectual

The introduction and diffusion of Lacanian psychoanalysis in Argentina is a complex and controversial subject. Critics emphasize the alleged political neutrality of this kind of psychoanalysis, and the fact that it expanded dramatically during the dictatorship that ruled the country between 1976 and 1983. Those were the years when politically active analysts were persecuted and killed. Lacanians heatedly deny this charge; they, too, they say, were victims of the brutal repression unleashed in the late 1970s. I do not propose to enter this debate; my interest here is in exploring how and to what extent Lacanianism was another means of spreading concern about psychoanalysis among the broad generality of intellectuals.

The early reception of Lacanianism in Argentina has been linked to the name of Oscar Masotta ever since the publication of his article on Lacan in 1965. In 1969 Masotta founded the Grupo Lacaniano de Buenos Aires, a group of leftist intellectuals (psychologists, philosophers, literary critics, and a few M.D.'s whom Masotta wooed in an effort to increase his project's legitimacy), devoted to the study of Lacan's theory.[46] Soon the group started its own journal, *Cuadernos Sigmund Freud,* and became the seed of the first formal Lacanian analytic institution in the Spanish-speaking world: the Escuela Freudiana de Buenos Aires. According to his former friend León Rozitchner, Masotta transformed himself from the bohemian Sartrean intellectual of the early 1960s into an authoritarian institutional leader in the early 1970s.[47] Soon after establishing his school (which suffered a split, in the typical Lacanian fashion), Masotta went into exile in Europe. He died there in 1979, after founding other Lacanian schools in Spain and "presenting" his Argentine school to the French master.[48]

Masotta's prestige attracted so many intellectuals to Lacanianism that it became quite fashionable in Buenos Aires. Not all members of the Lacanian community found Lacan through Masotta, however, and not all of them joined his institution. Many leftist intellectuals became interested in Lacan's works through their earlier independent interest in structuralism and all French intellectual fashions, and particularly through their reading of Althusser.[49] I am not suggesting that all Argentine readers of Althusser (or of his commentators) made the transition to Lacanianism, but Althusser's words carried such great weight among influential segments of the Argentine left that he certainly did make Lacanian psychoanalysis attractive to them.

In 1964 Althusser published an article on Freud and Lacan that was soon translated into Spanish.[50] That article legitimized psychoanalysis for the left as an autonomous science. Althusser had become such a cultural icon that his word of approval was akin to a papal imprimatur. Only Lacan, he claimed, had managed "to seek out, discern and delineate in [Freud] the theory from which all the rest emerged." Therefore, it was only through the key provided by Lacan that Freud's scientific theory could be understood. Althusser emphasized the nonhumanistic aspects of Lacan's theory: the little biological entity (the infant) becomes a human being under the Law of the symbolic Order that is external to him or her. "Where a superficial or tendentious reading of Freud saw childhood only as happy and without laws, the paradise of 'polymorphous perversity,' . . . Lacan shows the effectiveness of the Order, of the Law, lying in wait, from before birth, for every infant to be born and seizing on him from his very first cry to assign him to his place and role and thus his forced destination."[51] It is in submission to the Law of Order imposed by beneficent castration that "normality" resides. Finally, Althusser had sharp words for orthodox psychoanalysis as it was promoted by the IPA. According to Althusser, psychoanalysis could not be reduced to a therapeutic technique, as the Americans were doing. Rather, it was a full-fledged science with its own object of study: the unconscious, which was not reducible to the domain of any other science.

Althusser's reading of Lacan's reading of Freud—or, to be more precise, Argentine Lacanians' reading of Althusser's reading of Lacan's reading of Freud[52]—could not be further from Rozitchner's interpretation of the Freudian system (or from Bleger's, for that matter). It was also far from Plataforma's approach to psychoanalysis. The issue was neither to try to uncover the "concrete" elements of psychoanalysis in order to de-ideologize it nor to try to mix Marxism with psychoanalysis in order to put it at the service of revolution. Psychoanalysis' role was rather to uncover the unavoidable subjection of the subject to the symbolic order through castration. Psychoanalytic humanism had no place in the new system. As García pointed out, "from generation to generation [people have passed] through grids that produce men who cannot themselves produce those grids."[53] When Lacanians referred to culture, they were not talking about capitalist society in particular, as Rozitchner believed Freud was, but were concerned with an ahistorical symbol system. Psychoanalysis' revolutionary nature was essential to it as the science of the unconscious, which decentered the Cartesian subject. Any political revolution that ignored the subjection of the subject to the symbolic order through castration was therefore futile.[54] It is not surprising that while at least some members of the Plataforma group supported the armed struggle, few Lacanians were involved in it. For many analysts who had once been members of radical organizations, Lacanian psychoanalysis substituted for political militancy rather than complemented it.[55]

Lacanians started by defining themselves in opposition to orthodox psychoanalysis as it was practiced by the APA. The bases of their objections, however, were different from those of Plataforma or any other politicized group. The problem with the APA, according to the Lacanians, was not its claim to ideological neutrality but its abandonment of the real Freud in favor of such people as Melanie Klein and Ernest Jones, who claimed (wrongly) to have completed the master's theory.[56] Another of the Lacanians' targets was the ritualized psychoanalytic practice promoted by the APA, with its emphasis on the Kleinian "setting." The two technical issues the Lacanians contested most vehemently were the system of training analysis ("the analyst authorizes himself," said Lacan, although he himself considered the analyst's own analysis as a central element of his or her training) and the fixed duration of the analytic session.[57] Paradoxically, the Lacanians became great institution founders themselves, establishing a highly ritualized system of their own, which predictably led to multiple divisions and criticisms.

For Lacanians the only "right" reading of Freud was Lacan's. "Lacan's theory is psychoanalytic theory as it can and must be read in Freud's texts." Lacanians took their identification with the French master to an extreme. In their texts it is sometimes difficult to understand whose voice we are hearing. Is it Lacan's? Is it the Argentine Lacanian's? Or is it Lacan's through the Argentine Lacanian's? Here is Oscar Masotta on Melanie Klein: "What do we think about Melanie Klein? From the beginning it is easy to guess we are not Kleinians. . . . Lacan, however, is cautious."[58] It seems that Lacan's caution qualifies Masotta's reservations toward Melanie Klein.

If Lacanians had the magic key to the correct reading of Freud, however, there was one important dimension of the analytic experience that most of them missed, since their background was in most cases not medical: clinical experience. This limitation, in Masotta's view, was only partial: "Some will perhaps feel scandalized by our lack of clinical experience: we don't hide it, although in some of us it no longer exists, in others it's only temporary. In still others—the older ones, as in my case—it's a sentence. But who knows? . . . There are the texts, which are not so easy to read, and which in good Lacanianism are as levelheaded as clinical experience."[59] Thus the text substitutes for clinical experience. The lack of clinical experience surprised Maud Mannoni, an influential French analyst whom Masotta invited to Buenos Aires with her husband, Octave (another important analyst) in 1972.[60]

Their clinical limitations notwithstanding, Lacanians publicly attacked the official psychoanalytic institution. At least two themes converged in these attacks. Lacanians (especially psychologists) used Lacanianism as a battering ram against the APA's monopoly on legitimate psychoanalysis. Lacanian analysis offered itself as an alternative source of legitimacy and international connections for an analytic practice outside of the IPA.[61] Another line of attack was more theoretical. As early as 1969 Oscar Masotta published an article in the *Revista Argentina de Psicología* fiercely criticizing some writings of Emilio Rodrigué. The very beginning of the piece is a good example of the kind of rhetorical exercise on which Lacanians were so keen: "It is Althusser—who reads Marx not without having read Lacan—who suggests the task: to read Freud." As Germán García points out wittily, there was not much Rodrigué could do to Marx, Althusser, Lacan, and Freud all together in just one sentence.[62] The APA's version of psychoanalysis came in for its share of scorn: "What is repressed is Freud." Rodrigué responded with acid humor.[63] Masotta's debate with Rodrigué was probably the first time the APA had ever received such sharp criticism on *theoretical* grounds from someone who was totally outside the official psychoanalytic establishment; Masotta wasn't even a psychologist, and not only was he denying the APA's right to dictate what psychoanalysis was and was not, he was lecturing its president on how to read Freud.

Lacanian psychoanalysis quickly found a place in discussions carried on in other fields. Lacan's theory was seen as (and in fact was) one of the intellectual currents then in fashion. Many Lacanians had become well known in other fields before they discovered psychoanalysis. If Masotta was able to have his piece against Rodrigué published in a forum of psychologists, it was because he had been (in the words of Beatriz Sarlo) an "intellectual beacon" for a whole generation of Argentine intellectuals. Similarly, Germán García had become famous through his novels and works of criticism.[64] Such people could easily introduce Lacanian psychoanalysis into discussions that presumably were about something else altogether.

Masotta published numerous articles on Lacanian psychoanalysis in such cultural journals as *Los Libros,* where psychoanalysis was placed among the social sciences. In his articles psychoanalysis was a theory, not a therapy. To understand Lacanian psychoanalysis, according to Massota, one would do

well to have a good grounding in the problem of signification as it was debated not only in linguistics but also in the "intertextuality of Althusserian
Marxism, the epistemological debate of poststructuralism, the discussion
about the science of ideology, Derrida's antiphoneticism."[65] Later, however,
Lacanian psychoanalysts so effectively emphasized the clinical aspect of their
practice that they became central figures in the Argentine psychoanalytic establishment.[66] Whereas knowledge of Lacanian psychoanalysis in the United
States has been limited largely to the academic world (especially to depart-
ments of comparative literature), in Latin America, and in particular in
Argentina, it has become, in spite of its origins, a widely used therapeutic
technique.

Lacanian psychoanalysis opened a space for the convergence of psychoanalysis and literature. Grupo Cero, a semimarginal group of psychoanalyst-
poets who had remained outside the APA (though they claimed Pichon
Rivière as an intellectual mentor) and who supported Plataforma at the beginning, approached Lacanianism before moving to Spain in 1976.[67] More
consequences would flow from the writings of Germán García, who introduced Lacanian concepts in his writings on literature. In 1973 he launched a
literary journal, *Literal,* with a group of like-minded writers.[68] The language
of the journal was heavily loaded with Lacanian terminology and concepts,
and it also published fragments of Lacan's writings translated by Masotta.

The first issue of *Literal* included two articles that are worth examining
briefly. The first one, titled suggestively "No matar la palabra, no dejarse
matar por ella" ("Not to kill the word, not to allow oneself to be killed for
it"), is a kind of manifesto of autonomous literature. "The desire that literature talks about is not appropriate for the pleasures . . . that history pro-
poses." *Literal* dismissed the very idea of literature committed to a cause,
a matter that was at the core of the intellectual debates of the time. What
Literal proposed was not art for art's sake but art just because. While the general inclination was to subordinate literature (and intellectual activity in
general) to politics, *Literal* advised its readers not to allow themselves to be
killed for words. The second of the articles was a reference to the current
political situation dated July 1973; that is, after Perón's triumph. While most
leftist intellectuals were (briefly) euphoric about the Peronist utopia,[69] *Literal*
declared that "all objects proposed to fill a void only underline the inade-
quacy of the responses to the question they are intended to silence." The
project of (Peronist) restoration was impossible in itself.

Lacanians' attempt to separate the sphere of psychoanalysis from the
sphere of politics provoked sharp reactions from those who were trying to

erase the line between them. Lacanians had been colonized; they were petits bourgeois; they were trapped in the rigidities of science; and so on. It is true that Lacanians' identification with the French master and the movement he founded led many of them to ape debates that were taking place in France and that made sense only in the French context. As a prominent Lacanian put it, they covered their faces with the mask of Lacan. This "colonization" sometimes became grotesque, particularly after the terror unleashed by the military dictatorship established in 1976. Hugo Vezzetti claims that Lacanians gradually shut themselves up in their own institutional disputes, sheltered from social reality by their obscure jargon and their obsession with the signifier.[70] This tendency, however, was not evident at the beginning. Masotta, for one, never abandoned his political commitment. For him and others like him the value of psychoanalysis was still linked to its essential subversiveness. As Masotta himself declared in 1973, in one of the most political pieces he wrote during his Lacanian period, like it or not, psychoanalysis will always be an ally of any authentic liberation process.[71]

Psychoanalysis and the Discourse of Oppression

The discovery of mental patients as an oppressed group within the oppressive system of the mental hospital gave psychoanalysis another boost into the discourse of the intellectual left. By the early 1970s the discourse of oppression and liberation was widespread. Despite the long history of reforms, the situation in public mental hospitals was (and still is) deplorable. Up to the 1960s, discussions of conditions there were limited largely to medical circles; now politics entered into them. The antipsychiatry movement was gaining converts in Europe and the United States. The experiments and writings of Ronald Laing and David Cooper in England, Thomas Szasz in the United States, and Franco Basaglia in Italy, partially inspired by Erving Goffman's works on "total institutions," were discussed and read beyond the psy community. In 1969 Cooper visited Argentina to deliver a series of lectures.[72] Meanwhile the works of Michel Foucault, particularly his *Histoire de la folie*, and later Gilles Deleuze and Félix Guattari's *Anti-Oedipus* were translated into Spanish. From different starting points these authors converged on the claim that madness was a social construction and that mental hospitals were agents of social control rather than therapeutic institutions; they challenged the very concepts of schizophrenia and therapy.

Some leftists began to think of mental institutions in a general cultural context that placed emphasis also on "personal liberation," and on psychoanalysis as a means to attain it. In the national liberation to which all sectors of the left were committed, all oppressed groups had to be liberated, including mental patients. As *El Descamisado,* the journal of the young Peronists, proclaimed, the Peronist revolution had to be taken to the mental hospitals too.[73] *Crisis,* a widely read leftist magazine of the time that was published under the direction of Eduardo Galeano, the author of *The Open Veins of Latin America,* devoted a large part of one issue to poetry and other artistic works produced by mental patients. One of the patients represented had been a well-known poet in the 1920s, close to the literary avant-garde group associated with the journal *Martín Fierro.* Their contributions were presented as "cultural creations of oppressed men who are part of an oppressed social class and live in very painful conditions in a country that has also been oppressed."[74] The recovery of the voices of the mental patients fitted into *Crisis'* broader project of erasing the distinction between "popular" and "high" culture, and of giving visibility to those who were traditionally marginalized and oppressed by mainstream culture.

Mental health was at the convergence of political and theoretical concerns. As *Los Libros* pointed out, the mental health field had been aboil with political and professional mobilization and theoretical discussions on psychoanalysis, its relationship with Marxism, and so on.[75] Oppression, liberation, and dependency figured prominently in all the responses to a set of questions that *Los Libros* submitted to a group of mental health professionals. All the respondents saw the frightful conditions of the mental health system as a functional part of a society they defined as dependent. The liberation of mental health patients was just one more aspect of the national and social liberation project. Pichon Rivière, reversing his position of 1965, concluded that psychiatrists, sociologists, and other mental health workers were part of the "apparatus of domination," since madness was a social construction. Gregorio Baremblit and others reached similar conclusions.

How does psychoanalysis fit into these debates? The somatic therapies used in public mental institutions were perceived as instruments devised by the establishment to oppress people whose behavior deviated from the norm it prescribed. Neuropsychiatry was perceived as nothing but an instrument wielded by the dominant to maintain their dominance.[76] Miriam Chorne and others took Wilbur Grimson to task for using some somatic therapies in his therapeutic communities when he considered it necessary.[77] If the only possible nonrepressive therapy was psychotherapy and psychoanalysis was the only psychotherapy that had a solid scientific foundation, then clearly psychoanalysis was the therapy of choice. Moreover, most antipsychiatry movements either had psychoanalysis as their point of departure or were based on some aspect of psychoanalytic theory. Furthermore, traditional psychiatrists' opposition to psychoanalysis made it the necessary point of departure for any critical approach to mental health. The politicization of psychoanalysis and its legitimization by the left added a dimension to the opposition between traditional repressive psychiatry and liberating psychoanalysis. In his "Salud mental" Vezzetti discussed how the traditional psychiatry that rejected Freud was used as a mechanism of social control by the capitalist state.[78] Politicized psychoanalysis, according to Vezzetti and others, provided the only possible means for the liberation of mental patients. The discourse of oppression and liberation, then, was another way for the left to spread the message of psychoanalysis.

NINE

The Aftermath

The euphoria that greeted the return of Juan Perón and the restoration of democracy soon dissolved in blood. The violence that right- and left-wing Peronists unleashed against each other during the massive demonstration to welcome Perón back on June 20, 1973, was only a mild preview of what was to come. Terrorism had started before that. After Perón took power for the third time later that year, it became painfully clear to the young leftists who had fought for his return that their expectations had been badly misplaced. Far from being the revolutionary leader they wanted to see in him, Perón openly backed his right-wing supporters, particularly the deeply corrupt union bureaucracy.[1] In a heart-wrenching episode, during his last public appearance, on May Day 1974, Perón expelled the radical young Peronists from the Plaza de Mayo, a place of symbolic significance for the Peronist movement.

Perón's third wife, María Estela Martínez, known as Isabel, was his vice president. When he died in July 1974, she became the first female head of state in the hemisphere. During Isabel Perón's administration conditions deteriorated rapidly and Argentina descended into chaos. The most corrupt and reactionary of her husband's supporters were in total control of the state. The minister of social welfare, an obscure character who had been Perón's personal secretary and was known for his interest in black magic (he was nicknamed "El Brujo," the Witch), became the most powerful figure in the government. He organized the Anticommunist Argentine Alliance, the infamous Triple A, dedicated to the killing of leftist militants and sympathizers. The leftist guerrillas continued their operations against both military and civilian targets, turning the country into a battlefield. The economy collapsed and inflation soared.

In this situation it is not surprising that the military junta that took power on March 24, 1976, received broad support. The austere generals and admirals who overthrew Isabel Perón promised to reestablish morality in government, put order in the economy by freeing it from state constraints, and "eradicate" subversive (i.e., leftist) elements.[2] In fact, guerrilla activity was already in sharp decline when the military took power. A decree signed by the previous government had given them full authority to "exterminate" leftist subversion, and the army had mounted a full-scale offensive. The Proceso de Reorganización Nacional (Process of National Reorganization, the name the military gave to their government) opened a new and dark era in Argentine history.

Deeply influenced by the doctrine of national security, the generals placed terror at the center of their strategy for disciplining and demobilizing the population. During the eight years of military rule an undetermined number of people—estimates range from 9,000 to 30,000—disappeared without a trace. Most of them were tortured before being murdered by military or paramilitary groups.[3] The terror supposedly targeted "subversives"—a term that covered not only guerrillas but anyone who opposed or even questioned the new regime—but the Proceso's state terrorism gained a dynamic of its own. The terror was fed by a variety of factors, including conflicts within the armed forces. Under the aegis of a presumably centralized authoritarian state, armed bands operated with little control. Terror was also an instrument for personal gain. Illegal detentions were followed by the looting of the belongings of the victims, who were sometimes forced to sign documents transferring their property to the military officers who had kidnapped and tortured them. Nobody was exempt from the terror. The military tortured children in front of their parents or forced them to witness their parents' torture to extract information that often did not exist. Pregnant women were tortured, and when they finally delivered (if they did not miscarry during the torture), their babies were taken away and given to childless couples well connected to the military. Most such mothers were killed after delivery. The culture of terror served as a support for an economic program designed to redistribute income from industry and the working class to the financial interests. Speculation became the only rewarding economic activity. Economic policy and terror complemented each other in the Proceso's program of social control.[4]

Although the majority of victims of state repression were workers and union activists, the leaders of the Proceso made it clear from the beginning that they considered progressive intellectuals to be among the most dangerous groups. According to the generals, the war they were fighting was not limited to armed confrontations with guerrilla groups; it had to be fought also (perhaps principally) at the ideological level. Educators, from kindergarten teachers to university professors, and intellectuals in general had to be closely scrutinized because they were potential fifth columnists of international subversion. It is not by chance that 21 percent of the "disappeared" were students (including high school students);[5] professionals accounted for another 10 percent.[6] As the military governor of Buenos Aires Province declared, "The guerrilla is only the armed expression of an ideology that infiltrates and works within the university, in schools, in the press, in the arts, in industry, using a thousand deceitful modes of operation."[7] Suspect schoolteachers and university professors were dismissed and persecuted. Some of them went into exile; others disappeared or were brutally tortured. The educational system at all levels was soon placed in the hands of reactionaries who took it upon themselves to restore the "traditional Christian values" that supposedly were the basis of Argentine life.[8] As Juan Corradi points out, "right-wing Argentina offered the spectacle of a young country defending mythical old values, of a modern melting pot worshipping traditions it never had, of conservatives with little to conserve."[9] The universities were virtually placed under military control, particularly those schools and programs that were fertile ground for "subversion": the social sciences.[10]

For the psy professions the political wind had started to shift even before the coup of 1976. In 1975 Marie Langer was forced into exile for the second time in her life, this time to Mexico, when a patient revealed to her that her name had been placed on the Triple A's death list. Right-wing paramilitary groups raided the highly politicized APBA. The CDI was dissolved in part as a result of its own internal tensions, but when the Proceso was established, the situation could only become worse. Progressive psychiatric services that had been established in the 1960s were forcibly closed and their staffs summarily dismissed. Mauricio Goldenberg was forced to leave the country after two of his children were killed by the military. Dr. Valentín Baremblit, his successor in Lanús, was dismissed and later arrested and tortured; eventually he was released on condition that he leave the country. Since then he has lived in Spain. One staff member of the Lanús service disappeared and was never heard of again. Other progressive psychiatric services suffered a similar fate. The rationale behind this repression was made explicit by a naval officer in 1976: "Mental health centers had been turned into centers of subversive indoctrination.... [There the armed forces found] presses devoted to the preparation of pornographic material, sexual promiscuity among psychiatric patients encouraged by propaganda that justified it as a kind of liberation from psychiatric depression."[11]

Well-known progressive psychoanalysts who had been politically active were arrested and persecuted. Eduardo Pavlovsky escaped through a window of his consulting room in the middle of a group therapy session as heavily armed men in masks burst through the door. Others had to move their homes and consulting rooms periodically in order to avoid being abducted. Beatriz Perossio, president of the APBA, was not the only one who was kidnapped and never seen again. For the military any theory that questioned the traditional family and social models was a potential weapon in the hands of the subversives. As one of the generals in power declared, Freud and Marx were ideological criminals. An intelligence source consulted by *Somos,* a popular political and cultural magazine that provided unqualified support to the Proceso, revealed that "from the beginning of the war against subversion, among the information evaluated was the relationship of psychoanalysis to terrorism. . . . It has been proved that many subversives were enlisted in the active fight after spending time on the analyst's couch."[12]

Despite this kind of rhetoric, the actual consequences of the Proceso for the psy professions are not altogether clear. Although it has been said many times that psychologists and psychoanalysts were singled out for repression, the charge cannot be confirmed. Members of the psy professions who were persecuted, like the lawyers, artists, and journalists who suffered reprisals, were targeted less because of their profession than because of their real or alleged leftist sympathies or their opposition to the regime. Langer is a case in point. So is Pavlovsky. He had been anathema to the military since he ran for Congress as a Trotskyite and turned a spotlight on state-sponsored torture in his play *Señor Galíndez*.[13]

At the time of her disappearance, Perossio was a leading member of Vanguardia Comunista, a Maoist party that supported the Montoneros, the most powerful guerrilla group. The whole directorate of the party disappeared, while psychologists among the party's low-ranking members and former members were left alone.[14] In general the military targeted analysts who had participated in the Plataforma-Documento affair, particularly those who had been active in the CDI. But again, this selective repression seems to have been based more on those analysts' political allegiance than on their profession. Overall, between 30 and 60 psychologists and only a handful of psychoanalysts disappeared, a proportion that was similar to that of other professionals.[15]

During the military regime a second IPA-affiliated institution was created: the Asociación Psicoanalítica de Buenos Aires (APdeBA). The APdeBA was founded in 1977 by APA members who charged that the institutional changes

introduced in the 1970s, particularly the extension of the right to be training analysts to all full members, lowered the quality of analytic training. In
general they were much more conservative theoretically than politically.
The APdeBA is seen as a more orthodox Kleinian institution than the
APA.[16] Neither institution was singled out for repression by the military authorities. The APA even received a grant from the Ministry of Public Health
in May 1976 (two months after the coup) to cover the cost of organizing
a Latin American psychoanalytic conference.[17] Even after the Plataforma-
Documento crisis and the loss of 134 people to the APdeBA—38 full members, 26 associates, and 70 candidates—the APA continued to grow. In 1979
it was the fourth-largest IPA-affiliated analytic institution in the world. Moreover, APA and APdeBA analysts continued to travel freely throughout the
country to teach courses and train future analysts. In 1980 the APA president, a familiar figure in the media, could boast of the important place the
APA occupied in the nation's cultural life, beyond the analytic community.[18]

Psychologists did not fare so well as IPA analysts during the Proceso. The
psychology program was separated from the traditionally politicized School
of Philosophy and Literature and placed under direct control of the university's president through a delegate. The same happened to the sociology program. A high official of the Ministry of Education explained in 1980, "The
boom in programs like psychology, anthropology, sociology, and pedagogy is
unusual. Look, these are all disciplines that promote social change. That
boom is the result of a Marxist strategy, without any doubt."[19]

The first delegate to take charge of the psychology program was Luis Felipe García de Onrubia, a long-time faculty member who sympathized with
psychoanalysis.[20] He was soon replaced, however, by a series of functionaries
who had no connection with the program and were deeply suspicious of
the subversive potential of psychoanalysis and any other modern psychological theory. Enrollment in the program was drastically restricted and the
authorities attempted to shift its orientation away from psychoanalysis.
Their efforts had unexpected and unwelcome consequences. The private
universities that were springing up were happy to fill the demand for psychoanalytically oriented psychology programs.[21] As in earlier decades, the
deficiencies of the public universities forced students to rely more than ever
on private study groups, which once again became a kind of underground
university.

In 1980 the Ministry of Education passed a resolution reaffirming a law
passed by the previous military regime in 1967 that forbade psychologists in
areas under federal jurisdiction (that meant principally Buenos Aires) to

practice any kind of psychotherapy. Although the resolution introduced no change in the law, the psychology community felt the possibility of its enforcement as a humiliation and a threat. Talks between the APBA and the military authorities continued, however, and the feared enforcement never took place. Psychologists continued to practice psychoanalysis illegally even in some public hospitals.

At this point we must ask why, if prominent members of the military believed that psychoanalysis was really a threat to their cherished values, they did not act more firmly against the psy community. I can offer only speculation. The military regime, far from being a monolithic bloc, was cut through by all kinds of tensions. Promoters of traditional Catholic values had to coexist with modernizers who made efficiency their top priority. While some functionaries of the regime believed that psychoanalysis was essentially subversive, others feared that denying the importance of Freud's doctrine would be "obscurantist."[22] Moreover, psychoanalysis was such a well-established part of Argentine culture by that time that many high-ranking officers—including Gen. Leopoldo Galtieri, who would serve as president during the Falkland War—had children who were psychologists or were in psychoanalytic therapy themselves.[23] More important, the military authorities had themselves·appropriated some parts of the psychoanalytic discourse—the parts promoted by the most conservative psychoanalysts.

The family occupied a central place in the discourse of the military government. According to the Proceso authorities, Argentina would become immune to "subversive infection" when the family was firmly based on the values of hierarchy, discipline, and authority. If the existing social order was, as school textbooks characterized it, "emerging from a moral order based on the will of God," then the traditional family based on the authority of the father was the natural foundation for that social order. In the military's rhetoric, it was only by restoring the disciplinary role of the family that society could become "healthy again."[24] "Do you know what your child is doing at this moment?" was a message that was continuously broadcast on the state-controlled TV. If subversion had taken root in Argentine society, it was because parents did not properly perform their disciplinary role. An army officer announced: "I would ask each couple with an adolescent daughter, What are you doing to prevent your daughter from becoming a guerrilla? ... They do not control their [daughters'] friends, the books they read, the schools they go to...."[25] In the rhetoric of the military, politics was privatized and transformed into a family matter.

The rhetoric that emphasized a traditional model of family based on paternal authority, however, also had a more progressive side. Young people were in danger of becoming subversives when they could not find a nurturing environment at home. The same categories of analysis that progressive criminologists and psychologists have used for explaining youthful criminality were appropriated by the Proceso to explain "subversion." Parents should "talk" to their children, take care of them, and provide psychological support in times of trouble, in order to keep children safe from subversive temptation.[26] This rhetoric, which was aimed at middle-class parents deeply influenced by psychoanalytic concepts, appropriated some of the central elements of the most conservative aspects of psychoanalytic discourse.

At the beginning of the Proceso psychoanalysis all but disappeared from publications that supported or were controlled by the military regime. How could they give space to a doctrine that challenged the traditional family model? Soon, however, conservative psychoanalysts began to reappear in the media. Arnaldo Rascovsky, for instance, became a mainstay of widely read magazines that openly supported the Proceso, such as Somos and Para Tí, as well as of the state-controlled TV and radio. He was still insisting in the importance of the traditional family as the foundation of a healthy society. According to Rascovsky, terrorism (i.e., leftist subversion) was a mental disease in the same category as psychosis, neurosis, tobacco addiction, and drug addiction, all of which were the results of the crisis of the traditional family.[27]

The pathologizing of political activity was also a strategy of the military. Their fondness for medical metaphors has been noted many times. Subversion was a social "cancer" or "infection" that could be secretly carried by anyone, and therefore justified drastic treatment. It had to be "surgically removed." Subversives (broadly defined) were sick people with mental problems. The sickest subversives were the women. "The woman guerrilla is a psychopath," trumpeted Somos.[28] The language and some concepts of psychoanalysis—which, as Somos discovered with some pleasure, was forbidden in the Soviet Union—could be used by the military to construct a "modern" version of their discourse on the family.

Aside from the direct repressions suffered by the psychoanalysts and psychologists who were persecuted by the military, the Proceso had more general consequences for the psy world. Perhaps the most notable was the depoliticizing of psychoanalysis and the disruption of the ongoing dialogue between psychoanalysis and the left. Despite the terror, a few psychoanalysts and psychologists became active participants in the human rights movement, at the risk of their lives.[29] Both the APA and the APdeBA rejected any involvement in politics in the name of analytic neutrality. Like many other professional associations, the analytic institutions remained detached from social reality. This became pathetically evident when an APBA delegation asked the APA to support its demand for the liberation of Beatriz Perossio. According to one of the APBA officers who participated in the interview, the APA president regretted that it would be dangerous to present the Perossio case to the membership because there was no telling "what kind of elements could use the issue to make a mess in one of the APA's assemblies."[30] Similarly, according to Baremblit, the APA declined to plead for his own release after he was kidnapped, despite the fact that he was an APA member in good standing at the time.[31]

The APBA gradually took a more "professional" tack. Although it never stopped demanding Perossio's release, its priority became once again the lifting of the ban on the practice of psychotherapy: "We continued fighting for the law and we had interviews with the authorities, who at that time were the military."[32] The *Revista Argentina de Psicología* became totally psychoanalytic and apolitical in its orientation (with a growing Lacanian flavor). The articles on social issues and social applications of psychoanalysis that had proliferated until the mid-1970s gave way to more current and urgent concerns, such as how psychoanalysts and psychologists should deal with the never-ending and always increasing inflation.[33]

As long as psychoanalysis was once again confined to the analyst's couch, the regime did not perceive it as a threat, and in fact saw it as a potential ally in a social program that exalted individualism and aimed, as Corradi puts it, at the "corrosion of social networks." Psychoanalytic therapy provided a space in which all concerns could be dealt with privately. Even some psychoanalysts agreed that their role was to help patients to adapt to the environment in which they lived; the quality of that environment was not their concern.[34] And at a time of terror and uncertainty, for many people the analyst's couch was the only place where they could structure and discuss their daily experience.

Another development that had a lasting effect on the psy community was the expansion of Lacanianism. Although the depoliticizing potential of Lacanian psychoanalysis was clear from the beginning, it should be remembered that the appearance of Lacanianism in Argentina coincided with a general questioning of the orthodox analytic institutions and was deeply connected to the politicization of the late 1960s. During the Proceso Lacanian analysts, like many other intellectuals, had no place for real debate and theoretical controversy. Many Lacanians became what they had criticized years before: clinical practitioners of a highly ritualized version of psychoanalysis characterized by obscure jargon and total detachment from social reality. Moreover, according to Hugo Vezzetti, some Lacanians, in the absence of opportunities for real theoretical debate, became caught up in internal squabbles that were more relevant in Paris than in Buenos Aires. This may explain the proliferation of Lacanian groups, some with only a handful of members, during those years. Furthermore, Lacanians' focus on the "signifier" and on "discourse" (everything is discourse) over current reality, and over the social and political conditions of production of those discourses, also helped to dehistoricize psychoanalysis and weaken its ability to analyze reality. Now it was less of a threat. As one prominent psychoanalyst has pointed out, a certain synchrony—not necessarily causality—can be seen in the spread of Lacanianism, which emphasizes the illusoriness of cure, and an environment in which any attempt to restructure reality was clearly dangerous and doomed.[35]

What does the experience of the Proceso tell us about the possibility of psychoanalytic practice in a context of political oppression? Since Freud's day it has been said many times that an environment that guarantees a certain political and social freedom is necessary for the practice of psychoanalysis, a science that aims at the lifting of repression and whose practice is based on uncensored free association. Psychoanalytic theory is supposed to question central elements of our "world taken for granted." The historical development of psychoanalysis around the world, however, shows that it can be manipulated for many purposes. It can become part of mainstream culture and even a defining element of that "world taken for granted." Far from questioning accepted social values, some forms of psychoanalytic practice can reinforce those values or provide a new means to channel them, as the Proceso came to understand.

Moreover, it is important to distinguish between psychoanalysis as a body of knowledge, as a practice, and as a belief system. While there is a lot in Freudian thought that questions traditional values (it was probably to that aspect of psychoanalysis that the officer who called Freud and Marx ideological criminals was referring), the actual practice of psychoanalysis is another matter. A certain version of psychoanalytic practice can provide a place for the privatization of social relationships. If everything is psychological (including membership in a guerrilla organization), and if everything can be interpreted psychologically (including the refusal of the Mothers of the Plaza de Mayo to accept the death of their children and therefore to "work through the mourning process"), then there are very few incentives left to try to change the world.[36] The more insightful officers were probably aware of this potentially conservative aspect of psychoanalysis. Doubtless that was one reason why the practice of traditional psychoanalysis was not discouraged, whereas group therapy was suspect as potentially subversive. The fact that the military could find some parts of psychoanalysis useful for their purposes shows, once again, the flexibility of the Freudian system.

Some repressors were actually members of the psychoanalytic community. The most notorious case took place not in Argentina but in Brazil. In 1973 a candidate for membership in the Rio de Janeiro Psychoanalytic Society, an army doctor, was accused of torturing political prisoners. The case was hushed up by the Rio association and the torturer was allowed to continue his training. The matter was resolved only in the early 1990s.[37]

In Argentina, psychoanalysis has become a belief system for a large part of the population. It has become a map that orients and gives meaning to people's interpretations of reality. By the time the military took power, psychoanalysis was so deeply rooted in Argentine culture that any serious attempt to uproot it would have failed. By appropriating portions of it and by exalting individualism and turning social interaction into a trap to be avoided, the Proceso in fact generated the conditions for the diffusion of some kinds of psychoanalytic practice as a safety valve. It goes without saying that I am not arguing that the psychoanalytic community as a whole was an accomplice of the generals (some psychoanalysts may have been). I am arguing only that conditions under the Proceso favored the diffusion of certain kinds of psychoanalytic practices, just as the general conditions of the 1960s and 1970s promoted very different kinds. The Proceso experience confirms the general hypothesis that once psychoanalytic discourse takes root in a society and becomes widely available, different aspects of it can be easily appropriated without changing its identity. Thus during the Perón era of the 1940s and 1950s psychoanalysis was part of the system of cultural resistance to the regime. In the 1960s and early 1970s it gradually became simultaneously an instrument for cultural modernization and for revolution. In the late 1970s and early 1980s, under very different social and political conditions, the military used some portions of psychoanalysis to legitimize their social policies while suppressing other parts of it.

With the return of democracy in 1983, after the Falkland fiasco, the forces that had been repressed for seven years emerged again. Psychoanalysts tried to make sense of the traumatic experiences of recent years. In 1985 the APA organized an international conference on the psychological effects of state terrorism. The journals of both the APA and the APdeBA published many articles on the subject. It was clear that a neutral psychoanalysis that took no account of the social and political context was no longer possible.[38] Since 1983 psychoanalysts have been more prominent in public mental health centers, including traditional psychiatric hospitals, than ever before. Psychoanalysts were appointed to high positions in the public system of mental health services. As a result of an inertial dynamic generated during the Proceso but also of an aggressive policy of "occupying spaces," Lacanian psychoanalysis became mainstream and Argentina is today one of the world centers of Lacanian practice. Spanish is now one of the "official" languages of the Lacanian movement. Jacques-Alain Miller, Lacan's son-in-law and heir, has been making annual visits to Buenos Aires, where he delivers lectures on obscure topics of Lacanian psychoanalytic theory at the National Library and other public places. Those lectures draw literally thousands of people. Lacanian psychoanalysts who refuse to bow to the "tyranny of Miller" have also gathered large followings.[39] The expansion of Lacanianism should also be seen against the long-standing French influence in Argentine culture.

The importance of Argentina as a world center of psychoanalysis is by no means limited to the Lacanian movement. In the early 1990s a Latin American analyst was elected president of the IPA for the first time: Dr. R. Horacio Etchegoyen, of the APdeBA. It is not by chance that the first summit meeting ever to be held between the leaders of the two international psychoanalytic empires, Etchegoyen for the IPA and Miller for the Lacanians, took place in Buenos Aires.

In 1985, after lobbying Congress for two years, psychologists obtained their long-sought law, and now they are permitted to practice psychotherapy and psychoanalysis on equal terms with physicians. Some psychologists have been appointed to head psychopathology services at public hospitals. Soon after the law that "made legal what is legitimate" was passed, the APA and the APdeBA started admitting psychologists for analytic training. Psychologists are now accepted as full-fledged psychoanalysts. For the first time autonomous schools of psychology were created at the University of Buenos Aires and other public universities.

Today psychoanalysts are facing another challenge: the effects of a deep economic crisis and of the spread of alternative short therapies, New Age practices, and drug therapy.[40] Yet the place of psychoanalysis in the culture of the country remains unchallenged. Newspapers publish regular sections on psychology and psychoanalysts are still featured in the media. In 1995 when General Martín Balza, the army chief of staff, made a dramatic appearance on TV to apologize for the crimes committed by the military during the

Proceso, the language he (or his speech writers) chose to express his feelings was loaded with such concepts as the collective unconscious and the need to work through the mourning process. The fact that a military chief thought (probably rightly) that the language of psychoanalysis was the appropriate medium to transmit his message of reconciliation is significant in itself.

Reference Matter

Notes

1. For a discussion of the problems involved in doing archival research on the history of psychoanalysis, see Roudinesco, *Genealogies*.

Introduction

1. See Roudinesco and Plon, *Dictionnaire de la psychanalyse*, 63.

2. Figueira, *Nos bastidores de psicanálise*. See *Dispositio: Revista Americana de Estudios Comparados y Culturales / American Journal of Comparative and Cultural Studies* 18, no. 45 (1993), devoted to "the production of psychoanalysis in Buenos Aires."

3. A popular song by the Spanish singer Joaquín Sabina, "Estaban todos menos tú," includes among typical Madrid characters "an Argentine psychologist who shows you the way."

4. See, e.g., Kurzweil, *Freudians*, which does not even mention Argentina. Two exceptions are Roudinesco and Plon's *Dictionnaire*, which has nine entries on the Argentine psychoanalytic movement and six more on the Latin American, and Hollander, *Love in a Time of Hate*. Hollander's book, however, deals specifically with the politicization of psychoanalysis in Argentina, Chile, and Uruguay in the 1970s and the effects of the repressive regimes that ruled those countries. Two IPA analysts note that child psychoanalysis is more widespread in Argentina than in any other country in the world: Geissmann and Geissmann, *History of Child Psychoanalysis*, 275–84.

5. In 1978 the Lacanian analyst Germán L. García wrote the first (highly partisan) history of Argentine psychoanalysis, *Entrada del psicoanálisis en la Argentina*, designed to challenge the APA's official story. More recently Hugo Vezzetti has written two important volumes on the history of psychoanalysis in Argentina: a collection of primary sources preceded by a long preliminary study, *Freud en Buenos Aires*, and a monograph, *Aventuras de Freud*. Both focus

on the early years, before the APA was founded. A history of the APA and its most prominent members is Balán, *Cuéntame tu vida.*

6. Two prominent APA analysts who made notable contributions to psychoanalytic theory were Angel Garma, who reworked Freud's theory on dreams, and Heinrich Racker, a Polish-born immigrant educated in Vienna, who had his formal analytic training in Argentina under Garma. Racker is credited with making important contributions to the theory of countertransference.

7. For the Americanization of Gestalt psychology, see Harrington, *Reenchanted Science.* For the specific case of psychoanalysis, see Fuller, *Americans and the Unconscious.*

8. Emiliano Galende, quoted in "El psicoanálisis argentino: Un cuestionamiento," *Vuelta* (Mexico City) 2, no. 16 (November 1987): 39.

9. Forrester, "'A Whole Climate of Opinion,'" 174, and *Dispatches from the Freud Wars,* 2.

10. Stepan, *"Hour of Eugenics,"* 3.

11. See, among others, Berger, "Towards a Sociological Understanding"; Gellner, *Psychoanalytic Movement;* Turkle, *Psychoanalytic Politics.*

12. Geertz, "Religion as a Cultural System," 19.

13. Turkle, *Psychoanalytic Politics,* xvi.

14. For the history of psychoanalysis in France, see Roudinesco, *Bataille de cent ans.* For the United States, see Nathan Hale, *Beginnings of Psychoanalysis* and *Rise and Crisis.* For Russia, see Etkind, *Eros of the Impossible.* For a comparative perspective, see Kurzweil, *Freudians,* and the much less compelling Jaccard, *Histoire de la psychanalyse.*

15. This has been the argument of the "official history" of psychoanalysis since the times of Freud. For the particular case of Argentina, see the histories of psychoanalysis written by APA members: Aberastury, Aberastury, and Cesio, *Historia,* and the self-congratulatory volume published by APA on its fortieth birthday, *Asociación Psicoanalítica Argentina.*

16. See Demos, "Oedipus and America."

17. See Hellmich, "Plague or Passion." See also Harari, *Psicoanálisis in-mundo.*

18. Vezzetti, *Aventuras de Freud,* 11–12.

19. Borges, *El Aleph.*

1. The Beginnings of Psychoanalysis in Argentina

1. In his essays in *Histeria, estados baldeicos y baldeísmo,* some of which had been written in the 1930s, Gorriti cited Freud repeatedly. *Estado baldeico* and *baldeísmo* refer to a particular mental pathology (never described before, according to Gorriti) that appeared in a character in Rosa Bazán de Cámara's novel *El pozo de balde: Tragedia de los llanos de la Rioja* (1931). The use of

fictional characters to describe mental pathologies has been less uncommon in the medical profession. See Micale, *Approaching Hysteria,* esp. 235.

2. "A decir verdad mas que por los hombres de ciencia esta doctrina ha sido aceptada por los artistas y hombres de letras" (Sierra, "Sexualidad," 520). Elisabeth Roudinesco has identified a literary channel though which Freudian thought entered public discourse in France before it received attention in medical circles: *Bataille de cent ans,* chap. 1.

3. Greve, "Sobre psicología y psicoterapia."

4. Although many problems were later noted in this translation, it should be noted that it was the first collection of Freud's complete works published in any language and that Freud himself approved it.

5. See Alexim Nunes, "Da medicina social á psicanálise."

6. Argentine psychiatry is still waiting for a historian. For a general overview, see Guerrino, *Psiquiatría argentina;* Loudet and Loudet, *Historia de la psiquiatría argentina;* Balbo, "Argentine Alienism"; Vezzetti, *Locura en la Argentina.*

7. Piñero, "Psicología experimental."

8. The French cultural influence in Argentina surprised more than one French visitor. See, e.g., Janet, "Progrès scientifique."

9. For France, see Roudinesco, *Bataille de cent ans;* for Italy, see David, *Psicanalisi nella cultura italiana.*

10. See Carlson, "Medicine and Degeneration," 122.

11. Under the influence of José Ingenieros, some criminologists abandoned the notion of atavism. As Ricardo Salvatore points out in "Criminology," a psychological dimension was added to existing interpretations of crime, but Lombroso and degeneracy continued to be mentioned in forensic reports until well into the 1930s and even the 1940s.

12. The image of immigrants as idiots or degenerates can be seen in such novels as Eugenio Cambaceres's *En la sangre* (1887) and Julian Martel's *La bolsa (estudio social)* (1891).

13. Bosch, "Organización de la profilaxis."

14. See Stepan, *"Hour of Eugenics."*

15. See Nathan Hale, *Beginnings of Psychoanalysis,* 47.

16. See Zimmermann, "Racial Ideas and Social Reform."

17. Raitzin, "Locura y los sueños"; Régis and Hesnard, *Psychanalyse des névroses.* This became the standard version of psychoanalysis for many Argentine doctors. Hesnard later became a psychoanalyst himself and a founding member of the French association in 1926. The other source for psychoanalytic thought, also highly critical of Freud, was a book by an Italian positivist psychiatrist and follower of Lombroso: Morselli, *Psicanalisi.*

18. The first edition of Ingenieros's work was published as *Los accidentes histéricos y las sugestiones terapéuticas.* The title was changed for its 2nd ed. in 1906. Janet's text was originally presented at the 18th International Congress of

Medicine in London in 1913, and was translated and published in Buenos Aires as "El psico-análisis," *Archivo de Ciencias de la Educación* (La Plata) 1 (1914): 175–229. See Vezzetti, *Aventuras de Freud*, 16–17.

19. Discussions of neuroses as partially based on sexuality and of sexuality from the physiological point of view were common in Argentine journals. Even the concept of infantile sexuality was well accepted. See, e.g., Freidjung, "Sexualidad en los niños"; Tonina, "Educación sexual y el sexo"; Mandolini, "Sexualidad infantil."

20. Vezzetti, *Aventuras de Freud*, chap. 2.

21. Jackob, "Problemas actuales de psiquiatría."

22. The concept of intellectual field is borrowed from Pierre Bourdieu. See in particular his "Champ intellectuel." See also his *Field of Cultural Production*. For the crisis of positivism in the context of philosophy, see Dotti, *Letra gótica*, 72–73 and 150ff. For the constitution of a "literary field," see Altamirano and Sarlo, "Argentina del centenario."

23. Alberini, *Precisiones*, 145.

24. On Ortega's first visit to Argentina, see Medin, *Ortega y Gasset*, 15–22.

25. Among them were Manuel García Morente, "El chiste y su teoría" (September 1923); J. M. Sacristán, "Das Ich und das Es" (November 1923) and "Freud ante sus contradictores" (February 1925); Gonzalo Rodríguez Lafora, "La interpretación de los sueños" (October 1924). After 1925 the orientation of the journal changed. Freud almost disappeared from its pages and C. G. Jung became a regular contributor (seven contributions between 1925 and 1936). For a general overview of the journal, see López Campillo, *Revista de Occidente*.

26. Krausism was a philosophical system advanced by Karl Christian Friedrich Krause in early nineteenth-century Germany. It has been called Catholicism without the Church. See Rock, *Authoritarian Argentina*, 61–62.

27. Charles Hale, "Political and Social Ideas," 274–75. On the impact of immigration, see Halperin Donghi, "¿Para qué la inmigración?"

28. Nerio Rojas, for example, attempted to convince Freud that his ideas were compatible with Bergson's. See Rojas, "Visita a Freud" and "De Bergson y Freud." See also Fondani, "Conciencia desventurada."

29. "Palabras pronunciadas por el Dr. Gonzalo Bosch con motivo de la inauguración de la 1ra exposición de trabajos de alienados," in Liga Argentina de Higiene Mental, *Memoria*.

30. Austregesilo, "Errores del pan" and "Sexualidad y psiconeurosis."

31. Freud credited Delgado with introducing psychoanalysis to Latin America in *On the History of the Psychoanalytic Movement* and *Short Account of Psychoanalysis*, 202. See Rey Castro, "Freud y Honorio Delgado" and "Psicoanálisis en el Perú." The correspondence between Freud and Delgado is reproduced in "Lettres de Sigmund Freud à Honorio Delgado."

32. Interestingly enough, Freud condoned Delgado's eclecticism. At that point Freud was more interested in disseminating psychoanalysis in "exotic environments" than in an accurate understanding of his theories. He was much more tolerant of the deviations of followers far away than with small disagreements within his inner circle.

33. Delgado, "Ontogenia del instinto sexual" and "Rehabilitación de la Interpretación de los Sueños." See also Delgado, "Interpretación psicoanalítica."

34. *La Prensa,* June 6, 1923, 13. Other Spanish physicians who were influential in the spread of various unorthodox versions of psychoanalysis in Argentina were Gregorio Marañón, César Juarros, José M. Sacristán, José Sanchis Banus, and later Emilio Mira y López. Their works were regularly published in Argentine psychiatric journals. For a discussion of the impact of psychoanalysis in Spain in those years, see Glick, "Naked Science" and "Impacto del psicoanálisis."

35. E.g., Rodríguez Lafora, "Teoría y los métodos."

36. Dr. Emilio Mira y López, a Spanish exile from the Civil War, also contributed to the introduction of psychoanalysis in Argentina. Although he had some reservations about it, he lectured on psychoanalysis at the Medical School in the 1940s, before moving to Brazil.

37. See, for instance, Delgado, "Nueva faz de la psicología." For a general discussion of Freud's "biologism," see Sulloway, *Freud, Biologist of the Mind. Revista de Filosofía* 10, no. 2 (May 1924), for instance, contains an article by José Crespo, "Psicoanálisis," in which the author claims that only psychoanalysis has a meaningful conception of consciousness and of the unconscious, and a final article by Aníbal Ponce, "Psicología y clínica," which starts with a disdainful remark about psychoanalysis. Similarly, *Revista de Filosofía* published articles on Italian idealistic philosophy.

38. This idea made its way into his disciples' works. In 1908, Juan Antonio Agrelo submitted a dissertation titled "Psicoterapia y reeducación psíquica" under the supervision of Ingenieros. In a chapter titled "Reeducación psíquica" Agrelo emphasized the need to listen to the sick person. On p. 64 we read: "En el interrogatorio conviene seguir el método socrático, dirigiéndolo solamente en la exposición, tratando sobre todo de investigar las causas morales de la afección constatada. . . . [El médico] tratará de hacer renacer en él [el paciente] una confianza, una esperanza . . . mostrándole como los trastornos que experimenta están ligados a causas morales y analizando su mecanismo de formación puramente psíquico." Neither Freud nor psychoanalysis, however, is mentioned anywhere in the thesis.

39. Ingenieros's *Tratado del amor* is discussed in Vezzetti, *Aventuras de Freud,* 54–65.

40. For an account of Ingenieros, see Ponce, "Para una historia de Ingenieros." See also Bermann, "Obra científica de José Ingenieros."

41. See, e.g., Lambruschini, "Influencia del psicoanálisis." Lambruschini discussed Adler's and Jung's theories as well as Freud's. Following a well-established pattern, he distinguished between a psychoanalytic doctrine (questionable) and a psychoanalytic method (useful). He recognized, however, that psychoanalysis represented a big step forward with respect to psychotherapeutic methods, since it was the first one anchored in theory (although he disagreed with large portions of it).

42. For general assessments of somatic therapies, see Scull, "Somatic Treatments," and Merskey, "Somatic Treatments." For Argentina, see Ortega, "Tratamiento de la psicosis." Ortega recognized the effectiveness of insulin shock but also acknowledged "lo resbaladizo de sus bases teóricas." In the same vein, see Martínez Dalke, "Terapéutica convulsionante"; Castedo, "Electroshock en el Pabellón Charcot"; Krapf, "Doctrina y tratamiento de la alienación" (Krapf, a future short-term APA member, contrasted Freud's "truths" to the empiricism of the biologists); Pichon Rivière, "Contribución a la teoría psicoanalítica." On Pichon's conception of "single disease," see his "Grupos operativos."

43. In 1926 the psychologist Augusto Bunge, who was not sympathetic to psychoanalysis, chastised Alberto Palcos for neglecting to mention Freud in one of his books. See Bunge's review of Palcos's La vida emotiva in Nosotros 20, no. 203 (April 1926): 436–37.

44. Eduardo Gómez de Baquero, "Leyendo a Pérez de Ayala: Una novela y un problema" (May 4, 1923); Rómulo Cabrera, "Los precursores de Freud" (May 18, 1923); "El desarrollo de la psicología" (May 29, 1925); "Dionisio fue un precursor del Dr. Freud" (May 4, 1928). The purpose of most of these articles was to deny the originality of Freud's ideas (while acknowledging their importance). References to psychoanalysis could be found in El Hogar's short stories, too. See, e.g., F. Pelayo, "Un chico que tenía futuro" (Apr. 12, 1929). For a negative vision of psychoanalysis, see Aníbal Ponce, "Madame Sokolnicka." After the mid-1930s El Hogar published articles and notes that employed Freudian concepts without attributing them to Freud. See, e.g., A. Casal Castel, "El tema de la inquietud" (July 31, 1936), and two articles by Pizarro Crespo, "Por qué debe evitarse la violencia en los niños" and "Razones de la elección amorosa."

45. A woman who encounters difficulties on a sea voyage, for instance, is said to have problems that "not even Freud can explain" (E. Amorim, "Viajar es conversar" [Aug. 9, 1929]). Similarly, in a critical commentary on Ferenc Molinar's play La fábula y el lobo, which subtly links dreams to reality, Raúl Scalabrini Ortiz provided a short summary of Freud's ideas on dreams ("Desde la platea: La fábula del loco" [Nov. 29, 1929]).

46. Luis Campos Aguirre (Aníbal Ponce), "La divertida estética de Freud," Revista de Filosofía 9, no. 17 (1923): 89–93; Ponce, "Madame Sokolnicka."

47. See, e.g., Rocha, *Introdução ao nascimento de psicanalise.*

48. Whitley, "Knowledge Producers," 7.

49. Rojas, "Histeria después de Charcot."

50. Gorriti, *Psicoanálisis de los sueños.* In the same year Gorriti made an attempt at literary criticism using psychoanalysis in " 'Fuerza ciega.' "

51. In 1935 an Argentine third-year medical student wrote to Freud in Spanish criticizing some aspects of Freud's dream theory. Freud replied quickly and courteously. I thank Horacio Tarcus for giving me a copy of his father's letter to Freud and of Freud's reply.

52. On liberalism as a unifying myth, see Charles Hale, "Political and Social Ideas."

53. Glick, "Transferencia," 82. A case in point is Ortega y Gasset, who had developed strong philosophical reservations about psychoanalysis in the mid-1920s but felt forced to support it because those who opposed it were people of *mala catadura;* in other words, he didn't like the looks of them. "One could almost say that I am anti-Freudian except for two reasons: the first, because that would situate me among *mean-looking people;* the second, a decisive reason, is that in this epoch when everybody is 'anti,' I aspire to *be* and not to be *against*": "Vitalidad, alma, espíritu," in *Obras completas* (Madrid: Revista de Occidente, 1946), 2:452–53 (1924), quoted in Glick, "Naked Science," 542.

54. See Plotkin, "Freud, Politics, and the Porteños."

55. For Castelnuovo, psychoanalysis was more than a therapeutic method, and it was precisely its nature as a *Weltanschauung* that drew his criticism: "Porque el psicoanálisis no es una manera de encarar la patología del espíritu. Es una manera de encarar al hombre y al mundo, y por su intermedio, a la sociedad y a sus formas de existencia. Vale decir: es una filosofía, una interpretación del proceso histórico": *Psicoanálisis sexual,* 2. And a few pages later: "[Psicoanálisis] no se conforma ya con explicar el malestar de un enfermo del sistema nervioso. Quiere explicar hasta el malestar de la civilización . . . como si la civilización no fuese un conflicto político y económico, sino un conflicto de sanatorio" (8).

56. See Barrancos, *Escena iluminada,* 197.

57. González Tuñon was the editor of the magazine *Contra,* which was launched in 1933 and appeared only five times. Beatriz Sarlo says: "De las citas con que la dirección de *Contra* organiza el álbum de recortes de la izquierda, podría armarse un collage, muy de época, entre psicoanálisis y política en la versión de los tempranos años treinta": *Modernidad periférica,* 140.

58. E.g., "Patogenia de las neurosis obsesivas." Reversing the usual pattern, Bermann criticized Janet's theories in the light of Freudian psychoanalysis. See also his "Grave deficiencia."

59. Other editors were Arturo Ameghino, a traditional psychiatrist; Gonzalo Bosch; the psychologist and essayist Alberto Palcos; Enrique Mouchet, a

socialist leader, psychiatrist, and psychology professor; the Spanish physicians Emilio Mira y López and Gonzalo Rodríguez Lafora; Edoardo Weiss, an Italian psychoanalyst; and, interestingly enough, James Mapelli, a hypnotist who had arrived in Argentina from Italy in the 1920s with a reputation as an illusionist. More on him below.

60. "Programa," *Psicoterpia*, no. 1.

61. Ibid.

62. Prof. Segismundo [*sic*] Freud, "Dostoyevsky y el parricidio," *Psicoterapia*, no. 3 (September 1936); Prof. Dr. Sigmundo Freud, "Los tipos psicológicos," and C. G. Yung [*sic*], "Los símbolos religiosos de la madre y el renacimiento," *Psicoterapia*, no. 4 (May 1937). The same issue includes an obituary on Alfred Adler.

63. Garma, "Proyección" and "Evolución y nuevos problemas."

64. In 1948 Bermann wrote a foreword for Politzer's *Principios elementales de filosofía* (Buenos Aires: Problemas, 1948).

65. Balán, *Cuéntame tu vida*, 60.

66. Pizarro Crespo and Zeno, *Clínica psicosomática*.

67. Pizarro Crespo, "Rôle des facteurs psychiques."

68. Pizarro Crespo, "Movimiento psicoterápico en Francia." In "Neurosis obsesivas" he cited Lacan and also Jaspers and Jung.

69. Freud's response (addressed to Dr. Monteiro García of Córdoba), dated Jan. 18, 1934, is in the Sigmund Freud Collection, Box B17, Library of Congress. Pizarro Crespo's letter to Jones, dated Dec. 23, 1934, is in the archive of the British Psychoanalytic Society, doc. g07 / bc / f05 / 09. I thank the staffs of both institutions for facilitating my work in those archives. I could not locate the original letter sent to Freud.

70. See Pizarro Crespo, "Por qué debe evitarse la violencia en los niños" and "Razones de la elección amorosa."

71. Pizarro Crespo, "Neurosis obsesivas," 43.

72. Pizarro Crespo, "Narcicismo."

73. Pizarro Crespo, "Psicodiagnóstico y psicoanálisis," 782.

74. Cabral, "Jorge Thénon."

75. Thénon, "Thénon visto por Thénon." Freud's letter was lost when the police, searching for a militant anarchist, raided the printing house where it was being printed. A copy of it, however, was reproduced and translated in *Revista de Criminología, Psiquiatría y Medicina Legal* 17 (1930), in conjunction with an article by Thénon, "Contribuciones al estudio del sueño en las neurosis." The article and the letter are included in Vezzetti, *Freud in Buenos Aires*, 190–214. Thénon claimed that he received two more letters from Freud, but he never made them public.

76. Without apparent qualms, Thénon reports that he performed five unwarranted surgical operations with general anaesthesia to convince a patient

that a nonexistent tumor had been removed. He also tells of misleading a patient in order to plant a suggestion in his mind. It was easy to mislead her, Thénon says, because of her "[mental] simplicity": *Psicoterapia comparada*, 66–67, 74ff., 93ff.

77. Now Thénon cited Freud's works in French, Spanish, and German, as well as other recent developments in psychoanalytic theory such as a 1933 article by Melitta Schmideberg, Melanie Klein's daughter.

78. Thénon, *Neurosis obsesiva*, 48.

79. Ibid., 378.

80. Thénon, "Psiquiatría en el año 50," 352. It is interesting to compare this critical vision of psychoanalysis with the ideas Thénon had expressed earlier at the same institution. See, e.g., "Alfredo Adler" and "Sigmund Freud: Su influencia." Although Thénon was still supporting psychoanalysis in the late 1930s, he was already putting forward the idea that would become the basis for his criticism of it: psychoanalysis does not take into account the social factor. See Thénon, "Sigmund Freud," in Vezzetti, *Freud en Buenos Aires*, 280–93.

81. For Beltrán's biographical data, see Kohn Loncarica, "Juan Ramón Beltrán."

82. See Beltrán, "Tumba de Lombroso."

83. Beltrán, "Psicopatología de la duda," 161. See also Beltrán, "Psicoanálisis al servicio de la criminología."

84. Beltrán, "Contribución a la psicopatología de la personalidad." Beltrán included psychoanalysis among the methods of experimental psychology. See his "Freud," speech delivered in homage to Ramos Mejía, Freud, and Ribot, organized by the school of Philosophy of the University of Buenos Aires and the Sociedad de Psicología de Buenos Aires on Nov. 3, 1939, in *Anales del Instituto de Psicología* 3 (1941): 594–98.

85. On the right-wing ideology of some early French psychoanalysts, see Roudinesco, *Bataille de cent ans*, vol. 1.

86. Beltrán, "Psicoanálisis y el médico práctico." Among other serious misconceptions, Beltrán attributed free association to Jung. For a discussion on the uses of psychoanalysis in education, see Beltrán, "Psicoanálisis en sus relaciones con la pedagogía."

87. The society's minutes reveal that it was experiencing financial difficulties, and that the appointment of associate members was an important source of funds. See "Séance du 17 mars 1931" in "Comptes Rendus," *Revue Française de Psychanalyse* 4 (1930–31).

88. Enrique Pichon Rivière published his first article on psychotherapy (more on Jung and Adler than on Freud) in *Anales de Biotipología, Eugenesia y Medicina Social* in January 1934.

89. On Pende's ideas, see Stepan, *"Hour of Eugenics,"* 60.

90. A note on Germany in *Anales* 1, no. 7 (July 1, 1933), reads: "Tenemos,

pues, motivos para pensar que con el resurgir de Alemania, dentro del régimen de disciplina que caracteriza su actual organización política, los seguros sociales serán para ese país lo que previeron los estadistas del Imperio, y en consecuencia no podrían sino favorecer a las clases productivas."

91. Some of the contributors, however, were indeed far to the political right. One of them was Gustavo Martínez Zuviría, who under the pen name Hugo Wast wrote popular openly anti-Semitic novels. Martínez Zuviría became minister of education after the revolution of 1943 and was in charge of the introduction of mandatory Catholic education in the schools.

92. Although in 1935 the Spanish Republic was still under the control of a center-right coalition, as Mark Falcoff suggests, it was widely perceived as a radical break with the past. See Falcoff, "Argentina," in Falcoff and Pike, *Spanish Civil War.*

93. Federico Aberastury, "Medicina del espíritu." See also his "Teorías de Freud."

94. See the tribute to Adler in *Anales* 4, no. 71 (April 1937). See also Barilari, "Viena."

95. *Anales* 3, no. 88 (October 1939): 2. It is interesting to note that journals supposedly less ideologically committed did not publish obituaries when Freud died.

96. For a more thorough discussion that provides other examples of appropriations of psychoanalysis, see my "Freud, Politics, and the Porteños."

97. Foradori, *Perfiles de psicólogos argentinos,* 145.

98. See Carli, "Infancia, psicoanálisis y crisis."

99. Although Mercante claims he met Freud by chance, by the 1930s Freud's house had become a mandatory stop for any Argentine doctor with an interest in psychiatry who happened to be in Vienna.

100. "Psychoanálisis y criminología," *Boletín del Patronato de Recluídas y Liberadas* 2, no. 6 (January 1936). I am grateful to Lila Caimari for calling this source to my attention.

101. See, e.g., Jímenez de Azúa, "Valor de la psicología"; Rodríguez Lafora, "Paranoia ante los tribunales de justicia."

102. Roudinesco, *Bataille de cent ans,* 2:chap. 1. See also Breton, "First Manifesto of Surrealism." An interesting discussion of the similarities and differences between the Surrealists' and Freud's conceptions of the unconscious is Starobinski, "Freud, Breton, Myers."

103. Sagawa, "Psicanálise pionera." See, for instance, Mario de Andrade's "Prefácio Interessantíssimo" (1922) and Oswald de Andrade's "Manifesto Antropófago" (1928), both in Schwarz, *Vanguardas latino-americanas.* For an enlightening discussion of the differences between Brazilian and Argentine modernism, see Morse, "Multiverse of Latin American Identity."

104. Sarlo, "Vanguardia y criollismo."

105. "Modernism" here describes two different things. In Brazil it refers specifically to an avant-garde movement that originated in the "Modernist Week" of São Paulo in 1922. It represented rupture. In Argentina and elsewhere in Latin America, what is known as modernist literature originated with Rubén Darío. It was in opposition to Darío's modernism that the Argentine avant-garde defined itself. See Morse, "Multiverse of Latin American Identity."

106. While the "Futurist Manifesto" claimed that "a roaring automobile that seems to run over a machine gun is more beautiful than the Victory of Samothrace," *Martín Fierro* "maintains that a good Hispano-Suiza is a much more perfect WORK OF ART than a sedan chair from the times of Louis XV."

107. *Martín Fierro* 3 (June 8, 1926): 229–30.

108. Córdova Iturburu, *Revolución martinfierrista*, 38–39; Sarlo, *Modernidad periférica*, 107.

109. *Martín Fierro* 3, no. 30–31 (July 8, 1926): 10. This is one of very few references to psychoanalysis that I could find in *Martín Fierro*. The only one I could find in another avant-garde magazine is in an article critical of Surrealism: Guillermo de Torre, "Neodadaismo y superrealismo," *Proa* 2, no. 6 (January 1925). Many writers published in both magazines.

110. See, e.g., Roberto Giusti, "La polémica sobre Freud" (July 1924); Marcos Rabinovich, "Psicología freudiana" (January 1930). *Nosotros* also reproduced some sections of Giovanni Papini's *Gog,* including a mock interview with Freud, and a review by the philosopher Francisco Romero of vol. 14 of Freud's *Obras completas* (February 1931).

111. *Sagitario,* a cultural journal published in La Plata, published two articles on the topic: José Carlos Mariátegui's notorious "'Freudismo' en la literatura contemporánea" (July–August 1927) and Mariano Ibérico Rodríguez, "Bergson y Freud" (October–November 1926).

112. See also "El punto de vista de C. G. Jung y la 'realidad del alma'" (August 1935) and a review of Freud's *Moses and Monotheism* (June 1939).

113. Ocampo, *Autobiografía,* 140. Count Hermann von Keyserling, who was a friend of Jung and who also had a convulsed relationship with Ocampo, wrote about her to Jung.

114. See, e.g., Calimano, "Narcisismo." For a very critical use of Freudian concepts, see Gómez de Baquero, "Leyendo a Pérez de Ayala." See also Oría, "Teatro de Lenormand," and Gorriti, "Fuerza ciega."

115. See, for instance, the commentator's discussion of Erdosain's unconscious desires and their origins in his relationship and with father during childhood in Arlt, *Lanzallamas,* 312–13.

116. In 1969 Martínez Estrada said: "I had two guides . . . Spengler . . . and Freud. . . . Even the most nearsighted would have noticed that the configuration of *Radiografía de la Pampa* is owed to Spengler . . . [and] to Freud, with its

examination of the disturbance of the social psyche": "Sobre *Radiografía de la Pampa* (preguntas y respuestas)," in *Leer y escribir* (Buenos Aires, 1969), quoted in León Sigal, "La radiografía de la Pampa: Un saber expectral," in Martínez Estrada, *Radiografía de la Pampa,* critical ed., 503.

117. I recognize the problems involved in the category "popular culture." I use it in the sense described by Jean Franco: "a spectrum of signifying practices and pleasurable activities most of which fall beside the controlling discipline of official schooling. It is the area . . . which is traversed by class stratifications and subtle subcultural distinctions acquired largely in a non-institutional setting": "What's in a Name?" See also Burke, *Popular Culture,* Prologue.

118. Vezzetti, *Aventuras de Freud.*

119. Scobie, *Buenos Aires;* Romero and Romero, *Buenos Aires;* Walter, *Politics and Urban Growth.*

120. On cheap books, see Romero, "Empresa cultural."

121. For a perceptive contemporary view of the changes in the relations between the sexes, see Scalabrini Ortiz, *Hombre que está solo,* 55–56.

122. See, e.g., "¿Se debe decir a los niños siempre la verdad?" *El Hogar,* Jan. 19, 1923.

123. Sarlo, *Imaginación técnica,* 15.

124. In 1919 *El Hogar* published a series of articles titled "La ciencia al alcance de todos," which dealt with such topics as the nervous system of plants, experiments in physics, obesity, chemistry, and alchemy.

125. Sarlo, *Imaginación técnica,* 13.

126. Balán, *Profesión e identidad,* 9.

127. Mapelli, *Psicoinervación.* See also Bermann, "James Mapelli"; Balán, *Cuéntame tu vida,* 54–55.

128. Thénon, "Thénon visto por Thénon."

129. *Index* published eight of Arminda Aberastury's book reviews in one issue alone (November 1942).

130. Dreams had been a matter of interest long before psychoanalysis. Along with articles on scientific and psychological experiments, *El Hogar* published a number of articles on dreams in the 1920s; e.g., "Una teoría del ensueño" (Aug. 25, 1922); "Los sueños" (Oct. 31, 1924). Some of its short stories, too, dealt with dreams; e.g., J. García Gómez, "El extraño caso de Carlos Funes" (Nov. 21, 1924).

131. *Crítica's* combination of state-of-the-art technology and sensationalism attracted an enormous readership, particularly among the lower and middle classes. See Sarlo, *Imaginación técnica,* 68. Its staff included some of the country's top writers—Roberto Arlt, Conrado Nalé Roxlo, Enrique and Raúl González Tuñón, and Jorge Luis Borges. For a short time young Enrique Pichon Rivière wrote notes on sports and arts. See Zito Lema, *Conversaciones con Enrique*

Pichon Rivière, 127. For details on *Crítica / Jornada*, see Saítta, *Regueros de tinta;* Botana, *Memorias;* Talice, *100.000 ejemplares;* Llano, *Aventura del periodismo,* chap. 1.

132. Sarlo, *Imaginación técnica*, 68–69. A similar interest can be found in such publications as *El Hogar.*

133. In the early 1930s *Crítica* had a section on graphology run by Federico Aberastury (Talice, *100.000 ejemplares,* 466; Saítta, *Regueros de tinta,* 295–98). Aberastury introduced Pichon Rivière to psychoanalysis.

134. "In creating this column on spiritism, *Jornada* aims to turn people's attention from everything that may have any connection with charlatanry, [whose appeal is] easy to understand in people who do not know the seriousness of this kind of study" (Feb. 18, 1932, 7).

135. *Jornada,* Aug. 20 and 22, 1931.

136. To emphasize its scientific approach to psychoanalysis, on Aug. 25, 1931, *Jornada* published a long interview with the French psychologist George Dumas—he was visiting Buenos Aires at the time—on the importance of psychoanalysis.

137. *Jornada,* Aug. 25 and Nov. 28, 1931.

138. *Jornada,* Jan. 16 and Feb. 18, 1932.

139. *Jornada,* Oct. 24, 1931. Apparently a Cuban quack had named Thénon as co-author of one of his books. *Jornada* made clear that a serious psychoanalyst such as Thénon could have nothing to do with quackery.

140. *Jornada,* Jan. 30, 1932.

141. *Jornada,* Sept. 19, 1931.

142. *Jornada,* Aug. 20, 1931. On developments in psychiatry, see Plotkin, "Freud, Politics."

143. For a discussion of other examples of dream analysis in popular publications, see Plotkin, "Tell Me Your Dreams."

144. For details of the Hidalgo / Gómez Nerea book, see Vezzetti, *Aventuras de Freud,* 183–245.

2. The Founding of the APA and the Development of the Argentine Psychoanalytic Movement

1. There is some uncertainty about who the founding members of the APA were. It is generally thought that they were Angel Garma, Celes Cárcamo, the psychiatrist Enrique Pichon Rivière, the pediatrician Arnaldo Rascovsky, the otolaringologist Emilio Ferrari Hardoy, and the Austrian émigré Marie Langer, but Rascovsky denied that Langer was one of the founders. See "Entrevista a los fundadores," II. Of the original group only Garma, Pichon, and to a lesser extent Cárcamo had had formal psychiatric training.

2. During the APA's early years, avant-garde artists organized exhibitions of their paintings to raise money for it.

3. For a discussion of the early stages of institutional psychoanalysis, see Balán, *Cuéntame tu vida*.

4. Interview with Carlos Mario Aslán, Oct. 8, 1996.

5. E.g., Bosch and Aberastury, "Conceptos generales"; Aberastury, "Teorías de Freud." He also wrote a column on graphology in *Crítica*.

6. Gavrilov, *Reflexología*.

7. "Entrevista a los fundadores," I.

8. Garma was introduced to Cárcamo by Rof Carballo, another Spanish doctor who was waiting out the Civil War in France. See Rof Carballo to Thomas Glick, Sept. 20, 1974, Thomas F. Glick Papers. I thank Professor Glick for giving me access to this and other letters in his personal archive.

9. Garma had siblings who had immigrated to Argentina decades earlier. In fact, it seems that his father had died in Buenos Aires. Interview with Elizabeth Goode de Garma, Oct. 3, 1996.

10. Garma had been a member of the German Psychoanalytic Association. He resigned when it was taken over by the Nazis and thereafter was an independent member of the IPA.

11. Interview by Thomas Glick, Buenos Aires, Nov. 11, 1979. I am grateful to Professor Glick for permission to use this unpublished material. See also Grinberg, "Reseña histórica."

12. See, e.g., Garma, "Psicología del Suicidio," "Génesis del súper yo," and "Psicoanálisis e interpretación de los sueños"; Cárcamo, "Mecanismos patogénicos."

13. Interview with Dr. Carlos Mario Aslán.

14. Interview with Elizabeth Goode de Garma.

15. The only exception was Béla Székely, a Hungarian lay practitioner who had become an early diffuser of psychoanalysis and of Rorschach tests. See Balán, *Cuéntame tu vida,* 36–37.

16. Ibid., 71.

17. "Entrevista a los fundadores," II.

18. For the "foreignness" of U.S. analysts, see Kurzweil, *Freudians,* 290–92.

19. In time, however, the APA did become more Jewish. In 1971 the names of roughly half its members had a Jewish flavor.

20. Sagawa, "Durval Marcondes." For the early development of psycho-analysis in the United States, see Nathan Hale, *Beginnings of Psychoanalysis.*

21. In a small association, problems of "crossed analysis" multiply. Garma's first wife, Simone, was in analysis with Cárcamo. At some point Garma felt the need to undergo analysis again, and did so with Marie Langer; when Langer felt the same need, she went to Cárcamo. So Garma's analyst was in analysis

with Garma's wife's analyst. And all of them were training analysts who worked together in the APA. See Balán, *Cuéntame tu vida*, 185.

22. Howard Potter et al., "Problems Related to the Costs of Psychiatric and Psychoanalytic Training," *American Journal of Psychiatry*, no. 1131 (May 1957), 1013–19, quoted in Nathan Hale, *Rise and Crisis*, 227.

23. See Scull, "Somatic Treatments"; Merskey, "Somatic Treatments." See also Abbott, *System of Professions*, 300–307. For Argentina, see Ortega, "Tratamiento de la psicosis," in which the author recognizes the effectiveness of insulin shocks but acknowledges "the slipperiness of its theoretical basis." In the same vein, see Martínez Dalke, "Terapéutica convulsivante"; Castedo, "Electro-shock"; Krapf, "Doctrina y tratamiento."

24. A good analysis of the place of psychoanalysis in the evolving medical profession in Argentina can be found in Balán, *Profesión e identidad*.

25. See *Revista de Psicoanálisis* 2, no. 3 (1945): 562–65.

26. Similarly, after its first issues the *Revista de Psicoanálisis* did not publish reviews of works by Argentine nonpsychoanalysts. The upshot was that all Argentine works reviewed were written by APA members.

27. It is possible to see an anti-Perón bias in the *Revista de Psiquiatría y Criminología* from 1945 on. The only medical institution where psychoanalysts had a visible presence was the Sociedad de Psicología Médica y Psicoanálisis, which was literally taken over by the APA. Pichon Rivière was appointed chief of the Juvenile Psychiatric Service at the Hospicio de las Mercedes in 1947 but was dismissed shortly afterward, probably for political reasons.

28. Abadi, "Grupo psicoanalítico."

29. See Turkle, *Psychoanalytic Politics*, Preface.

30. *Archivos Argentinos de Psicología Normal y Patológica* 1, nos. 3–4 (November–December 1933).

31. Ibid. 2, no. 1 (January–March 1935). In 1929 Jesinghaus had made approving references to Freud and psychoanalysis. See his "Bases científicas."

32. Stocker, "Ley alemana."

33. Halperín Donghi, "Lugar del peronismo"; Buchrucker, *Nacionalismo y peronismo*.

34. On the impact of the Spanish Civil War on Argentine society, see Mark Falcoff, "Argentina," in Falcoff and Pike, *Spanish Civil War;* Rein, *Franco-Perón Alliance,* esp. chap. 5. On the impact of Nazism, see Newton, " 'Nazi Menace' ''; on Fascism, Newton, "Ducini, Prominenti, Antifascisti"; for a general overview, Buchrucker, *Nacionalismo y peronismo*.

35. Telma Reca to Robert Lambert, July 28, 1944, in Rockefeller Foundation Archives, ser. 301A, box 3, folder 34.

36. Irazusta, *Memorias*, 227.

37. A thorough analysis of the politicization of the scientific field is beyond

the scope of this work. Enlightening insights on this issue, particularly for the post-Peronist period and for the social sciences, can be found in Sigal, *Intelectuales y poder*, and in Neiburg, *Intelectuales*.

38. Yet both Bermann and Thénon took part in the 1940 preliminary meeting to plan the APA. Their reasons are not clear.

39. On the new identity of the working class under Perón, see James, *Resistance and Integration*, chap. 1.

40. I have dealt with this topic in detail in *Mañana es San Perón*.

41. José Uriburu, "Mensaje del 6 de septiembre de 1931," quoted in Sigal, *Intelectuales*, 40.

42. Neiburg, *Intelectuales*, 166.

43. For a history of the University of Buenos Aires in those years, see Halperín Donghi, *Historia de la Universidad*, and Walter, *Student Politics*.

44. Alejandro Korn, Narciso Laclau, Aníbal Ponce, Roberto Giusti, and Luis Reissig. For an enlightening discussion of CLES, see Neiburg, *Intelectuales*, chap. 4.

45. For a statement on CLES's political and cultural program, see Luis Reissig's address published in *Cursos y Conferencias*, July 1945. Many members of CLES's faculty in the 1930s also taught at the University of Buenos Aires. During the Perón regime professors expelled from the university for political insubordination could continue their academic careers at CLES.

46. CLES was so harassed that it had to cancel classes for a time.

47. In tune with Peronist ideology, Carrillo criticized psychoanalysis for failing to take into account the social, religious, and spiritual aspects of mental illness. See Carrillo, "Posición de la medicina psicosomática."

48. Other progressive pediatricians who had no training in psychoanalysis but were sympathetic to it, such as Florencio Escardó, a prominent professor at the medical school who suffered the consequences of Peronization, was also very influential in the diffusion of psychoanalysis among middle-class mothers.

49. "Entrevista a los fundadores," II.

50. Balán, *Cuéntame tu vida*, 123.

51. One of Muñoz's daughters married a psychoanalyst who would later be a president of APA.

52. Although Argentina became the main center for the diffusion of psychoanalysis in Latin America, it is less clear how much recognition it had in Europe and the United States. Few books by Argentine analysts were translated into other languages. The fragments of letters exchanged by Melanie Klein and Arminda Aberastury published by Silvia Fendrik reveal that Klein took an almost dismissive attitude toward Aburastury. Although in Argentina Aberastury was recognized as an authority on child analysis from the early 1950s, when she submitted a paper for publication in the *International Journal of*

Psycho-Analysis in 1948, Klein told her she still had work to do to bring it up to the journal's standards. Similarly, Klein questioned some of Aberastury's claims of originality. See Fendrik, *Desventuras del psicoanálisis,* 43ff. Céles Cárcamo received a similarly dismissive response when he invited Anna Freud to serve on the editorial board of a journal he was organizing in the early 1970s. Cárcamo seems to have led an Anna Freudian wing in the APA. See Anna Freud's papers, Library of Congress, box 13, for letters exchanged by Anna Freud and Cárcamo from the late 1940s through the 1970s. One more example: At the International Psychoanalytic Congress in Vienna in the early 1970s Marie Langer introduced a group of Uruguayan analysts who wanted to form an association. Despite her position in the APA and her reputation in Latin America, Langer recognized that she had to emphasize the fact that she was in fact Austrian when she introduced herself to Anna Freud. No one took a Latin American very seriously. See Langer, Guinsberg, and Palacio, *Memoria,* 104. I could not find a single book by an Argentine in the library of the Boston Psychoanalytic Institute.

53. In the minutes of APA meetings, Arminda Aberastury and Matilde Wenceblatt are usually referred to as "doctors."

54. When Pichon was dismissed from the Hospicio, students were still required to attend his lectures at his private institution. The requirement was later eliminated.

55. APA archive, "Libro de Actas," Acta 1, Dec. 15, 1942, and Acta 3, Mar. 18, 1943.

56. The regulation of 1948 was published in *Revista de Psicoanálisis* 5, no. 3 (1948): 850–54.

57. *Revista de Psicoanálisis* 1 (July 1943–April 1944): 2.

58. See Kurzweil, *Freudians,* 204.

59. See, e.g., Rosenthal and Rascovsky, "Formación psicoanalítica."

60. Garma, "Freud y la medicina contemporánea," 23.

61. Balán, *Cuéntame tu vida,* 116–17.

62. Rascovsky, "Interpretación psicodinámica."

63. Baranger, "Introducción al Grupo B."

64. *Revista de Psicoanálisis* 8, no. 4 (1951): 294.

65. Ibid. 16, no. 3 (July–September 1959).

66. Balán, *Cuéntame tu vida,* 149–51. It is interesting to note the large number of commercial establishments that advertised in the journal.

67. Eduardo Pavlovsky, letter to the editor, *Psique en la Universidad* 1, no. 1 (1958): 60.

68. Gradually the clinic deemphasized its clinical role and concentrated more on research. In 1964 its name was changed to the Enrique Racker Center of Orientation and Research. The clinical function was eliminated in 1968. In any case, the Racker clinic never had a large number of patients. In

1965, for instance, its staff interviewed 25 prospective patients and treated 14. See APA archive, "Libros de Actas," Acta 164, Mar. 23, 1965.

69. Wender, "Relaciones del analista con el medio ambiente."

70. Lustig de Ferrer, "Mis vivencias," 335. Most of the papers presented at the symposium proposed solutions within the analytic framework: more psychoanalysis for everybody.

71. Garma, "Como mejorar las relaciones." It is interesting to note that this symposium took place at a time of particular conflict in the APA. A group of analysts who had been experimenting with LSD had just been forced to resign. The APA issued a press release denying any connection between psychoanalysis and LSD.

72. Hernán Kesselman in "El psicoanálisis no existe," *Primera Plana,* Aug. 20, 1968, 50.

73. Mom, "Teoría psicoanalítica."

74. Nilda Sito, "Evaluación del II Congreso Panamericano de Psicoanálisis: Informe sociológico" (n.d.), APA archive, folder 12.

75. See the correspondence between Telma Reca and several officers of the Rockefeller Foundation in the Rockefeller Foundation Archive, R.G. 1.1, ser. 301A, box 3, folder 34.

76. On Telma Reca, see Fendrik, *Desventuras del psicoanálisis,* 193–262.

77. On the influence of Argentine and Kleinian psychoanalysis in Latin America, see Mallet da Rocha Barros, "Problem of Originality."

78. Aberastury is credited with discovering an "early genital phase" in the child's development, although Klein expressed doubt about the originality of the concept. See Fendrik, *Desventuras del psicoanálisis.* The organization of groups of mothers as a technique also departed from strict Kleinian thought. Other analysts, such as Willy Baranger and Heinrich Racker, modified Klein's theories further. A study of the development of Latin American psychoanalytic theory is still badly needed.

79. Interview with Goode de Garma.

80. To Klein's surprise, Goode presented a case of a twenty-one-month-old child whom she had treated following Klein's technique. Klein's youngest patient had been two years old. Klein invited Goode to spend a year in London studying with her, but Garma opposed the plan, and she acquiesced. The Garmas did, however, return to England for a short period of study and supervision in the early 1950s. See Angel Garma's "Prólogo" to Betty Garma's *Niños en análisis.*

81. Balán, *Cuéntame tu vida,* 189–90.

82. Betty Garma, "Psicoanálisis de un niño de 21 meses," in her *Niños en análisis.*

83. On Klein's technique and theory and its differences from Anna Freud's,

which provoked a political division within the British Psychoanalytical Association in the 1940s, see Donaldson, "Between Practice and Theory"; Viner, "Melanie Klein and Anna Freud"; Hughes, Judith, *Reshaping the Psychoanalytic Domain*. A critical edition of the texts of the Anna Freud–Klein controversy is King and Steiner, *Freud–Klein Controversies*.

3. Social Change and the Expansion of the Psychoanalytic World

1. Moscovici, *Psychanalyse*, 1–27.

2. See *Criterio* 35 (Mar. 22, 1962), 220–25. For an antipsychoanalysis and anti-Semitic book by an ultranationalist priest, see Castellani, *Freud en cifras*.

3. Ferrara and Peña, "Qué significa la salud mental."

4. The feeling of crisis was discussed in various forums. The structuring role that the Catholic Church was expected to play is discussed in José Enrique Miguens, "La Iglesia ante el cambio social en la Argentina," in Gera et al., *La Iglesia y el país*.

5. The debates can be followed in the Catholic magazine *Criterio* throughout the decade.

6. The multiple uses to which psychoanalysis was put is typical once it starts to spread, as Moscovici shows in *Psychanalise*.

7. "Una pregunta pocas veces respondida: ¿Por qué se sicoanalizan [*sic*] los jóvenes?" *Gente*, July 27, 1972, 68–70.

8. The middle class made up 38.4% of the urban population in 1947, 43.1% in 1970. Torrado, *Estructura social*, table 6.1, p. 146; table 8.2, p. 180.

9. Ibid., table 5.1, p. 124. By comparison, the service sector in Chile employed 23.8% of the workforce in 1960 and 28.1% in 1980. See Alan Angell, "Chile since 1958," in Bethell, *Chile Since Independence*, 129–202.

10. Torrado, *Estructura social*, table 5.3, p. 128; table 5.5, p. 134.

11. The new class of executives was conspicuous throughout popular culture. In the widely read comic strip *Mafalda*, Manolito, a grocer's son, advertises that his father's store is selling beans "for executives." The popular singer María Elena Walsh wrote an ironic song that starts: "How smart are the executives, / How smart they are. . . ."

12. "Las dueñas de casas padecen más el surmenage que los hombres de negocios," *Para Tí*, June 12, 1967.

13. Garma, "Algunos contenidos latentes." Thirty years later, R. Horacio Etchegoyen commented: "It's a fact that some analysts, not all, twisted things around (the business of making more money as the reason for going into analysis, and even as the criterion for judging its effectiveness)." See Stizman, *Conversaciones con Etchegoyen*, 14.

14. Torrado, *Estructura social*, table 3.10, p. 92. The growth rate of the

female economically active population was 22.3 per 1,000 in 1947–60 (the growth rate for men was 11.2 per 1,000 in the same period) and 29.6 per 1,000 in 1960–70 (12.8 for men).

15. Recchini de Lattes and Wainermann, *Estado civil y trabajo femenino*, 17.

16. By 1960 the percentage of illiterates among the Argentine population aged 14 and over was 8.9%.

17. Germani and Sautu, *Regularidad y origen social*, 14.

18. At the University of Buenos Aires, the number of students enrolled rose from 59,901 in 1958 to 90,251 in 1965. See Argentina, Secretaría de Estado de Cultura y Educación, *Educación en cifras*, table VI.I.3, p. 88.

19. See Plotkin, *Mañana es San Perón*, 333.

20. Fernández and Arata, *Series estadística*, table 1, p. 7.

21. The percentage of women attending national universities had been 32 in 1963. Cano, *Educación superior*, 69, and table 11, p. 132.

22. See Bianchi and Sachís, *Partido Peronista Femenino*, and Plotkin, *Mañana es San Perón*.

23. See Hollander, *Love in a Time of Hate*, 75–76. For a discussion of general attitudes toward women in Argentina, see Menéndez, *En búsqueda de las mujeres*.

24. Caimari, "Whose Prisoners Are These?"

25. It is interesting to note that Raquel Liliana Gelin, the first woman member of a guerrilla group to die in a clash with the military in 1970, was remembered as the *virgencita montonera*.

26. *Descamisado*, Nov. 6, 1973, 30, and Sept. 26, 1973, 25.

27. See the fascinating collection of interviews with former female members of the armed Guevarist / Trotskyite group ERP in Diana, *Mujeres guerrilleras*. The women were expected not only to take part in risky operations but also to carry out their "duties as women": taking care of children, preparing food, etc. In general women did not occupy leadership positions in revolutionary organizations, and they sometimes relied on traditional images of femininity (either as seductresses, as mothers, or as wives) to break loose from the police or the military.

28. "Encuestas: El hombre argentino cree en el amor pero subestima a su pareja," *Primera Plana*, Sept. 3, 1963.

29. Women remained legally dependant of their husbands until very recently. Only fathers had legal rights over their children until 1986. Until then, a mother who wanted to travel outside the country with her children needed written permission from their father. Moreover, only the husband could decide the location of the family home. In 1969 the military authorities passed legislation forcing married women to add their husband's last name preceded by "de" (which in Spanish connotes property) to their own family name. See Wainerman and Barck de Raijman, *Sexismo*, 85–86.

30. For an impressionistic but interesting discussion, see Sebreli, *Buenos Aires.*

31. James, *Resistance and Integration,* chap. 1.

32. For a discussion of the early interpretations of Peronism, see Plotkin, "Changing Perceptions of Peronism."

33. Neiburg, *Intelectuales,* 183–214.

34. *Primera Plana,* Nov. 13, 1962.

35. For middle-class perceptions of Peronism, see Plotkin, "Changing Perceptions."

36. For a discussion of the coup of 1966 and its consequences, see Sigal and Terán, "Intelectuales frente a la política."

37. In the School of Physical Sciences and Mathematics alone, 335 professors resigned in the aftermath of the coup. In the School of Philosophy and Letters, 300 resigned. See Oteiza, "Emigración," 225.

38. See, e.g., "El 'hippismo' no es un deporte," *Gente,* Jan. 11, 1968, 6; cf. "¿Qué está haciendo la policía?" *Gente,* Feb. 15, 1968, 4–5.

39. Halperín Donghi, *Larga agonía,* 41.

40. The comic strip, published in the magazine *4 Patas* in 1960, is discussed in Jorge Rivera, "Historia del humor gráfico argentino," in Ford, Rivera, and Romano, *Medios de comunicación,* 124–25.

41. For a general history of the University of Buenos Aires, see Halperín Donghi, *Historia de la Universidad.*

42. This tendency can be easily followed in the Peronist official press, particularly in *Mundo Peronista.*

43. The Lorraine, a theater that drew large audiences in the late 1950s and 1960s, when it showcased the films of Bergman and the Nouvelle Vague, had shown art films to a largely empty house in the 1940s. See Sebreli, *Buenos Aires,* 112. See also Goldar, *Buenos Aires.*

44. Among government institutions founded to promote the arts after the fall of Perón were the Fondo Nacional de las Artes, the Instituto Nacional de Cinematografía, and the Museo de Arte Moderno. In 1958 the government also created CONICET, an agency devoted to the support and promotion of scientific research.

45. In the late 1960s the leftist filmmaker Eduardo "Pino" Solanas, for instance, depicted the Instituto Di Tella as a bourgeois, decadent institution in *La hora de los hornos.* For an analysis of the Di Tella's public, see Marta Slemenson and Germán Kratochwill, "Un arte de difusores," in Marsal, *Intelectual latinoamericano.*

46. John King, *Di Tella,* 58–59.

47. *Primera Plana,* Oct. 10, 1964, mentions several famous psychoanalysts who purchased works of art exhibited at the Di Tella and other avant-garde galleries. One of them said he was going to remove some parts of the piece because otherwise they might disturb his patients.

48. "Buenos Aires 1966: ¿Que es eso del Hapening [*sic*]?" *Gente,* Aug. 25, 1966.

49. See John King, *Di Tella;* Woodyard, "Eduardo Pavlovsky."

50. See Aníbal Ford and Jorge B. Rivera, "Los medios masivos de comunicación en la Argentina," in Ford, Rivera, and Romano, *Medios de comunicación,* 24–45.

51. John King, *Di Tella,* 19–20.

52. The three shows featuring psychoanalysts were *Claudia mira la vida* (Mauricio Abadi), *Esta noche indagamos* (Enrique Pichon Rivière), and *El otro yo* (Alberto Fontana). See *Primera Plana,* Feb. 26, 1963, 45.

53. See *La narrativa: La generación del 55,* Capítulo: La historia de la literatura argentina, 53 (Buenos Aires: Centro Editor de América Latina, 1975). Also *Las últimas promociones: La narrativa y la poesía,* Capítulo, 55 (1975); and Rivera, *Apogeo y crisis.*

54. Sagastizábal, *Edición de libros,* 150. In 1964 EUDEBA issued 239 titles.

55. Gino Germani, "Sociografía de la clase media en Buenos Aires: Características culturales de la clase media en la ciudad de Buenos Aires estudiada a través del empleo de sus horas libres," *Boletín del Instituto de Sociología* 2 (1943), cited in Sebreli, *Buenos Aires,* 95.

56. Earlier and largely forgotten works by authors who had become fashionable were reissued and sold briskly. Cortázar's *Bestiario,* published in 1951, took more than ten years to sell out the first edition of 3,000 copies; in 1964 it sold 3,000 copies in less than a year, and by 1965 it was in its fifth edition. Rivera, *Apogeo y crisis.*

57. Borello, "Autores." For an insightful overview of Argentine literature in the 1960s, see Prieto, "Años sesenta"; Dellepiane, "Novela argentina."

58. García Canclini, "Movimientos artísticos."

59. Some of Puig's later novels, such as *The Buenos Aires Affair* (1975), deal more openly with psychoanalysis.

60. See, e.g., the examples cited in Anguita and Caparrós, *La voluntad,* 1:53, 248–50, 391.

61. See Buntig, *Catolicismo popular.*

62. Sylvia Bermann, "Verdad y mentira."

63. For this interpretation, see Schorske, *Fin-de-Siècle Vienna,* chap. 4; McGrath, *Freud's Discovery.* For an interpretation that emphasizes the role of psychoanalysis in depoliticizing modern society, see Castel, *Psychanalysme,* esp. 362, n. 9, and 378.

64. For a discussion of the political components of Freud's theories, see Brunner, *Freud and the Politics of Psychoanalysis.*

65. Martins, "A geração AI-5."

66. For an analysis of Brazilian intellectuals that stresses continuities in thought, see Pécault, *Entre le peuple et la nation.*

67. APA archive, "Libro de Actas," Acta 64, Mar. 23, 1964, 45.

68. Interview with Roberto Harari.

69. Its board of directors was composed of eight APA members: Juan Morgan, Emilio Rodrigué, Raúl Usandivaras, Jorge Mom, José Bleger, Alberto Fontana, León Grinberg, and Marie Langer. Mom, Usandivaras, and Morgan attended the First International Conference on Group Therapy in Toronto, 1954.

70. Giberti et al., "Técnica de abordaje psicológico."

71. Information on Germani can be found in Kahl, *Three Latin American Sociologists,* 23–74. Germani's introductions to Fromm's *Escape from Freedom,* Mead's *Mind, Self, and Society,* and Malinowski's *Myth in Primitive Psychology* were reprinted in Germani, *Estudios de psicología social.* Additional information can be found in Vezzetti, "Ciencias sociales." Germani's translation of Fromm's *Escape from Freedom* had sold 150,000 copies by 1969.

72. Germani, "Psicoanálisis y las ciencias del hombre."

73. Grinberg, Langer, and Rodrigué, *Psicoterapia del grupo,* 21, 27.

74. See also Langer, *Fantasías eternas,* Prologue and Epilogue.

75. Rodrigué, for instance, worked in the service of Dr. Juan Garraham at the Children's Hospital.

76. Langer, *Fantasías eternas,* 135, 137.

77. Ibid., 108, 100n.

78. Ibid., 112–15.

79. In 1967 Pavlovsky and Rojas separated because Rojas adhered more closely to Moreno's technique while Pavlovsky was more psychoanalytically oriented.

80. See, e.g., "Psicoanálisis, una candileja más," *Primera Plana,* Oct. 29, 1963, 43.

81. Balán, *Cuéntame tu vida,* 194. See also "Concluyó el sábado el Congreso Internacional de Psicodrama y Sociodrama. Y colorín colorado, mis complejos he curado," *Gente,* Sept. 4, 1969, 84–85. The conference was held at the medical school of the University of Buenos Aires.

82. Balán, *Cuéntame tu vida,* 192–93.

83. APA members who proposed technical deviations were ostracized, while members who proposed more daring theoretical deviations but continued to pledge allegiance to the Kleinian technical framework were left alone. An example, discussed in detail in Chapter 6, was José Bleger, who attempted to combine psychoanalysis and Marxism. Even Marie Langer and Arnaldo Rascovsky, as we shall see in Chapter 4, introduced important theoretical deviations.

84. Dr. Alberto Fontana told me that the reasons for the resignations and for Pérez Morales's punishment were related to internal politics, including sexual politics. He also claimed that many APA analysts continued to experiment with LSD in secret, despite the APA's prohibition.

85. *Revista de Psicoanálisis* 18, no. 2 (1961): 197.
86. "El psicoanálisis no existe," *Primera Plana*, Aug. 20, 1968, 39–51.
87. Cited in Brignardello, "Psicoterapias."

4. The Diffusers' Role in the Expansion of the Psychoanalytic Realm

1. See Langer, Guinsberg, and Palacio, *Memoria*, esp. 79–81.
2. See, e.g., "Psychoanalysis and Revolution." See also Langer, *From Vienna to Managua*.
3. See, e.g., her discussion of feminism in her *Maternidad y sexo*, chap. 1.
4. What follows is based on two papers by Hugo Vezzetti: "Marie Langer: De la maternidad" and "Marie Langer: La maternidad y la revolución."
5. Published in Spanish as *Matrimonio perfecto*.
6. Langer, *Maternidad y sexo*, Introduction.
7. Ibid., 48–49, 25–26, 232, 131. In the first edition Langer still left open the possibility of fulfillment through sublimation of the reproductive function.
8. Ibid., 130.
9. See Langer et al., *Memoria*, pt. 2.
10. See, e.g., "Proceso a la píldora anticonceptiva," *Gente*, Jan. 19, 1967, 12.
11. Langer, "La mujer, sus limitaciones y potencialidades," in her *Cuestionamos: 1971 Plataforma-Documento*, 183–208. The book is a condensed second edition of the two-volume *Cuestionamos* (1971–73), discussed in Chapter 8.
12. See Sigal and Verón, *¡Perón o muerte!*
13. See *Revista Latinoamericana de Psiquiatría* 1, no. 4 (July 1952): 80–83. In the early 1970s, after Langer's radicalization, she and Sylvia Bermann became personal friends and wrote articles together.
14. Langer, *Fantasías eternas*, 9, 91, 92.
15. Ibid., 95.
16. Ibid., 172.
17. Arnaldo Rascovsky, "Esquema autobiográfico," in his *Matanza de los hijos*, 64–65.
18. Rascovsky, "La matanza de los hijos," ibid., 27.
19. For a thorough discussion of Rascovsky's ideas in English, see his *Filicide*. Langer remembers that at a psychoanalytic congress in Vienna, journalists approached a senior member of the IPA to confirm that "psychoanalysts did not seriously believe that the cause of war was the filicidal tendencies of generals." See Langer et al., *Memoria*, 106.
20. A FILIUM poster explaining in mock seriousness "how to make a schizophrenic of your son" hung in my mother's bedroom.
21. Rascovsky opposed kindergartens on the grounds that children of that age should be at home with their mothers. See Carli, "Infancia," 269.
22. Rascovsky, "Matanza de los hijos," 14–15.

23. Rascovsky, *Conversaciones con Rascovsky,* 1:15.

24. Quoted in Hugo Vezzetti, "La situación actual del psicoanálisis," in Langer, *Cuestionamos: 1971 Plataforma-documento,* 221. On the official discourse of the military regime on family, see Filc, *Entre el parentesco y la política.*

25. The evaluations of Rascovsky's theories are uneven. In 1962 Horacio Etchegoyen, who was to become the first Argentine (and first Latin American) president of the IPA, said that "in general, few analysts outside of Dr. Rascovsky's group believe that the theory of fetal psychodynamics has enough basis to be operative in our clinical practice" (in Gregorio Bermann, *Psicoterapias y el psicoterapeuta,* 233).

26. Vezzetti, *Aventuras de Freud,* 265.

27. See his *Teoría del vínculo,* based on the notes for his classes on the technique of the therapy session taught at the APA in 1956 and 1957.

28. Cereijido, *Nuca de Houssay.*

29. Interview with Isidoro Vegh.

30. In the preface Pichon explicitly says that the development of his "link theory" and his shift of interest toward social psychology required a break with traditional psychoanalysis.

31. Interview with Ignacio Maldonado.

32. Ulloa, *Novela clínica psicoanalítica,* 55.

33. Marcelo Pichon Rivière, Introduction to Enrique Pichon Rivière, *Psicoanálisis del Conde de Lautréamont.*

34. His first article on psychology was on Adler and Jung, not on Freud. See Pichon Rivière, "Dos problemas."

35. Most of the articles are compiled in Pichon Rivière, *Psicoanálisis del Conde de Lautréamont.*

36. Enrique Pichon Rivière, "Grupos operativos y enfermedad única," *Del psicoanálisis,* 2:279.

37. Pichon Rivière and Etchegoyen, "Psiquiatría en el contexto de los estudios médicos."

38. In an interview Dr. Alberto Fontana claimed that it was he and not Pichon who introduced Lacan's works to Masotta. Fontana also said that Masotta spent time in his clinic, not at Pichon's house, as Masotta himself claimed.

39. Pichon Rivière, "Grupos familiares: Un enfoque operativo," in *Del psicoanálisis,* 2:205.

40. When I was a student in the late 1970s, the cool thing to do for students who were interested in psychology but not in the rigors of serious studies was to enroll in *la escuelita de Pichon.* The line for registration formed the night before.

41. "Reportaje: Doctor Enrique Pichon Rivière," *Revista Latinoamericana de Salud Mental* 10 (November 1966): 250–52.

42. See Pichon Rivière, *Teoría del vínculo,* 22. Elsewhere he wrote, "Nuestro esquema conceptual, referencial y operativo está constituído sobre todo en su aspecto genético, histórico y estructural, por las ideas de Freud y Melanie Klein, mientras en el aspecto social nos apoyamos en K. Lewin": Pichon Rivière, "Estructura de una escuela destinada a la formación de psicólogos sociales," in *Del psicoanálisis,* 2:318. For Lewin's theories on social psychology, see his *Field Theory in Social Science.*

43. Pichon Rivière, "Psicología social,"49.

44. In an interview Carlos Mario Aslán said, "Enrique inventaba cosas, inventaba palabras nuevas para las mismas cosas viejas. . . . Me acuerdo que en unas clases que él daba le pregunté: Decime, Enrique, qué diferencia hay entre lo que acabás de decir y la complacencia somática que hay en las histerias? Ninguna."

45. Pichon Rivière, "Prólogo" to Martelli, "Enfermedades de las empresas," 24–26.

46. At psychiatric conferences throughout the 1960s psychiatrists of the most disparate theoretical schools routinely claimed Pichon Rivière as their teacher. See, e.g., Gregorio Bermann, *Psicoterapias y el psicoterapeuta.*

47. For a description of Operación Rosario, see Pichon Rivière et al., "Técnica de los grupos operativos."

48. Ulloa, *Novela clínica,* 64.

49. Pichon Rivière, "Destino y computadora," *Primera Plana,* Nov. 22, 1966, 65.

50. Pichon Rivière, "Mirada, cuerpo y motivaciones," *Primera Plana,* June 7, 1966, 53. See also "Afiliación y pertenencia," ibid., Oct. 18, 1966, 49.

51. Pichon Rivière, "La psicología social," ibid., May 3, 1966, 49; and "Censor y censurado," ibid., Sept. 6, 1966, 49.

52. Pichon Rivière, "La elección de pareja," ibid., Oct. 25, 1966, 53.

53. *Para Tí,* Aug. 24, 1954.

54. In 1968 Giberti also took part in another TV show, *Tribunal de Apelación,* together with her husband and a lawyer, in which actual cases of family conflict presented by the audience were discussed and analyzed.

55. From the beginning Giberti and Escardó made use of modern technology to spread their message. In 1963 they put out a record album, *Exercises for the Baby,* sold at newsstands. The exercises were designed to help the baby "form his own corporal schema in the context of contact with the mother." The album liner read: "Modern science has discovered that there is no substitute for a mother's love in the growth and development of every human being." My thanks to Eva Giberti for granting me access to her personal archive.

56. According to Giberti, there were 30 editions of the book, each of which consisted of 5,000 copies, plus one unauthorized edition. See Eva

Giberti, "Psicoanálisis y divulgación: La experiencia de Escuela para Padres," *Todo Es Historia* 280 (1990): 64–72.

57. Giberti, *Escuela para padres,* 3:192.

58. *Para Tí,* Oct. 16, 1967.

59. Giberti, *Escuela para padres,* 1:15, 18.

60. Ibid., 23.

61. Elsewhere she urges parents to respect the "hierarchical labor of the doctor" and not put obstacles in his way: ibid., 2:294.

62. Ibid., 240–41.

63. Ibid., 70.

64. Quoted in Nathan Hale, *Rise and Crisis,* 286.

65. Giberti, *Escuela para padres,* 1:186, 2:64.

66. For a discussion of the debates on female labor by Argentine feminists during the first half of the century, see Lavrin, *Women, Feminism, and Social Change,* chap. 2.

67. *Para Tí,* Dec. 4, 1967; Jan. 1, 1968.

68. A mother who took part in one of Giberti's groups at the Children's Hospital asked her if her two-month-old baby could be considered neurotic (Giberti's personal archive).

69. Interview with Giberti, Nov. 6, 1996.

70. See, e.g., the review of Giberti's *Argentinos y el amor* in *Revista de Psicología* 8, no. 2 (June 1971).

71. Interview with Giberti, Nov. 6, 1996.

72. *Para Tí,* Mar. 8, 1960.

73. "Tribuna de la Juventud," *Nuestros Hijos,* March 1960, 58.

74. See Carli, "Infancia, psicoanálisis y crisis," 221–87.

75. In April 1962 *Claudia* consulted a psychoanalyst—"not a judge, a psychoanalyst"—on bigamy.

76. *Para Tí,* June 16, 1964.

77. On the discourse on women by the Catholic Church, see Wainerman, *Mujer y el trabajo.* On textbooks, see Wainerman and Barck de Raijman, *Sexismo en los libros.*

78. *Para Tí,* April 22 and May 2, 1950.

79. Ibid., Aug. 16, 1960.

80. Ibid., Jan. 19, 5, and 12, 1960.

81. Ibid., Apr. 28 and June 9, 1964.

82. Mafud, *Revolución sexual,* 12.

83. See, e.g., "Proceso a la píldora anticonceptiva," *Gente,* Jan. 1967, 12. The people interviewed included an unmarried actress, a gynecologist, a married actress, a housewife with seven children, a Jesuit priest, and a psychoanalyst. For a positive view of the pill, emphasizing the greater ability to enjoy sex that it allows, see "La verdad sobre la píldora," *Para Tí,* June 22, 1970.

84. *Gente,* Aug. 11, 1966.

85. Moscovici, *Psychanalyse.*

86. *Gente,* Feb. 29, 1968.

87. In the 1960s Argentine psychoanalysts typically charged their regular fees if patients missed their regular appointments while the analysts themselves were available. Therefore analysts forced patients to schedule their vacations to coincide with theirs.

88. *Gente,* Oct. 6, 1966; Mar. 9, 1967; Sept. 24, 1970.

89. "Una pregunta pocas veces respondida: ¿Por qué se sicoanalizan los jóvenes?" *Gente,* July 27, 1972, 68–70.

90. On *Primera Plana* see Alvarado and Rocco-Cuzzi, *"Primera Plana"*; Terán, *Nuestros años sesenta,* 81–84; and Mazzei, *"Primera Plana."*

91. Similar although less influential magazines published in the 1960s were *Confirmado* and *Panorama.* They also were full of psychoanalytic language.

92. Quoted in Mazzei, *"Primera Plana,"* 25.

93. *Primera Plana,* Jan. 1 and Feb.13, 1963.

94. Ibid., Nov. 20, 1962, 45–49.

95. Pichon Rivière, "Inundados."

96. *Primera Plana,* Apr. 9 and Feb. 18, 1963.

5. The Encounter Between Psychoanalysis and Psychiatry

1. Vezzetti, "Ciencias sociales."

2. The psychiatric branch of the Argentine Medical Association was never among the most active. Psychiatric journals complained that psychiatry was not being taken seriously: "La psiquiatría fue siempre una materia que incluída dentro del programa de los estudios médicos era mirada, y aun lo es por el estudiante, como una asignatura de escasa importancia, cuyo conocimiento mediocre excedía los límites de lo necesario, y que solo le bastaba que saber que un alienado debía ser recluído en un nosocomio de la especialidad, y allí que se entendieran": Vivaldo, "Breve reseña."

3. For a discussion of electroconvulsive therapy, see Berrios, "Scientific Origins." For a good general (although antipsychoanalytic) overview of the history of psychiatric methods, see Shorter, *History of Psychiatry.*

4. The degeneration paradigm, however, continued to thrive among the most conservative sectors of the psychiatric community. As late as 1940 forensic experts were still looking for "physical signs of degeneration" in criminal suspects. See, e.g., Ciafardo, "Homicidio." A year earlier a member of the Sociedad Argentina de Criminología had done an "anthropological study" of the skull of an anarchist who had been executed in 1931 and concluded that the anatomical piece "presenta anomalías de desarrollo, estigmas de degeneración y carácteres de regresión atávica que han preparado biológica-

mente un terreno favorable para que otro conjunto de factores, ya de naturaleza ambiente y social, pudieran complementarlos eficazmente para que la peligrosidad de Paulino Scarfo se manifestara de forma tan franca y decidida": *Revista de Psiquiatría y Criminología* 4, no. 22 (July–August 1939): 27.

5. In 1933, however, the assistant director of the national mental hospital recommended bloodletting for cases of manic excitement. See Esteves Balado, "Tratamiento de agitación," 39.

6. See, e.g., Krapf, "Sobre la despersonalización." Other contributors included Roque Orlando, Ramón Melgar, Mario Sbarbi, Atlántico Francia, and Gonzalo Bosch. Pichon Rivière was listed among the contributors but in fact he did not publish in the journal.

7. The "manifesto" of reflexology was Thénon's "Psiquiatría en el año 50." See also Gavrilov, *Psicoanálisis a la luz de la reflexología.*

8. Claudio Bermann, "La psicoterapia en el ambiente sanatorial," in Gregorio Bermann, *Psicoterapias y el psicoterapeuta,* 127–39. In the same vein, see Bleger, "Progresos farmacéuticos," 43.

9. Interview with Guillermo Vidal.

10. Argentina had 1,474 psychiatrists, Brazil 774, and Mexico 381. Brazil and Mexico had much larger populations than Argentina. See *Acta Psiquiátrica y Psicológica de América Latina* 16, no. 1 (March 1970): 5.

11. Sylvia Bermann, "Análisis de algunos datos."

12. See Ministerio de Salud Pública, *Informe,* 17.

13. See, among others, Sbarbi and Zipilivan, "Aspectos de la asistencia," 458–61; Esteves Balado, "Consideraciones"; Goldenberg, "Estado actual."

14. The minister of public health of Córdoba said at the Second Conference on Psychiatric Services in 1958: "Entiende mi gobierno que las soluciones de los problemas de la salud pública así como el resto de las cuestiones vinculadas a la seguridad social son inseparables de una política que aliente el desarrollo y el progreso económico. En otras palabras, que de no impulsarse y lograrse tal desarrollo, fallará la base económica que hace posible las soluciones más adecuadas": *Acta Neuropsiquiátrica Argentina* 14 (1958): 262.

15. For a general discussion of the differences between traditional mental hygiene and mental health, see Gregorio Bermann, "De la higiene mental mítica de ayer a la higiene mental racional," in his *Problemas psiquiátricos,* 391–403.

16. See Decreto Ley 12628, "Considerandos," *Boletín Oficial,* Nov. 18, 1957, 2–3.

17. "Programa," *Revista Latinoamericana de Psiquiatría* 1, no. 1 (October 1951).

18. Gregorio Bermann, "Sociopsiquiatría," 7.

19. See, e.g., "Polémica sobre el psicoanálisis," *Revista Latinoamericana de Psiquiatría* 1, no. 2 (November 1951). The debate consisted of a series of articles

(some of which had been published earlier in other journals), including Gregorio Bermann, "El psicoanálisis enjuiciado" (97–99); Arturo Capdevila, "El dios Freud: Diálogo con Gregorio Bermann" (99–101), and Bermann, "Las falacias del psicoanálisis: Respuesta a Arturo Capdevila" (101–6).

20. Gregorio Bermann, "Tratamiento de elección." For his view of psychoanalytic explications of reality see his "Etiopatogenia de las neurosis." Whereas Bermann emphasized social factors in the etiology of neurosis, Garma was denying their influence.

21. Interview with Guillermo Vidal.

22. In the 1970s the Communist psychiatrist César Augusto Cabral accused the journal of being *cientificista,* prompting a polemic with Sylvia Bermann. See *Acta Psiquiátrica y Psicológica Latinoamericana* 17, no. 3 (June 1971) and no. 4 (August 1971).

23. "Guillermo Vidal," in Alarcón, *Identidad de la psiquiatría latinoamericana,* 610, 620.

24. See, e.g., Verón, "Notas para una concepción estructural"; Korn and Kornblit, "Revisión de un concepto sociológico."

25. Rodrigué, "Bion y la psicoterapia de grupo."

26. Alvarez de Toledo, Fontana, and Pérez Morales, "Psicoanálisis y dietilamida."

27. Among the psychiatrists whom the journal published through the years were Honorio Delgado, Gregorio Bermann, Julio Endara, Enrique Pichon Rivière, Jorge Thénon, Angel Garma, and Mauricio Goldenberg.

28. During a conference on psychotherapy in Córdoba in 1964, Bermann said: "Yo me siento feliz con la compañía de psicoanalistas del rango humano de Etchegoyen y de Taragano y de otros miembros de la Mesa y del público. Ahora bien, el hecho real e incontrovertible es que tal vez el 90 o el 95 por ciento de los psicoanalistas permanecen encerrados tras de los muros de sus consultorios, ajenos a las otras cosas. La referencia va por ellos y por lo que pueda haber en el psicoanálisis que favorezca esa tendencia, de la que escapan los colegas nombrados y otros." Bermann, *Psicoterapia de la niñez,* 225.

29. José Bleger, "El tratamiento psicoanalítico," in Gregorio Bermann, *Psicoterapias y el psicoterapeuta,* 73.

30. Thénon in Gregorio Bermann, *Psicoterapia de la niñez,* 61.

31. See *Acta Psiquiátrica y Psicológica Argentina* 8 (1962): 177.

32. Balán, *Cuéntame tu vida,* 207.

33. "Asamblea de la Federación Argentina de Psiquiatras" (n.d. [1969]), mimeo, FAP archives.

34. *Boletín Informativo* 2, no. 6 (April–May 1971): 1.

35. Since 1983 Goldenberg has been appointed to several honorary positions at the University of Buenos Aires. The "Primeras Jornadas Encuentro del Servicio de Psicopatología del Policlínico Lanús" was held in 1992, with

Goldenberg and Valentín Baremblit, his successor at the Aráoz Alfaro, as guests of honor. In 1996 the School of Psychology of the University of Buenos Aires published a Festschrift dedicated to Goldenberg, *Testimonios para la experiencia de enseñar: Mauricio Goldenberg, maestro, médico, psiquiatra, humanista.* For an insightful analysis of the Goldenberg myth and its place in the collective memory, see Visacovsky, "Genealogías rompidas."

36. In *Testimonios,* 59–63, Goldenberg claims that he completed analytic training. He never did.

37. Sbarbi and Goldenberg, "Electroshock y psicoterapia intensivos."

38. Goldenberg, "Estado actual." For developments in the United States, see Boshes, "Function of the Psychiatrist"; Ayd, "Psychiatric Patients"; and Fairweather et al., *Community Life for the Mentally Ill.*

39. By 1966 the service included 48 M.D.'s, 18 residents, 16 psychologists, 2 sociologists, 2 educators, and an occupational therapist. Interestingly enough, only five of his team members received any salary.

40. Goldenberg et al., "Psiquiatría en el hospital general."

41. Ibid. See also Sluzki, "Informe estadístico." Sluzky attributed the increase in neurotic patients to "the public's better and more complete information and the subsequent lessening of resistance or prejudice toward mental disorders among the general population and among doctors. . . ."

42. For a sociological analysis of the patients carried out by members of Goldenberg's service, see Tarnopolsky et al., "Características sociológicas." For a description of the psychotherapeutic techniques used in Lanús, see Goldenberg, "Psicoterapia en el hospital general."

43. Goldenberg's response to a question at the Primeras Jornadas Argentinas de Psicoterapia, Córdoba, July 1962, in Gregorio Bermann, *Psicoterapias y el psicoterapeuta,* 155.

44. Ibid., 156.

45. Vezzetti, "Ciencias sociales."

46. Giberti et al., "Técnicas de abordaje psicológico."

47. Interview with Wilbur Ricardo Grimson.

48. Municipalidad de la Ciudad de Buenos Aires, *Plan de Salud Mental* (1969), 8.

49. "Sin muros, sin miedos: Los hospitales neuropsiquiátricos se transforman en centros modernos que se encargan de la prevención, asistencia y rehabilitación de los enfermos," *Gente,* Dec. 12, 1968, 10–11; "La sociedad espera," *Gente,* May 1, 1969, 46. See also Galende, *Psicoanálisis y salud mental,* 112, and *Acta Psiquiátrica y Psicológica de América Latina* 13 (1967): 285.

50. Jones, *Social Psychiatry.*

51. For an insightful discussion of therapeutic communities and an analysis of the experience of the Austen Riggs Center in Massachusetts, see Rodrigué, *Biografía de una comunidad terapéutica.* The experience of Lomas de Zamora is

discussed in Grimson, "Transformación del hospital psiquiátrico." For the experience at the Roballos Hospital, see Guedes Arroyo, "Hospital Dr. A. L. Roballos."

52. Grimson interview.

53. Grimson, "Transformación del hospital psiquiátrico," 358.

54. Interviews with Grimson and Jorge García Badaracco.

55. Goldenberg, "Estado actual"; Etchegoyen, "Nuestra cátedra."

56. *Testimonios para la experiencia de enseñar,* 218; interview with Etchegoyen.

57. Federación Argentina de Psiquiátras, "Ante la situación del Instituto Nacional de Salud Mental," November 1970, mimeo, FAP archives. The FAP also pointed out that the therapeutic community was an import with no roots in Argentine tradition. See also "Un balance de cinco años: Enjuician los especialistas la política oficial de salud mental," *La Opinión,* July 6, 1971, 18. FAP documents were kindly provided by Dr. Juan Carlos Stagnaro and Dr. Emiliano Galende.

58. This proposal was rejected in December 1966.

59. Patients and staff resisted the government interference and the police were called. Grimson had to jump over a wall to escape arrest.

6. Psychologists Take the Stage

1. See Litvinoff and Gomel, *Psicólogo y su profesión.* According to Rubén Ardila, "Psychology," on average only 9% of Latin American psychologists work in private practice.

2. According to Hornstein, "Return of the Repressed," "by the 1950s research on psychoanalysis had become so popular that . . . a new cottage industry was born of this demand." For a general overview of the development of psychology as a profession in the United States, see Capshew, *Psychologists on the March.*

3. Grego and Kauman, "Lugar del psicólogo," 72.

4. According to a survey conducted by the Asociación de Psicólogos de Buenos Aires in 1970, three out of five psychology programs at private universities in Buenos Aires had a definite psychoanalytical slant. APBA Archive, "Libro de Asambleas," vol. 2 (Oct. 19, 1970), 40–42.

5. There were 1,159 psychology students at the University of Córdoba, 699 in Rosario, 693 in La Plata, 360 in Tucumán, and 245 in Cuyo. See Chaparro, "Carrera de psicología." Although I have no figures for graduates, the combined total of licenciados in sociology and psychology graduated from the School of Philosophy rose from 78 in 1961 to 655 in 1967. In the latter year only 142 were men. The number of students enrolled in all programs of philosophy, literature, and the humanities in public universities rose from 9,732

in 1958 to 19,943 in 1965. See Argentina, Ministerio de Cultura y Educación, *Educación en cifras, 1961–1970,* table VI.I.8, p. 261, and *Educación en cifras, 1958–1967,* table VI.I.4, p. 89.

6. Not all of them, of course, were practicing at all. See Alonso, "Psicología en la República Argentina."

7. Argentina as a whole has 120 psychologists per 100,000 inhabitants. Brazil has 54 and the United States 56. See Acaso, "Psicología en la República Argentina."

8. Litvinoff and Gomel, *Psicólogo y su profesión,* 118. The remaining 7% presumably chose "wild analysts," those who practiced without having completed the proper training.

9. In that year 24% of all UBA students were in psychotherapy—28% of those in the upper-income group and 22% of the less affluent. See Toer, *Como son los estudiantes.* It is interesting that the researchers included a question about therapy in an investigation of the socioeconomic and cultural status of university students.

10. Ley 17,132, art. 91, reads as follows: "[Psicólogos] podrán actuar: en psicopatología únicamente como colaboradores del médico especializado en psiquiatría, por su indicación y bajo su supervisión . . . debiendo limitar su actuación a la obtención de tests psicológicos y a la colaboración en tareas de investigación. . . . Les está prohibido toda actividad con personas enfermas fuera de lo expresamente autorizado en los párrafos precedentes, asimismo como la práctica del psicoanálisis y la utilización de psicodrogas." See *Boletín Oficial,* Jan. 31, 1967, 2–9.

11. Toer, *Como son los estudiantes,* 15.

12. Now that psychologists are permitted to join psychoanalytic associations, 96% of the psychologists who belong to the APA and the Asociación Psicoanalítica de Buenos Aires (APdeBA) are still women. See Alonso, "Psicología en la República Argentina."

13. Ardila, "Psychology." Papini, "Psicología experimental," mentions a lab of experimental psychology established by Victor Mercante in the Escuela Normal de San Juan in 1891.

14. Alberini, *Precisiones,* 80. See also Klappenbach, "Recepción de Wundt."

15. For an enlightening introduction to the origins of Argentine psychology, see Vezzetti, "Estudio preliminar."

16. What follows is based on the syllabi of psychology courses at the University of Buenos Aires. For a more thorough discussion, see Plotkin, "Freud en la Universidad de Buenos Aires."

17. See Piñero, "Psicología experimental."

18. Interview with Reggy Serebriany, Oct. 2, 1996.

19. See Rossi et al., *Psicología antes de la profesión.*

20. Papini, "Psicología experimental."

21. Among the APA psychoanalysts were Willy Baranger, Angel Garma, Mauricio Knobel, and Emilio Rodrigué.

22. Vezzetti, "Orígenes de la Psicología."

23. Balán, *Cuéntame tu vida,* 146–47.

24. Similar programs were started in La Plata, Córdoba, Tucumán, and elsewhere. It is interesting to note that Buenos Aires granted the academic licenciado degree, whereas the other programs granted the professional psicólogo degree. A doctorate was proposed several times in Buenos Aires, but it did not materialize.

25. Balan, *Cuéntame tu vida,* 148.

26. Grego and Kauman, "Lugar del psicólogo," 71.

27. The idea of psychoanalysis as filling an empty theoretical space is suggested by Luis Felipe García de Onrubia, "Tres momentos en la constitución de la psicología argentina," in Rossi, *Psicología antes de la profesión,* 68.

28. See Goode, "Encroachment."

29. See Etchegoyen, "Estado actual."

30. On the reactions of psychiatrists to psychoanalysis, see Knobel, "Diagnóstico y psicoterapia."

31. Balán, *Cuéntame to vida,* 148.

32. Gregorio Bermann, "Los psicólogos en la práctica médica," in Bermann, *Nuestra psiquiatría,* 177.

33. On the evolution of the relationship between the medical corporation and the state in the 1960s, see Belmartino and Boch, *Sector salud.*

34. Knobel, "Diagnóstico y psicoterapia."

35. Galende, *Psicoanálisis y salud mental,* 252.

36. A poll taken among a representative group of psychologists in the early 1970s showed that a large proportion of psychologists not only were in therapy with psychoanalysts but also were controlling their cases with psychoanalysts. See Litvinoff and Gomel, *Psicólogo y su profesión,* 108.

37. *Acta Psiquiátrica y Psicológica Argentina* 8, no. 1 (March 1962).

38. In 1965 a chair in mental hygiene was established in the psychology department of the School of Philosophy, and Bleger was appointed to it. Bleger had to acknowledge that psychologists needed to work as independent professionals because most health care institutions that hired them (even the most progressive ones, such as the Hospital Aráoz Alfaro in Lanús) did not pay them. See Bleger, *Psicohigiene,* 41.

39. Ibid., 185; Bleger's emphasis.

40. Ibid., 172; Bleger, "Tratamiento psicoanalítico," 70.

41. Bleger, *Psicohigiene,* 186.

42. Grego and Kauman, "Lugar del psicólogo," 86.

43. The nonexistence of psychological research carried out by psychol-

ogists was noted by Eliseo Verón in 1965: "It should be taken into account that, in contrast to what happens in the field of sociology, in Argentina professional psychological activity in applied areas . . . increases in importance relatively quickly, while [psychological] research is in comparison nonexistent": "Coloquio," 118. In 1968 there were only three ongoing research projects at the Instituto de Psicología. Between 1969 and 1973 there was none. See Papini, "Psicología experimental."

44. Estudiantes delegados, "Producción del psicoanálysis," 36.

45. Knobel, "Función psicoterapéutica," 228, 239.

46. See, e.g., "Una pregunta pocas veces respondida: Por qué se sicoanalizan los jóvenes?" *Gente,* July 27, 1972, 68–70. Two of the young people interviewed claimed that they had more confidence in psychoanalysts because they were M.D.'s. One of them, however, said he was currently in therapy with a psychologist and that it was a good experience.

47. For instance, all senior teaching positions in Bleger's mental hygiene department were held by men (*adjuntos* and *jefes de trabajos prácticos*). All the teaching assistants and auxiliary staff were women. See Bleger, *Psicohigiene,* 202.

48. Ardila, "Psicología en Argentina."

49. *Revista Argentina de Psicología* 68 (January–February 1986), 7.

50. Ares, "'Fuerza' de una institución," 22; my emphasis.

51. When a group of psychologists petitioned for better working conditions at the Hospital Tornú in 1970, they were told they should be grateful to be allowed to work in a hospital at all. APBA Archive, "Libro de Actas," vol. 2 (Sept. 15, 1970), 33.

52. Confederación de Psicólogos de la República Argentina, "Declaración de principios y anteproyecto de estatutos," *Revista Argentina de Psicología* 3, no. 11 (May 1972): 193–97.

53. Grego and Kauman, "Lugar del psicólogo," 125.

54. For an example of this contradiction, see Estudiantes delegados, "Producción del psicoanális," 42, 44.

55. Knobel, "Función psicoterapéutica," 229.

56. Litvinoff and Gomel, *Psicólogo y su profesión,* 227.

57. Susana Bricht et al., "Para dialogar sobre el rol del psicólogo," in Bricht et al., *Rol del psicólogo,* 7–8.

58. In 1966 the APBA had 112 full members (graduates) and 14 associate members (students who had completed more than twenty courses).

59. Interview with Roberto Harari.

60. Masotta, "Leer a Freud."

61. Danis, "Psicólogo y el psicoanálisis."

62. Roberto Harari also gained legitimacy as a theoretician when he sent an article to Louis Althusser and received a letter of praise and encouragement

to continue working along the same lines. The article and Althusser's letter are reproduced in Bricht et al., *Rol del psicólogo*.

63. Harari, "Psicoanálisis y la psicoanalización del psicólogo."

64. Interview with Oscar Avelluto.

65. That was the general secretary of the University of Córdoba, a military officer on active duty.

66. One of them was a criminologist.

67. APBA archive, "Libro de Actas," vol. 2 (Sept. 15, 1970), 34.

68. The professionalization of Argentine psychologists and the influence of Lacan on Argentine psychoanalysis were mirrored by developments in Brazil; see Ana Cristina Figueiredo, "O movimento psicanalítico no Rio de Janeiro na década de 70: A produção de uma psicologia psicanalítica e seus efeitos sobre a formação profissional," in Birman, *Percursos*, 123–50.

69. Grego and Kauman, "Lugar del psicólogo," 118.

7. When Marx Meets Freud

1. On the importance of the role played by the intellectual left in Argentine culture in the 1960s, see Terán, *Nuestros años sesenta*.

2. Psychoanalysis revived only after the collapse of the Communist regime, when Freud's works were again published in Russian translation. For a fascinating cultural history of psychoanalysis in Russia, see Etkind, *Eros of the Impossible*.

3. During his last years in Vienna, Freud also distanced psychoanalysis from the left. As we saw in the case of Marie Langer, he prohibited members of the Viennese association from joining leftist parties or even providing psychoanalytic therapy to their members. See Langer, *From Vienna to Managua*, 78–79.

4. "La crisis del Marxismo," in *¿Qué es la izquierda?* (Buenos Aires: Documentos, 1960), 57, quoted in Sigal, *Intelectuales y poder*, 194.

5. *Escarabajo de Oro* 2 (July–August 1961): 2.

6. See, e.g., "Psicoanálisis: ¿Opio, terapéutica o idiotez?" *Escarabajo de Oro* 6 (February 1965): 3–5.

7. See Langer, Palacio, and Guinsberg, *Memoria*, 89.

8. Interview with Marta Rosenberg, Dec. 15, 1996.

9. For a discussion of similar developments on a much reduced scale in Great Britain, see Richards, "Eupsychian Impulse."

10. For an excellent discussion see Oscar Terán, "Rasgos de la cultura argentina en la década de 1950," in Terán, *En busca de la ideología argentina*.

11. Terán, *Nuestros años sesenta*, 65ff. The vogue of existentialism and the popularity of such books as Françoise Sagan's *Bonjour tristesse* may have contributed to this feeling.

12. After the fall of Perón a wave of books presenting more or less

politically tainted interpretations of Peronism flooded the Argentine market. For an overview, see Plotkin, "Perón y el Peronismo."

13. On *Contorno* see, among others, Terán, "Rasgos de la cultura"; Sarlo, "Dos ojos de *Contorno*"; and Katra, *"Contorno."*

14. Szusterman, *Frondizi,* 171.

15. Viñas, "Orden y Progreso," 23.

16. Altamirano, "Pequeña burguesía."

17. Sigal, *Intelectuales y poder,* 149.

18. Szusterman, *Frondizi,* 174.

19. In a telephone interview July 31, 1997, Ismael Viñas said: "We believed he was Lenin."

20. Sigal, *Intelectuales y poder,* 166.

21. *Contorno,* nos. 9–10 (April 1959), 4, quoted in Szusterman, *Frondizi,* 175.

22. See, e.g., the cautious response of such leftist magazines as *El Escarabajo de Oro,* nos. 30–31 (n.d.); *El Barrilete,* August 1966; *Hoy en la Cultura,* July 29, 1966. All the magazines agreed that liberal democracy was obsolete, so the generals at least deserved credit for having eliminated it. Again disappointment came quickly when the real nature of the so-called Revolución Argentina became evident.

23. Sábato, "Fin de una era," 30–31.

24. Torre, "A partir del Cordobazo," 16.

25. Telephone interview with Viñas, July 31, 1997.

26. Interview with Rafael Filipelli, June 18, 1997.

27. See Gitlin, *The Sixties,* esp. 203–14.

28. Filipelli interview.

29. Telephone interview with Viñas, Aug. 6, 1997; interview with Alberto Fontana.

30. Interview with Carlos Altamirano.

31. Terán, *Nuestros años sesenta,* 171.

32. *Cuestiones de Filosofía* 1, nos. 2–3 (1962): 3.

33. New enrollments in the sociology program rose from 483 in 1960 to 533 in 1966 to 1,032 in 1970. N. Rodríguez Bustamante, "La sociologie dans l'Amérique Latine contemporaine: L'expérience de l'Argentine," *Revue Internationale de Sciences Sociales* 31, no. 1 (1979): 105, cited in Sigal, *Intelectuales y poder,* 87.

34. Quoted in Aricó, *Cola del diablo,* 64.

35. Masotta, "Jacques Lacan."

36. For general discussions of the noninstitutional development of psychoanalytic thought in the 1960s, see Vezzetti, "Psicoanálisis" and "Ciencias sociales."

37. On the evolution of psychoanalysis in the United States and its connections with psychiatry see Nathan Hale, *Rise and Crisis.*

38. Herman, "Being and Doing," 90.

39. See Burnham, "From Avant-Garde to Specialism."

40. On the Freudian Marxists, see Wolfenstein, *Psychoanalytic Marxism,* chap. 3.

41. Bleger edited the first comprehensive translation of Politzer's psychological works published in Spanish: *Escritos psicológicos de Georges Politzer.* A translation of some of Politzer's works had been published in 1948 with a foreword by Gregorio Bermann.

42. Bleger, "Tratamiento psicoanalítico."

43. Bleger, *Psicoanálisis y dialéctica materialista,* 140.

44. Ibid., 121.

45. Ibid., 157.

46. See Bermann, "Psicoanálisis y materialismo dialéctico" (1960), in his *Nuestra psiquiatría,* 107–26; Cabral, "Algo sobre psicoanálisis y materialismo dialéctico" and "Algo más"; Bleger, "Crítica de la crítica." See also Vezzetti, "Querella Bleger."

47. See *Cuadernos de Cultura* 43 (September–October 1959).

48. See Langer, "Analizado del año 2000."

49. *Acta Neuropsiquiátrica Argentina* 5, no. 1 (January–March 1959).

50. After his expulsion from the Communist Party, Bleger, without abandoning his Marxist faith, became a committed Zionist.

51. Bleger, "Ideología y política."

52. Masotta, "Sur la fondation."

53. Interview with Oscar Terán, Nov. 11, 1996.

54. For a discussion of Rozitchner's position vis-à-vis the left, see de Ipola, "León Rozitchner."

55. For a discussion of Lacan, see Rozitchner, *Desventuras del sujeto político,* 225–28.

56. "Un enfoque de Lacan sobre la sexualidad femenina," *Rosa Blindada* 2, no. 8 (April–May 1966): 62. The article said: "A nosotros y para finalizar, nos parece también necesario agregar un enfoque que vuelva más totalizante la comprensión que el psicólogo obtiene de estos temas. Nos interesaría, por ejemplo, una comprensión más cabal sobre las contradicciones que recaen sobre la mujer actual que debe resolver un 'compañerismo' económico, social y político al lado de su pareja reteniendo aquellos atributos propios de su carácter de mujer."

57. The topic was certainly not new and had been on the agenda of the Freudian Marxists for a long time. See Jacoby, *Social Amnesia,* 76.

58. Although Rozitchner was working with a Spanish translation of Freud's works, my quotations throughout are from the Standard Edition. When referring to Rozitchner's quotations of Freud, I compared Rozitchner's version with the English translation for accuracy.

59. Rozitchner, *Freud*, 442, 103.

60. Ibid., 184, 337, 343.

61. Bleger, *Psicoanálisis*, 145n.

62. Rozitchner, Freud, 248. On this issue, Rozitchner's thought is similar to the late Fromm's in *Crisis del psicoanálisis*, 11–51.

63. Freud, *Civilization and Its Discontents*, 113; cf. 143. More specific and critical remarks on Marxism can be found in Freud's *New Introductory Lectures*, 176–82.

64. ". . . and I scorn to distinguish between culture and civilization": Freud, *Future of an Illusion*, 6.

65. For a view of Freud's "social writings" as apolitical, see Castel, *Psychanalysme*, 340–41.

66. Rozitchner, *Freud*, 283.

67. Ibid., 94, 351, 352, 95.

68. Rodrigues de Andrade, *Puzzle(s) Masotta*, 94.

69. García, *Oscar Masotta*, 22–23.

70. In addition to García's *Oscar Masotta*, the books are Correas, *Operación Masotta;* Rodrigues de Andrade, *Puzzle(s) Masotta;* and Izaguirre, *Oscar Masotta*. Correas told an interviewer that he chose his title "porque él hace como una operación; algo que él lleva a cabo y por lo cual, a partir de unos orígenes muy humildes, este muchacho de Floresta llega a ser el Oscar Masotta que está provocando este diálogo entre vos y yo": "Entrevista a Carlos Correas," in Rodrigues de Andrade, *Puzzle(s) Masotta*, 99.

71. Masotta, *Conciencia y estructura*, Prólogo.

72. Lacan was expelled from the IPA when he introduced his famous "short sessions"—too short for the IPA. For details, see Roudinesco, *Jacques Lacan & Co.*, 359–72.

73. *Temps Modernes* 13, no. 139 (September 1957): 339–417, and 140 (October 1957): 658–98.

74. ". . . permet de retrouver l'homme entier dans l'adulte, c'est-a-dire non seulement ses determinations présentes mais aussi le poids de son histoire": ibid., no. 139, 380.

75. Oscar Masotta, "Destrucción y promoción del marxismo contemporáneo" (1960), in his *Conciencia y estructura*, 49–63.

76. Masotta discusses his attempts at suicide in "Roberto Arlt, yo mismo," in his *Conciencia y estructura*. For his friends' impressions, see "Entrevista a Carlos Correas" and "Entrevista a Jorge Lafforgue" in Rodrigues de Andrade, *Puzzle(s) Masotta*.

77. Masotta, "Roberto Arlt, yo mismo," 197.

78. Dr. Alberto Fontana claims that he took care of Masotta and that in fact it was he who introduced Masotta to Lacan's works.

79. Masotta, "Roberto Arlt, yo mismo," 201.

80. Masotta, "Jacques Lacan," 15.
81. Masotta, "Roberto Arlt, yo mismo," 202.
82. On the reception of Althusser's ideas in Latin America, see Portantiero, "Marxismo latinoamericano."
83. Ollier, *Creencia y la pasión,* 196, 198. Analysts who assisted members of the guerrilla organizations had to work under conditions of strict security. They had to move their offices often. In some circumstances they had to hold the sessions in public places and without knowing the patient's identity. See Hollander, *Love in a Time of Hate,* 74, 75, 85.
84. Interviews with Isidoro Vegh and Evaristo Ramos. Ramos is a former Communist who sought in Lacan's teaching a way to connect psychoanalysis and Marxism "without mixing them."

8. Politics, Lacanianism, and the Intellectual Left

1. Jitrik, "Producción 'cultural.'" Interestingly enough, this issue of *Cuadernos de Marcha,* devoted to Argentina in the early 1970s, included an article by Enrique Guinsberg, "Marx y Freud, delincuentes ideológicos," on the trajectory of psychoanalysis there in those years.
2. The idea of "the world taken for granted" is Peter Berger's in "Towards a Sociological Understanding."
3. Piglia, "Literatura y sociedad," 1.
4. Marxism even became fashionable. See "El A.B.C. del marxismo," *Gente,* Aug. 5, 1971, 54–55.
5. The radical young people who devoured Frantz Fanon's works in the United States saw him as a black man preaching the liberation of oppressed people of color from domination by white society; Latin Americans, many of whom thought Fanon was Algerian, saw him as an apostle of national liberation of oppressed colonies.
6. Excellent discussions of unions and politics during those years are Brennan, *Labor Wars,* and James, *Resistance and Integration.* See also Anzorena, *Tiempo de violencia.*
7. Raimundo Ongaro, "1970: Año de la Organización," quoted in Anzorena, *Tiempo de violencia,* 111.
8. *Nuevos Aires* 6 (December 1971–February 1972): 73.
9. Langer, *Cuestionamos: Documentos,* 17.
10. See Ollier, *Creencia y la pasión.*
11. The Catholic center named for Pierre Teilhard de Chardin, which published the revolutionary magazine *Cristianismo y Revolución,* changed its name to Camilo Torres.
12. On the evolution of Peronist discourse, see Plotkin, "La ideología de Perón: Continuidades y rupturas," in Amaral and Plotkin, *Perón del exilio al poder.*

13. Nora Dottori's response on a questionnaire submitted to literary critics by the journal *Latinoamericana,* June 1973.

14. Ricardo Piglia maintained that intellectuals could play a role in revolution only by joining a revolutionary organization. Piglia himself was then a member of the Vanguardia Comunista.

15. See, e.g., the roundtable "Intelectuales y revolución: Conciencia crítica o conciencia culpable?" *Nuevos Aires* 6 (December 1971–February 1972): 3–81.

16. See "Punto de partida para una discusión," *Los Libros* 2, no. 20 (June 1971): 3–9. For a more nuanced position, see "Cuba: ¿Revolución en la cultura?" *Nuevos Aires* 5 (September–November 1971): 3–12.

17. On the discourse of dependency, see Panesi, "Crítica argentina."

18. The slogan of the neo-liberal *Nueva Fuerza* was GOLES (which brought to mind soccer goals), for "Grandeza, Orden, Liberación, Estabilidad, Seguridad."

19. See John King, *Di Tella,* 119–22.

20. Marta Harnecker's *Conceptos elementales del materialismo histórico* (she was a student of Althusser's) sold thousands of copies in Argentina and elsewhere in Latin America and went through many editions.

21. "Presentación," *Cuadernos de Psicología Concreta* 1, no. 1 (1969): 9.

22. Heroína was reviewed by Josefina Ludmer in *Los Libros* 7 (January 1970).

23. Caparrós, "Ideología y psicología," 15.

24. See Guinsberg, "Marx y Freud."

25. The differences between Plataforma and Documento were never clear. In an interview Fernando Ulloa, a Documento leader, described Documento as more moderate, the Mensheviks to Plataforma's Bolsheviks.

26. For an excellent discussion of the politicization of psychoanalysis, see Guinsberg, "Marx y Freud."

27. Plataforma, "A los trabajadores de salud mental," *Los Libros,* March 1972.

28. Langer wrote: "De esta manera dimos algunos pasos concretos en el tan debatido terreno de la interrelación entre marxismo y psicoanálisis, otorgando a la práctica el privilegio que le adjudican Marx, Gramsci y Mao." Quoted in Guinsberg, "Marx y Freud," 76.

29. *La Opinión,* Nov. 17, 1971, 12. *La Opinión,* a newspaper widely read by the middle class, devoted three articles to Plataforma.

30. Guinsberg, "Marx y Freud."

31. "En este número," *Los Libros* 3, no. 25 (March 1972): 2.

32. They could never clearly designate the place psychoanalysis would occupy in a future socialist society. See, e.g., the responses given by Emilio Rodrigué, Gilberte García Reinoso, and Marie Langer in an interview in April 1971, before the separation, in "Psicoanálisis: De Freud a Marx?" *Análisis,* Apr. 6–12, 1971.

33. A copy of Sciarreta's letter of resignation, dated Dec. 4, 1971, was kindly provided to me by Dr. Juan Carlos Stagnaro.

34. In an interview Pavlovsky said: "Para mí había una distorsión personal en la entidad del analista y su ser como intelectual latinoamericano, y creo que esta sola inquietud que te estoy diciendo justificaba nuestra renuncia . . . a nivel del devenir existencial. Queríamos militar, queríamos realizarnos, queríamos ser candidatos a diputados trotskistas, queríamos encontrarnos con otra gente y esto nos daba la intuición de ghetto, que reducía nuestro potencial, lo que llamaría la potencia de actuar."

35. In October 1971 Emilio Rodrigué, whose *Heroína* was about to be filmed, was featured together with Marie Langer in a popular magazine. The article was headed: "Dos grandes psicoanalistas, actores de cine. Emilio Rodrigué y Marie Langer 'vamos a hacer un desastre.'" It was subtitled "Como José María Rosa (historiador), Chunchuna VIllafañe (modelo), Jacobo Timerman (periodista), Amadeo Carrizo (futbolista) y antes Juan Carlos Paz (músico), ahora Emilio Rodrigué y Marie Langer, destacados psicoanalistas, actuarán en cine. Se representarán a si mismos. . . ." *Clarín,* Oct. 28, 1971, 18–19.

36. Pavlovsky interview.

37. *Nuevo Hombre* started as the project of a group of independent leftist intellectuals and lawyers linked to human rights organizations. Their original idea was an independent journal with professional standards. It gradually became more committed to armed leftist organizations and eventually was sold to PRT, the political wing of the powerful Guevarist-Trotskyite guerrilla group ERP. See Anguita and Caparrós, *Voluntad,* 1:488–92.

38. Kesselman, "Plataforma Internacional," 10.

39. Caparrós, "Perspectiva nacional," 10.

40. Guevara's invitation had come after Caparrós published an article on moral incentives. When Caparrós arrived in Cuba with a group of fellow psychiatrists, including his wife, Martha Rosenberg, Guevara was no longer there and apparently the Cuban government had no idea what to do with them. After a month of wandering about, they were sent to work with schoolteachers in the Sierra Maestra. Before returning, Caparrós received a mandate from Castro to organize a guerrilla movement in Argentina to support Guevara in Bolivia. Caparrós had quit the Communists because of the Party's reluctance to support armed struggle. See Anguita and Caparrós, *Voluntad,* 1:56.

41. Chorne and Torre, "Provenir de una ilusión."

42. Harari, "Psicoanálisis / stalinismo."

43. Harari took these ideas from Althusser. See Dosse, *History of Structuralism,* 2:164–90.

44. García, "Cuestionamos."

45. Ibid.

46. In an interview Isidoro Vegh, one of Masotta's early associates (they later had a falling out), said that since most members of the group had no clinical experience, Masotta tried to attract as many M.D.'s as possible to give his group "clinical legitimacy."

47. Rozitchner interview.

48. See Masotta, "Sur la fondation."

49. Interview with Roberto Harari.

50. There is an English translation, "Freud and Lacan," in Althusser's *Writings on Psychoanalysis*. The citations are to that edition.

51. Ibid., 18, 26.

52. The chain of signifiers is infinite for some Lacanians. In a polemic with Rodrigué, Masotta mentioned Rodrigué's quotation of Masotta's quotation of Lacan's citation of Freud. See Masotta, "Anotaciones," n. 3.

53. García, "Rozitchner," 7.

54. For a discussion of Lacan's attitude toward the events of May 1968 in Paris, see Dosse, *History of Structuralism,* 2:122–33.

55. Vegh interview.

56. Ironically, Lacan thought more highly of Melanie Klein than his Argentine followers did.

57. Lacanian analysts use "variable time" sessions, which in practice mean short sessions. Sessions of ten to fifteen minutes are typical among some Lacanian analysts.

58. "Presentación del Segundo Congreso Lacaniano" (October 1969), *Cuadernos Sigmund Freud* 1 (May 1971): 5, 6; ellipsis in original.

59. Ibid., 5.

60. According to Mannoni, the invitation was extended on condition that they stay away from the APA. In fact, many APA members and dissidents were invited to the discussions. Mannoni's recollections are often inaccurate. See Mannoni, *Ce qui manque,* 103–9.

61. This is the approach taken by Roberto Harari. See his "El objeto de la operación del psicólogo," in Bricht et al., *Rol del psicólogo,* 153–216.

62. García, "Nosotros los de entonces," 41.

63. Rodrigué, "Leer a Rodrigué." Masotta in turn responded to Rodrigué in "Anotaciones."

64. See, e.g., his review of Luis Gusmán's novel *El frasquito* in *Nuevos Aires* 10 (April–June 1973): 79–86.

65. Masotta, "Aclaraciones."

66. See, e.g., Levin, "Por el camino de Lacan"; Masotta, "Qué es el psico-análisis" and "Reportaje."

67. For a collection of sources on Grupo Cero, see Menassa, *Poesía y psicoanálisis.* See also Menassa, *Freud y Lacan hablados.*

68. Only two issues of *Literal* were published to my knowledge, in Novem-

ber 1973 and May 1975. My thanks to Germán García for allowing me to photocopy his copies of the journal.

69. See, e.g., "La larga marcha al socialismo en la Argentina," *Pasado y Presente*, n.s. 4, no. 1 (April–June 1973): 3–29.

70. Vezzetti, "Situación actual del psicoanálisis," in Langer, *Cuestionamos: 1971 Plataforma-Documento*, 215–26.

71. Oscar Masotta, "Sigmund Freud y la fundación del psicoanálisis," in his *Ensayos lacanianos*, 203.

72. In an interview Wilbur Grimson, who was involved in organizing the lectures, said that Cooper's visit was a fiasco. He was drunk most of the time and the lectures were disasters.

73. "¿Hospitales psiquiátricos o campos de exterminio?" *Descamisado*, July 10, 1973, 16–19.

74. "La emoción y el asombro," *Crisis* 11 (March 1974): 3–23.

75. *Los Libros* 34 (March–April 1974): 3. Most of the issue was devoted to mental health. Many professionals were interviewed, among them Pichon Rivière, Roberto Harari, Fernando Ulloa, Gregorio Baremblitt, and Wilbur Grimson. Earlier it had published Vezetti's "Salud mental," on the ideological foundations of current mental health policies.

76. Brain and Bertoldo, "Acerca de la psiquiatría biológica."

77. In a debate with Miriam Chorne, Irene Kauman, and Beatriz Grego about Grimson's review of Erving Goffman's *Internados (Asylums)*, in which Grimson defended therapeutic communities against charges that they did nothing to solve the mental health problem, the psychologists came close to the antipsychiatry position. See Grimson, "Apuntes sobre la locura," *Los Libros* 14 (December 1970), 14–15; Chorne, Kauman, and Greco, "Acerca de las comunidades terapeuticas," ibid., 29–30; Grimson, "Cerca de las comunidades terapeuticas," ibid. 15–16 (January–February 1971): 54–55; Chorne, Kauman, and Greco, "Cerca de la locura," ibid. 17 (March 1971): 29. It is interesting to note that neither Laing nor Cooper, the founding fathers of antipsychiatry, opposed a priori the use of somatic therapies when necessary.

78. Interestingly, Vezzetti introduces himself as "miembro de la tendencia PRACTICA REVOLUCIONARIA de Trabajadores de Salud Mental. Esta agrupación constituye no solo el marco de referencia político-ideológico sino el ámbito colectivo de producción y procesamiento de mi práctica específica."

9. The Aftermath

1. For a discussion of the pathetic misunderstanding between the Peronist left and the leader, see Sigal and Verón, *Perón o muerte*.

2. See Proceso de Reorganización Nacional, *Fundamentos de la decisión*. My

thanks to Andrew Wilson, a former student of mine at Harvard University, for giving me copies of the documents he collected on the Proceso.

3. The literature on the Proceso has grown in recent years. For a detailed account of the tortures, see Comisión Nacional, *Nunca más*.

4. For a perceptive analysis of economic policy as a tool for social discipline, see Canitrot, "Disciplina."

5. I personally remember when, as a third-year high school student, I saw two students taken from the school by force. One of them was killed; nobody knows the fate of the other.

6. Comisión Nacional, *Nunca más*, 296.

7. Saint Jean, *Mensaje del gobernador.* This is the same general who allegedly said: "First we will kill all the subversives; then we will kill their collaborators; then their sympathizers; then . . . those who remain neutral; and finally we will kill the timid!" *The Guardian*, May 6, 1977, quoted in Gillespie, *Soldiers of Perón*, 250.

8. See Tedesco, Braslavsky, and Carciofi, *Proyecto educativo autoritario*, 32.

9. Corradi, *Fitful Republic*, 126.

10. The zeal to uproot "subversion" led to some grotesque situations. The generals opposed the teaching of "modern mathematics" and requested the opinion of experts as to whether the word "vector" could be considered subversive.

11. "Declaraciones del capitán de navío Manuel Irán Campo," *Clarín*, Sept. 10, 1976, quoted in Vezzetti, "Situación actual del psicoanálisis," in Langer, *Cuestionamos: 1971 Plataforma-Documento*, 221.

12. "El psicoanálisis en la picota," *Somos*, Sept. 19, 1980, 6.

13. Pavlovsky told me that when the play was staged for the first time, Marie Langer, who was his analyst, told him, "They'll never forgive you for this. Never." Later, when he was in hiding and one of his brothers asked a friend in the navy what the situation was, the officer said, "Who, Galíndez? Is he still alive?"

14. Interview with Hugo Vezzetti. When Perossio was abducted, Vezzetti was vice president of the APBA. He had belonged to Vanguardia Comunista but had left it. He was not persecuted by the military and assumed the presidency of the APBA.

15. Interview with Oscar Avelluto. Lic. Avelluto is an active member of the APBA and was its president during the Proceso.

16. See Balán, *Cuéntame tu vida*, 210–12.

17. APA archive, "Libro de Actas," *Acta* 301, May 18, 1976, 132.

18. Ibid., *Acta* 437, Nov. 11, 1980, 171.

19. "Psicoanálisis en la picota," 6. The official used the English word "boom."

20. See "Que pasará con la carrera de psicología," *Actualidad Psicológica* 2, no. 21 (November 1976).

21. The Proceso promoted private universities as part of its policy to decentralize and privatize the educational system. See Tedesco, Braslavsky, and Carciofi, *Proyecto educativo autoritario.*

22. "Psicoanálisis en la picota."

23. One psychoanalyst remembers that during the Proceso a military officer deeply involved in illegal repression sought psychoanalytic assistance for sexual dysfunction. See Nélida Sakalik de Montagna, "El psicoanálisis y la represión política en la Argentina: Una visión como psicotarapeuta de grupo," in Abudara et al., *Argentina, psicoanálisis, represión política,* 142. Other cases are also discussed in the volume.

24. An insightful discussion of the Proceso's discourse on family can be found in Filc, *Entre el parentesco y la política,* chap. 1. Filc notes that while the private sphere was being politicized by the military's prying into family secrets, the political world was becoming privatized.

25. "Las guerrilleras: La cruenta historia de la mujer en el terrorismo," *Somos,* Dec. 10, 1976, 10–17.

26. Parents were also encouraged to inform the authorities about their children's suspicious activities.

27. "Psicoanálisis en la picota," 8.

28. "La guerrillera es una psicópata," *Somos,* Dec. 10, 1976, 16. A military officer consulted by the magazine explained that women were more dangerous than men because they used their "seductive power" to corrupt military officers and obtain information. By definition subversives were bad mothers, because they used their children as shields.

29. Some of them provided therapeutic services free of charge to the mothers who demonstrated daily in the Plaza de Mayo, carrying pictures of their children who had disappeared. See Hollander, *Love in a Time of Hate,* and Kordon and Edelman, *Efectos psicológicos.*

30. Vezzetti interview.

31. Interview with Dr. Valentín Baremblit, Barcelona, May 13, 1991, cited in Feldman, "Psychiatrie en Argentine," 123.

32. Avelluto inteview.

33. See Dubcovsky, "Inflación."

34. Arnaldo Rascovsky, cited in "Psicoanálisis en la picota," 8.

35. Emiliano Galende, interviewed in "El psicoanálisis argentino: Un cuestionamiento," *Vuelta* (Mexico City) 2, no. 16 (November 1987): 25–40.

36. For a general critique of the conformist aspects of contemporary psychoanalysis, see Jacoby, *Social Amnesia.*

37. The accusation against the doctor was made public in Langer and Bauleo, "Algo más sobre tortura," in Langer, *Cuestionamos: Documentos,*

1:151–52; see also Santiago Dubcovsky, "Follow-up de una denuncia: Psico-análisis, política y moral (1984), post-scriptum," ibid., 153–66, and Stitzman, *Conversaciones,* 211–20.

38. Raúl Jorge Aragonén, "Presentación," in Abudara et al., *Argentina, psicoanálisis y represión política,* 12–13.

39. For a discussion of the state of the Lacanian movement in France, which had a direct impact in Argentina, see Roudinesco, *Jacques Lacan & Co.,* pt. 3, and Turkle, *Psychoanalytic Politics,* 227–303.

40. On the diffusion of alternative therapies in Argentina, see Gorbato, *Competidores del diván.*

References

Archives

All archives not otherwise identified are in Buenos Aires.

Anna Freud Papers, Library of Congress, Washington, D.C.
Archive of the British Psychoanalytic Society, London
Archive of the Rockefeller Foundation, Tarrytown, N.Y.
Archive of the Asociación de Psicólogos de Buenos Aires
Archive of the Asociación Psicoanalítica Argentina
Archive of the Facultad de Medicina de la Universidad de Buenos Aires
Archive of the Facultad de Psicología de la Universidad de Buenos Aires
Archive of the Federación Argentina de Psiquiatras
Melanie Klein Trust Fund, Wellcome Institute for the History of Medicine,
    London
Personal archive of Dr. Martha Rosenberg
Personal archive of Eva Giberti
Sigmund Freud Papers, Library of Congress, Washington, D.C.

Other Primary Sources

Unless otherwise identified, all other primary sources are in Buenos Aires.

Argentina. Instituto Nacional de Salud Mental. "Ley de internación de
    enfermos mentales." 1966. Mimeo.
———. Ministerio de Cultura y Educación. *La educación en cifras, 1961–1970.*
    N.d.
———. Ministerio de Salud Pública y Asistencia Social. "Informe presentado
    por el consultor en Administración de Hospitales de la Oficina
    Sanitaria Panamericana, Dr. Odair Pedroso, 1956." 1968.
———. Secretaría de Estado de Cultura y Educación. *La educación en cifras,
    1958–1967.* N.d.

————. Secretaría de Salud Pública de la Nación. *Plan analítico de salud pública.* 1947.

Comisión Nacional sobre la Desaparición de Personas (CONADEP). *Nunca más.* EUDEBA, 1984.

Liga Argentina de Higiene Mental. *Memorias y balances.* 1940–1947.

Municipalidad de la Ciudad de Buenos Aires. *Plan de salud mental.* 1969.

Proceso de Reorganización Nacional. *Fundamentos de la decisión adoptada por las Fuerzas Armadas Argentinas el 24 de marzo de 1976.* Presidencia de la Nación, 1976.

Saint Jean, Ibérico. *Mensaje del gobernador de la provincia de Buenos Aires a los empresarios.* October 1976.

Interviews

Unless otherwise identified, all interviews were conducted in Buenos Aires.

Altamirano, Prof. Carlos (intellectual historian). Nov. 4, 1996.

Aslán, Dr. Carlos Mario (psychoanalyst). Oct. 8, 1996.

Avelluto, Lic. Oscar (psychologist). Dec. 10, 1996.

Baranger, Madelaine (psychoanalyst). Nov. 5, 1996.

Basz, Dr. Samuel (psychoanalyst). Oct. 7, 1996.

Berenstein, Dr. Adolfo (psychoanalyst). Oct. 23, 1996.

Civita, Césare (publisher). New York, Sept. 8, 1996 (by telephone).

Correas, Prof. Carlos (philosopher). Nov. 13, 1996.

Etchegoyen, Dr. R. Horacio (psychoanalyst, former president of IPA). Nov. 14, 1996.

Filipelli, Rafael (filmmaker, former member of MLN). June 18, 1997.

Fontana, Dr. Alberto (psychoanalyst). Mar. 17, 1998.

Galende, Dr. Emiliano (psychiatrist and psychoanalyst). Dec. 16, 1996.

García, Germán Leopoldo (psychoanalyst). Oct. 10, 1996.

Garcia Badaracco, Dr. Jorge (psychiatrist and psychoanalyst). Oct. 16, 1996.

García Reinoso, Dr. Gilberte (psychoanalyst). Dec. 16, 1996.

Giberti, Eva (psychologist). Oct. 23 and Nov. 6, 1996.

Goode de Garma, Elizabeth (psychoanalyst). Oct. 3, 1996.

Grismon, Dr. Wilbur Ricardo (psychiatrist). Nov. 28, 1996.

Harari, Dr. Roberto (psychologist). Nov. 11, 1996.

Maldonado, Dr. Ignacio (psychoanalyst). Mexico City, Apr. 15, 1997.

Pavlovsky, Dr. Eduardo (psychoanalyst and playwright). Dec. 16, 1996.

Paz, Dr. Rafael (psychoanalyst). Dec. 10, 1996.

Ramos, Dr. Evaristo (psychoanalyst). Oct. 30, 1996.

Rascovsky, Dr. Andrés (psychoanalyst). Oct. 7 and 22, 1996.

Rosenberg, Dr. Martha (psychoanalyst). Dec. 15, 1996.

Rozitchner, Dr. León (philosopher). Dec. 12, 1996.
Sarlo, Prof. Beatriz (literary critic). Apr. 5, 1998.
Sciarreta, Prof. Raúl (philosopher). May 19, 1997.
Serebriany, Dr. Reggy (psychoanalyst). Oct. 2 and 10, 1996.
Terán, Prof. Oscar (intellectual historian). Nov. 20, 1996.
Torre, Dr. Juan Carlos (sociologist). Oct. 15, 1996.
Ulloa, Dr. Fernando (psychoanalyst). Dec. 21, 1996.
Vegh, Dr. Isidoro (psychoanalyst). Nov. 19, 1996.
Vezzetti, Lic. Hugo (psychologist, historian of psychoanalysis and psychology).
    Oct. 10, 1996.
Vidal, Dr. Guillermo (psychiatrist). June 18, 1997.
Viñas, Dr. Ismael (lawyer). Miami. July 31 and Aug. 11, 1997 (by telephone).

Periodicals

Unless otherwise identified, all journals, magazines, and newspapers are or were published in Buenos Aires.

Acta Neuropsiquiátrica Argentina
Acta Psiquiátrica y Psicológica Argentina
Acta Psiquiátrica y Psicológica de América Latina
Actualidad Psicológica
Anales Argentinos de Medicina
Anales de Biotipología, Eugenesia y Medicina Social
Anales de la Sociedad Científica Argentina
Anales del Instituto de Psicología de la Facultad de Filosofía y Letras de la Universi-
    dad de Buenos Aires
Archivo de Ciencias de la Educación (La Plata)
Archivos Argentinos de Psicología Normal y Patológica; Terapia Neuro-Mental y
    Ciencias Afines (Paidotecnia, Psicotecnia, Orientación Profesional, Penología,
    Sexología, Medicina Legal y Social)
El Barrilete
Boletín del Patronato de Recluídas y Liberadas de Buenos Aires
Ciclo
Claudia
Contorno
Crisis
Criterio
Cuadernos de Psicología Concreta
Cuadernos Sigmund Freud
Cuestiones de Filosofía
Cursos y Conferencias

El Descamisado
El Escarabajo de Oro
Gaceta Psicológica
Gente
Grillo de Papel
El Hogar
Hoy en la Cultura
Humanidades (La Plata)
Index: Revista Ibero-Americana de Análisis Bibliográficos de Neurología y Psiquiatría
Latinoamericana
Los Libros
Literal
Literatura y Sociedad
La Nación
Neuropsiquiatría
Nosotros
Nuestros Hijos
Nuevo Hombre
Nuevos Aires
La Orientación Médica
Panorama
Para Tí
Pasado y Presente
La Prensa
Primera Plana
Proa
Psicoterapia: Revista de Psicoterapia, Psicología Médica, Psicopatología, Psiquiatría, Caracterología, Higiene Mental (Córdoba).
Psiquiatría
Punto de Vista
Revista Argentina de Higiene Mental
Revista Argentina de Neurología, Psiquiatría y Medicina Legal
Revista Argentina de Neurología y Psiquiatría: Organo Oficial de la Sociedad de Neurología-Psiquiatría y Especialidades Afines de Rosario (Rosario)
Revista Argentina de Psicología
Revista de Criminología, Psiquiatría y Medicina Legal
Revista de Filosofía
Revista de la Asociación Médica Argentina
Revista de la Universidad (La Plata)
Revista de Occidente (Madrid)
Revista de Psicoanálisis
Revista de Psiquiatría y Criminología

Revista Latinoamericana de Psiquiatría
Revista Latinoamericana de Salud Mental
Revista Latinoamericana de Sociología
Revista Martín Fierro, 1924–1927, facs. ed. (Fondo Nacional de las Artes, 1995)
La Rosa Blindada
Sagitario (La Plata)
La Semana Médica
Somos
Sur

Secondary Sources

Abadi, Mauricio. "El grupo psicoanalítico como sociedad secreta." *Revista de Psicoanálisis* 17, no. 2 (1960): 407–16.
Abbott, Andrew. *The System of Professions: An Essay on the Division of Expert Labor.* Chicago: University of Chicago Press, 1988.
Aberastury, Arminda, Marcelo Aberastury, and Fidias Cesio. *Historia, enseñanza y ejercicio legal del psicoanálisis.* Buenos Aires: Omega, 1967.
Aberastury, Federico. "Medicina del espíritu." *Anales de Biotipología, Eugenesia y Medicina Social* 1, no. 3 (May 1, 1931): 15–25.
―――. "Las teorías de Freud." *Anales de Biotipología, Eugenesia y Medicina Social* 7 (July 1, 1933).
Abudara, Oscar, et al. *Argentina, psicoanálisis, represión política.* Buenos Aires: Kargieman, 1986.
Acaso, Enrique. "La psicología en la República Argentina." Buenos Aires, n.d. Mimeo.
Agrelo, Juan Antonio. "Psicoterapia y reeducación psíquica." Thesis, School of Medicine, University of Buenos Aires, 1908.
Alarcón, Renato. *Identidad de la psiquiatría latinoamericana: Voces y exploraciones en torno a una ciencia solidaria.* Mexico City: Siglo XXI, 1990.
Alberini, Coriolano. *Precisiones sobre la evolución del pensamiento argentino.* Buenos Aires: Dolencia / Proyecto Cinae, 1981.
Alexim Nunes, Silvia. "Da medicina social á psicanálise." In *Precursos na história da psicanálise,* ed. Joel Birman, 61–122. Rio de Janeiro: Taurus, 1988.
Alonso, Modesto. "La psicología en la República Argentina." Buenos Aires, 1996. Mimeo.
Altamirano, Carlos. "La pequeña burguesía, una clase en el purgatorio." Paper presented to the symposium "Jornadas sobre Ideas, Intelectuales y Cultura en la 1ra Mitad del Siglo XX," Universidad Nacional de Quilmes, November 1995.
Altamirano, Carlos, and Beatriz Sarlo. "La Argentina del centenario: Campo intelectual, vida literaria y temas ideológicos." In Altamirano and

Sarlo, *Ensayos argentinos: De Sarmiento a la vanguardia*. Buenos Aires: Centro Editor de América Latina, 1983.

Althusser, Louis. *Writings on Psychoanalysis: Freud and Lacan*. Ed. Olivier Corpet and François Matheron. New York: Columbia University Press, 1996.

Alvarado, Maite, and Renata Rocco-Cuzzi. "*Primera Plana:* El nuevo discurso periodístico de la década del '60." *Punto de Vista,* December 1984, 27–30.

Alvarez de Toledo, Luisa G. de, Alberto Fontana, and Francisco Pérez Morales. "Psicoanálisis y dietilamida del ácido lisérgico: Fundamentos para una terapéutica combinada." *Acta Neuropsiquiátrica Argentina* 4, no. 1 (January–March 1958).

Amaral, Samuel, and Mariano Plotkin, eds. *Perón del exilio al poder*. Buenos Aires: Cantaro, 1993.

Anguita, Eduardo, and Martín Caparrós. *La voluntad: Una historia de la militancia revolucionaria en la Argentina, 1966–1973*. 3 vols. Buenos Aires: Norma, 1997.

Anzorena, Oscar. *Tiempo de violencia y utopía (1966–1976)*. Buenos Aires: Contrapunto, 1988.

Ardila, Rubén. "Psychology in Latin America Today." *Annual Review of Psychology* 33 (1982): 103–22.

Ares, Isabel. "La 'fuerza' de una institución: Crecimiento y participación." *Revista Argentina de Psicología* 68 (January–February 1986).

Aricó, José. *La cola del diablo: Itinerario de Gramsci en América Latina*. Buenos Aires: Puntosur, 1988.

Arlt, Roberto. *Los siete locos, Los lanzallamas*. Ed. Adolfo Prieto. Caracas: Biblioteca Ayacucho, 1978.

Asociación Psicoanalítica Argentina. *Asociación Psicoanalítica Argentina, 1942–1982*. Buenos Aires, 1982.

Ayd, Frank. "Pschiatric Patients on General Medical Wards." In *Frontiers in General Hospital Psychiatry,* ed. Louis Linn, 145–49. New York: International Universities Press, 1961.

Balán, Jorge. *Cuéntame tu vida: Una biografía colectiva del psicoanálisis en la Argentina*. Buenos Aires: Planeta, 1991.

———. *Profesión e identidad en una sociedad dividida: La medicina y el origen del psicoanálisis en la Argentina*. Buenos Aires: CEDES, 1988.

Balbo, Eduardo. "Argentine Alienism from 1852 to 1918." *History of Psychiatry* 2, no. 6 (June 1991): 181–92.

Baranger, Madeleine. "Introducción al Grupo B. Teoría e institución psicoanalítica. La formación psicoanalítica." *Revista de Psicoanálisis* 27, no. 2 (April–June 1970): 211–16.

Barilari, Mariano. "Viena, escuela de psicología individual de Adler." *Anales de Biotipología, Eugenesia y Medicina Social* 1, no. 6 (June 15, 1933).

Barrancos, Dora. *La escena iluminada: Ciencias para trabajadores (1890–1930).* Buenos Aires: Plus Ultra, 1996.

Belmartino, Susana, and Carlos Boch. *El sector salud en la Argentina: Actores, conflictos de intereses y modelos organizativos, 1960–1985.* Buenos Aires: Organización Panamericana de la Salud, 1994.

Beltrán, Juan Ramón. "Contribución a la psicopatología de la personalidad: La despersonalización." *Anales del Instituto de Psicología de la Facultad de Filosofía y Letras de la Universidad de Buenos Aires* 1 (1935).

———. "Freud." *Anales del Instituto de Psicología* 3 (1941): 594–98.

———. "La psicoanálisis al servicio de la criminología." *Revista de Criminología, Psiquiatría y Medicina Legal* 10 (1923): 442ff.

———. "La psicoanálisis en sus relaciones con la pedagogía." *Humanidades* (La Plata) 5 (1922): 29–42.

———. "Psicoanálisis y el médico práctico." *Psicoterapia* 3 (September 1936).

———. "Psicopatología de la duda." *Semana Médica,* Jan. 20, 1927, 160–62.

———. "La tumba de Lombroso." *Semana Médica,* Oct. 31, 1929.

Berger, Peter L. "Towards a Sociological Understanding of Psychoanalysis." *Social Research* 32 (1965): 25–41.

Bermann, Gregorio. "La etiopatogenia de las neurosis y el doctor Garma." *Orientación Médica,* Apr. 22, 1956, 313–17.

———. "Una grave deficiencia en la medicina argentina." *Semana Médica* 47, no. 19 (May 9, 1940).

———. "James Mapelli." *Revista Latinoamericana de Psiquiatría* 1, no. 2 (1952).

———. *Nuestra psiquiatría.* Buenos Aires: Paidós, 1960.

———. "Patogenia de las neurosis obsesivas." *Semana Médica,* Mar. 4, 1927.

———. *Problemas psiquiátricos.* Buenos Aires: Paidós, 1966.

———. "Sociopsiquiatría: Desintegración social y deterioración mental." *Revista Latinoamericana de Psiquiatría* 1, no. 1 (October 1951).

———. "Tratamiento de elección en las esquizofrenias." *Revista Latinoamericana de Psiquiatría* 2, no. 8 (July 1953): 11–22.

———, ed. *La psicoterapia de la niñez a la senectud.* Buenos Aires: Paidós, 1971.

———, ed. *Las psicoterapias y el psicoterapeuta.* Buenos Aires: Paidós, 1964.

Bermann, Sylvia. "Análisis de algunos datos de estadística psiquiátrica." *Acta Neuropsiquiátrica Argentina* 5 (1959): 150–60.

———. "Verdad y mentira del psicoanálisis." *Primera Plana,* Oct. 24, 1967.

Berrios, G. E. "The Scientific Origins of Electroconvulsive Therapy: A Conceptual History." *History of Psychiatry* 8, no. 29 (March 1997): 105–19.

Bethell, Leslie, ed. *Chile Since Independence.* Cambridge: Cambridge University Press, 1992.

Bianchi, Susana, and Norma Sachis. *El Partido Peronista Femenino.* Buenos Aires: Centro Editor de América Latina, 1986.

Birman, Joel, ed. *Percursos na história da psicanálise.* Rio de Janeiro: Taurus, 1988.

Bleger, José. "Crítica de la crítica a *Psicoanálisis y dialéctica materialista.*" *Anales Argentinos de Medicina* 4, no. 4 (October–December 1959).

———. "Ideología y política." *Revista de Psicoanálisis* 30, no. 2 (April–June 1973).

———. "Progresos farmacéuticos en psiquiatría: Tratamientos farmacológicos." *Revista Latinoamericana de Psiquiatría* 1, no. 2 (December 1951): 43.

———. *Psicoanálisis y dialéctica materialista: Estudio sobre la estructura del psico-análisis.* Buenos Aires: Paidós, 1958.

———. "Psicoanálisis y Marxismo." *Cuestiones de Filosofía* 1, nos. 2–3 (1962): 60–73.

———. *Psicohigiene y psicología institucional.* Buenos Aires: Paidós, 1976.

———. *Psicología de la conducta.* Rev. and enl. ed. Buenos Aires: Centro Editor de América Latina, 1969.

———. "El tratamiento psicoanalítico." In *Las psicoterapias y el psicoterapeuta,* ed. Gregorio Bermann. Buenos Aires: Paidós, 1964.

Borello, Rodolfo. "Autores, situación del libro y entorno material de la literatura argentina del siglo XX." *Cuadernos Hispanoamericanos,* nos. 322–23 (April–May 1977), 35–52.

Borges, Jorge Luis. *El Aleph.* In Borges, *Ficciones: El Aleph; El informe de Brodie.* Caracas: Biblioteca Ayacucho, 1986.

Bosch, Gonzalo, and Federico Aberastury. "Conceptos generales sobre la profilaxia neurótica." *Psicoterapia* 1, no. 2 (1936).

Boshes, Benjamin. "The Function of the Psychiatrist in the General Hospital." In *Frontiers in General Hospital Psychiatry,* ed. Louis Linn, 27–35. New York: International Universities Press, 1961.

Botana, Helvio. *Memorias tras los dientes del perro.* Buenos Aires: Pena Lillo, 1985.

Bourdieu, Pierre. "Le champ intellectuel: Un monde à part." In Boudieu, *Choses dites,* 167–78. Paris: Minuit, 1987.

———. *The Field of Cultural Production: Essays on Art and Literature.* Ed. Randal Johnson. New York: Columbia University Press, 1993.

Brain, Andrés, and Carlos Bertoldo. "Acerca de la psiquiatría biológica." *Los Libros* 38 (November–December 1974): 16–19.

Brennan, James. *The Labor Wars in Córdoba, 1955–1976: Ideology, Work, and Labor Politics in an Argentine Industrial City.* Cambridge: Harvard University Press, 1994.

Breton, André. "First Manifesto of Surrealism." In *Art in Theory, 1900–1990: An Anthology of Changing Ideas,* ed. Charles Harrison and Paul Wood, 432–39. Oxford: Blackwell, 1992.

Bricht, Susana, Isabel Calvo, Frida Dimant, Susana Pravaz, María T. Calvo de Spolansky, Estela Troya, Juana Danis, Beatriz Grego, Irene Kauman, Roberto Harari, Edgardo Musso, Mauricio Knobel, Ricardo Malfé,

León Ostrov, and Isabel Palacios. *El rol del psicólogo.* Buenos Aires: Nueva Visión, 1973.

Brignardello, Luisa. "Psicoterapias y psicoterapeutas en Argentina." *Revista Interamericana de Psicología* 9, nos. 1–2 (1975): 187–211.

Brunner, José. *Freud and the Politics of Psychoanalysis.* Oxford: Blackwell, 1995.

Buchrucker, Cristián. *Nacionalismo y peronismo: La Argentina en la crisis ideológica mundial (1927–1955).* Buenos Aires: Sudamericana, 1987.

Buntig, Aldo. *El catolicismo popular en la Argentina.* Buenos Aires: Bonum, 1969.

Burke, Peter. *Popular Culture in Early Modern Europe.* New York: Harper & Row, 1978.

Burnham, John C. "From Avant-Garde to Specialism: Psychoanalysis in America." *Journal of the History of Behavioral Science* 15 (April 1979): 128–34.

Cabral, César Augusto. "Algo sobre *Psicoanálisis y materialismo dialéctico.*" *Anales Argentinos de Medicina* 4, nos. 2–3 (April–September 1959).

———. "Algo más sobre *Psicoanálisis y materialismo dialéctico.*" *Anales Argentinos de Medicina* 4, no. 4 (October–December 1959).

———. "Jorge Thénon y la psiquiatría argentina." *Acta Psiquiátrica y Psicológica de América Latina* 15 (1969): 367–81.

Caimari, Lila. "Whose Prisoners Are These? Church, State, and Patronatos and Rehabilitation of Female Criminals (Buenos Aires, 1890–1970)." *The Americas* 54, no. 2 (October 1997): 185–208.

Calimano, E. Luis. "El narcisismo en la poesía femenina de Hispano-America." *Nosotros* 25, no. 264 (May 1931).

Canitrot, Adolfo. "La disciplina como objetivo de la política económica: Un ensayo sobre el programa económico del gobierno argentino desde 1976." *Estudios CEDES* 2, no. 6 (1979).

Cano, Daniel. *La educación superior en la Argentina.* Buenos Aires: FLACSO, 1988.

Caparrós, Antonio. "Perspectiva nacional: Psicoanálisis o anti-imperialismo." *Nuevo Hombre* 1, no. 10 (Sept. 22–28, 1971).

Capshew, James H. *Psychologists on the March: Science, Practice, and Professional Identity in America, 1929–1969.* New York: Cambridge University Press, 1999.

Cárcamo, Celes. "Mecanismos patogénicos de la impotencia psíquica masculina." *Revista de Psiquiatría y Criminología* 7, no. 39 (September–October 1942): 367–80.

Carli, Sandra. "Infancia, psicoanálisis y crisis de generaciones: Una exploración de las nuevas formas del debate en educación (1955–1983)." In *Dictaduras y utopías en la historia reciente de la educación argentina (1955–1983),* ed. Adriana Puiggrós, 221–88. Buenos Aires: Galerna, 1997.

Carrillo, Ramón. "Posición de la medicina psicosomática." *Archivos de Salud Pública,* nos. 6–8 (September 1949–December 1950), 213–19.

Castedo, César. "Electro-shock en el pabellón Charcot del Hospital Melchor Romero." *Revista de Psiquiatría y Criminología* 7, no. 39 (September–October 1942).

Castel, Robert. *Le psychanalysme: L'ordre psychanalytique et le pouvoir.* 2nd ed. Paris: Union Générale d'Editions, 1976.

Castellani, Leonardo. *Freud en cifras.* Buenos Aires: Cruz y Fierro, 1966.

Castelnuovo, Elías. *Psicoanálisis sexual y psicoanálisis social: Examen de una nueva teoría de desorientación política y económica.* Buenos Aires: Claridad, 1938.

Cereijido, Marcelino. *La nuca de Houssay: La ciencia argentina entre Billiken y el exilio.* Buenos Aires: Fondo de Cultura Económica, 1990.

Chamberlin, J. Edward, and Sander L. Gilman, eds. *Degeneration: The Dark Side of Progress.* New York: Columbia University Press, 1985.

Chaparro, Félix. "La carrera de psicología en las universidades nacionales." *Revista Argentina de Psicología* 1, no. 2 (December 1969): 147–54.

Chorne, Miriam, and Juan Carlos Torre. "El provenir de una ilusión." *Los Libros* 25 (March 1971): 3–4.

Ciafardo, Roberto. "Homicidio cometido por un epiletico-imputabilidad." *Revista de Psiquiatría y Criminología* 5, no. 28 (July–August 1940).

Córdova Iturburu, Cayetano. *La revolución martinfierrista.* Buenos Aires: Ediciones Culturales Argentinas, 1962.

Corradi, Juan E. *The Fitful Republic: Economy, Society, and Politics in Argentina.* Boulder: Westview, 1985.

Correas, Carlos. *La operación Masotta (cuando la muerte también fracasa).* Buenos Aires: Catálogos, 1991.

Danis, Juana. "El psicólogo y el psicoanálisis." *Revista Argentina de Psicología* 1, no. 1 (September 1969): 75–82.

David, Michel. *La psicanalisi nella cultura italiana.* Turin: Boringhieri, 1966.

Delgado, Honorio. "Nueva faz de la psicología." *Revista de Filosofía* 6, no. 4 (July 1920): 31–37.

Dellepiane, Angela. "La novela argentina desde 1950 a 1965." *Revista Iberoamericana* 34, no. 66 (July–December 1968).

Demos, John. "Oedipus and America: Historical Perspectives on the Reception of Psychoanalysis in the United States." In *Inventing the Psychological: Toward a Cultural History of Emotional Life in America,* ed. Joel Pfister and Nancy Schnog, 63–78. New Haven: Yale University Press, 1997.

Diana, Marta. *Mujeres guerrilleras: La militancia de los setenta en el testimonio de las protagonistas femeninas.* Buenos Aires: Planeta, 1996.

Dispositio: Revista Americana de Estudios Comparados y Culturales/American Journal of Comparative and Cultural Studies 18, no. 45 (1993).

Donaldson, Gail. "Between Practice and Theory: Melanie Klein, Anna Freud, and the Development of Child Analysis." *Journal of the History of the Behavioral Sciences* 32, no. 2 (April 1996): 160–76.

Dosse, François. *History of Structuralism.* Trans. Deborah Glassman. 2 vols. Minneapolis: University of Minnesota Press, 1997.

Dotti, Jorge. *La letra gótica: Recepción de Kant en Argentina desde el romanticismo hasta el treinta.* Buenos Aires: Facultad de Filosofía y Letras, Universidad de Buenos Aires, 1992.

Dubcovsky, Santiago. "La inflación." *Revista Argentina de Psicología* 9, no. 25 (October 1979): 25–52.

"Entrevista a los fundadores": I, "Angel Garma"; II, "Arnaldo Rascovsky." *Revista de Psicoanálisis* 40, nos. 5–6 (1983); 41, nos. 2–3 (1984).

Esteves Balado, Luis. "Consideraciones sobre la organización de la asistencia de alienados en la República Argentina." *Psiquiatría* 1 (April–June 1958): 26–33.

———. "Tratamiento de agitación." *Archivos Argentinos de Psicología Normal y Patológica* 1, no. 1 (August 1933): 39.

Estudiantes delegados de materia (Psicoanalítica II) y docentes de la Asociación de Docentes de la Facultad de Filosofía y Letras de la UNBA, Primer cuatrimestre de 1971. "La producción del psicoanálisis en Buenos Aires y la relación entre el psicoanalísta y el psicólogo." In Susana Bricht et al., *El rol del psicólogo.* Buenos Aires: Nueva Visión, 1973.

Etchegoyen, R. Horacio. "Nuestra cátedra de psiquiatría." *Acta Neuropsiquiátrica Argentina* 4 (1958): 231–32.

Etkind, Alexander. *Eros of the Impossible: The History of Psychoanalysis in Russia.* Boulder: Westview, 1997.

Fairweather, George W., et al. *Community Life for the Mentally Ill: An Alternative to Institutional Care.* Chicago: Aldine, 1969.

Falcoff, Mark, and Fredrick Pike, eds. *The Spanish Civil War, 1936–1939: American Hemispheric Perspectives.* Lincoln: University of Nebraska Press, 1982.

Feldman, Nelson Roberto. "La psychiatrie en Argentine: Tendances et evolution au XIXème et au XXème siècle. Psychiatrie et psychanalyse. Le service de l'Hôpital de Lanus." Mémoire de spécialisation en psychiatrie. Université René Descartes–Paris V, 1992.

Fendrik, Silvia Inés. *Desventuras del psicoanálisis: Donald Winicott / Arminda Aberastury / Telma Reca.* Buenos Aires: Ariel, 1993.

Fernández, Marta, and Silvia Arata. *Series estadísticas universitarias argentinas.* Vol. 1, *Estadísticas internacionales sobre educación superior: América Latina y Europa, 1950–1978.* Buenos Aires: ISIS-CONICET, n.d.

Ferrara, Floreal, and Milcíades Peña. "Qué significa la salud mental para los argentinos: Resultados de una encuesta por muestro." *Acta Neuropsiquiátrica Argentina* 5, no. 4 (October–December 1959): 361–65.

Figueira, Servulo. *Nos bastidores de psicanalise: Sobre historia, estrutura e dinamica do campo psicanalitico.* Rio de Janeiro: Imago, 1994.

Filc, Judith. *Entre el parentesco y la política: Familia y dictadura, 1976–1983.* Buenos Aires: Biblos, 1997.

Fondani, Benjamin. "La conciencia desventurada: Freud, Bergson y los dioses." *Sur* 5, no. 15 (December 1935): 30–80.

Foradori, Américo. *Perfiles de psicólogos argentinos.* Buenos Aires, 1944.

Ford, Aníbal, Jorge Rivera, and Eduardo Romano. *Medios de comunicación y cultura popular.* Buenos Aires: Legasa, 1985.

Forrester, John. *Dispatches from the Freud Wars: Psychoanalysis and Its Passions.* Cambridge: Harvard University Press, 1997.

———. "'A Whole Climate of Opinion': Rewriting the History of Psychoanalysis." In *Discovering the History of Psychiatry,* ed. Mark S. Micale and Roy Porter. New York: Oxford University Press, 1994.

Franco, Jean. "What's in a Name? Popular Culture Theories and Their Limitations." *Studies in Latin American Popular Culture* 1 (1982).

Freud, Sigmund. *Civilization and Its Discontents.* Vol. 21 of *The Standard Edition of the Complete Psychological Works of Sigmund Freud* (S.E.), ed. James Strachey et al. London: Hogarth, 1955.

———. *The Future of an Illusion.* Vol. 21 of S.E., 1962.

———. *Group Psychology and the Analysis of the Ego.* Vol. 18 of S.E., 1959.

———. *New Introductory Lectures on Psycho-Analysis.* Vol. 23 of S.E., 1933.

———. *On the History of the Psycho-Analytic Movement.* Vol. 14 of S.E., 1914.

Fromm, Erich. *La crisis del psicoanálisis.* Barcelona: Paidós, 1970.

Fuller, Robert. *Americans and the Unconscious.* New York: Oxford University Press, 1986.

Galende, Emiliano. *Psicoanálisis y salud mental: Para una crítica de la razón psiquiátrica.* 3rd ed. Buenos Aires: Paidós, 1994.

García, Germán Leopoldo. "Cuestionamos: Las aventuras del bien social." *Los Libros* 3, no. 25 (March 1972): 12–13.

———. *La entrada del psicoanálisis en la Argentina: Obstáculos y perspectivas.* Buenos Aires: Catálogos, 1978.

———. "Nosotros los de entonces." *Gaceta Psicológica* 93 (October–November 1993): 41–43.

———. *Oscar Masotta y el psicoanálisis en castellano.* Buenos Aires: Puntosur, 1991.

———. "Rozitchner y los límites del individualismo burgués." *Latinoamérica* 2 (June 1973): 86–91.

García Canclini, Néstor. "Movimientos artísticos y transformaciones sociales en la Argentina (1960–1975): Informe sobre una investigación." *Cuadernos Americanos* 35, no. 6 (November–December 1976): 24–41.

Garma, Angel. "Algunos contenidos latentes de las discordias entre psicoanalistas." *Revista de Psicoanálisis* 16, no. 4 (October–December 1959): 354–61.

———. "Como mejorar las relaciones entre psicoanalistas." *Revista de Psico-análisis* 16, no. 4 (October–December 1959): 362–67.

———. "Evolución y nuevos problemas en la teoría." *Psicoterapia,* no. 3 (September 1936).

———. "Freud y la medicina contemporánea." *Psique en la Universidad* 1, no. 1 (1958).

———. "La génesis del super yo y la angustia." *Revista de Psiquiatría y Criminología* 7, no. 36 (January–April 1942).

———. "La proyección y la vuelta de los instintos contra el yo en el sueño." *Psicoterapia,* no. 3 (September 1936).

———. *Psicoanálisis de los sueños.* Buenos Aires: Ateneo, 1940.

———. "Psicoanálisis e interpretación de los sueños." *Revista de Psiquiatría y Criminología* 7, no. 38 (July–August 1942).

———. *Psicoanálisis: Presente y perspectiva.* Buenos Aires, 1942.

———. "Psicología del suicidio." *Revista de Psiquiatría y Criminología* 10, no. 28 (July–August 1940).

Garma, Betty [Elizabeth Goode]. *Niños en análisis: Clínica psicoanalítica.* Buenos Aires: Kargieman, 1992.

Gavrilov, Konstantin. *El psicoanálisis a la luz de la reflexología.* Buenos Aires: Paidós, 1953.

———. *Reflexología.* Buenos Aires: Vázquez, 1944.

Geertz, Clifford. "Religion as a Cultural System." In *Anthropological Approaches to the Study of Religion,* ed. Michael Banton. London: Tavistock, 1966.

Geissmann, Pierre, and Claudine Geissmann. *A History of Child Psychoanalysis.* London: Routledge, 1998.

Gellner, Ernest. *The Psychoanalytic Movement; or, The Cunning of Unreason.* London: Grafton Books, 1985.

Gera, Lucio, Alberto Sily, José Miguens, Francisco Suárez, and Justino O'Farrel. *La Iglesia y el país.* Buenos Aires: Búsqueda, 1967.

Germani, Gino. *Estudios de psicología social.* Mexico City: Biblioteca de Ensayos Sociológicos, Universidad Nacional de México, n.d.

———. "El psicoanálisis y las ciencias del hombre." *Revista de la Universidad* (La Plata) 3 (January–March 1958): 61–67.

Germani, Gino, and Ruth Sautu. *Regularidad y origen social en los estudiantes universitarios.* Buenos Aires: Instituto de Sociologia, Universidad de Buenos Aires, 1965.

Giberti, Eva. *Escuela para padres.* 3 vols. Buenos Aires: Losada, 1961.

Giberti, Eva, Roberto Baretto, Irene Meter, and Silvia Zeigner. "Técnicas de abordaje psicológico en una sala de pediatría." *Revista Latinoamericana de Psicología* 2, no. 3 (1970): 343–51.

Gillespie, Richard. *Soldiers of Perón: Argentina's Montoneros.* Oxford: Clarendon, 1982.

Gitlin, Todd. *The Sixties: Years of Hope, Days of Rage.* New York: Bantam, 1987.

Glick, Thomas. "El impacto del psicoanálisis en la psiquiatría española de entreguerras." In *Ciencia y sociedad en España: De la Ilustración a la Guerra Civil,* ed. Ron Sánchez and José Manues, 205–21. Madrid: Arquero, 1988.

———. "The Naked Science: Psychoanalysis in Spain, 1914–1948." *Comparative Studies in Society and History* 24 (1982): 534–71.

———. "La transferencia de las revoluciones científicas a través de las fronteras culturales." *Ciencia y Desarrollo* (Mexico City) 12, no. 72 (January–February 1987).

Goldar, Ernesto. *Buenos Aires, vida cotidiana en la década del 50.* Buenos Aires: Legasa, 1980.

Goldenberg, Mauricio. "Estado actual de la asistencia psiquiátrica en nuestro país." *Acta Neuropsiquiátrica Argentina* 4, no. 4 (October–December 1958): 401–10.

Goldenberg, Mauricio, Valentín Barenblit, Octavio Fernández Moujan, Vicente Galli, Hernán Kesselman, Anatolio Muller, Aurora Pérez, Lía G. Ricon, Carlos Sluzki, and Gerardo Stein. "La psiquiatría en el hospital general: Historia y estructura actual del servicio de psicopatología y neurología del policlínico 'Profesor Dr. Gregorio Aráoz Alfaro.'" *Semana Médica,* Jan. 4, 1966, 80–102.

Gómez de Baquero, Eduardo. "Leyendo a Pérez de Ayala: Una novela y un problema." *El Hogar,* May 5, 1923.

Goode, William. "Encroachment, Charlatanism, and the Emerging Profession: Psychology, Sociology, and Medicine." *American Sociological Review* 15 (December 1960): 902–14.

Gorbato, Viviana. *Los competidores del diván: El auge de las terapias alternativas en la Argentina.* Buenos Aires: Espasa-Calpe, 1994.

Gorriti, Fernando. "*La fuerza ciega* del Dr. Vicente Martínez Cuitino desde el punto de vista freudiano." *Semana Médica,* Aug. 1, 1929, 320–23.

———. *Histeria, estados baldeicos y baldeísmo en la histeria y en la constitución histérica respectivamente.* Buenos Aires: Ideas, 1948.

———. *Psicoanálisis de los sueños en un síndrome de desposesión: Estudio psicosexual freudiano de 74 sueños de un alienado que terminó por curarse de este modo.* Buenos Aires: Talleres Gráficos Argentinos, 1930.

Grego, Beatriz, and Irene Kauman. "El lugar del psicólogo en el proceso de producción del psicoanálisis en Buenos Aires." In Bricht et al., *El rol del psicólogo.* Buenos Aires: Nueva Visión, 1973.

Grimson, Wilbur Ricardo. "La transformación del hospital psiquiátrico: Una experiencia de comunidad terapéutica." *Acta Psiquiátrica y Psicológica de América Latina* 16, no. 4 (December 1970): 354–60.

Grinberg, León. "Reseña histórica de la Asociación Psicoanalítica Argentina: Discurso pronunciado por el Doctor León Grinberg el día 29 de junio de 1961." *Revista de Psicoanálisis* 18, no. 3 (1961): 259–303.

Grinberg, León, Marie Langer, and Emilio Rodrigué. *Psicoterapia del grupo: Un enfoque psicoanalítico.* Buenos Aires: Paidos, 1957.

Guedes Arroyo, Luis César. "Hospital Dr. A. L. Roballos, primer centro piloto psiquiátrico regional: El hospital como comunidad terapéutica." 1968. Mimeo.

Guerrino, Alberto Martín. *La psiquiatría argentina.* Buenos Aires: Cuatri, 1982.

Guinsberg, Enrique. "Marx y Freud, delincuentes ideológicos." *Cuadernos de Marcha* (Mexico City), 2nd ser., 1, no. 2 (July–August 1979): 73–81.

Hale, Charles. "Political and Social Ideas." In *Latin America: Economy and Society, 1870–1930,* ed. Leslie Bethell, 274–75. Cambridge: Cambridge University Press, 1989.

Hale, Nathan G., Jr. *The Beginnings of Psychoanalysis in the United States, 1876–1917.* New York: Oxford University Press, 1971.

———. *The Rise and Crisis of Psychoanalysis in the United States: Freud and the Americans, 1917–1985.* New York: Oxford University Press, 1995.

Halperín Donghi, Tulio. *Historia de la Universidad de Buenos Aires.* Buenos Aires: EUDEBA, 1963.

———. *La larga agonía de la Argentina peronista.* Buenos Aires: Ariel, 1994.

———. "El lugar del peronismo en la tradición política argentina." In *Perón, del exilio al poder,* ed. Samuel Amaral and Mariano Plotkin. Buenos Aires: Cántaro, 1993.

———. "¿Para qué la inmigración? Ideología y política inmigratoria en la Argentina (1810–1914)." In Halperin Donghi, *El espejo de la historia: Problemas argentinos y perspectivas hispanoamericanas.* Buenos Aires: Sudamericana, 1987.

Harari, Roberto. *Psicoanálisis in-mundo.* Buenos Aires: Kargieman, 1994.

———. "El psicoanálisis y la psicoanalización del psicólogo (a partir de 'El psicólogo y el psicoanálisis' de Juana Danis)." *Revista Argentina de Psicología* 1, no. 3 (March 1970): 147–59.

———. "Psicoanálisis / stalinismo." *Nuevo Hombre* 1, no. 14 (Oct. 20–26, 1971): 14–15.

Harrington, Anne. *Reenchanted Science: Holism in German Culture from Wilhelm II to Hitler.* Princeton: Princeton University Press, 1996.

Hellmich, Renate. "Plague or Passion: Commentary on Some Notes and a Possible Hypothesis." *Dispositio* 18, no. 45 (1993): 164–72.

Herman, Ellen. "Being and Doing: Humanistic Psychology and the Spirit of the 1960s." In *Sights on the Sixties,* ed. Barbara Tischler. New Brunswick: Rutgers University Press, 1992.

Hollander, Nancy Caro. *Love in a Time of Hate: Liberation Psychology in Latin America.* New Brunswick: Rutgers University Press, 1997.

Hornstein, Gail. "The Return of the Repressed: Psychology's Problematic Relations with Psychoanalysis, 1909–1960." *American Psychologist* 47, no. 2 (February 1992): 254–63.

Hughes, Judith. *Reshaping the Psychoanalytic Domain: The Work of Melanie Klein, W. R. D. Fairbairn, and D. W. Winnicott.* Berkeley: University of California Press, 1989.

"Ideología y psicología concreta," pts. 1 and 2. *Cuadernos de Psicología Concreta* 1, no. 1 (1969): 11–41, and no. 2 (1969): 7–32.

Ingenieros, José. *Los accidentes histéricos y las sugestiones terapéuticas.* Buenos Aires: Librería J. Menéndez, 1904.

———. *Tratado del amor.* Buenos Aires: J. L. Rosso, 1940.

Ipola, Emilio de. "León Rozitchner: La especulación filosófica como política sustituta." *Punto de Vista,* November 1986, 9–14.

Irazusta, Julio. *Memorias: Historia de un historiador a la fuerza.* Buenos Aires: Ediciones Culturales Argentinas, 1975.

Izaguirre, Marcelo, ed. *Oscar Masotta: El revés de la trama.* Buenos Aires: Atuel / Anáfora, 1999.

Jaccard, Roland, ed. *Histoire de la psychanalyse.* 2 vols. Paris: Hachette, 1982.

Jacoby, Russell. *Social Amnesia: A Critique of Contemporary Psychology.* (1975.) New Brunswick, N.J.: Transaction, 1996.

James, Daniel. *Resistance and Integration: Peronism and the Argentine Working Class, 1946–1955.* New York: Cambridge University Press, 1988.

Janet, Pierre. "Le progrès scientifique." *Journal des Nations Américaines: Argentine,* n.s. 1, no. 7 (June 8, 1933).

Jesinghaus, Carlos. "Las bases científicas de la orientación profesional." *Nosotros* 23, nos. 236–37 (January–February 1929).

Jiménez de Azúa, Luis. "Valor de la psicología profunda en ciencias penales (psicoanálisis y psicología individual)." *Revista de Criminología, Psiquiatría y Medicina Legal* 22, no. 131 (1925): 596–630.

Jitrik, Noé. "La producción 'cultural,' 1972–1974: Las desventuras de la crítica." *Cuadernos de Marcha* (Mexico City), 2nd ser., 1, no. 2 (July–August 1979): 39–48.

Jones, Maxwell. *Social Psychiatry: A Study of Therapeutic Communities.* London: Tavistock, 1952.

Kahl, Joseph. *Three Latin American Sociologists: Gino Germani, Pablo González Casanova, Fernando Henrique Cardoso.* New Brunswick, N.J.: Transaction, 1987.

Katra, William H. *"Contorno": Literary Engagement in Post-Peronist Argentina.* Rutherford, N.J.: Fairleigh Dickinson University Press, 1988.

Kesselman, Hernán. "Plataforma Internacional: Psicoanálisis y anti-imperialismo." *Nuevo Hombre* 1, no. 6 (August 1971): 25–31.

King, John. *El Di Tella y el desarrollo cultural argentino en la década del sesenta.* Buenos Aires: Arte Gaglianone, 1985.

King, Pearl, and Ricardo Steiner, eds. *The Freud-Klein Controversies, 1941–1945.* London: Tavistock / Routledge, 1991.

Klappenbach, Hugo. "La recepción de Wundt en la Argentina, 1907: Creación del segundo curso de psicología en la Universidad de Buenos Aires." *Revista de Historia de la Psicología* 15 (1994).

Knobel, Mauricio. "Diagnóstico y psicoterapia: Una concepción psicodinámica de la psiquiatría de urgencia y del rol del psicólogo." *Revista Interamericana de Psicología* 6, nos. 1–2 (1972): 111–20.

———. "La función psicoterapéutica del psicólogo." In Susana Bricht et al., *El rol del psicólogo.* Buenos Aires: Nueva Visión, 1973.

Kohn Loncarica, Alfredo. "Juan Ramón Beltrán (1894–1947): Datos biográficos y bibliografía histórica." *Actas de las Segundas Jornadas de Historia del Pensamiento Científico Argentino* (Buenos Aires), July 5, 6, and 7, 1984.

Kordon, Diana, and Lucila Edelman. *Efectos psicológicos de la represión política.* Buenos Aires: Sudamericana / Planeta, 1986.

Korn, Francis, and Analía Kornblit. "Revisión de un concepto sociológico de la normalidad." *Acta Psiquiátrica y Psicológica de América Latina* 9, no. 4 (December 1963): 292–97.

Krapf, E. Eduardo. "Doctrina y tratamiento de la alienación a través de los siglos." *Anales de la Sociedad Científica Argentina* 128, no. 5 (November 1939).

———. "Sobre la despersonalización: Estudio psicopatológico." *Neuropsiquiatría* 2, no. 1 (March 1951): 64–72.

Kurzweil, Edith. *The Freudians: A Comparative Perspective.* New Haven: Yale University Press, 1989.

Langer, Marie. "El analizado del año 2000." *Revista de Psicoanálisis* 25, nos. 3–4 (July–December 1968): 617–40.

———. *Fantasías eternas a la luz del psicoanálisis.* 2nd ed. Buenos Aires, 1966.

———. *From Vienna to Managua: Journey of a Psychoanalyst.* London: Free Association Books, 1989.

———. "Ideología e idealización." *Revista de Psicoanálisis* 16, no. 4 (October–December 1959): 417–22.

———. *Maternidad y sexo: Estudio psicoanalítico y psicosomático.* Buenos Aires: Nova, 1951.

———. "El mito del niño asado." *Revista de Psicoanálisis* 7, no. 3 (1950).

Langer, Marie, ed. *Cuestionamos: Documentos de crítica a la ubicación actual del psicoanálisis*. 2 vols. Buenos Aires: Granica, 1971–73.

————. *Cuestionamos: 1971 Plataforma-documento, ruptura con la APA*. Buenos Aires: Búsqueda, 1987.

Langer, Marie, Enrique Guinsberg, and Jaime del Palacio. *Memoria, historia y diálogo psicoanalítico*. Mexico City: Folio, 1981.

Lavrin, Asunción. *Women, Feminism, and Social Change in Argentina, Chile, and Uruguay, 1890–1940*. Lincoln: University of Nebraska Press, 1995.

"Lettres de Sigmund Freud à Honorio Delgado, présentées par Alvaro Rey Castro." *Revue Internationale d'Histoire de la Psychanalyse* 6 (1993).

Levin, Roberto. "Por el camino de Lacan, regreso a Freud." *Los Libros* 1 (July 1969).

Lewin, Kurt. *Field Theory in Social Science: Selected Theoretical Papers*. Ed. Dorwin Cartwright. New York: Harper, 1951.

Liga Argentina de Higiene Mental. *Memoria y balance correspondiente al 12 ejercicio*. Buenos Aires, 1941.

Litvinoff, Norberto, and Silvia de Gomel. *El psicólogo y su profesión*. Buenos Aires: Nueva Visión, 1975.

Llano, Francisco Luis. *La aventura del periodismo*. Buenos Aires: Peña Lillo, 1978.

López Campillo, Evelyne. *La Revista de Occidente y la formación de minorías (1923–1936)*. Madrid: Taurus, 1972.

Loudet, Osvaldo, and Elías Loudet. *Historia de la psiquiatría argentina*. Buenos Aires: Troquel, 1971.

Lustig de Ferrer, Susana. "Mis vivencias de pregraduada frente a las relaciones entre analistas." *Revista de Psicoanálisis* 16, no. 4 (October–December 1959): 333–36.

Mafud, Julio. *La revolución sexual argentina*. Buenos Aires: Americalee, 1966.

Mallet da Rocha Barros, Elias. "The Problem of Originality and Imitation in Psychoanalytic Thought: A Case Study of Kleinian Thinking in Latin America." *International Journal of Psycho-Analysis* 76, no. 4 (August 1995): 835–43.

Mannoni, Maud. *Ce qui manque à la verité pour être dite*. Paris: Denoël, 1988.

Mapelli, James. *La psicoinervación: Estudio de la acción psíquica sobre las funciones vitales*. Buenos Aires: Ateneo, 1928.

Marsal, Juan, ed. *El intelectual latinoamericano: Un simposio sobre la sociología de los intelectuales*. Buenos Aires: Editorial del Instituto, 1970.

Martelli, Juan Carlos. "Las enfermedades de las empresas." *Cuadernos de Mr. Crusoe: Arte-Ciencia-Ideas* 1 (November 1967).

Martínez Dalke, Luis. "La terapéutica convulsivante en las enfermedades mentales." *Revista de Psiquiatría y Criminología* 4, no. 20 (March–April 1939).

Martínez Estrada, Ezequiel. *Radiografía de la Pampa.* (1933.) Buenos Aires: Hyspamerica, 1986. Critical ed., ed. Leo Polman. Mexico City: Consejo Nacional para la Cultura y las Artes, 1993.

Martins, Luciano. "A geração AI-5 (Un ensaio sobre autoritarismo e alienação)." *Ensaios de Opinião* (Rio de Janeiro) 11 (1979): 72–102.

Masiello, Francine. "Argentine Literary Journalism: The Production of a Critical Discourse." *Latin American Research Review* 20, no. 1 (1985): 27–60.

Masotta, Oscar. "Aclaraciones en torno a Jacques Lacan." *Los Libros* 10 (August 1970): 6–7.

———. "Anotaciones para un psicoanálisis de E. Rodrigué." *Cuadernos Sigmund Freud* 1 (May 1971): 60–75.

———. *Conciencia y estructura.* (1968.) Buenos Aires: Corregidor, 1990.

———. *Ensayos lacanianos.* Barcelona: Anagrama, 1976.

———. "Jacques Lacan, o El inconsciente en los fundamentos de la filosofía." *Pasado y Presente* 3, no. 9 (April–September 1965): 1–15.

———. "Leer a Freud." *Revista Argentina de Psicología* 1, no. 1 (September 1969): 19–25.

———. "Qué es el psicoanálisis." *Los Libros* 5 (November 1969).

———. "Reportaje: Tres preguntas sobre Jacques Lacan." *Los Libros* 9 (July 1970): 10.

———. "Sur la fondation de l'Ecole Freudienne de Buenos Aires." *Ornicar?* (Paris) 20–21 (1980): 227–35.

Mazzei, Daniel Horacio. "*Primera Plana,* modernización y golpismo en los sesenta." In Asociación Argentina de Editores de Revistas, *Historia de revistas argentinas.* Buenos Aires, n.d.

McGrath, William. *Freud's Discovery of Psychoanalysis: The Politics of Hysteria.* Ithaca: Cornell University Press, 1986.

Medin, Tzvi. *Ortega y Gassett en la cultura hispanoamericana.* Mexico City: Fondo de Cultura Económica, 1994.

Menassa, Miguel Oscar. *Freud y Lacan hablados.* Madrid: Escuela de Psicoanálisis Grupo Cero, 1987.

———. *Poesía y psicoanálisis (1971–1991): Veinte años de la historia del Grupo Cero.* Madrid: Grupo Cero, 1995.

Menéndez, Susana. *En búsqueda de las mujeres: Percepciones sobre género, trabajo y sexualidad, Buenos Aires, 1900–1930.* Amsterdam: CEDLA, 1997.

Mercante, Víctor. *La paidología: Estudio del alumno.* Buenos Aires: M. Gleizer, 1927.

Merskey, H. "Somatic Treatments, Ignorance and the Historiography of Psychiatry." *History of Psychiatry* 5, no. 19 (1994): 387–91.

Micale, Mark S. *Approaching Hysteria: Disease and Its Interpretations.* Princeton: Princeton University Press, 1995.

Micale, Mark S., and Roy Porter, eds. *Discovering the History of Psychiatry*. New York: Oxford University Press, 1994.

Mom, Jorge. "Teoría psicoanalítica y forma de vida." *Revista de Psicoanálisis* 27, no. 2 (April–June 1970).

Morse, Richard. "The Multiverse of Latin American Identity, c. 1920–c. 1970." In *Ideas and Ideologies in Twentieth-Century Latin America,* ed. Leslie Bethell, 3–132. New York: Cambridge University Press, 1996.

Moscovici, Serge. *La psychanalyse, son image et son public: Etude sur la représentation sociale de la psychanalyse*. Paris: Presses Universitaires de France, 1961.

Neiburg, Federico. *Los intelectuales y la invención del peronismo*. Buenos Aires: Alianza, 1998.

Newton, Ronald. "Ducini, Prominenti, Antifascisti: Italian Fascism and the Italo-Argentine Collectivity, 1922–1945." *The Americas* 51, no. 1 (July 1994).

———. *The "Nazi Menace" in Argentina, 1931–1947*. Stanford: Stanford University Press, 1992.

Ocampo, Victoria. *Autobiografía*. Vol. 5, *Versailles-Keyserling-Paris-Dreiu*. Buenos Aires: Sur, 1983.

Ollier, María Matilde. *La creencia y la pasión: Privado, público y político en la izquierda revolucionaria*. Buenos Aires: Ariel, 1998.

Orgambide, Pedro, ed. *Crónicas del psicoanálisis*. Buenos Aires: Jorge Alvarez, 1966.

Oría, José. "El teatro de Lenormand, antes y después de la influencia de Freud." *Revista de Criminología, Psiquiatría y Medicina Legal* 22 (1935): 554–72.

Ortega, Luis. "El tratamiento de la psicosis por el shock insulínico." *Revista de Psiquiatría y Criminología* 3, no. 13 (January–February 1938).

Oteiza, Enrique. "La emigración de personal altamente calificado de la Argentina: Un caso de 'brain drain' latinoamericano." In *El intelectual latinoamericano,* ed. Juan Marsal. Buenos Aires: Editorial del Instituto, 1970.

Panesi, Jorge. "La crítica argentina y el discurso de la dependencia." *Filología* 20 (1985): 171–95.

Papini, Mauricio. "La psicología experimental argentina durante el período 1930–1955." *Revista Latinoamericana de Psicología* 10, no. 2 (1978): 227–58.

Pécault, Daniel. *Entre le peuple et la nation: Les intellectuels et la politique au Brésil*. Paris: Maison des sciences de l'homme, 1989.

Pichon Rivière, Enrique. *Del psicoanálisis a la psicología social*. 2 vols. Buenos Aires: Galerna, 1970–71.

———. "Dos problemas psicológicos." *Anales de Biotipología, Eugenesia y Medicina Social* 1, no. 18 (1934).

————. "Inundados: Las reacciones psicológicas ante el desastre." *Primera Plana,* Mar. 29, 1966.

————. *Psicoanálisis del Conde de Lautrèamont.* Ed. Marcelo Pichon Rivière. Buenos Aires: Argonauta, 1992.

————. "La psicología social." *Primera Plana,* May 3, 1966.

————. *Teoría del vínculo.* Buenos Aires: Nueva Visión, 1985.

Pichon Rivière, Enrique, with José Bleger, David Liberman, and Edgardo Rolla. "Técnica de los grupos operativos." *Acta Neuropsiquiátrica Argentina* 6 (1960).

Pichon Rivière, Enrique, and Ricardo Horacio Etchegoyen. "La psiquiatría en el contexto de los estudios médicos." *Revista de la Asociación Médica Argentina* 71, nos. 11–12 (November–December 1957): 442–46.

Piglia, Ricardo. "Literatura y sociedad." *Literatura y Sociedad* 1, no. 1 (October–December 1965).

Piñero, Horacio. "La psicología experimental en la República Argentina." In *El nacimiento de la psicología en la Argentina,* ed. Hugo Vezzetti, 43–54. Buenos Aires: Puntosur, 1988. First published in *Bulletin de l'Institut Géneral Psychologique* 1 (1903).

Pizarro Crespo, Emilio. "El narcicismo: De una actitud psíquica a una enfermedad social del erotismo." In *Freud en Buenos Aires, 1910–1939,* ed. Hugo Vezzetti, 240–44. Buenos Aires: Puntosur, 1989.

————. "El movimiento psicoterápico en Francia." *Psicoterapia,* no. 1 (January 1936).

————. "Las neurosis obsesivas y las fobias: Aportaciones psicoterapéuticas y metodológicas de cinco casos clínicos." *Psicoterapia,* no. 2 (May 1936).

————. "Por qué debe evitarse la violencia en los niños." *El Hogar,* Jan. 1, 1937.

————. "Psicodiagnóstico y psicoanálisis: Aportaciones clínicas y terapéuticas." *Semana Médica,* Mar. 7, 1935.

————. "Las razones de la elección amorosa." *El Hogar,* Oct. 15, 1937.

————. "Le rôle des facteurs psychiques dans le domaine de la clinique (Communication faite à la Société Psychanalytique de Paris, le 2 mai 1935)." *Revue Française de Psychanalyse* 8 (1935).

Pizarro Crespo, Emilio, and Lelio Zeno. *Clínica psicosomática.* Buenos Aires: Ateneo, 1945.

Plotkin, Mariano. "The Changing Perceptions of Peronism: A Review Essay." In *Peronism and Argentina,* ed. James Brennan, 29–56. Wilmington, Del.: Scholarly Resources, 1998.

————. "Freud en la Universidad de Buenos Aires: La primera etapa hasta la creación de la carrera de psicología." *Estudios Interdisciplinarios de América Latina y el Caribe* 7, no. 1 (January–June 1996): 23–40.

————. "Freud, Politics, and the Porteños: The Reception of Psychoanalysis in Buenos Aires, 1910–1943." *Hispanic American Historical Review* 77, no. 1 (May 1997): 45–74.

————. *Mañana es San Perón: Propaganda, rituales políticos y educación en el régimen peronista (1946–1955)*. Buenos Aires: Planeta, 1993.

————. "Perón y el peronismo: Un ensayo bibliográfico." *Estudios Interdisciplinarios de América Latina y el Caribe* 2, no. 1 (January–June 1991).

————. "Tell Me Your Dreams: Psychoanalysis and Popular Culture in Buenos Aires, 1930–1950." *The Americas* 55, no. 4 (April 1999).

Politzer, Georges. *Escritos psicológicos de Georges Politzer*. Trans. Evaristo Ramos. Ed. José Bleger. 3 vols. Buenos Aires: Jorge Alvarez, 1965–66.

Ponce, Aníbal. "Madame Sokolnicka y el psicoanálisis francés." *El Hogar*, May 10, 1929.

————. "Para una historia de Ingenieros." *Revista de Filosofía* 12, no. 1 (January 1926): 1–82.

————. "Psicología y clínica." *Revista de Filosofía* 10, no. 2 (May 1924).

Portantiero, Juan Carlos. "Il marxismo latinoamericano." In *Storia del marxismo*, vol. 4, *Il marxismo oggi*. Turin: Giulio Einaudi, 1982.

Prieto, Adolfo. "Los años sesenta." *Revista Iberoamericana* 34, no. 66 (July–December 1968).

"Psychoanalysis and Revolution in Latin America: Marie Langer Interviewed by Arturo Varchevker." *Free Associations* 15 (1989).

Rascovsky, Arnaldo. *Conversaciones con Rascovsky, acerca de la vida, el amor, el sexo, y la libertad*. 3 vols. Buenos Aires: Dobledía, 1987.

————. *Filicide: The Murder, Mutilation, Denigration, and Abandonment of Children by Parents*. Northvale, N.J.: Jason Aronson, 1995.

————. "Interpretación psicodinámica de la función tiróidea: Observaciones sobre disfunciones tiróideas en psiconeuróticos." *Revista de Psicoanálisis* 4, no. 3 (January 1947): 413–50.

————. *La matanza de los hijos y otros ensayos*. Buenos Aires: Kargieman, 1975.

Recchini de Lattes, Zulma, and Catalina Wainermann. *Estado civil y trabajo femenino: Un análisis de cohortes*. Buenos Aires: Centros de Estudios de Población, 1983.

Régis, Emmanuel, and Angelo Hesnard. *La psychanalyse des nevroses et des psychoses, ses applications médicales et extra médicales*. Paris: Alcan, 1914.

Rein, Raanan. *The Franco-Perón Alliance: Relations Between Spain and Argentina, 1946–1955*. Pittsburgh: Pittsburgh University Press, 1993.

Rey Castro, Alvaro. "Freud y Honorio Delgado: Crónica de un desencuentro." *Hueso Húmero* 15/16 (January–March 1983).

————. "El psicoanálisis en el Perú: Notas marginales." *Debates en Sociología* 11 (1986).

Richards, Barry. "The Eupsychian Impulse: Psychoanalysis and Left Politics since 1968." *Radical Philosophy* 48 (1988): 3–13.

Rivera, Jorge. *Apogeo y crisis de la industria del libro: 1955–1970*. Capítulo: La historia de la literatura argentina, 99. Buenos Aires: Centro Editor de América Latina, 1975.

Rocha, Gilberto Santos da. *Introdução ao nascimento de psicanalise no Brasil*. Rio de Janeiro: Forense Universitaria, 1989.

Rock, David. *Authoritarin Argentina: The Nationalist Movement, Its History, and Its Impact*. Berkeley: University of California Press, 1993.

Rodrigué, Emilio. *Biografía de una comunidad terapéutica*. Buenos Aires: EUDEBA 1965.

———. "Bion y la psicoterapia de grupo." *Acta Neuropsiquiátrica Argentina* 1, no. 1 (October 1954): 108–13.

Rodrigué, Emilio, and Martha Berlin. *El antiyo-yo*. Buenos Aires: Fundamentos, 1977.

Rodrigues de Andrade, Rosangela. *Puzzle(s) Masotta. Oscar Masotta: Lo imaginario (búsqueda teórica y búsqueda de imágenes matrices)*. Rosario: Homo Sapiens, 1997.

Rodríguez Lafora, Gonzalo. "La paranoia ante los tribunales de justicia." *Revista de Criminología, Psiquiatría y Medicina Legal* 22, no. 131 (1925): 631–50.

Rojas, Nerio. "De Bergson y Freud." *La Nación*, Nov. 26, 1939.

———. "La histeria después de Charcot." *Revista de Criminología, Psiquiatría y Medicina Legal* 12 (1925): 458ff.

———. "Una visita a Freud." *La Nación*, Mar. 17, 1930.

Romero, José Luis, and Luis Alberto Romero, eds. *Buenos Aires, historia de cuatro siglos*. 2 vols. Buenos Aires, 1983.

Romero, Luis Alberto. "Una empresa cultural: Los libros baratos." In *Sectores populares cultura y política: Buenos Aires en la entreguerra*, ed. Luis Alberto Romero and Leandro Gutiérrez. Buenos Aires: Sudamericana, 1995.

Rosenthal, Ludovico, and Arnaldo Rascovsky. "La formación psicoanalítica: Consideraciones sobre el desarrollo del movimiento pscoanalítico en América Latina." *Revista de Psicoanálisis* 4, no. 4 (April 1947).

Rossi, Lucía, et al. *La psicología antes de la profesión: El desafío de ayer: Instituir las prácticas*. Buenos Aires: EUDEBA, 1997.

Roudinesco, Elisabeth. *La bataille de cent ans: L'histoire de la psychanalyse en France*. 2 vols. Paris: Seuil, 1986.

———. *Généalogies*. Paris: Fayard, 1994.

———. *Jacques Lacan & Co.: A History of Psychoanalysis in France, 1925–1985*. London: Free Association Books, 1990.

———. *Lacan: Esbozo de una vida, historia de un sistema de pensamiento*. Mexico City: Fondo de Cultura Económica, 1994.

Roudinesco, Elisabeth, and Michel Plon. *Dictionnaire de la psychanalyse*. Paris: Fayard, 1997.

Rozitchner, León. *Las desventuras del sujeto político: Ensayos y errores*. Buenos Aires: Cielo por Asalto, 1996.

———. *Freud y los límites del individualismo burgués*. Buenos Aires: Siglo XXI, 1972.

———. "La izquierda sin sujeto." *Rosa Blindada* 2, no. 9 (September 1966): 30–44.

Sábato, Ernesto. "El fin de una era." *Gente*, July 28, 1966.

Sagastizábal, Leandro de. *La edición de libros en la Argentina: Una empresa de cultura*, Buenos Aires: EUDEBA, 1995.

Sagawa, Roberto Yutaka. "Durval Marcondes e o início do movimento psicanalítico brasileiro." *Cadernos Freud Lacanianos* 2 (São Paulo), 1980, 99–118.

———. "A psicanálise pioneira e os pioneiros da psicanálise em São Paulo." In *Cultura da psicanálise*, ed. Servulo A. Figueira. São Paulo: Brasiliense, 1985.

Saítta, Sylvia. *Regueros de tinta: El diario "Crítica" en la década de 1920*. Buenos Aires: Sudamericana, 1998.

Salvatore, Ricardo. "Criminology, Prison Reform, and the Buenos Aires Working Class." *Journal of Interdisciplinary History* 23, no. 2 (Autumn 1992): 279–99.

Sarlo, Beatriz. "Los dos ojos de *Contorno*." *Punto de Vista* 4, no. 13 (November 1981): 3–8.

———. *La imaginación técnica: Sueños modernos de la cultura argentina*. Buenos Aires: Nueva Visión, 1992.

———. *Una modernidad periférica: Buenos Aires, 1920 y 1930*. Buenos Aires: Nueva Visión, 1988.

———. "Vanguardia y criollismo: La aventura de *Martín Fierro*." In Carlos Altamirano and Sarlo, *Ensayos argentinos: De Sarmiento a la vanguardia*, 211–60. Buenos Aires: Centro Editor de América Latina, 1983.

Sbarbi, Mario, and Mauricio Goldenberg. "Electroshock y psicoterapia intensivos." *Neuropsiquiatría* 1, no. 1 (November 1949): 32–39.

Sbarbi, Mario, and Mario Zipilivan. "Aspectos de la asistencia en nuestros establecimientos psiquiátricos." *Orientación Médica* 4 (1955): 458–61.

Scalabrini Ortiz, Raúl. *El hombre que está solo y espera*. (1931.) Buenos Aires: Hyspamérica, 1986.

Schorske, Carl. *Fin-de-Siècle Vienna: Politics and Culture*. New York: Vintage Books, 1981.

Schwarz, Jorge. *Vanguardas latino-americanas: Polemicas, manifestos e textos críticos*. São Paulo: Editora da Universidade de São Paulo, 1995.

Scobie, James. *Buenos Aires: Plaza to Suburb, 1870–1910.* New York: Oxford University Press, 1974.

Scull, Andrew. "Somatic Treatments and the Historiography of Psychiatry." *History of Psychiatry* 5, no. 18 (1994): 1–12.

Sebreli, Juan José. *Buenos Aires: Vida cotidiana y alienación.* 15th ed. Buenos Aires: Hyspamérica, 1986.

Shorter, Edward. *A History of Psychiatry: From the Era of the Asylum to the Age of Prozac.* New York: Wiley, 1997.

Sigal, Silvia. *Intelectuales y poder en la década del 60.* Buenos Aires: Puntosur, 1991.

Sigal, Silvia, and Oscar Terán. "Los intelectuales frente a la política." *Punto de Vista* 14, no. 42 (April 1992): 42–48.

Sigal, Silvia, and Eliseo Verón. *Perón o muerte! Los fundamentos discursivos del fenómeno peronista.* Buenos Aires: Legasa, 1986.

Sluzki, Carlos. "Informe estadístico del servicio de psicopatología y neurología del policlínico de Lanús." *Acta Psiquiátrica y Psicológica Latinoamericana* 11, no. 2 (June 1965): 145–47.

Starobisnki, Jean. "Freud, Breton, Myers." In Starobinski, *La relation critique,* 320–41. Paris: Gallimard, 1970.

Stepan, Nancy Leys. *"The Hour of Eugenics": Race, Gender, and Nation in Latin America.* Ithaca: Cornell University Press, 1991.

Stitzman, Jorge. *Conversaciones con R. Horacio Etchegoyen.* Buenos Aires: Amorrortu, 1998.

Stocker, Hector. "La ley alemana de esterilización." *Semana Médica,* Aug. 8, 1935.

Sulloway, Frank. *Freud, Biologist of the Mind: Beyond the Psychoanalytic Legend.* Cambridge: Harvard University Press, 1992.

Szusterman, Celia. *Frondizi and the Politics of Developmentalism in Argentina, 1955–1962.* London: Macmillan, 1993.

Talice, Roberto. *100.000 ejemplares por hora: Memorias de un redactor de "Crítica," el diario de Botana.* Buenos Aires: Corregidor, 1977.

Tarnopolsky, Alejandro, Gabriel del Olmo, and Dora Orlansky. "Características sociológicas de pacientes psiquiátricos en tratamiento hospitalario: Estudio exploratorio." *Acta Psiquiátrica y Psicológica de América Latina* 14, no. 3 (September 1968): 217–28.

Tedesco, Juan Carlos, Cecilia Braslavsky, and Ricardo Carciofi. *El proyecto educativo autoritario: Argentina, 1976–1982.* Buenos Aires: FLACSO, 1983.

Terán, Oscar. *En busca de la ideología argentina.* Buenos Aires: Catálogos, 1986.

———. *Nuestros años sesenta.* Buenos Aires: Punto Sur, 1991.

Testimonios para la experiencia de enseñar: Mauricio Goldenberg, maestro, médico, psiquiatra, humanista. Buenos Aires: Facultad de Psicología, Universidad de Buenos Aires, 1996.

Thénon, Jorge. "Alfredo Adler (1870–1937): Las proyecciones de su teoría en la psiquiatría moderna." *Cursos y Conferencias* 7 (April 1937): 69–83.

———. *La neurosis obsesiva: El sado-masoquismo en el pensamiento obsesivo y en la evolución sexual.* Buenos Aires: Ateneo, 1935.

———. *Psicoterapia comparada y psicogénesis: Contribución al estudio psicoanalítico del sueño en las neurosis.* Buenos Aires: A. López, 1930.

———. "La psiquiatría en el año 50 del siglo XX." *Cursos y Conferencias* 21 (October–December 1952): 337–66.

———. "Sigmund Freud: Su influencia en la psiquiatría moderna." *Cursos y Conferencias* 9 (December 1939): 61–73.

———. "Thénon visto por Thénon." *Acta Psiquiátrica y Psicológica de América Latina* 15 (1969): 381–85.

Toer, Mario. *Como son los estudiantes: Perfil socioeconómico y cultural de los estudiantes de la UBA.* Buenos Aires: Catálogos, 1990.

Torrado, Susana. *Estructura social de la Argentina, 1945–1983.* Buenos Aires: Flor, 1992.

Torre, Juan Carlos. "A partir del Cordobazo." *Estudios* 4 (December 1994): 15–24.

Turkle, Sherry. *Psychoanalytic Politics: Jacques Lacan and Freud's French Revolution.* 2nd ed. London: Free Association Books, 1992.

Ulloa, Fernando. *Novela clínica psicoanalítica: Historia de una práctica.* Buenos Aires: Paidós, 1995.

Velde, Th. H. van de. *El matrimonio perfecto: Estudio de su fisiología y su técnica.* Buenos Aires: Claridad, 1939.

Verón, Eliseo. "Coloquio sobre las relaciones entre psicología y sociología." *Revista Latinoamericana de Sociología* 1, no. 1 (March 1965).

———. "Notas para una concepción estructural en psiquiatría social." *Acta Psiquiátrica y Psicológica de América Latina* 9, no. 4 (December 1963): 287–92.

Vezzetti, Hugo. *Aventuras de Freud en el país de los argentinos: De José Ingenieros a Enrique Pichon Rivière.* Buenos Aires: Paidós, 1996.

———. "Las ciencias sociales y el campo de la salud mental en la década del sesenta." *Punto de Vista,* April 1995, 29–33.

———. *La locura en la Argentina.* Buenos Aires: Folios, 1983.

———. "Marie Langer: De la maternidad y de los mitos sobre Eva Perón." Paper delivered at LASA International Congress, Washington, D.C., Sept. 28–30, 1995.

———. "Marie Langer: La maternidad y la revolución." *Tres al cuarto* 3 (Spring 1994): 38–41.

———. "Orígenes de la Psicología." *Gaceta Psicológica,* no. 93 (October–November 1992), 23–25.

———. "El psicoanálisis y la cultura intelectual." *Punto de Vista,* November 1992, 33–37.

———. "La querella Bleger: Psicoanálisis y cultura comunista." *Ciudad Futura* 27 (February–March 1991).

———. "Salud mental: Ideología y poder." *Los Libros* 32 (October–November 1973): 28–32.

Vezzetti, Hugo, ed. *El nacimiento de la psicología en la Argentina.* Buenos Aires: Puntosur, 1988.

———, ed. *Freud en Buenos Aires, 1910–1939.* Buenos Aires: Puntosur, 1989.

Viñas, Ismael. "Orden y Progreso." *Contorno,* nos. 9–10 (April 1959).

Viner, Russel. "Melanie Klein and Anna Freud: The Discourse of the Early Dispute." *Journal of the History of the Behavrioral Sciences* 32, no. 1 (January 1996): 4–15.

Visacovsky, Sergio Eduardo. "Genealogias rompidas: Memória, política e filiação na psicanálise argentina." *Mosaico, Revista de Ciêncas Sociais* (Espírito Santo, Brazil) 1, no. 1 (1998): 197–225.

Vivaldo, Carlos. "Breve reseña sobre la terapéutica de las enfermedades mentales." *Anales de la Sociedad Científica Argentina* 128, no. 5 (November 1939).

Wainerman, Catalina. *La mujer y el trabajo en la Argentina desde la perspectiva de la Iglesia Católica.* Buenos Aires: CENEP, 1980.

Wainerman, Catalina, and Rebeca Barck de Raijman. *Sexismo en los libros de lectura de la escuela primaria.* Buenos Aires: IDES, 1987.

Walter, Richard. *Politics and Urban Growth in Buenos Aires, 1910–1942.* New York: Cambridge University Press, 1993.

———. *Student Politics in Argentina.* New York: Basic Books, 1968.

Wender, Leonardo. *"Relaciones del analista con el medio ambiente."* *Revista de Psicoanálisis* 16, no. 4 (October–December 1959): 333–36.

Whitley, Richard. "Knowledge Producers and Knowledge Acquirers: Popularization as a Relation Between Scientific Fields and Their Publics." In *Expository Science: Forms and Function of Popularization,* ed. Terry Shinn and Richard Whitley. Dordrecht: Reidel, 1985.

Wolfenstein, Eugene Victor. *Psychoanalytic Marxism: Groundwork.* London: Free Association Books, 1993.

Woodyard, George. "Eduardo Pavlovsky, los años tempranos." In *Teatro argentino de los sesenta: Polémica, continuidad, ruptura,* ed. Osvaldo Pellettieri. Buenos Aires: Corregidor, 1989.

Zimmermann, Eduardo. "Racial Ideas and Social Reform: Argentina, 1890–1916." *Hispanic American Historical Review* 72, no. 1 (February 1992): 23–46.

Zito Lema, Vicente. *Conversaciones con Enrique Pichon Rivière sobre el arte y la locura.* Buenos Aires: Cinco, 1992.

Index

In this index *passim* is used to indicate a cluster of references in close but not consecutive sequence.

Abadi, Mauricio, 65
Aberastury, Arminda, 20, 40, 44, 48; correspondence with M. Klein, 67. *See also* Child analysis
Aberastury, Federico, 33, 40, 45
Aberastury, Pedro, 46
Acta Neuropsiquiátrica Argentina (later *Acta Psiquiátrica y Psicológica Argentina*, then *Acta Psiquiátrica y Psicológica Latinoamericana*), 129–31, 178
Adler, Alfred, 26, 29, 33
Agosti, Héctor, 167
Alberini, Coroliano, 148, 150
Alcalde, Ramón, 172
Allende, Salvador, 194
Allendy, René, 26
Alliance for Progress, 80
Althusser, Louis, 164, 180, 188, 189, 196, 202, 203, 206, 208; on Freud and Lacan, 209
Alvarez de Toledo, Luisa, 46, 89
Anticommunist Argentine Alliance (Triple A), 216
Anti-imperialism. *See* Dependency theory
Aramburu, Pedro, 193
Archivos Argentinos de Psicología Normal y Patológica, 54

Ardila, Rubén, 158
Argentine Communist Party, 26, 29, 30, 130, 153, 166–69, 174, 176; *Cuadernos de Cultura*, 178
Argentine Medical Association, 31, 49
Argentine Psychoanalytic Association (APA), 1–4, 8, 9, 13, 20, 22, 23, 27, 44; and Kleinianism, 64, 67–69; institutional consolidation, 59–65
Arlt, Roberto, 37, 82. *See also* Psychoanalysis in Argentina, and literature
Aslán, Carlos, 45
Asociación Argentina de Psicología y Psicoterapia de Grupo, 85
Asociación de Biotipología, Eugenesia y Medicina Social, 13, 32, 53, 55; *Anales*, 33, 55
Asociación de Psicólogos de Buenos Aires (APBA), 146, 159–63, 218, 221–23
Asociación de Psiquiatras de la Capital Federal, 133
Asociación Psicoanalítica de Buenos Aires (APdeBA), 164, 219, 220, 223
Asylums. *See* Mental hospitals
Ateneo Psiquiátrico de Buenos Aires, 132
Atlántida, 118, 119
Austregesilo, Antonio, 20, 129

Balán, Jorge, 67, 134
Baranger, Madeleine, 62
Baremblit, Gregorio, 214

Patronato de Recluídas y Liberadas
(Argentina), 35
Pavlov, Ivan, 26, 29, 46, 167
Pavlovsky, Eduardo (Tato), 81, 89, 197,
200, 202, 219
Peluffo, Julio, 126
Pende, Nicola, 19, 32, 33
Pérez Morales, Francisco, 89
Perón, Isabel, 197, 216, 217
Perón, Juan D., 52, 54, 55, 61, 62, 71, 72,
76, 84, 85, 97, 163, 170, 195, 216; and
education system, 74
Peronism, 25, 74, 77, 93, 121; and the
New Left, 168, 169, 180, 181, 192,
193; political polarization of, 54–57,
78, 79; and the professionalization of
psychoanalysis, 69; revolutionary
groups in, 193, 194
Perossio, Beatriz, 159, 219, 223
Piaget, Jean, 143
Picarel, Julio, 32
Pichon Rivière, Enrique, 19, 20, 23, 40,
44, 45, 47, 52, 58, 61, 62, 80, 85, 89,
91, 102–7, 120, 122, 125, 128, 133,
135, 167, 175, 176, 187, 197; science
and ideology of, 198, 200, 214
Piglia, Ricardo, 192, 193, 196
Piñero, Horacio, 15, 33, 34, 147, 148
Pizarro Crespo, Emilio, 26–29, 30–32,
53, 54
Plataforma (secession of APA), 62, 94,
200–205, 207, 209, 210, 219. *See also*
Documento
Politzer, Georges, 27, 176–78, 181, 198
Ponce, Aníbal, 21, 23, 25, 26, 30, 42
Porto Carrero, J. P., 35
Positivism (in Argentina), 14, 21, 22;
displacement/crisis of, 55, 18, 19, 22,
34, 42, 147
Prieto, Adolfo, 2
Primera Plana, 71, 73, 75, 77
Psicoterapia, 26, 27, 28, 31, 39, 46, 53, 54
Psique en la Universidad, 63
Psychiatry, 12–14, 16, 17, 19, 22–24, 27,
29–33, 35, 52; care, 135–40 (*see also*

Goldenberg, Mauricio); and ideology, 132–35
Psychoanalysis in Argentina, 1–3, 5–15,
17; and criminology, 21, 35, 45; and
cultural modernization, 79–81; and
depoliticization, 218–23; and
existentialism, 79; French influences
on, 13, 17, 22, 24, 27–29, 31, 32, 35,
82, 154; and literature, 35, 82; and
Marxism, 54, 173, 175–90, 202 (*see
also* New Left); and politicization,
197–215; and politics, 83, 84, 166;
and popular culture, 38, 114, 115, 118,
119; and psychiatry, 104, 107, 124–42;
and psychology, 143–46; and social
changes, 70–73 *passim*, 76–77; and
social sciences, 85–90, 175; U.S.
influences on, 52, 60, 61, 66, 68, 69
Psychoanalysis in Brazil, 8, 13, 49, 50,
127; and Modernism, 35–36; and
political repression, 225; and politics,
83, 84; and psychiatry, 14
Psychoanalysis in France, 3, 4, 6, 13, 35
Psychoanalysis in U.S., 3, 4, 6, 49, 51,
87, 92, 124–26, 137, 140, 141, 143,
146, 152, 175, 176, 213
Psychologists: and gender, 158–62; and
medical corporation, 152–54; and
psychoanalysts, 154–58
Psychology: humanistic (in U.S.), 175;
and social sciences, 144, 145; as
synonymous with psychoanalysis,
150, 151, 197
Psychotherapy, 17, 21, 23, 27, 28, 29;
group therapy, 85–90, 131, 137;
psychodrama, 89, 141
Puig, Manuel, 82. *See also* Psychoanalysis in Argentina, and literature

Quiroga, Ana, 105

Rabinovich, Paulina H. de, 26
Racker Clinic, 63
Raitzin, Alejandro, 17, 20
Ramón y Cajal, S., 21, 46